# FOUNDATION

# Also by Peter Ackroyd

## Fiction

*The Canterbury Tales: A Retelling*
*The Trial of Elizabeth Cree*
*The Last Testament of Oscar Wilde*
*Chatterton*
*First Light*
*English Music*
*Dan Leno and the Limehouse Golem*
*Milton in America*
*The Plato Papers*
*The Clerkenwell Tales*
*The Lambs of London*
*The Fall of Troy*
*The Casebook of Victor Frankenstein*

## Nonfiction

*The Collection: Journalism, Reviews, Essays, Short Stories, Lectures*
(edited by Thomas Wright)
*London Under: The Secret History Beneath the Streets*
*Dressing Up: Transvestism and Drag: The History of an Obsession*
*London: The Biography*
*Albion: The Origins of the English Imagination*
*Thames: Sacred River*
*Venice: Pure City*
*T. S. Eliot*
*Dickens*
*Blake*
*The Life of Thomas More*
*Shakespeare*
*Chaucer*
*J. M. W. Turner*
*Newton*
*Poe: A Life Cut Short*

*Peter Ackroyd*

# FOUNDATION

## THE HISTORY OF ENGLAND FROM ITS EARLIEST BEGINNINGS TO THE TUDORS

THOMAS DUNNE BOOKS
*St. Martin's Press*
*New York*

THOMAS DUNNE BOOKS.
An imprint of St. Martin's Press.

FOUNDATION. Copyright © 2011 by Peter Ackroyd. All rights reserved.
Printed in the United States of America. For information, address
St. Martin's Press, 175 Fifth Avenue, New York, N.Y. 10010.

www.thomasdunnebooks.com
www.stmartins.com

The list of illustrations on pages vii–ix constitute an extension of this copyright page.

Library of Congress Cataloging-in-Publication Data

Ackroyd, Peter, 1949–
 Foundation : the history of England from its earliest beginnings to the Tudors /
Peter Ackroyd. — 1st U.S. ed.
     p. cm.
 "First published in Great Britain by Macmillan" —T.p. verso.
 Includes bibliographical references and index.
 ISBN 978-1-250-00361-4 (hardcover)
 ISBN 978-1-250-01367-5 (e-book)
1.  Great Britain—History—To 1485. 2.  Great Britain—History—Henry VII,
1485–1509.  I. Title.
 DA130.A45 2012
 942—dc23

                                                              2012028305

First published in Great Britain by Macmillan,
an imprint of Pan Macmillan, a division of Macmillan Publishers Limited

First U.S. Edition: October 2012

10   9   8   7   6   5   4   3   2   1

# Contents

*List of Illustrations* vii

1. Hymns of stone 1

2. The Roman way 25

3. Climate change 42

4. Spear points 45

5. The blood eagle 61

6. The measure of the king 77

7. The coming of the conquerors 81

8. The house 92

9. Devils and wicked men 97

10. The road 119

11. The law is lost 122

12. The names 128

13. The turbulent priest 130

14. The lost village 151

15. The great charter 154

16. Crime and punishment 177

17. A simple king 183

18. The seasonal year 204

19. The emperor of Britain  210

20. The hammer  225

21. The favourites of a king  229

22. Birth and death  247

23. The sense of a nation  251

24. The night schools  269

25. The commotion  278

26. Into the woods  305

27. The suffering king  308

28. Old habits  317

29. The warrior  320

30. How others saw us  331

31. A simple man  333

32. Meet the family  351

33. The divided realm  359

34. The world at play  370

35. The lion and the lamb  378

36. The staple of life  394

37. The king of spring  398

38. Come to town  411

39. The zealot king  415

40. The king of suspicions  425

41. A conclusion  442

*Further reading*  449

*Index*  465

# List of Illustrations

1. Stonehenge, from an illuminated manuscript (© akg-images/ British Library)
2. A silver relief of Cernunnos, the horned god of Iron Age worship (© akg-images/Erich Lessing)
3. A mosaic from the Roman villa at Bignor in West Sussex (© akg-images/Florian Monheim/Bildarchiv Monheim)
4. A stylized depiction of some protagonists in the Roman conquest of Britain (© Mary Evans Picture Library)
5. The helmet of a great Germanic overlord, from Sutton Hoo (© akg-images/British Museum)
6. A nineteenth-century print of a Saxon manor (© akg-images/ North Wind Picture Archives)
7. Saxon soldiers about to engage in battle (© Mary Evans Picture Library)
8. 'Alfred in the Danish Camp' (© Mary Evans Picture Library)
9. Aethelbert, the great king of Kent (© akg-images)
10. The Venerable Bede in his scriptorium (© akg-images/British Library)
11. The *incipit* of the Gospel of Saint Matthew from the Lindisfarne Gospels (© akg-images/British Library)
12. A Viking ship (© akg-images/British Library)
13. An image of Ethelred, commonly known as 'the unready' or 'the ill-advised' © akg-images/British Library)
14. Edward the Confessor, king of England from 1042 to 1066 (© akg-images/British Library)
15. The Normans crossing the Channel for the invasion of 1066 (© Getty Images/Bibliothèque Nationale)
16. The death of Harold in battle, from the Bayeux Tapestry (© Mary Evans Picture Library)

17. A man wielding an axe, taken from *Topographia Hibernica* (© akg-images/British Library)
18. An image of man and dogs from the Luttrell Psalter (© akg-images/British Library)
19. A nineteenth-century woodcut of a medieval manor (© akg-images/North Wind Picture Archives)
20. An image of Matilda, de facto queen of England from March to November 1141 (© akg-images/British Library)
21. Henry II confronting Thomas Becket (©akg-images/British Library)
22. Richard I, more commonly known as 'Richard the Lionheart' (© akg-images/Erich Lessing)
23. 'John Lackland' on horseback (© akg-images/British Library)
24. The season of March as seen in The Bedford Book of Hours (© akg-images/British Library)
25. The varied labours of the agricultural year (© Mary Evans Picture Library)
26. The abbots, and monks, of a medieval monastery (© akg-images/British Library)
27. The building of a monastery (© akg-images)
28. Edward I addressing one of his parliaments (© Mary Evans Picture Library)
29. A view of Harlech Castle (© IAM/akg-images)
30. Queen Isabella, errant wife of Edward II (© Mary Evans Picture Library)
31. The Black Death (© Mary Evans Picture Library)
32. A woman who has contracted leprosy (© akg-images/British Library)
33. A blood-letting (© akg-images/British Library)
34. The Battle of Crécy (© akg-images/British Library)
35. The tomb of the Black Prince (© akg-images/Erich Lessing)
36. The image of Richard II from the 'Wilton Diptych' (© akg-images/Erich Lessing)
37. A page from Wycliffe's Bible (© IAM/akg-images)
38. The cloisters of Gloucester Cathedral (© akg-images/Bildarchiv Monheim)
39. A scene from the Peasants' Revolt of 1381 (© akg-images/British Library)

40. The coronation of Henry IV in Westminster Abbey (© IAM/ (akg-images)
41. The Battle of Agincourt (© akg-images/Bibliothèque Nationale)
42. The wedding of Henry V and Katherine of Valois (© akg-images/British Library)
43. Joan of Arc (© akg-images/Archives Nationales, Paris)
44. Henry VI in full martial array (© Mary Evans Picture Library)
45. The Warwick family tree, from John Rous of Warwick's *De Regius Angliae* (© akg-images/British Library)
46. Edward IV (© Mary Evans Picture Library)
47. Elizabeth Woodville (© Mary Evans Picture Library)
48. Edward V (© Mary Evans Picture Library)
49. Richard III standing on a white boar (© Mary Evans Picture Library)
50. Elizabeth of York and Henry VII, from a nineteenth-century illustration (© Sarah, Countess of Essex/Getty Images)
51. An allegory of the Tudor dynasty (© akg-images/British Library)

# 1

# Hymns of stone

When the first sarsen stone was raised in the circle of Stonehenge, the land we call England was already very ancient. Close to the village of Happisburgh, in Norfolk, seventy-eight flint artefacts have recently been found; they were scattered approximately 900,000 years ago. So the long story begins.

At least nine distinct and separate waves of peoples arrived from southern Europe, taking advantage of warm interglacial periods that endured for many thousands of years; they are races without a history, leaving only stones or bones as the evidence of their advance and retreat. Against the wall of a cave of the Gower Peninsula has been found the body of a man laid down 29,000 years ago. His bones were stained with a light patina of red, suggesting either that they were sprinkled with red ochre or that his burial garments were deeply dyed. He also wore shoes. Around him were various items of funereal tribute, including bracelets of ivory and perforated shells. His head had been removed, but his body had been placed in alignment with the skull of a mammoth.

He was young, perhaps no more than twenty-one, but in that far-off time all men and women were young. He was clearly some kind of clan leader or tribal chieftain. At the beginning of the human world, a social hierarchy already existed with marks of rank and status. The cave in which he was interred was visited by many generations, but we do not know what secrets it contained. The people whom he represented passed from the face of the earth.

Only the last of the arrivals to England survived. These people came some 15,000 years ago and settled in places as diverse as the areas now known as Nottinghamshire, Norfolk and Devon. In a Nottinghamshire cave the figures of animals and birds were carved 13,000 years ago into the soft limestone ceiling; the stag and the bear, the deer and the bison, are among them.

Generations passed away, with little or no evidence of change. They persisted. They endured. We do not know what language they spoke. Of how or what they worshipped, we have no idea. But they were not mute; their intellectual capacity was as great, or as small, as our own. They laughed, and wept, and prayed. Who were they? They were the forebears of the English, the direct ancestors of many of those still living in this nation. There is an authentic and powerful genetic pattern linking the living with the long dead. In 1995 two palaeontologists discovered that the material from a male body, found in the caves of Cheddar Gorge and interred 9,000 years ago, was a close match with that of residents still living in the immediate area. They all shared a common ancestor in the maternal line. So there is a continuity. These ancient people survive. The English were not originally 'Anglo-Saxon' or 'Celtic'; they were a prehistoric island people.

The study of prehistory must also be the study of geography. When the settlers arrived in England, 15,000 years ago, the North Sea was a great plain of lakes and woodland. It now lies submerged, rich in the unseen evidence of the past. Yet we can in part rescue that which has been lost. Oak woods, marshes covered by reeds, and open grasslands covered the land. It was a warm and humid world. Red deer and voles inhabited the landscape; but they shared it with elephants and macaque monkeys. Among them wandered groups of humans, twenty-five or more in each group, pursuing their prey. They fired upon the animals with flint arrowheads, and used carved reindeer antlers as axes; they carried wooden spears. We do not know how they were organized but the discovery of 'butchery sites', where tools were manufactured and food prepared away from the main settlements, suggests a measure of social control.

We can still see the people walking towards us. On the sand at Formby Point, on the north-west coast of England, there are human footprints continuing for 32 feet (9.75 metres). The prints of many children are among them. The men were approximately 5 feet and 5 inches in height (1.55 metres), the women some 8 inches shorter (20 centimetres). They were looking for shrimps and razor shells. Footprints are found in other parts of England. Some appear on the foreshore of the Severn estuary; they fade away at the point where, 7,000 years before, the dry land became swamp. Now, on the flooding of the tide, they are gone.

These are the prints of what have been called Mesolithic people. The term, like its counterparts Palaeolithic and Neolithic, is loose but convenient. These people cleared the woods and forests by burning, in order to make way for settlements or to render the hunt for game more effective. Pine was also burned to make way for hazel, whose autumnal nuts were a popular source of food; they knew how to manage their resources. The early English have been called 'hunter-gatherers', with dogs employed for hunting, but their life was not that of undisciplined nomadic wandering; their activities took place within well-defined boundaries. They ranged through group territories that adjoined one another. They liked the areas where land and water meet.

Some 11,000 years ago a great lake covered what is now the Vale of Pickering in Yorkshire. On the bank of this lake was built a platform of birch wood. It might have been used to expedite fishing, but it is more likely to have been a site of ritual ceremonial; the people wore amber beads, and left behind the bones of pig and red deer, crane and duck. A round house has also been discovered, 11.5 feet in diameter (3.5 metres), that has been dated to approximately 9000 BC; it was constructed of eighteen upright wooden posts, with a thick layer of moss and reeds to furnish a sleeping area.

Its inhabitants used barbed antler points, flint knives and scrapers; they started fires by means of iron pyrite. The house itself seems to have possessed a hearth. They used canoes to travel over the lake; one paddle has been found, but no craft is now visible. It has disintegrated through time. But there are survivals. At this site, known as Star Carr, were discovered twenty-one fragments of deer skull, some of them still with antlers. Were they a form of disguise for hunting? More likely, they were part of a shamanistic covering to enter the spirit of the deer. It might have been an early form of morris dancing, except that the numinous has now become simply quaint.

The Mesolithic English lived in settlements such as that found at Thatcham in Berkshire; the modern town itself is in fact the latest version of human community on the same site. Some atavistic impulse keeps habitations in the same place. 10,000 years ago the people lived on the shore of a lake. Burnt bones, burnt hazelnuts and patches of charcoal used for fires, were found; here, in other words, was all the panoply of daily domestic life. Cleared spaces represented the floors of small huts. The first English house was made of flexible saplings, bent over and covered with hides. It measured approximately 20 feet by 16 feet (6 metres by 4.8 metres).

Hundreds of other such settlements existed, many of them in coastal regions that now lie upon the seabed. The coasts were once between 70 and 100 feet (between 21 and 30 metres) higher than their present level and, as the seas rose, so the settlements were lost in the deluge. We may never know very much more about the Mesolithic English because their remains are beneath the waves. One submerged village came to light when some divers peered into a burrow made by a wandering lobster off the Isle of Wight; the crustacean was flinging out pieces of worked flint. A settlement of craftsmen and manufacturers, as well as hunters and fishermen, was then revealed. A wooden pole, with a flint knife embedded in it, was rescued from the waters. A canoe was found, carved from a log. The remains of structures like houses could clearly be seen. They were workers in wood as well as in stone. This is part of the lost English world under water.

The water rose so much that, after the melting of the ice sheets of the glacial era, it encircled what had become the archipelago of England, Scotland and Wales. 8,000 years ago, the marshes and forests of the plain lying between England and continental Europe were obliterated by the southern North Sea. It may not have come as a tidal wave, although earthquakes can precipitate great masses of water. It is more likely to have happened gradually, over 2,000 years, as the land slowly became swamp and then lake. In earlier ages of the earth, two catastrophic floods had already created the Channel between England and France. With the influx of new waters the archipelago (we may call it an island for the sake of lucidity) was formed; 60 per cent of the land surface became what is now the land of England.

The land then becomes the object of topographical enquiry. Where, for example, is the exact centre of England? It is marked by a stone cross at the village of Meriden in Warwickshire; the consonance of Meriden with meridian or middle of the day is striking, and that may indeed have been reason enough for a cross to be raised there. In fact the true centre of the country is to be found on Lindley Hall Farm in Leicestershire. The property was recently owned by a couple with the surname of Farmer.

The effects of this novel insularity eventually became evident in the tools which were fashioned in England. They became smaller than those shaped on the continent, and certain types of microlith were in fact unique to this country. Yet the island was no less inviting to the travellers who came across the waters in boats manufactured of wood or of osier covered with stitched skins. They came from north-western Europe, proving that the Anglo-Saxon and Viking 'invasions' were the continuations of an ancient process.

They also came from the Atlantic coasts of Spain and south-western France, but that migration was not a recent phenomenon. The Atlantic travellers had been colonizing the south-western parts of England throughout the Mesolithic period, so that by the time of the formation of the island a flourishing and distinctive civilization existed in the western parts of the country. The travellers from Spain also settled in Ireland; hence the relationship between 'Iberia' and 'Hibernia'. The Iron Age tribe of the Silures, established in South Wales, always believed that their ancestors had come from Spain in some distant past; Tacitus noted that these tribal people had dark complexions and curly hair. These are the people known later as 'Celts'.

So differences between the English regions already existed 8,000 years ago. The flint tools of England, for example, have been divided into five separate and distinct categories. The artefacts of the south-west had a different appearance to those of the south-east, encouraging trade between the two areas. Individual cultures were being created that reinforced geographical and geological identities. There is bound to be a difference, in any case, between those cultures established upon chalk and limestone and those built upon granite.

A division is to be observed within England, established upon two broad zones. The Lowland Zone – comprising the midlands, the Home Counties, East Anglia, Humberside and the south central plain – is built upon soft limestone, chalk and sandstone. This is a place of low hills, plains and river valleys. It is a place of centralized power and settlement. It is soft, and various, and pliable. The Highland Zone in the north and west – comprising the Pennines, Cumbria, North Yorkshire, the Peak district of Derbyshire, Devon and Cornwall – largely consists of granite, slate and ancient hard limestone. This is a place of mountains, high hills and moors. It is a region of scattered groups or families, independent one from another. It is hard, and gritty, and crystalline. These two regions do not face each other; they face outwards, towards the seas from where their inhabitants came. We can see the changes upon the ground itself. In Wessex the border of the 'finds' from one settlement stops at the point where the chalk meets the Kimmeridge clays. These people would move no further west. So regional differences began to spread.

Differences, in accent and in dialect, may already have existed. There was an original language in the south-east of which traces still survive in contemporary speech – the words 'London', 'Thames' and 'Kent' have no known Germanic or Celtic root. It is possible that the people of East Anglia and the south-east began to speak a language that developed into Germanic, and that the people of the south-west spoke a language that would become Celtic. The Germanic tongue became Middle English before flourishing as standard English; Celtic speech diverged into Welsh, Cornish and Gaelic. It is pertinent that in Wales and Cornwall Celtic inscriptions can be found in stone, carved during the Roman age, while in southern England there are none. Tacitus reports that, at the time of the Roman colonization, the south-eastern English spoke a language not unlike that of the Baltic tribes. But there can be no certainties in the matter. All lies in mist and twilight.

When the mist rises, we see extraordinary things. Beneath a

burial mound in Wiltshire, near Avebury, was discovered what had once been a surface layer of soil dating from 3500 BC; it had been preserved by the construction of the barrow. The significance of this ancient ground was confirmed by the discovery of tiny grooves running at right angles, one to another, so that they form a criss-cross pattern. These grooves were cut by a plough. It was a forked tree branch, strengthened by a stone tip, pulled by an ox. It is the first evidence of a field in England. It represents the beginning of farming. We have entered what has become known as Neolithic England. This small patch of land was cleared by the destruction of dense woodland; it was cultivated with the plough; it then became pasture for sheep and cattle; a boundary fence or hedge was erected; the barrow was then built some 1,500 years later. In this sequence of events we see the slow changes of prehistory.

The transition from hunting to farming was itself a very gradual one; there was no agricultural revolution in any meaningful sense, just the increments of days and years and centuries of habitual practice. Custom was the keystone of life. In this long period flint tools were replaced by sickles and polished axes; pottery was introduced to England; new forms of communal ritual emerged. But in the space of an individual generation, which we may estimate between twenty and thirty years, it must have seemed that nothing had changed. When we use terms like 'Mesolithic' and 'Neolithic', we should remember the underlying deep continuity that represents the nature of England itself.

The slow expansion of farming can be dated from 4000 BC. The woods and forests of the country were cleared, at first sporadically but then extensively; the moors of northern and south-western England, and the heaths of East Anglia, were in part created by human activity. On this newly open ground wheat and barley crops were harvested. Domesticated pigs and cattle were kept, as well as sheep and goats. But sheep were not originally English. All of these animals were brought over in ships, not being native to the island, emphasizing the extent to which seafaring visitors contributed to the now familiar landscape.

This was a time of rising temperature, and in the glowing sun the people expanded; during the entire Neolithic period, from approximately 4700 BC to 2000 BC, the population trebled and has been estimated at 300,000. The pressure of ever-increasing numbers helped to accelerate the intensity of cultivation, and by 3000 BC the available countryside was marked out in small rectangular fields. Where there are fields there will be fences and ditches; there will be stone walls. Fences have been found beneath prehistoric burial mounds, testifying to their ancientness.

The presence of the barrows, where the dead reside upon the landscape, is a further sign of a settled society with its own forms of ritual and worship. Evidence can be found for the construction of houses and of scattered farmsteads with settlement pits, for enclosures where cattle might be herded or fairs and meetings held. One such enclosure, built in Cornwall before 3000 BC, was guarded by a great stone wall; the remains of houses were found here, sufficient accommodation for approximately 200 people. So the beginning of the English village, or of the English town, is to be found in the Neolithic period.

Roads and trackways were built from settlement to settlement. The Icknield Way took the prehistoric traveller from Buckinghamshire to Norfolk. Lanes led from farmstead to farmstead. The Pilgrims Way linked the great religious centres of Canterbury and Winchester. Ermine Street is now known, in part, as the Old North Road. The Jurassic Way goes from Oxfordshire to Lincolnshire. Watling Street ran between Canterbury and St Albans, passing through what may have been prehistoric London. Long causeways were built across the soft fens of Somerset, from timber that was felled in approximately 3800 BC; the varieties of wood used in their construction, from ash and lime to hazel and holly, suggest that they were especially grown for the purpose. The specific properties of the wood, utilized by the Neolithic English, are not known to us. Their technology is lost.

Many of the roads loosely known as 'Roman roads' are much more ancient; the Romans simply made use of the prehistoric paths. Modern roads have been built along the routes of these ancient lines, so that we still move in the footsteps of our ancestors. They created a network of communication that extended throughout England. This was a populous and busy civilization, much more sophisticated than was once generally thought. Along these routes were transported axe-blades for the use of farmers or house-builders, pottery of all kinds, and leather goods. Flint was mined in underground galleries entered by hundreds of shafts reaching a depth of 50 feet (15.2 metres); then it was sent over the country.

Yet the great division was steadily growing more pronounced. On the Atlantic side rose up megalithic portal tombs and passage tombs, unknown in East Anglia, the midlands and the south-east. These great stone hymns to the dead, erected for 600 years from 3800 BC, are the emanations of a distinctive culture that originally came from south-western Europe. The same tombs are found in Portugal and Brittany, Scotland and the Orkneys, suggesting that there was in essence a shared European religion inscribed in the siting of stone.

Causewayed enclosures of the same period are to be found predominantly in southern and eastern Britain; these are oval or circular spaces surrounded by a ditch cut into segments. They were used for the purposes of ritual, but the system of belief and practice was different from that of the south-west. Unlike the massive gateways of death revealed in the excavation of portal tombs, the open spaces suggest a more egalitarian or at least communal faith.

From the same epoch emerge the long parallel lines of ditches that have become known as cursus monuments; they cross what must have been cleared countryside, and can extend as far as 6 miles (9.6 kilometres). They are part of a ritual landscape of which the significance is now lost. Yet we know well enough that in this age of England the ground was holy; the stones, and the earth, were sacred. The English of the early Neolithic age had some direct communion with the terrain, and with the creatures that lived upon it, beyond the reach of the modern imagination.

All roads lead to Stonehenge, part of the greatest of all sacred sites. It began with a circle of fifty-six timbers, erected in approximately 2800 BC and placed in a ritual landscape that had already been in existence for 500 years. A cursus, 1½ miles long (2.4 kilometres), runs just to the north. Also found were pieces of rock crystal that must have been carried from Alpine regions. Salisbury Plain was then the spiritual centre of the island. From here radiate the chalk and limestone ranges of lowland Britain. A network of ridgeways and trading routes converged upon it. It was the largest area of habitable land. It was accessible by rivers. It was a great cauldron of human energy and purpose.

At some point, around 2200 BC, the first stone circle was being formed. The change from wood to stone has been related to a profound cultural movement, resulting in the building of monumental enclosures elsewhere, in the decline of ancestor worship and in bouts of warfare between opposing groups. In Peterborough a male and a female, with two children, were found within the same grave; the male was killed by an arrow in the back. In Dorset several bodies were found lying in a ditch, with a rampart fallen upon them; one of them had been killed by an arrow.

The building of Stonehenge was the largest and most protracted programme of public works in the history of England. A series of bluestones was first erected in 2200 BC; these stones were largely igneous in origin and were considered to have magical healing properties. The bluestones were then dismantled after a life of approximately 100 years and replaced by thirty sarsen stones; they formed a circle around five pairs of trilithons arranged in horseshoe pattern. At approximately the same time a wooden henge, or circular monument, of twenty-four obelisks was erected less than half a mile (0.8 kilometres) from its stone companion; it may have been a burial centre or the site of some other ritual activity.

Another henge and stone circle, known as Bluestonehenge, was erected a mile (1.6 kilometres) to the south-east along the bank of the Avon. A large village was also constructed, less than 2 miles away (3.2 kilometres), variously interpreted as a lodging for pilgrims, a ritual centre, a place of healing, or a home for those who erected the sarsen stones. Whatever the explanation, Salisbury Plain was the site of communal and spiritual settlement on a very large scale. It was once conceived to be a largely empty field, but now we find it to have been a field full of folk.

From this period was found the body of a man variously called 'the Amesbury archer' and 'the king of Stonehenge'; his grave contained over 100 artefacts, including gold hair ornaments, copper knives, pots and boars' tusks. Over his body, crouched in a foetal position, were scattered flint arrowheads. This was the last resting place of a tribal chieftain. Oxygen isotope analysis revealed that he had been brought up in the colder regions of northern Europe. What was a foreign king doing on Salisbury Plain? Was he on pilgrimage? There is evidence of an abscess and a painful bone infection. Had he crossed the sea to be healed? Or did he reign here as one of the tribal chieftains who, in an era without countries or nations, were not necessarily confined to one region?

In the final phase of building, approximately 1600 BC, the pits or holes for two circles of standing stones were hollowed out; but they were never filled. So the shape, and therefore possibly the nature, of Stonehenge has changed over a period of 1,200 years. It would be strange if it were not so. The same distance of time separates us from the Saxon age. It has been argued that the stones were a burial ground, a centre of pilgrimage and of ritual healing, a great observatory and a celestial clock, a place of public ceremonial and ritual. There is no reason why they could not have fulfilled all of these, as well as other, functions in the various eras of their existence. At the time of their erection these great stones seemed magnificent and immoveable in the earth; now, from a distance of 4,000 years, they dance in a pattern before us.

In all these eras, however, the stones are evidence of a controlling power that could organize vast numbers of people in a shared project. This was a hierarchical society with an elite, tribal or priestly, that could coerce or persuade many thousands of people into fulfilling its ritual will. The inhabitants of Salisbury Plain, to put it no broader, were under the guidance and protection of leaders who were rich in land and in cattle; the more we understand the material remains of this Neolithic culture, the more impressed we become by its range and authority. The construction of Silbury Hill, in the same region as Stonehenge, would have taken the labour of 1,000 men working every day for five years. The construction of Stonehenge itself would have entailed millions of hours of labour. Its bluestones were transported from the Preseli Hills in south-west Wales, some 200 miles distant. So great parts of England were already under organized administration long before the Romans and the Anglo-Saxons came; land, labour and material resources were governed by some form of central control.

It is suggestive that, in the course of the formation of Stonehenge, communal burials were being replaced by individual burials. The 'king of Stonehenge' is just one example. In some graves the body of the chieftain is accompanied by weapons, and in others the corpse is surrounded by goods. These are the graves of leaders and high priests, often with their immediate families. England had become an aristocratic, rather than a tribal, society.

The contours of the Bronze Age, succeeding the Neolithic in the standard time-lines of prehistory, are still to be found everywhere. They have endured for almost 4,000 years, and can be seen in a certain light. In the hour before sunset, when the rays of the sun lie across the English fields, the old patterns of the earth rise up and the land seems to return to its origins. The banks and ditches of hundreds and hundreds of small rectangular fields can be discerned. The sweep and extent of these fields are truly extraordinary; they can only really be comprehended from the air and, seeing aerial photographs for the first time in 1929, the historian G. M. Trevelyan was moved to declare that 'the discovery of these old Celtic fields, from under the palimpsest of later agricultural systems, is the most romantic thing that has come to stir our historical imaginations since the first Cretan finds'.

A lost world was revealed. The uplands and downlands of southern Britain were laid out in fields, with hedges and stone walls stretching for mile after mile; drove-ways and waterholes can be seen among these rectangular ditched fields. It is a feat of organization to rival that of the building of Stonehenge, and bears all the marks of powerful central planning. It seems likely that many thousands of square miles of land were laid out in one significant single act or set of acts, an example of land planning that has never since been rivalled in English history. In the process the English landscape was created.

This intensive cultivation is the best possible evidence for a steady rise in population. By 1900 BC there were as many as a million people, rising to more than 2 million by the time of Julius Caesar's invasion in 55 BC. It was of course an agricultural society, with its own regional variations. More and more territory was brought into cultivation, and has continued as productive arable land ever since. The woodland was cleared. Grass for pasture was created. There were more sheep than there would be in the sixteenth century AD. There was little appetite, or perhaps leisure, for monumental construction; working the land had become a more important activity.

Settlements were to be found everywhere, most of them located away from the monumental sites. Single households, and small hamlets, abounded. Enclosures were surrounded by a fence or ditch. 'Hut circles' were in fact groups of round stone houses with beehive roofs where the perfume of burning peat mingled with the smells of the farmyard. If every settlement was a light, then the whole of England was now ablaze. The island people were settled on Dartmoor, in the Lake District and on the North York moors.

They buried their dead in family units, the bodies cremated and laid in decorated urns. So the cemeteries of the Late Bronze Age, from approximately 1300 BC, have become known as 'urn fields'. Their discovery in the middle of the seventeenth century inspired the antiquary, Sir Thomas Browne, to compose *Hydriotaphia, Urn Burial, or a Discourse of the Sepulchral Urns lately found in Norfolk*. He was moved to declare that 'what time the persons of these ossuaries entered the famous nations of the dead, and slept with princes and counsellors, might admit a wide solution. But who were the proprietaries of these bones, or what bodies these ashes made up, were a question above antiquarism; not to be resolved by man, nor easily perhaps by spirits.' In this he has caught the remoteness of the long-dead, of whose rituals and customs we can have no conception.

Yet in certain respects they are not so distant as the philosopher implied. The men wore woollen cloaks, above a tunic known as a kirtle; the kirtle was still being worn in the sixteenth century. The women wore tunics and jackets, covered also by a woollen cloak. Shoes were made of skin, and men wore woollen caps. The women of more elevated status wore elaborate necklaces of jet, in the manner of Victorian ladies. One grave has yielded evidence of a woman who had a concealed 'pad' to bolster her hair. Men and women of the higher class sported ornaments of gold and bronze, as well as blue beads imported from Egypt. Amber jewellery was imported from the Baltic region, testifying to the range of international trade in Bronze Age England. Browne did not know that the people of this ancient period ate soups and stews as well as dressed meat; they consumed a kind of dried porridge made of wheat, barley and oats. Beer, wine and other alcoholic drinks were an integral part of the diet. Varieties of berry as well as hazelnut, herbs and seaweed, were eaten.

In his disquisition Browne went on to note that 'the iniquity of oblivion blindly scattereth her poppy, and deals with the memory of men without distinction to merit of perpetuity'. In the matter of their faith, at least, he has proved to be correct. The devotions of these people cannot be divined except in the broadest terms. The focus of ceremony and worship shifted from the sky to the earth; the steady exploitation of the land by Bronze Age farmers would have increased the significance of fertility rituals. There was in particular a pronounced attention to water and to watery places – springs, rivers, fens and marshes among them. The Thames, for example, became the home of Bronze Age weapons and other artefacts. In the Thames itself the offerings of weapons, bones and ornaments were kept separate and distinct; at Eton there are many skulls but no metal. Tools were left in dry, and weapons in wet, locations. An intricate taxonomy of worship cannot now be comprehended. Wooden platforms and causeways were built beside the river, part of the sacred space in which the priests of the people dwelled.

The significance of water is apparent throughout prehistory, with burial mounds and henge monuments sited by the rivers of England. For example, 368 Neolithic axes have been found in the Thames. It has been surmised that the deposition of Bronze Age work was part of a rite in propitiation of the dead and therefore a form of ancestor worship. If the dead were believed to cross between two worlds, they would have a particular affinity with the river; the river gains access to the underworld through a myriad passages, and springs ever fresh and renewed from its source. There is another, and perhaps more prosaic, explanation for the fervour elicited by water. There was literally water in the air. In the late Bronze Age the weather was growing cooler and wetter.

So we see the Bronze Age English in glimpses. A stirrup is found in a grave. Some seeds are deposited at the base of a bowl.

The bones of a sheep are excavated from the refuse pit of a settlement. Weapons are uncovered everywhere – spearheads, socketed axes, rapiers and, at a slightly later date, swords. There is evidence of harnesses, and bronze fittings, for horses. And there were chariots. In Peterborough have been uncovered the traces of wheel ruts that would have supported a vehicle with a width of $3^{1}/_{2}$ feet (1 metre).

From all these traces and tokens we can infer the presence of a warrior aristocracy, in a kingdom or group of sub-kingdoms that stretched from Dorset to Sussex. The culture of the middle and late Bronze Age is roughly contemporaneous with that of Troy, as depicted by Homer, and it had the same predilection for kings and warriors, feasting and ritual battle. It was a warrior society with small-scale sporadic fighting between elites, with gift exchanges between leaders, and tribute from the subject population in the form of food. That was one of the reasons why the land was so extensively farmed.

Defended settlements, and other enclosures containing buildings, were ubiquitous. These are the prototypes for the hill forts that are characteristic of southern England in the Iron Age. In Dorset, for example, a fence made out of great tree trunks – set in a trench some 10 feet (3 metres) deep – was built around an area of 11 acres (4.4 hectares).

Strong regional identities were already being formed, as well as regional divisions. The trading advantage of the Thames Valley region with its access to the European mainland, for example, helped to eclipse the agricultural wealth of Salisbury Plain. The north was engaged in stock-raising, while the south tended to concentrate upon cereal production. Trade encouraged interdependence.

Commerce of all kinds was increasing throughout this long epoch. Trade is the key to the growth of civilizations. Trade is the motor of wars. Trade fosters technologies. Trade creates towns and cities. Certain types of sword were manufactured in western France and found their way to England's eastern counties. Highly embellished barbecue spits were fashioned in Spain and exported to England. Metal work from the ancient city of Mycenae, in Greece, has also been found. Gold ornaments were sent from

Ireland. Linen and woollen fabrics were in turn exported to Europe, together with slaves and hunting dogs. Children worked in the tin mines of Cornwall, digging out the precious ore with bones and hammer-stones; the metal was then despatched to the coastal ports for shipment.

And of course when tin was added to molten copper, the metal from which this age is named was formed. Bronze implements changed everything, from the cutting down of forests to the building of houses. They made fighting more efficient. Bronze ornaments, bronze spears, bronze shields, bronze buckets, bronze chisels, bronze skewers and bronze knives were in abundant supply; the Bronze Age Englishman could shave himself with a bronze razor, using oil as the lubricant.

There is a theory that once a new process has been discovered and utilized, it appears in many other places simultaneously. Once something has been learned, it is conveyed across the whole human species. This is likely to explain the manufacture of bronze, since it could not have emerged from one source. Bronze of the same date has been found from Switzerland to Thailand. So people of approximately the same culture met on equal terms. We imagine visitors of high status sailing to England; there may have been embassies from Troy itself or from the court of the pharaoh Akhenaten in Egypt.

The Bronze Age did not come to an end; the movement from bronze to iron reflects a change in technology leading to slow cultural change. The process took hundreds of years, during which period bronze and iron were simultaneously in use. Of course none of these 'ages' existed in the minds of those who experienced them. The Neolithic inhabitants of England lived in the same places as the Mesolithic people. Bronze Age fields and cemeteries are on the same sites as their Neolithic forebears; Bronze Age settlements were continuously in use through the Iron Age, and the people of the Iron Age consistently respected the burial mounds and boundary lines from the previous age of the human world. They honoured the structure of the landscape around them.

*

From the beginning of the Iron Age in approximately 700 BC, therefore, an advanced concept of territoriality governed relations between the land and the people. It had gathered strength over thousands of years. Leaders, and tribes, were firmly and specifically associated with certain regions. We see this in the laying out of boundaries and in the location of settlements. Yet through the Iron Age there was an intensification of this natural development. Engels once described iron as 'the last and most important of all the raw materials that have played a revolutionary role in history'. New forms of alliance, and new networks of trade, were gradually established. Objects of ritual and ceremonial value were often made out of the new metal. The trade in iron contributed to the ultimate shape of England, where the various regions were becoming more intensely organized and controlled.

Hierarchy was marked out with chieftains and sub-chieftains, warriors and priests, farmers and craftsmen, workers and slaves. Slave irons have been found at a site near St Albans. A gang chain has been discovered on Anglesey. The funereal practices for the elite dead became more and more elaborate. In the burial places of the Iron Age chieftains the body was surrounded by molten silver, cloth of gold, ivory, suits of iron chain mail, precious cups and bowls. They pre-date the wealth of Sutton Hoo by a thousand years. Trampled earth was uncovered around the base of one mortuary chamber, suggesting dancing. The graves of women of high status contained many ornaments, including mirrors, brooches, bangles, beads, tweezers and bowls. In one burial a great bowl of bronze had been placed over the woman's face.

Strong regional identities were in place. In the east undefended settlements, very much like villages, lay among open fields. In the south-west small communities lived in defended homesteads, together with unenclosed settlements sited at a distance; this has been interpreted as a division between tribal leaders and their subject people. In the north-east was found a pattern of defended homesteads, while in the north-west a tradition of roundhouses known as beehive huts existed. The culture of Salisbury Plain, sometimes known as 'Wessex culture', demanded a pattern of large territorial groupings based around hill forts. There are of course variations on all these themes, from the pit dwellings carved out of the chalk in Hampshire to the lake villages of Somerset where round huts were built upon floating islands of logs.

The hill forts themselves are evidence of a strongly ranked society. They seem to have originated in the neighbourhood of the Cotswolds and then spread over the whole of central southern England. They demonstrated the mastery of land and resources, and were therefore a symbol of proprietorship. Linear earthworks often mark out the boundaries of the territory controlled by each fort. They became more heavily defended over the period of the Iron Age and were sometimes occupied for hundreds of years. They resembled towns as much as forts, with clusters of buildings, streets, temples, storage facilities and 'zones' for separate industrial activities. The houses were circular, built of upright posts, woven together with wattle and sticks of hazel; they had doors and porches, facing east, and the roofs were generally thatched with reeds or straw. The thatch was held in place with a daub of dung, clay and straw; since soot from the peat fires was a valuable manure, it is likely to have been replaced each year. Archaeologists, reconstructing the interiors of these houses, have found small cupboards in which weapons were stored. Although their populations ranged only from 20 to 200 people, we may see in them the beginnings of urban life in England. The author believes that London was once just such a hill fort, but the evidence for it is now buried beneath the megalopolis it has become. All the evidence suggests, however, the existence of many small tribes living in a state of constant alert against rivals.

There were indeed cattle raids, conflicts between warriors and large-scale wars. Some hill forts were stormed and burned. Bodies have been found in the ramparts, their bones marked and hacked. We can expect a tradition of heroic songs and tales in which the exploits of an individual warrior or leader were celebrated. They are to be found in the early Irish epics, for example, which may incorporate stories and refrains from the prehistoric age of Irish tribes. An analogy with Homer's *Iliad* can be made. Indeed it has been suggested that the epic poem in fact adverts to events in England, in myths and tales that were then carried by bards eastward to Anatolia.

Yet the various tribes or regional groupings did come together in a network of alliances and ties of kinship; how else could trade in commodities such as iron and salt flourish throughout the country? Many of these smaller clans were in time integrated and, perhaps in the face of threat, became large units of territory. These were the tribes of England whom the Romans confronted in their slow progress towards ascendancy. By the end of the Iron Age certain hill forts had become dominant and assumed the role of regional capitals. As the population steadily increased, so agriculture became ever more intensive. The clearance of woodland and forest continued without a break. The farmers began to work the thick clay soils in earnest, with the help of the heavy wheeled plough. This was the solid basis for the agricultural economy of England over the next 2,500 years. Wheat was grown in Somerset, and barley in Wiltshire; that broad pattern is still the same.

A visitor sailed to England's shores. The Greek merchant and explorer Pytheas made landfall in 325 BC. He named the island as Prettanike or Brettaniai. This is the origin of the name of Britain. The land of the Picts was known by the diminutive of Prydyn. Pytheas visited Cornwall, and watched the inhabitants work the ore and purify the metal. On another stage of his journey he was told by the natives that the mother of Apollo, Leto, was born on this island 'and for this reason Apollo is honoured among them above all other gods; and the inhabitants are looked upon as priests of Apollo'.

He also reports that he had seen 'a wonderful sacred precinct of Apollo and a celebrated temple festooned with many offerings'; it was 'spherical in shape' and close by there was a city 'sacred to this god' whose kings are called 'Boreades' after the god of the cold north wind. The identity of this precinct, temple and city have long been a matter of debate. Some argue that Pytheas was describing the sacred landscape of Stonehenge and Silbury Hill; others believe that it refers to a temple of Apollo where Westminster Abbey now stands, and the adjacent 'city' of London.

It is clear, however, that Pytheas was reporting the claims of a people deeply imbued in ritual worship, with the names of Apollo and Boreas simply being used by him as tokens of holiness. The Parthenon had already been built in Athens, and all foreign gods were seen by the Greeks in classical terms. The religion of the Iron Age in England, however, has always been associated with the cult of Druidism.

It may also be glimpsed within the sacred geometries of Iron Age art (still known inaccurately as Celtic art). It was an art of vision, penetrating beyond the appearances of things. It traced living lines of energy and purpose with spirals and swastikas, curves and circles, whirling together in an intricate network of shapes and patterns. It is in no sense primitive or barbaric; on the contrary it is ingenious and complex, showing a mastery of artificial form and linearity. These intricate patterns are clearly related to the whorls, spirals and concentric circles carved upon Mesolithic passage graves several thousand years earlier; they suggest a broad continuity of belief and worship throughout the prehistoric age.

At the core of Iron Age religion were the persistent and continuing native beliefs of England, enshrined in certain sacred places. Caves were often holy. The Druids themselves are known to have congregated in sacred groves, where ancient trees provided the setting for ritual practice. Powerful gods had to be propitiated. An early Bronze Age barrow in Yorkshire yielded up certain drum-shaped idols carved out of chalk, with what seem to be human eyebrows and noses. 2,000 years after these images were carved a British writer, Gildas, was still moved to condemn the 'diabolical idols ... of which we still see some mouldering away within or without the deserted temples, with the customary stiff and deformed features'. So there was a long tradition of worship that may have had its earliest origins in the Neolithic period. The image of the horned god Cernunnos has been found at Cirencester. The horse goddess Epona has been discovered in Wiltshire and in Essex. A carving of the hammer god Sucellus has been unearthed in East Stoke, Nottinghamshire. The mysterious god, Lud or Nud, is still commemorated by Ludgate Hill and Ludgate Circus in London.

Religious sanctuaries were established all over the land, and it is safe to assume that even the smallest settlement had its own central shrine. They have been discovered in hill forts, within ditched enclosures, along boundaries, and above barrow graves; they are often marked by the subsequent presence of Roman temples or early Christian churches. Certain places were deemed to be blessed. Many English churches will be lying upon prehistoric originals. In Iron Age England, it was believed that the cock served as a defence against thunderstorms; that is why cocks are still to be found on church steeples. They became known as weathercocks.

Human sacrifice helped to sanctify the land. A male body was found in a bog in Cheshire; he had been bludgeoned in the head, and his throat cut before being deposited in the marsh. Many skeletons have been found at the bottom of pits in southern England, their bodies flexed in an unnatural posture. There is also the known prehistoric affinity for severed heads, believed to be the site of the soul or spirit. Skulls have been found lined up in a row. The bodies of defeated enemies were often beheaded, and their heads buried or placed in running water. Three hundred skulls, dating from the Neolithic to the Iron Age, have been found in the Thames. The river was once an English Golgotha, the place of skulls.

Caesar's account of the high priests of England, the Druids, adverts to the practice of human sacrifice. They created images of wicker-work which 'they fill with living men and, setting them on fire, the men are destroyed by the flames'. In his account the Druid priests are the lawmakers of the land who determine rewards and punishments. They settle disputes over boundaries and over property.

The Roman writer Pliny records that they 'esteem nothing more sacred than the mistletoe'; the high priests 'select groves of oak, and use the leaves of the mistletoe in all sacred rites'. The sacrificial victim was tied to the trunk of the oak tree, and his priestly killers wore chaplets of oak leaves. They practised divination, magic and astrology; they believed in the immortality of the soul that passes through various incarnations. This doctrine of immortality was considered by the Roman writers to make clear the contempt for death revealed by the native English; the English were noted for this quality of indifference in subsequent centuries.

The Druids worshipped the sun and moon also, but their solar belief persisted long after the passing of the priestly caste. A butcher from Standon in Hertfordshire was accused, in 1452, of proclaiming that there was no god except the sun and the moon. In the second chapter of *Tess of the d'Urbervilles* Thomas Hardy remarks that 'old customs' last longer on clay soils. The power of the Druids was retained by the bishops of the Anglo-Saxon church, just as the tonsure of early Christian monks may reflect Druidical practice.

By 100 BC, at the very latest, the eyes of Rome were turned towards England as a source of wealth and of trade. What did they see? They saw a land made up of tribal kingdoms, large and small, that had kept to the old tribal boundaries. The Dumnonii inhabited the south-west peninsula, while the Durotriges were the people of Dorset; the Cantii of Kent comprised four separate kingdoms; the Iceni were of Norfolk. The Brigantes controlled the smaller tribes of the entire northern area from the Irish Sea to the North Sea; they occupied the Pennines and their tribal name means 'the high ones'.

There were altogether fifteen large tribes in England, now coming under the control of leaders who were being described as kings. Suetonius named Cunobelinus, the leader of the Catuvellauni in the years preceding the main Roman invasion of Claudius, as '*rex Britannorum*'. From his capital at St Albans he controlled a great area north of the Thames – including Cambridgeshire and Bedfordshire and Oxfordshire – and has since entered English mythology as the Cymbeline of Shakespeare's play. His was a fully formed elite culture of warriors and priests, with its traditions going back to the early Bronze Age. One or two more recent tribal migrations have been identified. Members of a tribe from North Gaul, the Parisii, had settled in Yorkshire at some time in the fifth century BC and created an archaeologically distinctive community. More recent visitors arrived in Kent; a tribe known as the Belgae launched a small invasion in the first century BC and eventually settled in Hampshire, Essex and Kent. The Roman name for Winchester is Venta Belgarum, or the market of the Belgae.

The population of England in the late Iron Age has been estimated at approximately 2 million, rising to 3 million by the end of the Roman dominion. It was in every respect a wealthy and flourishing country. That is why the Romans chose to invade it. They wished to exploit the surplus of corn. There was in particular a spread of settlements in the south-east and central southern regions with extensive fields, shrines, cemeteries, industries, markets, towns and villages. In his *Commentarii de Bello Gallico* Julius Caesar remarked that 'the population is very large, their homesteads thick on the ground and very much like those in Gaul, and the cattle numerous. As money they use either bronze or gold coins or iron bars with a fixed standard of weight.' Coins, in particular, facilitated trade between tribes and bore the stamp of a powerful leader. The further north a traveller progressed, however, the fainter was the evidence for these material benefits.

That is because the southern tribes were engaged in extensive trade with Rome and Romanized Gaul long before Caesar's invasion. They had, in a sense, already become Romanized with their predilection for certain foods and luxury goods. Yet, if you look beneath the surface, you find ancient tribal ways. There seems to have been consistent inter-tribal warfare, for example, with various leaders appealing to Rome for assistance. Large earthworks were created as boundaries. The warriors came to battle in chariots, their naked bodies covered with blue woad and pierced with tattoos. 'They wear their hair long', Caesar wrote, 'and shave all their bodies with the exception of their heads and their upper lips.' They had not quite left the domain of prehistory.

Nor have we yet. The legacy of prehistory is all around us. The clearances of prehistoric farmers helped to create the English landscape, and there are still places where the division of the land follows its prehistoric boundaries. In southern England the field systems of the Bronze Age and Iron Age inform and maintain the layout of modern farming. Modern roads follow the line of ancient paths and trackways. The boundaries of many parishes follow ancient patterns of settlement, and their irregular outlines enclose land sufficient to maintain a small farming community; ancient burials are often to be found on the boundaries of such a parish, and even the orientation of the church may obey old laws. Churches and monastic communities were placed close beside the sites of megalithic monuments, as well as sacred springs and early Bronze Age ritual spaces. The churchyard of the parish church of Rudston, in East Yorkshire, harbours the tallest Neolithic standing stone in England. The pilgrim routes of medieval Kent trace the same

pattern as the prehistoric tracks to holy wells and shrines. We still
live deep in the past.

Many villages, and towns, are built upon the sites of prehistoric
originals. Leicester and Lincoln, Cambridge and Colchester, Rochester and Canterbury – to name only a few examples – were settled
in the Iron Age or earlier. Village communities endure through
recorded and unrecorded history. They may begin as simple family
units, surrounded by ancestral spirits, before the natural process of
extension. But we cannot dig down to the prehistoric origins of
most English villages precisely because they are still in thriving
occupation. Many Iron Age settlements became the market towns
of the twenty-first century, where surplus produce has always been
traded.

Certain customs, and festivals, belong to the prehistoric past.
The celebrations of the Iron Age were incorporated into the
Christian calendar, with the festival of the dead or 'Samain'
becoming All Souls' Day, and the midwinter solstice commemorated as Christmas. The Bronze Age practice of scattering white
quartz stones upon freshly dug graves was still being observed in
early twentieth-century Wales. In nineteenth-century Scotland
many inhabitants still lived in stone 'beehive' houses from the
Neolithic period. The famous public house beside Hampstead
Heath, Jack Straw's Castle, stands on the site of an ancient
earthwork. The historic and the prehistoric exist simultaneously.
Catterick in North Yorkshire remains a military base, just as it was
when the mead-drunk warriors of the Gododdin assailed it at the
end of the sixth century AD. There is scarcely one spot in England
that does not contain memorials of an ancient past.

# 2

# The Roman way

Julius Caesar's 'invasion' of 55 BC was more in the nature of a preliminary patrol; he said that he wanted to acquaint himself with 'the lie of the land'. The Romans did not like the sea, but the pull of the island was irresistible. Britain was already a trading partner, and was rumoured to be rich in metal and wealthy with wheat. Some of its tribes had allied themselves with the northern Gauls whom Caesar was fighting. So there was every reason for a visit.

Several of the tribal leaders, informed in advance of his preparations, sent emissaries to treat with him; he in turn despatched an envoy who urged them to collaborate with their putative conqueror. Then Caesar set sail with two legions, each of approximately five thousand men, transported in eighty ships; when they eventually landed near Deal, the English were watching them. A skirmish took place on the beach, in which the Romans were victorious, and once more the tribal leaders sued for peace. Yet it was of short duration. A storm blew up, compounded by the force of a high tide at a time of full moon. The Romans were not aware of the phenomenon. All the ships were damaged.

The English tribes now broke the vow of peace, and a number of skirmishes took place in the immediate vicinity of Deal where Caesar was hard-pressed. His one thought now was of retreat across the water. He managed to repair the ships, and sought material aid from Gaul. Then, taking many hostages from the English, he sailed back vowing to return.

In the following year he kept his promise. On this occasion he was more determined and more resourceful. He brought with him 800 ships, 25,000 infantry and 2,000 cavalry. It was a true invasion. In the face of this threat the warring tribes of the region were animated by a single purpose and chose Cassivellaunus, king of territory north of the Thames, as their war leader. The English fought the Romans just as they fought each other − warriors on foot, warriors on horseback and warriors in chariots, each attacking and withdrawing at opportune moments. Cassivellaunus had an army of 4,000 chariots; the charioteer would drive to the front line, and the warrior would jump out while the driver retired and waited for his return. Caesar reported that, by steady practice, 'they attain such proficiency that even on a steep incline they are able to control the horses at full gallop, and to check and turn them in a moment'. They were a difficult and formidable force, motivated by sheer courage and ingenuity.

Yet the steady and disciplined army of the Romans withstood them. After a number of battles, the English retreated into the woods. Caesar followed them, and laid waste to Cassivellaunus' stronghold. The chieftains of the various tribes sought peace, and in the end Cassivellaunus himself capitulated. Taking hostages and exacting tribute, Caesar returned to Rome.

There was to be no subsequent invasion for ninety years, but the advent and victory of the Roman forces had left their mark. Their success, ironically, can be seen in the gradual Romanization of southern Britain where tribal leaders began to import wine and luxury goods from the Roman Empire. When old ways of life have been defeated, they begin to lose their potency. The dwellings of the elite were beginning to change their shape, from round to rectilinear; this is profound evidence of cultural transition. The tribal leaders of the south, at least, wished to imitate the victors.

Some of them changed their allegiance altogether, and became the client kings of Rome. According to one Greek historian, Strabo, they procured the friendship of the first master of the Roman Empire, Augustus, 'by sending embassies and paying court to him'. They exported grain and iron and slaves, while in return obtaining glass vessels, amber ware and other goods on which they were obliged to pay duty to the Roman state. No better way could be found of binding them to mainland European culture.

The Romans had become well aware of the material benefits to be found on the island. They simply needed the right moment to strike. This was given to them when the leaders of the tribe or kingdom of the Atrebates appealed to Rome for assistance against one of their hostile neighbours. It is clear that certain tribes welcomed the intervention of Rome. The new emperor, Claudius, needed an opportunity to prove himself in the field. He had small military reputation and, in the words of Cicero, 'glory in war exceeds all other forms of success'. Glory was also to be found on English soil.

In AD 43, under the leadership of Aulus Plautius, four legions comprising some 20,000 men landed in two separate locations, thus confusing any English counter-attack. The tribes dispersed in front of them, but rallied for a major battle by the Medway; the fighting lasted for two days but the native forces under the leadership of Caratacus were eventually defeated. It was one of the most significant battles in English history, but its precise site is not known. Plautius now sent for Claudius to deliver the final and triumphant *coup de grâce*. Two months later the emperor arrived, together with twenty-eight elephants; he stormed the native capital of Camulodunum, and Caratacus fled westward. When Claudius returned to Rome, he was celebrated for having received the surrender of eleven kings. The conquest of the country had begun. It would take almost forty years before it was complete.

Camulodunum, or Colchester, became the first Roman capital; a great fort was built on the site of the native earthworks as a token of dominion. From here the Roman army spread outwards; they advanced in three directions, north and west and north-west. The leader of the western army, Vespasian, fought thirty-three battles in his drive towards Wales and the south-west peninsula. On the banks of a hill fort in Dorset, Maiden Castle, has been found the body of a man with a Roman bolt from a crossbow in his spine. By AD 49 Roman soldiers were supervising mining operations in Somerset.

The armies to the north and north-west proceeded slowly along existing roads, such as Ermine Street, attempting to pacify or subdue the various tribes in their path. They built forts in the conquered areas, so that each tribal zone was dominated by at least one military settlement. By AD 51 the queen of the great northern tribe of the Brigantes, Cartimandua, was receiving Roman wine in Roman vessels as well as building tiles. She had become a client queen. The historians of Rome describe a smooth progress of colonization, but the natives are unlikely to have surrendered without a fight; the process was one of steady advance beset by tribal rebellions and occasional army mutinies. Ambushes, raids and battles were commonplace. All the land south of the Fosse Way, running from Exeter to Lincoln, was under Roman control; the land north of it was more treacherous. Some tribes had divided allegiances; other tribes fought one against another.

A revolt in AD 47 by members of the tribe of Iceni, living deep within the pacified zone of East Anglia, was an indication of continuing uncertainty. The uprising, over the right to bear arms, was put down easily enough; but it was a harbinger for a much more serious rebellion that occurred thirteen years later. The name of Boudicca, or Boadicea, has now become part of English folklore. She was the wife of the king of the Iceni, Prasutagus, whose death prompted the agents of the Roman provincial government to attempt a wholesale appropriation of Iceni wealth. Boudicca was flogged, and her two daughters were raped. It was a signal instance of imperialist brutality.

So Boudicca rose and fought. She gathered into her confederacy other English tribes and launched an attack upon the Roman capital of Colchester. It was a particular object of offence because it harboured hundreds of military veterans who had taken control of adjacent land. The tribal army went southward, burning and pillaging any evidence of incipient Romanization. Villas were destroyed, their inhabitants put to the sword. When the warriors descended upon Colchester itself, they were ferocious. The city was destroyed by fire, the shops looted. The veterans took shelter in the central temple but after two days they were overwhelmed and hacked to pieces. A great statue of Claudius was beheaded and thrown into the river. The temple itself was destroyed. Boudicca then proceeded to move further south in the direction of London;

Chelmsford and St Albans were sacked, and an entire legion massacred.

The Roman military governor, Suetonius Paulinus, was aware of the gravity of the threat posed to his regime. He had marched quickly back from Wales, where he had been campaigning, but his arrival in London did not save the city. He could not yield to the demands and supplications of the citizens; it was his duty to save the whole imperial province by a battle at a place and time of his own choosing. Many Londoners left the city in haste, going further south to find haven with pro-Roman tribes; those who remained were destroyed. Tacitus reports that 70,000 people were killed in the attack. The city itself was razed by fire, and there still exists beneath the City of London's streets a red level of oxidized iron. Towards the end of the twentieth century forty-eight human skulls were found embedded in the track of the river Walbrook.

Boudicca now went after Suetonius Paulinus, on the evident assumption that the time was right for a final blow against the Roman occupation. The site of the ensuing battle is not certainly known; it may have been near the village of Mancetter in Warwickshire, or at Messing in Essex. Whatever the location, it was drenched in blood. Suetonius Paulinus had 10,000 troops, but they were ranged against a force of 100,000. The legionaries had a forest behind them, a plain before them; the native warriors ran against them, across the plain, but many of them were struck down by a hailstorm of javelins. The Romans then began to move forward with their shields and short swords. Their discipline held them steady, and slowly Boudicca's men were turned. General carnage ensued, with 80,000 of her forces dead by the end of the battle. Some 400 Romans were killed. It was one of the most bloody massacres on English soil. Some say that Boudicca then took poison, so that she would avoid capture by the enemy; other sources report that she fell ill and died. Her monument now stands on Westminster Bridge as a token of the fight for native independence.

The Romans wished to extirpate another particular enemy. The Druids, the guardians of the old faith, had to be silenced before the full work of pacification could be completed. They had been harried and pursued as they had retreated steadily westward; their last stand took place on the island of Anglesey in AD 61. The

Roman historian Tacitus reports that the troops, crossing from the mainland, were confronted by a 'dense line of armed warriors along the foreshore, while women were rushing about between the ranks garbed in black like the Furies, holding up lighted torches'. Close to them stood the Druids, offering sacrifices, holding their arms in the air and screeching terrible curses. Yet their gods did not come to their rescue; they were all cut down and their sanctuaries put to the flame.

After the east and south had been pacified the next Roman governor of the province, Julius Agricola, turned his attention to the western and northern regions. In AD 78 he conquered Wales. In the following year he sent his legions to the north-east, through Corbridge, and to the north-west, through Carlisle. He divided the enemy, and built up a network of forts to supervise those tribes that had surrendered to him. These tribes were more hostile and aggressive than those of the south, and there were according to Tacitus 'many battles, some not unbloody'. The ultimate aim was to create and control a northern frontier, and as a result troops were sent in to subjugate what is now southern Scotland.

The general shape of militarized England was also now created; permanent fortresses, each harbouring a legion, were built at York and Chester. Manchester and Newcastle were also built around the site of Roman forts. The original name for Manchester was Mamucio, after the Latin word for a hill shaped like a breast; this was then misread as Mancunio, giving its name to the modern inhabitants of the city. A series of virtually straight roads were constructed, linking fort to fort. Garrison towns, inhabited by retired legionaries, were created at Lincoln and at Gloucester. The imposing colonial presence was emphasized by a network of encampments, forts, watchtowers and defensive walls. Posting stations were set up on the principal roads, and these staging posts eventually became villages. So the country was organized by military power into a landscape of farmsteads and villas, fields and settlements, drove-ways and enclosures. It was not unlike the vista of the Iron Age; yet it was more coherent.

This was not necessarily a benign process. One tribal chief is reported by Tacitus to have complained that 'our goods and money are consumed by taxation; our land is stripped of its harvest to fill their granaries; our hands and limbs are crippled by building roads through forests and swamps under the lash of our oppressors'. The military zone, including Wales and the north of England, required a standing force of 125,000 men. It would be wrong to think of the legionnaires as Romans; in the first century of occupation 40,000 soldiers were recruited from Gaul, Spain and Germany. The English also joined the army of occupation. The troops mixed and mingled with the indigenous population so that, within two or three generations, it had indeed become a native army.

One other pertinent development took place. A great wall, dividing Romanized England from the tribes of Scotland, was built on the orders of the emperor Hadrian. Twenty years later another wall was constructed, effectively separating south from north Scotland. The Romans had no intention of venturing into the Highlands, just as they dropped any plans for the invasion of Ireland. The Roman Empire had ceased to expand, and it became necessary to protect its borders so that it might enjoy the pleasures of peace. The territory just south of the wall was intensively cultivated. A great agricultural regime was established on the Cumbrian Plain. England was no longer a province easily shaken by tribal rebellion. It became prosperous once again, as rich and as productive as it had been during the Iron Age.

The process of Romanization was gradual and local. The conditions of the Iron Age still prevailed in the countryside, where the people largely remained faithful to old customs and habitual practice. The evidence of change comes from the towns, and from the administrative elite of English leaders who worked in them. These were the men who had welcomed, or at least exploited, the ascendancy of the Roman officials in their country. With the advice of these officials they began to erect temples, public squares and public buildings; they learned the Latin language, and took to wearing togas as an indication of their new identities. They put down their weapons and attended more to the abacus. The children of the leading English families were educated in the 'civilized arts' and some were sent to Rome. Bathing establishments and assembly rooms were built and, according to Tacitus, the natives began to attend 'smart dinner parties'. There were many more plates, dishes, drinking vessels and bowls than in the Iron Age. Amphorae or storage vessels were imported; they contained wine and olive oil, olives and fish sauce. Tacitus went on to write, cuttingly enough, that 'they called it civilization when in fact it was part of their servitude'.

The old hierarchies were still in existence, but now they were wearing Roman brooches and rings. The landowner had tenants, known as *coloni*, who were tied to the land. At the top of the scale were the tribal leaders who owned extensive territory and property; at the bottom was the large community of slaves. The word for slave, *servus*, eventually became serf. So the old bonds were perpetuated through the centuries. The social patterns of the Bronze Age and Iron Age were strengthened and deepened by the rule of a strong central power.

As part of the organization of the country, the Romans converted the old tribal regions into government districts or *civitates*. Each district had its own central town which, in many cases, was the old tribal capital or *oppidum* re-dressed in stone rather than in wood. A forum 'complex' of civic buildings represented the centre where all the affairs of the town were administered. The colonial power imposed its own forms of architecture, with monumental arches, sculptures, altars and bathhouses bringing order to what were once irregular settlements. Many of these public buildings were part of a state initiative that continued well into the second century AD. The forum and the basilica, the temple and the amphitheatre, rose above closely packed shops, houses and workshops still generally built out of timber and clay and with floors of earth. Many of the houses were in fact single-room lodgings; other buildings consisted of a shop at the front, a workshop behind it, and a room for accommodation at the back. The area of settlement was pitted with wells and hearths. Beyond the streets lay the cemeteries, the kilns, the quarries and the enclosures for livestock.

The government of the towns was controlled by a council or *curia* of the larger landowners, with a complement of clerks and other officials. All the elements of social differentiation, and specialization, are to be found here as kinship and tribal ties slowly gave way to group relations on an economic basis. The larger towns were independent and self-governing, with the magistrates and councillors taking care of such matters as drainage, sanitation and the repaving of roads. The most common 'find' for archaeologists of Roman England is the writing tablet.

Villas in the Roman style were soon rising in the countryside. The earliest of them, such as that discovered at Fishbourne in Sussex, were of very high status and were presumably designed for the convenience of Romanized tribal leaders or great officials of the empire. The fashion for luxury spread to the other leaders of the indigenous population, and more modest villas were built in the south-east; these would have been appropriate for a prosperous landowner or the chief family of an agricultural community. Villas were essentially farming establishments that enjoyed surplus wealth to be lavished upon display and decoration; they copied the Roman style, with walls of stone and costly mosaics. They might have had roofs of ceramic tiles, quite different from the thatch and wattle of the English roundhouse. Mosaics, underfloor heating and window glass, all carried the stamp of imperial civilization. Even the smaller houses might be plastered and decorated with wall-paintings; plain or painted plaster was also used as external protection from the elements. But it would be unwise to overestimate their presence in the English landscape. Hill forts were also to be found, for example, especially for the leading families of England who had remained in closer contact with their social and cultural traditions.

An Iron Age farm was still in use at the beginning of the second century AD at Keston in Kent. By the middle of that century a new wooden farmhouse had been erected, decorated with painted walls. At the beginning of the third century a house of stone rose upon the site, complete with a bathhouse in the Roman style. Wooden barns occupied part of the farmyard, and one of them was later rebuilt in stone. Ovens were in use for malting or corn-drying, and it is likely that the owner or owners of the villa also employed potters, blacksmiths and workers in bronze. An early Roman cremation cemetery has also been uncovered. A circular mausoleum was created at a later date. So by degrees a small Romanized community was created.

In the farming of the soil itself, the practices of the Bronze and Iron Ages were still maintained. In certain regions, such as the south-west, native habits persisted without change of any kind. Only in the south-east is there evidence of altering taste, albeit confined to the leaders of society. The Romans brought in cherries, mulberries and figs, previously unknown. Turnips, cabbages and peas first appeared under the aegis of Roman rule. One sticking point remained; the natives even of the Romanized areas still preferred beef to pork.

It can be said with some certainty that the majority of the people were still living in the Iron Age, and would continue to do so for several hundreds of years. One agricultural innovation, however, occurred as a direct result of imperial decree. The fenlands of East Anglia were drained, and the reclaimed soil made productive with hundreds of villages and farms planted in a pre-ordained manner. The whole area became an imperial estate, taxed for the benefit of the central government. The prosperous Salisbury Plain became another imperial estate.

Taxation, including a land tax and a poll tax, was the key of Roman exploitation. As the costs of maintaining the army, in the face of northern invaders, became ever higher so the burden of taxation increased. The Roman occupation hastened the process by which a tribal economy gave way to a monetary economy. The tribal coinage, more significantly, was replaced by imperial coinage. The Romans of course also levied taxes on the fruits of trade. Industrial centres, such as the potteries at the village of Castor in Cambridgeshire, altered parts of the landscape. Ironworks were established in all areas of the country from the coast of Kent to the banks of the Wye. Lead mines were in continuous use throughout the Roman period. Under the twin stimuli of demand and innovation, English production was never more buoyant. Coal was used for working iron and heating the bathhouses; it was also the fuel for the sacred fire at Minerva's temple in Bath.

Two native woollen products were in demand by the subjects of the empire; one was known as the *birrus Britannicus*, a type of waterproof cloak and hood. The other, the *tapete Britannicum*, was a woollen rug. Other forms of merchandise included bears and bulldogs for the Roman arena. The men wore jackets of cattle hide and leather breeches. It was said that Caesar had invaded England so that he could get his hands on some excellent oysters.

In the early third century the country was divided into two

provinces, Britannia Superior with London as its capital and Britannia Inferior with York as its centre. 'Superior' and 'Inferior' were geographical, not qualitative, terms. The two areas were later subdivided into four and then five provinces, emphasizing the fact that the country was being closely administered and exploited.

As the country became a settled part of the empire, its role changed. The armies of occupation became armies of defence; they became naturalized, with a self-conscious local or regional identity. Over one-tenth of the entire imperial army was stationed in the colony, which meant that its forces had extraordinary power over events in distant Rome. Mutinies, and uprisings, were not uncommon. In AD 268, one governor of England, Carausius, proclaimed himself emperor. He took his forces to the continent and, in his absence, the various towns and cities of the country took measures to defend themselves against possible reprisals from Rome. One hundred years later another Roman commander seized the province and declared it to be independent. He was disabused of this notion in a battle somewhere in central England, but it is a measure of the significance of the country in imperial calculations.

England was worth a fight. Its ports, its metals, its taxes, helped to sustain the vast engine of Roman commerce. Yet it remained wealthy and productive largely because of its agriculture. In AD 359 the emperor, Julian, organized a fleet of 600 ships to transport corn from England to the war zones of the Rhine. The country had become one of the bread baskets of Europe, and by the fourth century it had never been more prosperous. The villas of the grandees became larger and more luxurious, and there can be no doubt that the social stratification of the country grew ever more pronounced under the auspices of imperial rule. The Roman English controlled the Iron Age English.

The northern borders were always a source of conflict, with the weight of the Scots and the Picts pressing against them, but the general frontiers of the province soon came into jeopardy. There is a curious alignment of forts in southern England known generally as the 'Saxon Shore', but their purpose is not altogether clear. Were they a means of defending the coast against Saxon invaders from the north-west of Europe, or were they perhaps designed to harbour

Saxon fighters and traders? They may thus have been designed to protect the seaways between England and Europe from pirates and other marauders.

Yet, as with so many aspects of England under imperial control, the evidence is fragmentary and inconclusive; we rely on chance inscriptions, the indications of archaeology and the occasional commentaries of Roman historians. The Roman governance of England lasted for 350 years – the same span of time that separates the contemporary reader from the Great Fire of London – and yet it is the least-known phase in the country's history.

In particular we cannot see the people – the Romanized leaders in their fashionable and luxurious villas, the smaller landowners in farmsteads built of stone or timber, the townsmen inhabiting one- or two-room houses along narrow and squalid lanes, the civil servants working in offices while wearing their official togas and military belts, the landless labourers living in dormitories set well away from the villas, the whole general tide and swell of population unmoved by purges and coups and counter-purges that are evident in the pages of Roman histories.

There is much unknown, also, about the advance of Christianity. England had been introduced to that faith in the second century, but it was perforce a minority religion. The Roman English had been reconciled to the Roman gods, while the Iron Age English no doubt still venerated the ancient deities of hill and forest. Christianity was not an indigenous faith. Nevertheless, Christian vessels and plaques from the third century have been found in Huntingdonshire, close to the river Nene, and are clear evidence of a local shrine; they are in fact the earliest examples of such vessels from the whole of the empire. A Christian cemetery, of approximately the same date, has been uncovered at Poundbury in Dorset. Christianity had penetrated as far north as Carlisle by the fourth century.

Christianity only became the sacerdotal face of the empire after Constantine the Great's conversion in AD 312; Constantine had in fact been acclaimed and appointed emperor at York in AD 306 and in subsequent years seems to have considered England to be one of the spiritual centres of his rule. York itself was refashioned in honour of his elevation, and he made three further visits to the province. He styled himself on Britannicus Maximus, and it seems likely that London itself was for a while renamed Augusta in his honour. So the Christianity of England was an important element of its later development.

It was a monotheistic faith in a period when the emperor himself aspired to single rule, and it assumed a uniform set of values and beliefs that could be transmitted across the empire. It helped to support the legislative and bureaucratic forces of the centre. Its adherents were, unsurprisingly, drawn from the governing class. There can be no doubt that in England, for example, the Romanized population were quick to embrace the delights of an institutionalized faith. That is why Christianity became associated with the culture of the villas. It was also a religion of the administrative elite in the towns and cities, where a bishop was charged with the care of his urban flock.

In AD 314 three English bishops, together with a priest and a deacon, were attending an ecclesiastical council at Arles in southern France. The bishops came from York, London and Lincoln; the deacon and priest arrived from Cirencester. Evidence for what may be a Christian cathedral, complete with marble and painted walls, has been found at excavations near Tower Hill. A holy well was located in the centre of the nave. This may have been the diocesan centre for Bishop Restitutus of London. There is precious little evidence for other churches of the third and fourth centuries (although one has been found at Silchester), but there is good reason for this. The earliest churches lie concealed beneath more recent ones in the long history of sacred spaces. We would find the churches of early English Christianity only if we could uproot the cathedrals and churches of the modern world.

No empire can last forever; no state can remain steady and unscathed. The frontiers of the Roman polity were steadily being threatened and, in many places, overwhelmed. The pressure of the northern tribes grew ever more insidious. The Franks had entered northern Gaul. The Visigoths were to settle in Aquitania. The threat to England was posed by the Picts and the Scots in the north, together with their tribal allies among the Franks and the Saxons. In AD 367 a force overcame Hadrian's Wall, and then in dispersed bands moved southward to ravage the country;

the commander of the forts of the Saxon Shore was murdered and the provincial leader known as *Dux Britanniarum* was captured. It was a notable defeat for the English. Roman intervention and rebuilding, including the refortification of key posts, helped to maintain prosperity and peace for forty years; but then the northern tribes came back.

A series of bids for imperial power by various pretenders meant that, at the beginning of the fifth century, England was effectively stripped of its military forces. They had gone off in search of glory. Civil war between the various pretenders to the imperial throne weakened the self-discipline and orderliness that had always been the sign of Roman rule. The administrative machinery was beginning to break apart. In 408 the northern tribes were emboldened once more to attack, and the Roman English had no choice but to defend themselves. A contemporary historian, Zosimus, records that they 'took up arms and, braving danger for their own independence, freed the cities from the barbarians threatening them'. He also reports that they then expelled their Roman governors and established their own administrations.

Various levels of intrigue are embedded in this simple narrative. There would have been some Roman English who wished to retain the Roman administration from which they derived great benefits; there would have been others who wished to be rid of the burden of taxation and coercion associated with the central government. Two years later, in 410, one section of the English appealed to the emperor for arms and men; it is not clear whether they were needed against an external army of Saxons, or against an internal English enemy. In any case the emperor, Honorius, replied that the English must now fend for themselves. This was effectively the end of Roman England.

Another historian, Procopius of Caesarea, further reveals that after the disappearance of the Roman officials the various cities and regions were taken over by 'tyrants' or 'usurpers'. They may have seemed like usurpers from Rome, but in actual fact they are likely to be the familiar English leaders descended from tribal chiefs or large landowning families. As the hand of Rome was lifted the English tribes and polities reacted in several significant ways. The Romanized English in the towns and cities, with the dependent estates all around them, are likely to have formed themselves into self-governing administrative units; the leaders of these small states were still known as 'magistrates'. In the civil zone of the country – in the east and south-east – there rose small kingdoms that were defended by mercenaries. The kingdoms of eastern England, for example, were obliged to use Germanic soldiers; these troops would pose problems in subsequent years. The tribes in the more distant regions of the country, never properly Romanized, reverted to pre-Roman forms of social organization. The remaining detachments of the armies of the north were grouped under a commander who became their chieftain. One of the first Roman leaders of the north, Coelius or Coel Hen, became in English folk rhyme 'Old King Cole'.

So the pattern of English life is localized and various in this period after the withdrawal of the Roman *imperium*. Signs of a more general change, however, can be found. The taxation system of Rome was dismantled, and the countryside was now controlled by an aristocracy of landowners. With the abandonment of taxation, the circulation of coinage diminished rapidly. By 410 the large centres of pottery manufacture had gone out of business; the demand no longer existed. Brick-making did not return to England until the fifteenth century. Villas were neglected or abandoned, becoming unused sites for later settlers.

The days of public and monumental display in the cities had gone. But this does not necessarily mean that the cities decayed or were in decline; they had simply changed their function. They remained centres of administration for the immediate area, and housed the local bishop and the local leader, but they no longer wanted or needed the imperial facades of the third century. The basilica at Silchester, for example, was converted into a centre for metal-working. The urban population remained, and there is evidence of rebuilding at York and Gloucester in the fifth century. A new water supply, with timber pipes, was introduced to Verulamium in the latter half of that century. So a civic organization was still in operation. The Roman city of Wroxeter has been unearthed from the fields of Shropshire. It did not disappear after the Romans had left. The basilica was razed, and in its place a large wooden hall was erected; this hall became the centre for a complex of timber buildings based on Roman models. A prosperous and busy life continued well into the medieval period.

Archaeologists have discovered, from the strata of the fifth century, a deposit spread over many towns and cities; they have named it 'dark earth'. This was once thought to be evidence of abandonment and desolation. Now it is more correctly interpreted as the residue of wattle-and-daub dwellings. The towns and cities of the fifth century may have been heavily populated, maintaining a commercial life that never left them.

Self-sufficiency was established upon barter and local trading. There is evidence of hand-made pottery, and quantities of raw clay that might have been used for the building of walls. The lives of the farmers and labourers of the country were changed not at all by the dislocation of leaders.

The *Confession* of St Patrick, who was taken by Saxon slavers at the end of the fourth century, shows that the affluent life of the villa owner continued into the early decades of the fifth century. On Patrick's return to England, six years after his capture, his father urged him to enter public service; local rhetoricians were employed, for example, to guide the populace. Some kind of working polity was based upon a Roman original. When Bishop Germanus came to England from Gaul in 429 he was greeted by the leading men of Verulamium in a gesture of civic unity. These are likely to have been the members of the diocesan or provincial council who had taken over the administration of the city. In the life of Germanus they are reported to have been 'conspicuous for their wealth, fashionable in their dress, and surrounded by an adoring multitude of people'. This was not a country denuded of its prestige or affluence.

Germanus had come in part to assist the English in their fight against the Picts and Saxons, adding weight to the suggestion that there was some sudden or overwhelming Saxon 'invasion'. But in fact the Saxons were already here. They had been in England from the third century. They were already part of the fabric of English life. The urban and tribal elites needed Saxon warriors to defend their property; many of these soldiers married native women, and settled down with their families. Germanic forces remained among the Roman army in the north. Saxon traders lived in the towns and cities. Saxon workers cultivated the lands of Kent in exchange for occasional military service.

Here we must confront questions of nomenclature. By common consent the native English, from the Iron Age forwards, have been called 'Britons'. But the term is really only pertinent to the Atlantic English of the western coasts; these are the Britons who migrated to Gaul and established the province of Brittany. They are the people who spoke Celtic and Gaelic. The Britons were also strong in the north, as a permanent reminder of old tribal groupings. In the centre, south and east of the country were native English, too, but they inhabited the regions where Saxon settlers came to dominate, sometimes by peaceful and sometimes by violent means. It was from one band of these settlers, the Angles, that the name of England itself first emerged. 'Engla land' was the Viking description. It is characteristic of a country that, from the first century to the thirteenth century, was subject to almost continual foreign occupation. The 'empire race' was once a colonized and exploited people.

# 3

# Climate change

The climate of England has been characterized as generally damp and relatively sunless but, as every native knows, the weather is as various as the land. In the south-east the summers are warm and the winters are cold, while in the north-west the winters are mild and the summers are cool. In the north-west four and a half hours of sunshine light up an average July day, while on the south coast six and a half hours can be anticipated; the western seaboard attracts 40 per cent more rainfall than the eastern. The predominant wind of autumn and of winter is from the south-west; in the spring it is the east. This was the weather that created a land of damp forests of oak and ash, of marshes and heath wrapped in mist. In the north and the west lay the moors and the mountains, where the soil was thin. This was the land of pasture rather than of crops, and the local farmers grew only as much corn as they needed for themselves. The south and east were the lowlands, with gradual undulations in the rich earth; this was ground as fit for corn as for cattle. It was the territory of 'mixed farming'.

In the history of England these patterns of climate are of the utmost importance; if there is a drop in temperature of two degrees, as in the period from 500 to 300 BC, the prospect of adequate harvests in the north is noticeably curtailed. A difference of one degree made a failure of the harvest seven times more likely. In this period, then, we see the abandonment of upland farms and settlements. The southern land was warmer, and more stable; it was the home of the plentiful harvest, and the general dampness meant that crops could even be grown on lighter soils where sand and chalk prevailed. It is a general truth, therefore, that in the south-east the land was devoted to wheat whereas in the north it was given over to oats. But important regional variations were still found. Oxfordshire and north-east Suffolk grew wheat, whereas Norfolk grew more rye. Oats were the main crop in Lancashire, while rye was dominant in Yorkshire. Wheat and barley shared the ascendancy in Wiltshire whereas, in the rainier country west of that shire, barley predominated.

The people of the south were wealthier if not healthier than their counterparts in the north. So the climate is active in human history. It may also be that the drier east creates human communities different from those of the rainier west; marked contrasts of social systems in the first millennium BC are in fact evident, with small centres of lordly power in the west and more scattered settlements in the east. The isolated farmhouse and the small hamlet were characteristic of the north and west; the village and the manorial system of common cultivation were more usual in the south and east.

At the time of the Roman occupation the weather was warmer than at any period in subsequent history, but this was succeeded by colder and wetter conditions by the end of the fourth century. For ten years, beginning in AD 536, there was a very low level of sunlight; this would have been a time of dearth and famine, hitherto unrecorded. It might also be noted that Alfred was credited with the invention of a clock that allowed him to tell the time when the prevailing fogs obscured the sun.

The climate of 1009 and 1010 was recorded by a Benedictine monk, Byrhtferth, who dwelled in East Anglia; the winter lasted from 7 November to 6 February, being cold and moist; the spring from 7 February to 8 May was moist and hot; summer from 9 May to 6 August was hot and dry; autumn from 7 August to 6 November was dry and cold. He was only one of the clerics who kept a detailed record of the conditions of the weather.

The eleventh and twelve centuries were in fact warmer than

those immediately preceding them, but a deterioration of climate took place in the thirteenth and fourteenth centuries; the annals of these later centuries also mention the increasing incidence of floods and droughts, suggesting greater instability. Hard frosts lasted into spring, and violent gales brought down the trees of the forests. The Thames froze in the winter of 1309–10, and the years 1315 and 1316 were marked by endless rain. The harvests failed, and the dead were buried in common graves. It was a time of epidemic disease. Crime rates rose proportionately.

The increase of rainfall, in the fourteenth century, is marked by the construction of drainage ditches and house platforms; church floors were raised, and the lower halves of some villages were deserted. The carpenter in Chaucer's 'The Miller's Tale' reveals an obsessive fear of another Great Flood covering the earth. The extraordinary wind of 14 January 1362 was widely believed to be a harbinger of the Day of Judgment. In the medieval period the weather is the lord of all. Outer weather creates inner weather. It would be possible to write the history of England as the history of the English climate.

# 4

# Spear points

The *Anglo-Saxon Chronicle*, composed long after the events related, reports that in 449 'Hengist and Horsa, invited by Wyrtgeorn' arrived in England; they had come to help the English against invaders, but they stayed only to fight against their hosts. Hengist and Horsa mean respectively 'horse' and 'mare'. Wyrtgeorn, or Vortigern, is simply the term for an overlord or over-king. In some of the Welsh annals he is also known as Vortigern 'of the repulsive mouth'. So, as always, there are elements of mythology embedded within the history. The dates are also wrong.

The evidence suggests that in 430 Vortigern, the leader of the confederacy of small kingdoms into which much of the country had divided, called in Saxon mercenaries to defend England against the Picts from Scotland and various marauding bands from Ireland. This was an old and familiar strategy, used by the Romanized English at various points in their history.

The Irish landed on the west coast, within easy reach of the Cotswolds; the central part of Vortigern's kingdom lay in that hilly region, which may account for his leading role in the struggle. It is reported that the Picts had landed in Norfolk. The Pictish sailors painted their ships, and their bodies, the colour of the waves so that they could less easily be seen. So the decision to call in the Saxons was born out of fear and urgency. According to historical legend they came in three ships, holding at best only a few hundred men. There are likely to have been more ships but, in any case, these mercenaries were known for their ferocity as well as for their valour. The bands of warriors, under a war chieftain, worshipped the sun and the moon. They adored Woden, god of war, and Thor, god of thunder. They practised human sacrifice. They drank from the skulls of their enemies. The fronts of their heads were shaved, the hair grown long at the back, so that their faces might seem larger in battle. 'The Saxon', a Roman chronicler of the fifth century wrote, 'surpasses all others in brutality. He attacks unforeseen, and when foreseen he slips away. If he pursues, he captures; if he flees, he escapes.'

The most significant elements of the Saxon force were stationed in Kent, and were given the island of Thanet in the Thames estuary. Other bands of soldiers were placed in Norfolk, and on the coast of Lincolnshire. The Icknield Way was guarded. London and the Thames estuary were defended. The remains of the Romanized armies, still in the north, were stationed in a strongly fortified York. Then, on the invitation of Vortigern, more Saxon mercenaries were brought to England. The show of strength seems to have been enough. The Picts abandoned their plans for the invasion. The Irish were in turn checked by the tribal armies of the west and the west midlands; the kingdom of the Cornovii, with its capital at Wroxeter, was instrumental in that repulse to the invaders.

Yet now a more insidious threat to Vortigern's leadership emerged. His allies, alarmed at the cost of the Saxon presence, could not or would not pay them. They also refused to yield land in exchange for payment. After the immediate threat had passed, they declined to subsidize their defenders. According to the Kentish chronicles they declared that 'we cannot feed and clothe you, because your numbers have grown. Leave us. We no longer need your assistance.'

The reaction of the mercenaries was immediate and strong. Their insurgency began in East Anglia, and then spread down to the Thames Valley. They took over many of the towns and countryside areas in which they had been stationed. They appropriated large estates, and enslaved many of the native English. They had seen at first hand the prosperity of the land and had acquired a taste for it. Thanet itself, as a granary, was a golden prize. The Saxon federates then sent out a call to their compatriots. Come and settle here. Together we can master the natives.

So the Germanic migrants kept on coming. Among them were four predominant tribes – the Angles from Schleswig, the Saxons from the territories around the river Elbe, the Frisians from the northern coast of the Netherlands, and the Jutes from the coast of Denmark. There were no such people as 'Anglo-Saxons' until the chroniclers invented them in the sixth century. The routes of settlement were already established by the river system. The settlers pushed along the Thames, the Trent and the Humber.

The Jutes settled in Kent, Hampshire and the Isle of Wight; the New Forest was once Jutish land. The Saxons were established in the Upper Thames valley. The Frisians were scattered over the south-east, with an important influence in London. The Angles settled in eastern and north-eastern England; by the early sixth century the people of east Yorkshire were wearing Anglian clothes. These were small tribes, small communities under a leader or leading family. Some were resisted; some were welcomed. Others were simply accepted by a working population who had no real love for their earlier native masters. All were accommodated and, according to the best genetic evidence, eventually made up 5 per cent of the population we now call English; in the eastern regions it may have reached approximately 10 per cent, but there is no hint of deliberate genocide and replacement of the native population.

They came because they were being pushed by other tribes in the great westward migrations of that era, but they also came because their ancestral lands were in peril from the rising sea. This was the period in which the northern European coastline was sinking, as the archaeological evidence from Germany and the Netherlands testifies; there was urgent need to find land elsewhere.

The revolt of the Saxon federates was a decisive blow to the prestige and authority of Vortigern. He was overthrown by another Romanized English leader, Ambrosius Aurelianus, who led a counter-attack upon the Saxons and for ten years engaged in a series of strenuous battles. In 490 the English won a great victory at a place known to posterity as Mons Badonicus, believed to be near modern Bath. The leader of the English forces on that occasion is not recorded, but in this period the name of Arthur emerges as over-king. He is a shadow in the historical record, known only as *dux bellorum* or 'leader of warfare'. He is said to have participated in twelve battles against the Saxons, but the places cannot now be identified. In the pages of the medieval romances he is a great king with a shining court at Camelot, otherwise known as Winchester; in truth he may have been a military commander whose head-quarters were within the hill fort of Cadbury. 18 acres (7.2 hectares) of that hill fort were enclosed in the period of Arthur's supposed lifetime.

The English had survived but, as part of the spoils of war, the Saxons retained their control over Norfolk, East Kent and East Sussex. There was a division in the country, perhaps marked by the construction of the Wansdyke designed to keep the Germanic people from crossing into central southern England. On one side of that barrier were small English kingdoms; on the other, Germanic tribes with their warrior leaders. What had previously been some of the most Romanized parts of the country had become the home of 'barbarians'. The town and villa life of these regions was, therefore, in abeyance. An English chronicler of the early sixth century, Gildas, laments that 'the cities of our country are still not inhabited as they were; even today they are squalid deserted ruins'. This was the process of the Saxon 'invasion'.

Yet some towns and cities were still in active use, as markets and places of authority. It is well known that the Saxons set up their own trading area outside the walls of London, in the district now known as Aldwych, but the old city was still a place of royal residences and public ceremonial. In the countryside, there is even greater evidence for continuity of settlement. It is not to be expected that any change in agricultural practice took place. The same field systems were laid out by the Germanic settlers; the new arrivals respected the old boundaries and in Durham, for example, Germanic structures were set within a pattern of small fields and drystone walls created in the prehistoric past. More surprisingly, perhaps, the Germanic settlers formed groups that honoured the boundaries of the old tribal kingdoms. They respected the lie of the land. The sacred sites of the Saxons, at a slightly later date, follow the alignment of Neolithic monuments. All fell into the embrace of the past.

The Germanic settlers were kept within their boundaries by the English for two or three generations. It should not be forgotten that, in this period, the average life expectancy was thirty-five years. It was a country of young men and women, with all the energy and thoughtlessness of the young. The leaders of the country were brash, vibrant and energetic.

By the middle of the sixth century the Germanic people wished to move further west, and to exploit the productive lands that had previously been beyond their grasp. There are many reasons for this sudden efflorescence of activity, but one of the most convincing lies in the onset of deadly plague in the 540s. Bubonic, and perhaps pneumonic, plague spread from Egypt all over the previously Romanized world. It seems that it struck down the native English rather than the settlers, with a force and scope that rival the great plagues of the thirteenth and seventeenth centuries. Some actuarial experts suggest that a population of 3 or 4 million now dropped to 1 million. The land was left vacant, and fewer men were available to defend it. So the Angles, and the Saxons, moved westward. Anglo-Saxon civilization was created by a pandemic.

One of the leaders of the Saxons, Ceawlin, had reached as far as Cirencester, Gloucester and Bath by 577; seven years later his forces had penetrated the midlands. The native kings were thereby deposed. This was the pattern throughout the country. The pressure was growing on the Durotriges of Somerset and Dorset and as a result there was an exodus of native people to Armorica, on the Atlantic coast of north-western France, where their leaders took control of large tracts of land. They may have been welcomed. They were perhaps part of the same tribe. So the region of Brittany emerged. The Bretons in fact retained their old tribal allegiances, and never really thought of themselves as part of the French state. Some of them came back. A Breton contingent was among the forces of William the Conqueror, which chose to settle in south-west England. They had come home at last.

In the end the natives would be so mixed and mingled with the new settlers that the term Saxon or Angle ceased to have any meaning. All would become English. Yet it was a slow process. Much of western England was still under the rule of native kings 200 years after the first Saxons arrived; the native kingdom of Elmet, now known as the West Riding of Yorkshire, survived until the early seventh century and the 'Anglo-Saxon invasion' only came to an end with the capture of Gwynedd by Edward I in 1282. Celtic speakers were to be found in Cornwall at the beginning of the sixteenth century, and the language did not wholly die until the eighteenth century.

The settlements of the Germanic tribes took the form of small folk territories, made up of groups of warriors and marked off by river boundaries. So the followers of Haesta created Hastings and the followers of Gilla established Ealing. The people of the Peak district, the people of the Chilterns, and the people of the Wrekin, were all given distinct topographical names. Jarrow means 'among the Jyrwe', a small tribe found in the fen district as well as in Northumberland. The immense number of small tribes was gradually aligned for the purposes of defence or warfare. Over-kings emerged as the leaders and protectors of tribal chiefs, and by 600 the recognizable kingdoms of Anglo-Saxon England begin to enter recorded history. The kingdom of the East Angles was formed together with those of the East Saxons and the Mercians.

These were societies of rank, based upon a structure of burdens and obligations imposed by the warlords and their entourage. There were slaves, there were landless workers, there were *ceorls* or free heads of households, and there were *thegns* or noblemen, with all possible divisions and distinctions within each rank. The financial penalties for murder, for example, were graded according to the 'worth' of the victim. It was a harsh and divisive society, only made possible by the continuous exploitation of the unfree. In that respect, it may not have differed very much from any previous English polity. There never was any Rousseau-esque state of equality in nature. There always was a system of lordship and vassalage.

And what of the native English? They endured the change of leadership. Most of them worked the soil, as before, and paid tax or tribute to the local lord. The ordinary routines of life are never chronicled by the historian, but they make up almost the whole of experience. The artisans and merchants were still here. It was in the interest of the Angles and the Saxons to utilize what remained of Romanized English civilization. They did not exterminate the native population because they needed it. They had no aversion to the practices of the open field and could quickly accustom themselves to working the land according to the traditional methods of the English.

In the first years, however, there may have been a form of separation or apartheid between settlers and natives. The Germanic *walh* means Celtic speaker or Latin speaker; it also came to mean a serf or a slave. The name of Wales derives from this. So we have Corn*wall*, and places known as *Wal*ton, *Wal*sall and *Wal*cot. We can also deduce the presence of native English in what is now north-east London in *Walth*amstow and elsewhere. The reader will be able to identify many other examples. The native population survived.

Christianity was not driven out of England by the invaders. Early churches have been found in London, embedded within Roman edifices, as well as in York, Leicester and Exeter. Churches were located in other towns, and of course in western England – beyond the reach of the Germanic tribes – the religion flourished with the appearance of small monastic communities. One was situated on top of Glastonbury Tor.

The eventual shape of England itself was becoming clear as the Germanic tribes continued their expansion. In the north the settlers were first confined to East and South Yorkshire; these areas may already have harboured Germanic troops, and may therefore have welcomed their arrival. They formed the kingdom of Deira, roughly comprising what is now Yorkshire from the Humber to the Tees. An Anglian community was established at Bamburgh, where the castle still stands. A great Anglo-Saxon cremation cemetery is to be found by the village of Sancton, in the East Riding of Yorkshire, and as late as the nineteenth century the villagers used pots and urns taken from the site. The native tribes, the Parisii and the Brigantes, tried to contain these powerful Germanic settlers, but they proved unsuccessful.

Under the leadership of their king, Aethelfrith, according to the history of the Venerable Bede, the settlers conquered many territories and many peoples by the end of the sixth century; they 'either drove out their inhabitants and planted them afresh with their own people, or subdued them and made them tributary'. That was the familiar process of colonization. Aethelfrith became king of both Deira and Bernicia, the kingdom to the north of Deira that stretched from Durham to Edinburgh and from Derwentwater to Ayrshire. He can thus be truly considered the first king of Northumberland.

The native tribes and kingdoms were divided among themselves, and could not arrest the momentum of the invaders. The old kingdoms – Rheged (north-western England), Strathclyde (south-western Scotland), Gododdin (north-eastern England and south-eastern Scotland) – fell. The warbands slowly moved northward and westward. The Germanic settlers may have been few in number, but they eventually controlled a huge territory of moorland and hill with scattered farmsteads and cottages. Yet the old traditions survived in the fastness; that is why Yorkshire and Northumberland retained much of their ancient organization and custom.

Out of these battles between invaders and native tribes emerged the pure poetry of war. Aneirin's poem *Gododdin* has made him the Homer of the north. Written in the language of the Britons, it records the defiance of the natives in stern cadences:

> Swift horses and stained armour with shields,
> Spear shafts raised and spear points honed,
> Sparkling chain mail and radiant swords.

It records a world of warriors, wearing beads and collars of amber, and of councils of war; it is a world of battles, with banners held high by the opposing forces; of crows and ravens waiting for the slaughter, climbing like clouds in the sky; of feasting with cups of mead and sweet wine; of hounds and hawks; of drinking horns passed round in candlelight; of a landscape of wolves and sea-eagles; of a lord, decked with jewels, sitting at the head of a table. It is a poetry of assonance and internal rhyme. It is avowedly and unrepentantly aristocratic. It is not as fearful or as mournful as

Anglo-Saxon poetry, with the latter's longing for a haven and the safety of the hall against the forces of a wild world.

On the death of Aethelfrith his rival, Edwin, became the king of Northumberland. Towards the end of his reign he was powerful enough to conquer the Isle of Man, to invade North Wales and to occupy Anglesey. He aspired to over-kingship of the entire country, and according to Bede 'in the days of Edwin a woman with a baby at her breast might have travelled over the island without suffering an insult'. Along the principal highways of the country he also instituted a system of stone cisterns, designed to collect water from the nearest fountains, together with cups of brass. The drinking fountain has a long history.

Two memorials of his reign survive. Edwin's fortress, Edwin's burgh, is now known as Edinburgh. And, in recent years, evidence of Edwin's palace has been recovered. At Yeavering, in Northumberland, have been found the traces of a great hall with other buildings clustered around it; this suggests the presence of a king with his warriors and councillors. A temple was later converted into a Christian church. Since the palace was built upon a Bronze Age cemetery, it must always have been considered a sacred site. An open-air wooden theatre or meeting-place, with concentric rows of seats before a raised platform, has also been recognized; this was used for regional assemblies where the over-king could address 300 of his followers. It was the place of public pronouncement and public judgment. There was a large enclosure, where animals were herded before being killed and eaten in elaborate feasts. Other such palaces, with the complex of attendant buildings, have been found in other parts of the country.

They represent a life of feud and warfare, of lordship and dynastic marriage. Young warriors would congregate around the king and enter his service; the good lord would distribute land and gifts. It was a rich and intense culture based upon violence and covered with a sheen of gold. The clothes worn by the noblemen were opulent in the extreme, and the men as well as the women were lavishly bedecked with jewels. The men wore linen tunics, fastened at the wrists and waist with shining clasps; their cloaks were ornamented with brooches. Gold was the key. In the early Christian Church statues of the saints, larger than life-size, were covered in gold. There were thrones of gold, and great crucifixes of gold. It was in no sense a barbaric culture, but one based upon formal ostentation.

The territory of the East Angles also had great kings. Their land was large, taking within its compass what are now Norfolk, Suffolk and the Isle of Ely. It was all of a piece, the invaders having overlain the kingdom of the Iceni from which Boadicea had come. There are no annals of this people, but Bede records that one of their early kings claimed dominion over the whole of southern England. Redwald reigned in the early seventh century, and at a burial site in Sutton Hoo have been found relics of his magnificence. It is presumed to be Redwald's tomb, based upon the elaborate funereal rites of the Germanic tribes of Sweden.

This was a boat burial. The boat itself was 90 feet in length (27.4 metres) and within its central space were found a helmet of Scandinavian style, a coat of mail, a battleaxe, a sword with gold fittings, several spears and a shield ornamented with the shapes of birds and dragons; there seems to have been a sceptre crowned with a bronze stag, as well as a great gold buckle. Relics were also found of a tunic with gold clasps in the Roman fashion, as well as silver bowls, coins, cauldrons and a lyre. This was the resting place of a king. We have the words of *Beowulf* as an epitaph. 'There they laid the dear lord, the giver of rings, in the bosom of the ship, a marvellous prince by the mast. Men brought from distant lands a trove of treasure and ornament.' In another mound upon the site (there are seventeen of them) were uncovered the skeletons of a warrior and his horse. They are the tokens of a society of force and conquest.

Yet no body was found within the boat. It may have been a cenotaph, an empty tomb erected as a memorial. But it is more likely that a wooden coffin and its occupant have been eaten by the acid sand all around. There is one memory of Redwald, however. It resides in the helmet; it is silver plate on a base of iron, with ornamentation of bronze. It is monstrous, savage, a thing out of nightmare.

The life of the people under his rule was harsh and unremitting. It was, for the poor, one of incessant labour; their food was coarse and their clothes were made out of rough woollen fabrics. They

lived in earth-floored cottages of wicker or wattle. They knew only
the rake and the sickle, the plough and the pick and the spade.
The rich engaged in a life of hunting and of warfare. They ate
voluminous quantities of pork and venison. They drank to excess
and were celebrated for doing so. Their faces were often painted or
tattooed. Men as well as women dyed their hair; blue, green and
orange were the colours favoured by the male. Both sexes were
heavily adorned with gold bracelets. Young boys were trained in
bravery by being placed on steep sloping roofs; if they held fast,
without screaming out in fear, they were deemed to be fit for
purpose. The sports were those of leaping, running and wrestling;
at the age of fourteen a boy had the right to bear arms.

The kingdom of Mercia occupied what is now known as the
midlands; the East Saxons gave their name to Essex, the Middle
Saxons to Middlesex and the South Saxons to Sussex. The West
Saxons created Wessex, of course, but that territory has not survived
as an administrative entity. Mercia was until the time of Alfred
always a mixture of kingdoms, and the tribal name of the West
Saxons was Gewissae, meaning 'confederates'. These allied tribes
moved further westward, conquering Devon and Cornwall. But the
Germanic tribes did not move against the native kingdoms alone;
they fought among themselves, and there were some ferocious
struggles between the tribes of Wessex and the tribes of Kent.

Kent offers an interesting case of continuity. It was the first
part of England to be settled by Germanic mercenaries and traders,
who may have obtained a permanent presence there as far back as
the time of Roman rule. That is why the administrative structures
set up by the Romanized English survived intact. The settlers and
natives did not need to confront one another. So the native name
for the area was maintained even after the Jutes and others had
acquired supremacy. The people were known as 'Cant-ware', but
the origin of 'Cant' lies somewhere in prehistory. The names of
Canterbury and Dover date back at least to the Iron Age. There is
abundant evidence for continuity of use, in settlements and in
sacred sites, from the Iron Age to the Jutes; the churches of many
Kentish neighbourhoods are linked by prehistoric roads. They are
also characteristically associated with holy wells, springs and female
saints, all of which point towards prehistoric worship.

Another continuity can be noticed. When the first Germanic settlers came they were planted as freeholders, following the custom of their country. That is why the land of Kent is marked by individual farmsteads and hamlets rather than manorial villages; no tradition of co-operative farming under a lord existed. There was no room in Kent for powerful magnates or great mansions. There are few of the 'common fields' found throughout the rest of the country. The county bears all the signs of the 'free folk' whom Tacitus recognized among the northern peoples.

That tradition was maintained over the centuries. In *The Perambulation of Kent*, written in 1570, William Lambarde wrote that 'the Yeomanrie, or common people is no where more free and jolly than in this shyre ... in manner every man is a freeholder, and hath some part of his own to live upon. And in this their estate they please themselves and joy exceedingly.' In fact the legal custom of Kentish land tenure was not abolished until 1926, the only known example of specifically county law surviving into the twentieth century. That independence has taken other forms. In the Peasants' Revolt of 1381 'the men of Kent' were the first to take up arms behind Wat Tyler. Seventy years later, under the leadership of Jack Cade, they provoked a popular revolt against unfair taxation; their petition was entitled *The Complaint of the Poor Commons of Kent*. The men of Kent were the first to rise against Richard III. In the miners' strike of 1984 the miners of Kent were the most militant and vociferous. The old history still manifests itself. It still matters.

These continuities underlie the changing patterns of lordship. Small kingdoms gave way to greater kingdoms. The earliest fiscal document for the whole of England, dated to the early seventh century, lists nineteen kings and fifteen peoples. Yet even the great kingdoms were based upon English originals. The Jutes of Hampshire and the Isle of Wight took over the prehistoric lands of the Belgae; the East Saxons held the ancient territory of the Trinovantes; and the South Saxons established themselves within the prehistoric borders of the Regnenses. They even retained the same capitals. There are many other examples testifying to the fact that the roots of the country go very deep.

The great king of Kent, Aethelbert, who ruled from the end of the sixth century to 616, is prominent in English history as the king who greeted Augustine and supported his Christian mission among the Germanic tribes. Aethelbert was aligned with the Frankish kings of the continent, and it may be that he welcomed Augustine in deference to them. He was in any case what the Venerable Bede called 'rex potentissimus', an over-king of English lands stretching to the Humber. He was also the first English king to become converted to Christianity; he was followed by the king of Essex and, more ambiguously, by the king of East Anglia. But his example was crucial to the success of Augustine's mission. Augustine converted the king's household, and thus the area under the control of Aethelbert's lords. The people came creeping to the cross under the twin pressures of deference and emulation. They flocked to the rivers of Kent, where they were baptized en masse.

It should be remembered that this saint had not come to convert the native English, the large majority of whom were already Christian. He had not come to evangelize the whole island; he had come to baptize the Germanic settlers and their leaders. In 597 he landed at Thanet, and then led a solemn procession singing hymns behind a silver cross. Aethelbert duly obliged with his conversion. He could see the advantage of being associated with the institution that had succeeded Roman *imperium*. The important part of the Christian contribution to England was in fact the re-imposition of old forms of authority. After Augustine had converted Kent and Essex his fellow missionary, Paulinus, brought the gospel to Northumberland. With the conversion of heathen Sussex and the Isle of Wight, in the late seventh century, all England had entered the Christian communion. Many of the old native churches were extended or rebuilt in Anglo-Saxon style, and many large churches were erected in the walled towns inherited from Rome. The same sacred sites were still in use, with a continuity of worship that goes much deeper than the choice between a native or a Roman affiliation. Many of today's cathedrals will retain at their core a small Anglo-Saxon church superimposed upon a temple used by the Romanized English.

The leaders of the native Church did not look kindly upon this usurper who had come to convert their Saxon-Jutish-Frisian oppressors. When Augustine summoned the Welsh bishops he did not rise to greet them, and his arrogance struck them as character-istic of the old Roman ways. The native priests had in any case come to despise the Germanic leaders; they did not attempt to convert them. They were monks and missionaries who had been educated in the worship of the Celtic saints (think of all the small churches in Cornwall), and saw no authority or beauty in what was essentially a church of bishops and administrators – administrators, indeed, who were willing and prepared to work for the alien kings. Priests on the other side of the Severn would not eat from the same dishes as the Romanized priests; they would not even let their dogs lick them. Yet they lost the battle of faiths. The Roman Church became England's Christian Church, and the old faith of the English withered on the vine. It is not the first, or the last, example of cultural amnesia.

For their part the kings were aware of all the advantages of the Roman faith. Christ was a more powerful support in war than Woden, and the Christian God offered more effective lordship than Thor. One hitherto pagan priest went to the trouble of destroying his own temple to prove the point. The Roman Church preferred the rule of strong kings and unified governments; it made the work of religious control much easier. The priests were the literate members of the kingdom and, at a time when legal documents and title deeds and proclamations of every kind were being published, they became the indispensable administrators of the state. Almost as soon as the first missionaries set foot on Thanet, the kings of the vicinity began to issue laws. 'If anyone kills a man, he is to pay as ordinary wergild 100 shillings. If hair-pulling occurs, 50 sceattas [silver pennies] are to be paid as compensation.'

The kings were also happy to adopt a quasi-liturgical role as the embodiment of the people in public ritual. This was a way of enhancing authority. It was a way of enforcing respect and ensuring obedience. Kings and saints appear, in England, within the same period. And they are often the same thing. King Edwin and King Aethelbert are known to posterity as St Edwin and St Aethelbert. There were occasional reactions. King Sigeberht of Kent was killed by two of his kinsmen for the tiresome practice of forgiving his enemies.

Yet on the whole Christianity helped to bring unity to a kingdom. To adapt the old Catholic motto, a people who pray together stay together. The encouragement of moral discipline, by the priests, had a material effect upon the social discipline of the country. In the graveyard remains of great ladies in the seventh century, from Kent and Wessex, from Mercia and East Anglia, there is a much greater uniformity of ornament. The various regions of the country were slowly coming together. A single English Church seemed to require a single English nation as its stage. It was the time of the Christian conversion that turned all the people of the country, in the words of Pope Gregory the Great, into 'Angelcynn, of English race'. Soon after a list was compiled of 'the Saints of God who rest in Engla lond'. Bede wrote of 'the Holy Church of the English nation', implicitly excluding the Welsh and the Picts. England, as we understand it today, was created by the Christian Church.

So the Church was an essential aspect of government. That is why the boundaries of the dioceses followed the frontiers of the old tribal kingdoms. Worcester followed the same area as the district of the Hwicce, for example, and Hereford of the Magonsaetan. The lines of authority had been passed on. The diocesan synods were like parliaments, where laws were debated and where kinfolk could meet. Bishops were in any case aristocrats, members of the various royal families of the land. When the king called a Church synod in London, secular as well as spiritual lords would attend.

The king's edicts invariably took an ecclesiastical tone. The archbishops, of York or of Canterbury, drew up the national law codes in consultation with the king. Only after the arrival of the Normans in England was there any formal separation between Church and State. In a similar spirit abbots and bishops were often part of the war-bands of the great magnates; one bishop of Sherborne, Heahmund, was killed in a bloody battle against northern invaders. He may have fulfilled the former role of the pagan high priest guiding companies of warriors.

There existed large organizations known as minsters, communities of priests and monks that, as the word suggests, ministered to their surrounding areas. Between the seventh and ninth centuries many hundreds of such foundations were planted so that every district had its minster. They represent the original expression of Christian England, with all the energy and power of first things. They acted as centres of patronage and learning; they maintained trade and agriculture. They organized the surrounding countryside with their constant demand for food rents. They were essentially royal courts, their abbots and abbesses an integral part of the aristocracy, where Christ was overlord. They housed golden treasures, and the relics of the saints. The priests would travel through their areas, preaching; that is why England is still dotted with stone crosses that mark the places of worship.

The religious power of the minsters was gradually lost, as villages and parish churches became the pattern of the land. But the minsters survived. Some of them became great churches and cathedrals. Others took on new life as burgeoning towns. Their names are part of the fabric of the country, in Axminster, Kidderminster, Westminster and a thousand others. Many other towns – Hexham, Barking, Godalming, Oundle, Reading, Woking – are also the direct survivors of these early foundations. England is still filled with minsters.

# 5

# The blood eagle

By the beginning of the ninth century there were in general terms three predominant kingdoms in England; Wessex, Mercia and Northumbria vied for mastery, while around them struggled the smaller kingdoms of East Anglia, Kent, Sussex and Essex. Northumbria was pre-eminent in the seventh century, Mercia in the eighth century, and Wessex in the ninth century. These were sophisticated states with complex systems of administration and taxation, capable of huge communal enterprises such as the building of the 98 miles (158 kilometres) of Offa's Dyke. In that sense, they resembled their prehistoric forebears. A mass currency was in circulation, with the ubiquitous silver penny or *sceat*, as a result of voluminous trade.

These three kingdoms were eventually forged together by fire and slaughter, and the growth of a unified kingdom can in part be seen as a desperate response to an external threat. In 790 three boats of Norwegian men landed upon the Dorset coast at Portland; an official rode from Dorchester, believing them to be the familiar merchants of that country, and prepared to escort them into the town. They turned around and killed him. They were warriors, not traders.

Three years later men from Norwegian ships attacked the monastery of St Cuthbert on the island of Lindisfarne. The attacks

were as unexpected as they were unwelcome. The monastery was
ransacked and many of the monks were put to the sword. 'Never
before has such a terror appeared in Britain as we have now suffered from a pagan race,' a chronicler wrote, 'nor was it thought
that such an inroad could be made from the sea.' A year later
the monastery at Jarrow was attacked. No one had feared such an
invasive force because the people of the north had previously come
as peaceful traders. They were masters of commerce, as their later
settlements in York and Dublin would testify. Long before the
raids commenced, there had been Scandinavian settlers in East
Anglia. The location of the eighth-century poem *Beowulf* is to be
found in southern Scandinavia.

The men of Norway were better known at the time as Norsemen or, in the English sources, as Vikings; the name was also
applied to the men of Denmark, but at the beginning the Norwegian warriors were the dominant force. The *víkingar* were 'the
men from the fjords'. They came because their own territories
were unsettled by the emergence of new and centralized kingdoms;
these kingdoms in turn encouraged the formation of warrior bands
ready to kill and pillage. The land of Denmark was also being
threatened by Charlemagne, king of the Frankish Empire, further
undermining the powers of the ruling elite. It takes only one
moment of fear to launch a hundred ships. This was the period,
too, when the design of the longboat was perfected. The wind was
literally in the sails of the Norsemen.

Another cause can be found for these bloody expeditions. The
monasteries of Lindisfarne and Jarrow were not attacked at random;
they were chosen as examples of revenge. The onslaught of the
Christian Charlemagne on the 'pagans' of the north had led to the
extirpation of their shrines and sanctuaries. The great king had cut
down Jôrmunr, the holy tree of the Norse people. What better
form of retaliation than to lay waste the foundations devoted to the
Christian God? The Christian missionaries to Norway had in fact
set out from Lindisfarne. So its destruction was nicely calculated.
It was the beginning of what might be called an anti-Christian
crusade. In the year the monastery burned, premonitions passed
across the tremulous English sky. The *Anglo-Saxon Chronicle* records that in 793 'terrible omens appeared over the Northumbrians

and miserably distressed the people: there were immense lightning flashes, and fiery dragons were seen flying in the sky'.

Yet these early raids were really only a warning, a seismic shudder before the fire burst forth. The English people were becoming more nervous, and the archaeological evidence suggests that more of them chose the safety of the walled towns. The earliest monastic chronicle was written at this time, to be incorporated later into the first version of the *Anglo-Saxon Chronicle*. The hand of the monk may have been guided by a sense that the world was changing for the worse.

In 830 the raids began once more. The forces of 'heathen men' had come for land and slaves and women. They fell upon the island of Sheppey, off the coast of North Kent, in 833. As its name implies, it was filled with sheep and good pasture. That was the prize. The Norsemen were well known for their skills in stock-breeding. Over the next thirty years a score of other attacks took place, from the men of Denmark in particular. Kent and East Anglia were an attractive target; the first sea battle in English history took place off Sandwich, in Kent, when the invaders were rebuffed. But the port at Southampton was ravaged by them. London and Rochester were attacked. The army of Northumberland was defeated in battle. The threat came from all sides.

Some of the warriors were known as 'wolf-coats' from their mode of dress and from the howls they sent up in battle. They brandished long kite-like shields, and wielded ferocious battleaxes against their prey. Others were known as 'berserks' because they wore no armour and charged the enemy in the throes of blood frenzy. The sagas tell of one warrior known as 'the children's man'; unlike his companions, he refused to impale children on the tip of his lance. These men were the terror of England.

The raids were simply the prelude to a true invasion. In 865 a great host of Danes descended upon East Anglia. This was the region their ancestors knew best and where many of them already lived. These men had not come to raid; they had come to settle. It is no coincidence that in this period there was a marked increase in the population of Scandinavia, where land was becoming more scarce.

They came in their thousands, aboard hundreds of ships; each ship could carry no more than thirty men. They dwelled in East Anglia for twelve months, taking command of the local resources and in particular marshalling a regiment of good horses. They established fortresses, or defensive encampments, from which they ruled the surrounding land. In 866 they rode against York, and took the city. Their control lasted for almost one hundred years. From York they gained mastery of Northumberland. Then they rode south and captured Nottingham. The king of the Mercians appealed to the king of Wessex for assistance, but eventually he was obliged to buy off the enemy.

The Danes had now acquired the two kingdoms of Northumberland and East Anglia. The kings of these territories were executed in the ritual of the 'blood eagle', whereby the lungs were ripped out of the body and draped across the shoulders so that they resembled an eagle's folded wings. The charters, the ornamented books, the diocesan records, of the two kingdoms disappear. It was a time of devastation for the landed proprietors of the soil.

In 870 the Danes set up a great camp in Reading, and began preparations to invade the kingdom of Wessex. At this stage in the history of England there emerges Alfred. He had encountered the Danes before, when his older brother came to the aid of the Mercians. Now he was king. It cannot be said, however, that his first actions were entirely heroic. After a series of defeats, he bought off the Danish forces with coin and treasure. He incurred the wrath and hatred of the monks at Abingdon for purloining their wealth in the process; in their history he is named as a 'Judas'. The Danes retired to London which they now also controlled. For a period Alfred was reduced to the role of a tributary king, and was obliged to take silver from the Danes to coin his own currency.

Further attacks and incursions were organized by the invaders, who were still intent upon complete mastery of Wessex; it was the largest surviving English kingdom, and thus the key to supremacy. For the most part Alfred's army seem to have shadowed the forces of the Danes as they conducted raids or acquired more territory and, after one particularly bloody defeat at Chippenham, Alfred was forced to take refuge in the Somerset marshes. Here at Athelney he built a fortress; from his sojourn in the marshes springs the story of his burning the cakes, once known to generations of English schoolchildren, but it is an eleventh-century fiction designed to emphasize the wretchedness of his plight before his final victory. And a victory came.

In the spring of 878 he rallied the forces of Somerset, Wiltshire and part of Hampshire at a place known as 'Egbert's Stone'. He fought a great battle at Edington in Wiltshire against Guthrum, the Danish leader, and the Danes were defeated. Guthrum accepted the outcome, and with several of his commanders was baptized into the Christian communion. Alfred stood as his sponsor in this signal act of conversion, where Guthrum took the Wessex name of Athelstan. In the battle between the pagans and the Christians, Christianity had won. This had become a war about faith as much as land.

Why was it that Alfred and Guthrum could enter such a holy or unholy alliance? They were both of the same blood. Guthrum and the Saxon, Alfred, were great kings in the same sacred tradition. Alfred may have been a Christian leader but he also traced the descent of his royal house from Woden. The Germanic and Scandinavian peoples were deeply related. They had much more in common than anything they shared with the men of Cornwall or of Devon. They were, in a sense, relatives. So they came to an agreement to divide England between them.

Alfred was not in a position to dictate terms. The negotiations took place in the shadow of the Danish forces that were still within Wessex. Guthrum was already king of the land in the east, from the Thames to the Humber, and had no intention of abandoning England. So he kept what he had conquered by force of arms. No doubt Alfred also gave him money. One phrase of the treaty establishes that 'all of us estimate Englishman and Dane at the same amount'. Equality reigned between them, in other words.

So was set up the region of the country known by the eleventh century as 'the Danelaw'. This essentially comprised the largest part of northern and eastern England, with a colony of Norwegians in north-western England. The process of settlement was made more intense, with successive waves of immigration from the coastline of north-western Europe being organized by the leaders of the Danish army in England. The chronicles use the phrase of the lands being 'shared out', suggesting some high authority. The later settlers were obliged to take up poorer land than that of their predecessors; but land in England was still available. The Danish farmers were situated by fortified towns or 'burghs' manned by the Danish army, from which we derive the term for borough. These forts could be used for the purposes of defence or of public assembly.

The most important territorial divisions of the Danelaw were the five boroughs of Nottingham, Leicester, Derby, Stamford and Lincoln. Those boroughs of course still survive, all except Stamford becoming county towns. Yet the evidence of Scandinavian loan-words suggests that the entire region of north and east was assimilated by the new settlers. There are hundreds of place names of Danish and Swedish origin, the most notable being those that end with -by or with -thorpe. Streoneshalch was renamed as Whitby, and Northworthig became Derby. The plethora of Kirbys or Kirkbys in the area of the Danelaw suggests that 'settlements by the church' were recognized by the invaders. The survival of English place names, however, sometimes in close proximity to the newly named settlements, suggests that the native people of humble stock were left undisturbed.

The Danes brought trade and prosperity to the areas under their control. It is not at all surprising that in the eleventh century the three most wealthy shires were Norfolk, Suffolk and Lincolnshire, which had all been part of the Danelaw. York itself was one of the richest and most flourishing cities in the kingdom. It was guarded by strong walls, and excavations have revealed streets of narrow and tightly packed wooden houses complete with workshops and warehouses. Jewellers and metalworkers lived beside workers in wood and in textiles. And everywhere there were merchants, trading with Ireland, with France and, of course, with Scandinavia. They were engaged in the business of pepper, and of vinegar; of fish, and of wine; of salt, and of slaves.

After the treaty was concluded with Guthrum, Alfred had the opportunity to rebuild the defences of his kingdom against any further incursion. Throughout southern and western England he set up a system of fortified towns similar to those established in the Danelaw. An elaborate network of these towns was created to ensure that no one lived more than 20 miles (32 kilometres) from a refuge. It was the beginning of the first true or systematic urbanization within England, springing from the urgent military necessities of the moment, since the Roman epoch. Within a hundred years most of the burghs had become fully ordered towns with courts and markets.

Iron Age hill forts such as those at Hastings and Southampton, and early Romanized settlements like those at Bath and Winchester, were restored with stronger walls. New towns were built, employing a grid system of streets that still survives in towns such as Wallingford and Cricklade that are sited by the Thames. Alfred knew the importance of guarding the major rivers that flowed through his land. Each burgh had a large force of defenders, placed there with their families. In addition Alfred began the formation of a permanent navy to deter any further hostilities from Scandinavian war-bands. An early warning system of beacons, set on hilltops, was put in place. His territories, therefore, were militarized in a great programme of public works.

But, for a while, Alfred's protection did not seem enough. In 896, six years after the death of Guthrum, another Danish king invaded East Kent with a force of 4,000 or 5,000 warriors; they had brought their women and children with them, and their purpose once again was to settle. Alfred led his army into the region and forced them to retreat to their encampments. But he then became aware of a greater threat. The arrival of these new settlers destroyed the uneasy peace between the English and the people of the Danelaw; ships from East Anglia and from Northumbria sailed around the coast and attacked the northern reaches of Devon. Another Danish contingent besieged Exeter. All the parties of the Danes colluded. The plan was to force Alfred to concentrate in the west, while the new invaders took over Kent and Essex.

In the course of the next few months Alfred defeated the Danish forces in the west, while sending reinforcements to the support of south-east England. The chronology of what became known as Alfred's 'last war' is not entirely clear, but the result is not in doubt. The invading Danes gave up their attempt to acquire the territories of the south-east and instead settled among their compatriots in East Anglia and Northumbria. They may have been bribed to leave Essex and elsewhere. They may have bowed to the inevitability of the strong defence set up by the system of burghs. In any event, Alfred had defended his kingdom.

Yet he also defined his kingdom. He generally termed himself 'the king of the Angles and of the Saxons', but one of his newly minted pennies uses for the first time the legend 'REX ANGLO'. With the pagans settled on the very borders of his land, he did his best to assert English identity. He was a Christian king in the face of heathen warlords. The Danes had attempted to extirpate the spiritual civilization of the English; Alfred would do everything within his power to cultivate English learning and the study of English history. Even as he was creating the system of burghs and building a navy, he was fostering a programme of translating major Latin texts into the West Saxon vernacular. He wished to commission books 'which are most necessary for all men to know'. He is one of the very few kings of England who himself wrote books. He translated Pope Gregory's *Pastoral Care*, the *Consolation of Philosophy* by Boethius and the *Soliloquies* of St Augustine; he caused to be translated Bede's *Ecclesiastical History of the English People* and *Histories against the Pagans* by Orosius, thus defining the context for his devoted scholarship. The English, at least according to their sacred historians, were the people of God.

In the reign of Alfred's son, Edward the Elder, the English began to conquer the territories of the Danelaw and to absorb its people into the larger society. The Danes were more vulnerable because they had settled; they were no longer the roving war-bands that had threatened Alfred, and they had always been more skilled at attack than at defence. In 917 and 918 Edward's soldiers marched out into the Danelaw, building fortresses as they moved forward. They seized Derby and Nottingham; then the men of Lincoln submitted to King Edward. By 920 all of the country south of the Humber had recognized him as overlord. This was a true conquest, since the rulers of Wessex had never before been lords of the eastern lands. The battles were remembered for many centuries, and it was said that the purple pasqueflower grew in the meadows where Danish blood had been spilled.

The people of the Danelaw were converted to Christianity

within two or three generations, and their old burial customs were forgotten. They were in any case so close to the Angles and the Saxons in custom and character that they effortlessly mingled with them. The English language is filled with Scandinavian words such as 'sky' and 'die', 'anger' and 'skin' and 'wing', 'law' and 'birth', 'bread' and 'eggs'. There is scarcely a phase of human activity that has not been deeply influenced by Danish nomenclature.

The memory of the Danish occupation survived. The Orkney islands and the Shetlands were in fact not surrendered to Scotland until the latter half of the sixteenth century, and Norwegian was still being spoken in the Shetlands at the end of the eighteenth century; the island accent is still much closer to Norwegian than to Scots or English. In the middle of the nineteenth century the people of Northamptonshire, according to a local historian, maintained 'a traditional remembrance of their oppression'. In Cornwall, at the end of the same century, a colony of red-headed people were called 'Danes' with whom the local population would not marry. Samuel Pepys was informed that the west door of Rochester Cathedral was covered with 'Dane-skins'. All this suggests that the viciousness of the early invasions and battles had left a deep and abiding mark.

After the partial unification of England by Edward there followed a line of powerful kings whose names have faded from the collective consciousness of the English; yet the memory of one of them, Athelstan, was revered for many centuries. His name means noble stone, like the throne in Kingston upon which in 924 he was crowned and anointed with holy oil. In the fourteenth century he was still invoked when land was granted:

> This land and twig I give to thee,
> As free as Athelstan gave it to me,
> And I hope a loving brother you will be.

He was the son of Edward the Elder, and became heir to a great dynasty; he was intent, however, upon augmenting the kingdom that he had inherited. He defeated in battle the king of York and his ally, the king of Dublin; Dublin and York were the twin engines of a Norse trading empire that was now coming to an end. Athelstan seized York, and subdued Scotland. The forces of the north then launched a counter-attack, but in 937 were decisively beaten at a place known only as Brunanburgh. 'From this period,' a chronicler wrote, 'there was peace and abundance of all things.' Many years later the period of Athelstan's struggle was still known as 'the great war', just as the First World War is now remembered.

Alfred had been generally characterized as king of the Angles and of the Saxons, but Athelstan was hailed as king of England. His family became linked by marriage with the kingdom of France and the province of Aquitaine as well as the empire of Germany. Poets and scholars flocked to his court; he established one coinage for the entire realm; he refurbished many of the towns. He called truly national assemblies of bishops and lords. He imposed strict controls over buying and selling; he set out a code of laws. 'I have learned that our peace is worse kept than I should like it,' he wrote, 'and my councillors say I have borne it for too long.'

There is a painting of him in the company of St Cuthbert, the holy man known as 'the wonder-worker of England'. It is the first English royal portrait, and shows Athelstan wearing an imperial crown. Towards the end of his reign he styled himself *monarchus totius Britanniae*, and the *Annals of Ulster* declared him to be 'the roof-tree of the dignity of the western world'. The tomb of this now forgotten king is to be found in Malmesbury Abbey. In life he wore his hair in ringlets entwined with threads of gold.

By the tenth century the polity of the Anglo-Saxon realm had taken an enduring shape. If the monarch was to guarantee order and stability, it was necessary for him to act in a formal and deliberate manner. He assembled a council of religious men and of wise men. He created structures of authority to supervise the exploitation of royal land and the dispensing of royal justice. A bureaucracy already existed, issuing what became an unbroken succession of charters and writs. (The charters can still be used in unravelling the English landscape.) They came in the first place from the king's scriptorium, staffed by a handful of priests, but the emergence of a centralized monarchy prompted the growth of new institutions and procedures. So from this foundation there would spring a civil service, a judiciary and a parliament. The nation was becoming conscious of its own identity. That is part of the story of this volume.

It was taken for granted that every man must have a lord. Lordship was no longer dependent upon tribal relations, but on the possession of land. Mastery was assumed by those who owned the most territory. No other test of secular leadership was necessary. Land was everything. It was in a literal sense the ground of being. Land granted you power and wealth; it allowed you to dispense gifts and to bend others to your will. It was inevitable that, under the reign of a strong king, the hierarchy of the country would also be strengthened; the divisions would be sharper, the evidence of status more pronounced. When in 1086, according to the chronicles, 'all men of property in England' swore an oath of allegiance to William the Conqueror they were following an established procedure.

The landless man was either a slave or a pauper. He was not to be trusted. This represents the crucial difference between medieval and early modern England. The names of slaves are given for the first time within a document of 880; 'Almund, Tidulf, Tidheh, Lull, Lull and Gadwulf' are being transferred to land belonging to the bishop of Winchester. Slavery was in fact a legal punishment inflicted on those, for example, who could not pay their fines. A penniless farmer might sell his children. It has been estimated that 12 per cent of the English population were slaves. So land created economic subjection. Slaves, like oxen and sheep, were known as 'live money'.

By the time of Athelstan the country was divided into shires, hundreds and vills or townships, precisely in order to expedite taxation. The shires of England were unique, their boundaries lasting for more than a thousand years until the administrative reorganization of 1974. The earliest of them date from the late seventh and early eighth centuries, but many of their borders lie further back in the shape of the Iron Age tribal kingdoms. So the essential continuity of England was assured. Hampshire is older than France. Other shires, like those in the midlands, were constructed later; but they are still very ancient.

The shire was originally a military district, but it also served royal purposes as a centre of taxation and a source of justice. Each shire had a court, and a *burgh* or major town; it could muster its own army, and was ruled on behalf of the king by a shire-reeve whose name became sheriff. The shire was then divided into 'hundreds'; each hundred was supposed in theory to support one hundred households or to supply one hundred fighting men in times of war. The hundreds were further subdivided into 'tithings' made up of ten households. The administration of the entire country could be devolved upon small groups of individuals who led the 'hue and cry' against thieves and who were responsible for each other's conduct. It was the essential basis of local government in England for at least the next thousand years.

The men of the hundred met in the open air at ancient places of assembly, and some of the hundreds are named after a prehistoric tumulus or barrow in the immediate neighbourhood. Hundreds-barrow and Loosebarrow, for example, are to be found in Dorset. The hundred of Doddingtree in Wiltshire is 'Dudda's tree'. The hundred of Brixton is derived from 'Brihtsige's stone'. This suggests that the roots of the hundreds go very deep, and that they reflect the primeval organization of the country. Since they still survive unaltered, although now rarely used for administrative purposes, they are another indication that we live in a prehistoric landscape. The rural district council is very old indeed.

In the tenth century the lie of the land was being changed. The country had been generally divided into very large estates governed by king, noble, or bishop; these estates of many thousands of acres are likely to have been the original territories of a tribe, their boundaries preserved by the burial mounds of ancient leaders. Yet in the reign of Athelstan they were being fragmented. Parcels of land were being granted to the clients of the king, or noble, in reward for service; an approximate size of the grant was 600 acres (243 hectares), upon which the new proprietor built his residence and organized his agricultural workforce. In the tenth century the new lords were known as thegns; they became the lords of the manor in the fourteenth century, the squires of the eighteenth century, and the country gentlemen of the nineteenth century.

The thegns had a much more direct relation to their land than had the great absentee landlords of the previous epoch. They created villages on their estates, taking the place of scattered farms and hamlets, so that their workers could be more easily housed and controlled. Villages were in existence in the period of Roman dominance, and similar settlements could be found in the Iron Age. Continuity is once more the key. But the village became the defining feature of a large part of the English countryside only in the ninth and tenth centuries. There is no village still in existence (except for those formed during the Industrial Revolution) that was not established by the twelfth century. If you dig deep into the village soil, you will find its ancient roots. Some of them, not the majority, have been in existence for thousands of years. But they are absent from certain territories. Down the middle of England, from Northumberland to Wiltshire, numerous villages are to be found; beyond that great expanse, in the north and in the west, the Iron Age landscape of scattered farms and hamlets survived.

The thegn built his wooden halled residence with smaller outbuildings; this manor was defended with a bank and ditch together with a palisaded fence. He built a small church, also of wood, with a bell tower to call his workers to prayer and to divide their day. Eventually he set up his own court. A well was sunk and before long a mill was built for grinding corn. The country village was not some comfortable and affable idyll; for its poorest residents it was a form of outdoor prison. The agricultural workers lived in buildings that were little more than wooden huts that they shared with their livestock. The ploughman, in a text of the eleventh century, laments his cruel life; he lives in fear of 'my lord' and must plough an acre or more in even the coldest weather. The boy who drives the oxen with his goad is hoarse from shouting.

The labourers were slowly reduced in status; for two days each week they performed services for the lord in return for a house and for a smallholding of land from which they could feed their families. Their duties included harvesting and ploughing, carting and haymaking, shearing sheep and constructing the stalls for oxen. Somebody would be ordered to uproot the weeds or to dig a ditch, to run an errand or mend a hedge. Independent farmers still existed, of course, but a large section of the peasantry was ground down by need, misfortune, or misjudgment. Taxes had to be paid. The threat of murrain, to the crops and to the oxen, was constant. Life, for small farmers, was very uncertain. Undoubtedly many of their farms were bought up by the larger landowners. It would be impossible to convey the sheer complexity of the grades and divisions among the working population. It is enough to understand that this was a society of intricate divisions with nice variations in degrees of freedom and unfreedom, where every single person was susceptible to certain claims from superiors.

The history of the village is so entwined with the history of the fields that they cannot be separated. As villages replaced hamlets, so in many shires large fields divided into strips supplanted the older rectangular fields. The lord of the manor had the most land, of course, but the rest was assigned by lot to the individual villagers. This was the most just and methodical way of sharing out the territory. It was also the only way that the land could be efficiently ploughed, by being made available to large plough-teams. The interest of the community, and of the lord, came before that of the individual. The procedure was also accompanied by a form of crop rotation, so that land left fallow for one year was sown the next. This system of common fields lasted until the passing of the Enclosure Acts in the eighteenth century, maintained by the force of custom and communal arrangement.

Other aspects of English life were also being more sharply defined. Towns, small and large, were acquiring unique identities. Some of them grew out of the Romanized towns, and some of them emerged from the burghs established by Alfred; others occupied the sites of large trading settlements on the coast or along the routes of the rivers, while yet more were simply part of the expansion of the large Christian minsters. By the last three decades of the tenth century they were bursting into life, taking advantage of a general rise in population and prosperity throughout the country.

The towns were crammed with buildings and with workshops. In Canterbury the houses stood 2 feet (0.6 metres) apart, enough room for the rain to drip freely from the eaves. The evidence of glassware and pottery, of metalworking and leatherworking, suggests a true urban community. The populations of Norwich and Lincoln were approximately 6,000, while those of London and York were appreciably higher. The people of other towns may be numbered in hundreds rather than thousands. Yet they were living together without agricultural or proprietary ties; this is nowhere more evident than in the fact that the inhabitants of the towns were deemed to be free. They had no lord except the king. The hand of the monarch is in fact evident everywhere, since most towns were royal creations with their streets and defences laid out by royal command. They became engines for making money from taxes and trade. Where there is money, there is power and hierarchy. The towns became self-governing, with the administration of their courts and markets in the hands of 'elders' or 'seniors' who formed themselves into guilds. It was a new form of kinship in a country that was redefining its tribal nature.

It is no accident that the English parish emerges in this period. It is part of the same appetite for definition and control – for discipline – that accompanied the growth of a united kingdom under a powerful king. You cannot separate religion from social restraint. The chapel of the thegn became the parish church, and the parish system itself arose directly out of the manors and villages that had spread across the country. By the twelfth century, the organization was complete. The parish became the centre of communal action. It survived unchanged until the last decades of the nineteenth century. The great minsters and monasteries decayed, or changed their function, and by the ninth century little churches had begun to fill the countryside. They were generally built of timber, unplastered, and enclosed a rectangular space divided into one or two 'cells'. In the eleventh century the wood was replaced with a fabric of stone, and the interiors of the small churches began to be ornamented and painted.

The church was not always used for sacred purposes. The contemporary literature suggests that it might be used as a meeting-place, a covered market, or even as an alehouse. The parish priests themselves were often illiterate, and many complaints were made about their drunkenness and violence. They were often married. They might be slaves employed by the lord of the manor. They were in any case little better than the lord's servants, who worked in the fields when they were not in their churches. They carried knives. They exercised control over the villagers in every sense. These 'Mass priests', as they were known, were supposed to catechize children, administer the sacraments and repeat the rudimentary truths of the Christian faith. But in many parishes they also were treated as 'cunning men' who practised rural magic. They were as experienced in pagan customs as in Christian practice. It is hard to realize the sheer earthiness of life in these centuries, where people and cattle slept beneath the same roof and where the priest might be an unshaven scoundrel.

The men of the ninth and tenth centuries wore their hair long. If you pulled it you merited a fine, and forcible cutting of the hair was considered to be as criminal as cutting off a nose or ear. The clothes were simple, consisting principally of cloaks and tunics made of woollen cloth; yet the wealthy were heavily adorned with rings and brooches. When some Englishmen were imprisoned in Syria, during the eighth century, the native inhabitants came to see them and to wonder at the beauty of their clothes. The arms and faces of both men and women were tattooed. The richer women wore long flowing tunics, ornamented with gold, and their heads were covered with silk or linen that was wrapped around the neck. Both sexes loved bright colours such as scarlet and green and pink. And both sexes delighted in perfume. Heavy drinking was commonplace, as it has been in all stages of English history. 50 per cent of the people died before the age of thirty, and 90 per cent before the age of fifty. Death was always close at hand.

# 6

# The measure of the king

At the beginning of the twelfth century, in the reign of Henry I, it was declared that the measurement of the yard (0.9 metres) should be 'the distance from the tip of the king's nose to the end of his outstretched thumb'. Yet what gave the kings of England such significance and control? They represented the country in a physical, as well as a spiritual, manner. They embodied the country, in its coinage and in its judicial process, in its land tenure and in its religious life. The history of England cannot be written without a careful account of its sovereigns. For many centuries it was impossible to imagine a country without a king. It was believed that a king's health would affect the health of the kingdom as a whole, and that the private vices of the king could provoke a public calamity. The image of England might be that of the king outstretched.

The origins of kingship cannot be found. We may deduce from the evidence of the Neolithic monuments that there was power in the land from the fourth millennium BC. Who once lay in the great works of Sutton Hoo or Avebury? The kings of the dead have also gone down into the earth.

And then we begin to see flashes of regal pre-eminence. The early Saxon kings claimed that they were descended from the gods, in particular from Woden, and it was believed that they possessed magical powers. Even the supposedly saintly Edward the Confessor traced his descent from pagan Woden. In some more remote age of the world the king might also have been the high priest of the tribe. It is likely that, his true wife being a goddess, he was allowed to have intercourse with whomever he chose. This may help to account for the excessive promiscuity of later English kings; even until recent times they were always permitted and even expected to keep mistresses.

The Saxon kings were violent men, warlords in all but name, but they clothed themselves in the panoply of divine power. Their banners were carried before them wherever they walked. From the tenth century the kings took on classical and imperial titles such as *caesar*, *imperator*, *basileus* and *Augustus*. In their magnificence we may see traces of ancient British kings, combining wrathfulness and vengeance with spells and rituals. In essence it was the same authority wielded by Henry VIII and Elizabeth I.

The continuity is there. The promises made by King Edgar at his coronation in 973 were repeated in the coronation charter of Henry I, beginning with the words 'In the name of the Holy Trinity! I promise three things to the Christian people subject to me! First, that God's Church and all Christian people of my dominions shall keep true peace!' The ceremony, devised by Archbishop Dunstan to crown Edgar at Bath, has been at the centre of every subsequent coronation. Much of it was employed, for example, at that of Elizabeth II in 1953. In his writings, particularly in his preface to the soliloquies of St Augustine, King Alfred reflects upon the divine power of the king, who is closer to God than anyone else in the realm; indeed, God Himself can be seen as 'an exceedingly powerful king'. The damned souls of doomsday are compared to men 'condemned before some king'.

From generation to generation the same message has been passed. The monarch has been anointed with holy oil, and is invested with divine power; he or she has been elected by God, rather than the people, and has been blessed by the Holy Spirit. That is why, from the tenth century, the king organized and controlled both the monasteries and the bishoprics; the strength and unity of the nation were materially assisted by the union of secular and ecclesiastical authority. The leading clergy were the king's servants, assisting him in times of peace and war. He was a Christus.

The main task of the king was indeed to lead his people into battle. By the aggrandizement of land and wealth he rendered the country more powerful and more worthy of God's grace. All the land was his. He owned all highways and bridges, all monasteries and churches, all towns and rivers, all markets and fairs. That is why from the earliest times England was controlled by a minute and complex system of taxation. The coin itself was minted in the king's name. The voice of the king was the voice of law; it could be said that he held the laws of the land in his breast. This was also the claim of Richard II, many centuries after his Saxon ancestors.

William the Conqueror did not need to create the role of a powerful and centralizing king, therefore; he simply had to take up the part acquired by him. He adopted his crown three times a year at a ceremony known as the festal crown-wearing; we may imagine a tableau in which the king, in silent possession of his majesty, receives the homage of his great lords. There had been such crown-wearings in the eighth century but the practice may lie further back. These three days of the year – Christmas, Easter and Pentecost – were also the days when the pagan kings of the north used to perform a ritual sacrifice for the sake of the people. So kingship had very ancient roots. It has been said that William borrowed from the customs of the Frankish or Roman or Byzantine civilizations; yet it may be that his true ancestors are to be found in those who ordered the building of Stonehenge.

The Angevin kings, the line of Henry II, Richard I and John I, chose instinctively to espouse and even to exaggerate the sense of divine kingship. They were all wilful and ruthless sovereigns who systematically exploited the resources of the country to bolster their own sense of significance. Richard was the first king to use the plural 'we' in the composition of royal charters. John was the first to call himself the king of the land rather than the king of the people. The premise of absolute power was of course challenged by the barons in the course of John's reign, but it did not disappear with his death. It lay beneath the confused inheritance and dynastic struggles of the later generations; royal power was still a question of what was possible rather than what was just or right. In the thirteenth century the principle of primogeniture or the hereditary right of the eldest son was first advanced. The power of the Crown was secure in the reigns of Henry IV, Henry V and Edward IV. Richard II was the monarch most inclined to emphasize the divine rights of kingship.

There was no progress towards a more liberal or benevolent concept of monarchy working in partnership with the great magnates of the land. As soon as the conditions were right, at the beginning of what has become known as the Tudor period, the king reasserts all of his authority and power with as much forcefulness as any Norman monarch.

The belief that the king's touch could cure the skin disease of scrofula emerged at some point in the twelfth century, although Edward the Confessor was accredited with miraculous powers at an earlier date. It is possible that Henry II was the first king to make a ritual out of healing those afflicted by the disease, and one of his courtiers wrote that the 'royal unction' was manifest 'by the diminution of groin disease and the cure of scrofula'. The tradition continued until at least 1712, when Queen Anne touched the three-year-old Samuel Johnson for the latter disease. Johnson remained a staunch royalist for the rest of his life.

# 7

# The coming of the conquerors

By the end of the tenth century England was a rich and prosperous country. So the men of Denmark still came in search of treasure and of slaves; they fought against naturalized Danes as well as Englishmen. Sporadic raiding took place in the 980s, and in the course of one attack London was put to the torch. It was one of the many great fires of London. In 991 a Danish army overwhelmed a native force in Essex, giving rise to a great English poem of lament entitled 'The Battle of Maldon':

> Our thoughts must be the braver, our hearts the steadier,
> Our courage the greater, as our strength grows less.

It is a poem containing all the stoicism and valour of the tenth-century warrior. He rode to the battlefield and then dismounted in order to fight on foot; he killed, rather than captured, the enemy. The English monarch Ethelred II was obliged to sue for peace after the signal defeat at Maldon. The Vikings wanted money, and Ethelred agreed to buy them off with £22,000 of silver and gold. The negotiations were helped by the fact that the English king could understand Old Norse. The taxation system of the nascent state was put into operation to provide what has become known as Danegeld or 'the Danish tax'.

This had been precisely the method used by Alfred when faced with victorious foes, but Ethelred was not so fortunate or perhaps as sagacious as his ancestor. He was given the nickname 'unready' or more precisely 'ill-advised', and it may be that his real fault lay in taking bad counsel. The leaders of the realm, the earls who controlled the shires, were divided among themselves on the best way of confronting the Danish threat. In legal and administrative affairs he was better served, however, and his reign is notable for its law-codes and charters. His was also a court of poetry and music as well as of war. We might call him Ethelred the Unlucky, with the proviso that kings are obliged to make their own luck.

The king of Denmark was in that fortunate position. When he laid siege to London in 994, Ethelred again poured money into his purse. This was getting to be a habit. And the Danes now knew that England was as craven as it was wealthy. That is why all their attacks were now aimed against it. The raids continued over succeeding years, until the time came when a Danish king gained the throne. Ethelred materially affected the history of England in another sense, when in 1002 he married the daughter of the count of Normandy. It was a way of securing the protection of the south-east coast but, by that union, the fate of the English became inseparable from the fate of the Normans.

In the early years of the eleventh century a storm of blood fell across England. The chroniclers write of nothing except the savagery and violence of the Viking raiders, of monasteries ransacked and towns put to the torch. In the same year as his marriage Ethelred ordered a general massacre of the Danes in England in retaliation for the attacks; it was said at the time of the slaughter that 'every parish can kill its own fleas'. Ten years later the archbishop of Canterbury was murdered by a Danish force, and became one of the first martyrs of the English Church.

In 1013 the king of Denmark, Swein Forkbeard, deemed that England was on the point of chaos and collapse. The various shires were in disarray, with their leaders unable to agree on a coherent strategy. Ethelred himself seemed to waver between paying and killing the enemy. One English bishop, Wulfstan, who called himself 'Lupus' or the Wolf, delivered a sermon to the nation in which he declared that 'soldiers, famine, flames, and effusion of blood, abound on every side. Theft and murder, pestilence, disease, calumny, hatred, and rapine, dreadfully afflict us.' It was the punishment of God on a sinful people. The nobles had squandered their strength in luxury.

So Swein Forkbeard sailed with his son, Canute, in a great fleet. They came in splendour, their ships ornamented with gold and silver, their shields brightly burnished; when the sun shone on them, the eyes of the spectators were dazzled. Admiration, and dread, were mingled. All the people of the Danelaw submitted to him, and Ethelred fled to the protection of the walls of London before taking refuge in Normandy. He came back to England, on the death of Swein, but the young Canute proved too much for him and his sons. On their prone bodies Canute climbed to the throne in 1016. With the death of Ethelred and of the son who succeeded him, Edmund Ironside, the long lineage of the early English kings came to an end. The descendants of Alfred, the sons of Woden, had ruled the country for 145 years. Not one of them was ever proclaimed to be a tyrant.

The first acts of King Canute were bloody indeed. He slaughtered the leading nobles of England, together with their children, so that his own sons could retain their dominion. When he took hostages, he often mutilated them before releasing them. He was as cunning as he was cruel; power often uses piety for its own deep purposes and, after his conversion to Christianity, he gave unstintingly to churches. When he entered the great monasteries, according to a chronicler, his eyes were fixed on the ground and he overflowed with 'a true river of tears'. The tears were not idle ones. He needed the English Church as a way of maintaining his spiritual authority as a legitimate king. He also strengthened an already strong position by marrying Ethelred's widow, Emma from Normandy. But he had acquired a country that had suffered almost continual warfare and raiding for more than thirty years, and the universal call was for peace at any price. The price was vast. Canute exacted more than £82,000 from the shires of England in order to pay off his army.

Then he began to set his kingdom in order. He divided the country into four military districts, and scattered his chosen men – his housecarls – over the shires in place of the English thegns. The English were once more a subject race. Canute was now a great emperor in his own right. He claimed to be the overlord of Scotland, of Ireland and of Wales. One of the Scottish nobles who paid homage to him was Maelbeath, better known to posterity as Macbeth. Canute was also lord of Denmark and of Norway, thus forming a Scandinavian empire of which England was a part. He married his daughter to the German emperor, whose coronation he had attended in Rome. He was known as Canute the Great, but he knew where his greatness ended. The setting for the story of the king failing to command the waves was the bank of the tidal Thames at Westminster, where his palace was situated. He died in the winter of 1035, and it is believed that his bones still lie buried somewhere within Winchester Cathedral.

The reigns of Canute's two sons, Harold Harefoot and Hartha-canute, were short and inglorious, reinforcing the perception that the sons of a powerful father are often weak and insecure. Hartha-canute was half a Canute. He and his brother serve only as a prelude to the longer rule of Edward, known as 'the Confessor'. The new sovereign was the son of Ethelred and Emma; he was therefore part English and part Norman. He was related to King Egbert of Wessex, grandfather of Alfred, but he was also a Viking; the Normans had once been Viking settlers.

In any case his real sympathies lay with the duchy of Nor-mandy, in which he had lived for twenty-eight years. He arrived in London with a Norman escort, thus marking the true beginning of the Norman invasion. Within a few years of his coronation on Easter Day 1043, three Norman clerics were given English bish-oprics, and Edward also planted a number of foreign magnates on English soil; they followed their native tradition and built castles rather than halls. The new king granted the Sussex ports to Fécamp Abbey, situated on the coast of Normandy, and gave the merchants of Rouen their own London port at Dowgate. The first act of the eleventh-century drama had begun. The invasion of 1066 was the end of a long process.

The earls of England, however, the powerful magnates who controlled the shires, were instinctively hostile to the Norman interlopers. Among their number were Godwin, earl of Wessex, and Leofric, earl of Mercia; Godwin was married to a Danish noblewoman, while Leofric had been connected by marriage to the wife of Canute. The Danes and the English were close to becoming one people. It is a pertinent fact that the Danes fought alongside the English at the battle of Hastings.

The two earls have long passed from memory but, curiously enough, the wife of Leofric survives in legend. Lady Godgifu is better known as Lady Godiva; her ride through the marketplace of Coventry, naked but with her long hair covering her honour, has become one of the most famous of English stories. She essayed the journey on condition that her husband alleviated the taxes of the citizens. It was also said that she commanded all windows to be closed and covered, so that she would be heard but not seen; one person disobeyed the rule, and he became known ever afterwards as 'peeping Tom'. So another phrase has entered the vocabulary. There is no truth in the legend, of course, except for the fact that Godiva was indeed 'lady of Coventry' in the eleventh century. Almost a thousand years later, the 'black eagle' of Leofric is still part of the city's coat of arms.

If the earls of England were hostile to the Normans in their midst, they were also averse to war and disorder. When Godwin of Wessex led an insurgency against Edward, the other magnates joined forces with the king and obliged Godwin to flee to Bruges. The leaders of the nation feared open civil war, and they also feared another Viking invasion. That is why they would not fight one another. This bond of shared loyalty helped to stabilize the realm, and to ensure Edward's survival. When Godwin died his son, Harold, took the earldom of Wessex; he would become one of England's most short-lived kings.

As a monarch Edward the Confessor made singularly little impression on the English chroniclers. He also made hardly any impression at all upon the course of English life. Of his character and nature, very little is known. The fact that he survived at all in such a ruthless and violent society suggests that he possessed shrewdness as well as resilience. He was called 'the Confessor' because he was deemed to have borne witness to the efficacy of the Christian faith, but in life he was not a particularly pious king. In one eulogistic poem he is described as 'claene and milde': he was 'claene' because he was not licentious, and he had no child; he was 'milde' because he was merciful. But he was not devout. His grants to the abbeys and monasteries were no more than what was expected. He showed no particular talent for diplomacy or administration. He had no grand plan; he worked by hazard and necessity, responding to each crisis in a measured manner. He had no principles other than those of self-interest and survival. Chance, and fortune, were his mentors. In this he was not unlike any other English king. It is perhaps the most important lesson of the nation's history.

With his death the life of England passes to a new stage. In the period from the eighth to the eleventh centuries, the identity of the nation was formed. Edward the Confessor had been *rex Anglorum*, 'king of the English', and his people were the *anglica gens*; he controlled *Anglorum exercitus*, 'the army of the English', and *anglicanum regnum*, 'the kingdom of the English'. In this period, too, the fundamental components of the English state – the shire, the hundred and the tithing – were complete. England was unique and distinctive in its possession of a strong state. English law was propounded and drawn up in elaborate codes, with laws on property and inheritance that remained fundamentally unaltered for many hundreds of years. The art and literature of the period, including *Beowulf* (tentatively dated to the eighth century) and the Lindisfarne Gospels (early eighth century), have become part of the English heritage. Most importantly, the customs of the land were maintained and its traditions were preserved. The essential continuities of the English nation were passed on.

To whom did Edward leave his crown? The question has never been satisfactorily resolved. It is reported that on his deathbed he pronounced Harold, son of Godwin, as his successor. Harold was not in fact the rightful heir; that honour was held by the king's great-nephew, Edgar Atheling, who was only fourteen years old. In turn William, duke of Normandy, claimed that Edward had offered him the crown and that Harold had sworn on the relics of the saints to submit to William. Since history is written by the victor, that account became generally accepted. It is likely to be completely untrue.

In any case Harold believed himself to have the greater claim, even though he was not part of any royal dynasty. He was the senior earl in the country, earl of East Anglia and earl of Wessex, possessed of vast estates and a great fortune. He was brother-in-law to the dead monarch and in Edward's lifetime he was deemed to be a *sub-regulus* or 'under-king'. The chroniclers report that he was of a free and open nature, and his own acts prove that he was skilful and brave in matters of war. With his brother, Tostig, he subdued Wales in 1063. So on 6 January 1066, the day of Edward's burial, Harold was crowned as king of the English; it was the first coronation in the newly consecrated Westminster Abbey. Yet this happy precedent did not necessarily augur well. His reign, lasting nine months and nine days, was one of the shortest in English history.

Two threats were raised against his kingdom. One came from the Scandinavian kings of northern Europe, eager to restore Canute's empire, and the other now came from Normandy, where Duke William seems to have felt himself slighted or humiliated by the choice of Harold as king. It is alleged that, on hearing the news, he was much agitated. He could not sit still. He raged. He was driven by greed and desire for power.

William was a child of violence and of adversity. In his earlier years he was known as William the Bastard, being the illegitimate child of his father's relationship with the daughter of a tanner. He himself said that 'I was schooled in war since childhood', when he succeeded to the duchy at the age of seven or eight. He came to power in a region that was noted for private feud and vendetta with ensuing public disorder. But by force of character he subdued his enemies. He won his first victory on the battlefield at the age of nineteen, and reduced the neighbouring regions of Maine and Brittany to feudal dependency. He was a man of formidable power and ruthlessness, greedy for lands and for money. But he had one great gift; he had the power of command and was able to bend men to his will. If they refused to be persuaded, he broke them.

That is why he was able to recreate the Norman state in his own image. It was still essentially a Norse state, fashioned from the early tenth century when Norwegian invaders forced their way into the territory and were allowed to settle there. The Normans were indeed the North men. They were part of a warrior aristocracy, their culture and society far less sophisticated than those of England. But they were learned in the new arts of war, which the English armies had not yet mastered. Duke William took the disparate regions of his duchy and, through a potent mixture of bellicosity and cunning, forged them into a centralized state under his leadership. He is a pre-eminent example of the 'strong man', the maker of the state, who emerges in all periods of the world's history. He was 5 feet and 10 inches in height (1.7 metres), corpulent by middle age, with a harsh and rough voice. He had enormous strength and physical stamina. It was said that he could bend on horseback the bow that other men could not even bend on foot.

This was the enemy that King Harold most feared. William had no possible claim to the English throne except by right of conquest. And that is what he set out to achieve. It was in many respects a hazardous enterprise. The Normans had no fleet; the ships for the invasion, more than 500, would have to be built. William was also confronting a formidable adversary; the English state was wealthier and more powerful, with the potential of raising far more soldiers for the fight. The fortunes of battle were in any case uncertain, which was why the pitched conflicts of armies were avoided at all costs; it was better to harass, and to ravage, than to rely upon the outcome of one event.

Yet the force of the duke's will was insurmountable; he persuaded the lords of Normandy, and certain French allies, to follow him across the sea. He promised in return innumerable riches from a country as prosperous as it was fruitful. William also enlisted the help of a higher power. He persuaded the pope to give his blessing to the enterprise, on the dubious grounds that Harold had violated a sacred oath taken in his submission to the duke. The pontiff sent William a ring containing one of the hairs of St Peter. In the same period William placed his daughter, Cecilia, into a nunnery at Caen. He had in effect sacrificed his daughter to God in the hope of a victory, just as Agamemnon sacrificed Iphigenia before sailing to Troy.

William made preparations for the great fleet to be collected on the Channel coast at Dives-sur-Mer by the middle of June 1066. 14,000 men were summoned for the onslaught. Harold, knowing of the naval threat, stationed his fleet at the Isle of Wight and posted land forces along the Channel coast. Yet the French army was kept in port by contrary winds. On eventually taking sail for England it was blown off course and was obliged to take shelter in the port of Saint Valéry-sur-Somme. There it remained until the last week of September. Never has an invasion been so bedevilled by bad luck, and it must have seemed to William's commanders that divine help would not necessarily be forthcoming.

Meanwhile, Harold waited. For four months he kept his forces prepared for imminent attack. Then on 8 September, he disbanded them. Provisions were running out, and the men needed urgently to return to their farms. He may have been informed of the abortive sailing of William's fleet and calculated that, with the season of storms approaching, there would be no invasion this year. Soon after his return to London, he learned of a more immediate danger. As the *Anglo-Saxon Chronicle* puts it, 'Harald, king of Norway, came by surprise north into the Tyne.' On 20 September, Harald Hardrada descended upon York. On hearing this unwelcome news Harold mustered his retainers; he marched north very swiftly, riding night and day, picking up local forces as he went forward. The first that the Danish army knew of his arrival was the sight of the dust thrown up by the horses. On 25 September he engaged the enemy at Stamford Bridge where he obtained a complete victory. It was a measure of his competence as a military commander. Harald Hardrada was killed in the course of the battle, marking the end of the Viking interest in England. 'A great man,' Harold said of Hardrada, 'and of stately appearance. But I think his luck has left him.'

Harold's own luck was soon dissipated. He was, in effect, the last of the English kings. As soon as he had celebrated the victory over the Norwegians, he received news that William had launched his invasion force. The duke had put a lantern on the mast of his ship, leading the way across the Channel. The Norman force landed in Pevensey Bay at nine o'clock in the morning on Thursday, 28 September 1066. It was the most fateful arrival in England's history. From Pevensey Bay the Normans rowed around the coast to Hastings, which they considered to be more favourable terrain. William built a makeshift castle here, and proceeded to ransack the adjacent villages. But he did not march along the road to London; his position was essentially defensive, close to his ships.

Harold received word of William's invasion two or three days after the event and immediately marched southward with the core of his army to meet the enemy in Sussex. He acted very promptly, but his troops had just fought an arduous battle in the course of which their numbers had been reduced. Haste may have precipitated defeat. He was hoping, perhaps, to catch the Normans by surprise just as he had surprised Harald Hardrada; he was undoubtedly trying to confine them on the little peninsula of which Hastings was a part. He knew the territory well; Sussex was his native country, and he possessed large estates there. By 13 October he had attained this objective. He had told the local Sussex militia to meet him at 'the hoary apple-tree' on Caldbec Hill, but William received word of the forthcoming assault. He was able to lead his forces against an English army that was not properly assembled.

The Norman troops were marched in sight of the English force waiting on Caldbec Hill, the highest ground available; the Normans took up battle order on the southern slope of the hill, in what was theoretically an inferior position. The location of the English, on the summit, was later marked by the high altar of Battle Abbey; they were pressed tightly together, whereas the Normans were in more military formation. The English had some 6,000 or 7,000 men, but they were outnumbered by the Normans. The English were on foot, according to their normal practice, whereas the Normans had a large force of cavalry waiting in the rear.

So battle was joined. The Normans cried out 'God is our help' as they ran against the enemy, while the English called upon 'Christ's rood, the holy rood!' William wore sacred relics around his neck. As the Normans advanced upon them, the English put up their shields in order to form a 'wall'. They were essentially in a defensive formation, and it seemed that they were rooted to the spot. But the Normans had another tactic. On two occasions they pretended to flee from the enemy, only to wheel around and cut off their pursuers. The core of the English army, however, held its ground and fought all day. Then Harold was killed, at dusk, by a stray arrow. With their leader gone, the soldiers weakened. They fled into the night. If Harold had not fallen, his forces might have prevailed. But 'if' is not a word to use in history.

William and his army rested for five days, and then advanced on London by way of Dover and Canterbury. He was now in a foreign country still governed by men who were unwilling to submit to him; he was surrounded by foes. The earls of the northern shires were implacably opposed to him, as were the people of London itself. So he trusted his violent instincts; he took the offensive and began a campaign of terror. He was beaten back at London Bridge, and in revenge he burned Southwark to the ground. He then lit a circle of fire around London, ravaging the countryside all around; he left a trail of destruction and rapine through Hampshire, Surrey and Berkshire. The entries for 'waste lands' in *Domesday Book* tell the story of his progress. The leaders of the English, trapped in London, now agreed to submit. A delegation came to Berkhamsted, in Hertfordshire, and formally yielded to his power. The English were accustomed to foreign kings, after all, and the transition from Canute and the half-Norman Edward the Confessor to William was not considered unacceptable. Surrender was preferable to resistance and further bloodshed. With the death of Harold, too, they lacked an effective war leader.

William then led his troops into the capital. There may have been some local resistance among the Londoners, but his victory was complete. He was crowned king of England on Christmas Day in Westminster Abbey. As duke of Normandy, however, he was still in theory a vassal of the king of France. This dual status would bear bitter fruit in the years, and centuries, to come. From this time forward England would be involved in the affairs of France, and of western Europe, with many bloody battles and sieges that did not really come to an end until the defeat of Napoleon in 1815.

# 8

# The house

The British roundhouse, the Roman villa and the Anglo-Saxon hall – many of them built in the same place through successive centuries – have gone into the earth. A few ruined villas remain as evidence of ancient civilization, but most of them are now part of the land on which they once rested.

In the eleventh and twelfth centuries the standard house consisted of one square room on the ground floor, with another square room built above it; access to the latter was generally granted by means of an external staircase. The furniture was simple, and scarcely varied at all from that of the Anglo-Saxons. A board laid on trestles acted as a dining table, and a wooden bench was the primary form of seating. In the houses built of stone, alcoves or recesses in the wall could be used for the same purpose. There were very few chairs or stools, except for the chair of state in noble households. Some of the richer families might own chests, coffers and cupboards; the bed was essentially a bag of straw laid upon a carved frame.

Only the wealthy possessed houses of stone with a 'hall' on the ground floor. A larger proportion of families owned houses built of wood and thatched with straw or reeds or heather; the windows boasted no glass, but wooden shutters could be barred at night for safety and comfort. Nevertheless the wooden house was always draughty and smoky. It was generally on two floors, like its stone counterpart, with a living room and kitchen on the ground floor; on the upper storey was a bedroom for the master of the house and his family. In the poorer dwellings the inhabitants would sleep on the floor, with heather or straw as their bedding. There might be a wooden booth in front of the house, where goods and produce could be sold; behind the house might be located a warehouse or small factory where those goods were manufactured.

The poorer sort had no such resources, most of them living in huts of wattle and daub that were little different from those of the early Britons. At the level of absolute need, there are no variations. Peasant buildings, in the countryside, had a limited rate of survival; they either crumbled, or were pulled down, within two generations. They rise from the land and return to it. A form of tenure in Hampshire was known as 'keyhold tenure'; if a person could build a hut or house in one night, and have his fire lit before morning, then his residency was assured.

The style and method of peasant construction survived for many hundreds, if not thousands, of years. At the beginning of the twentieth century, for example, Thomas Hardy recalled the method of building used in his childhood. 'What was called mud-wall', he wrote, 'was really a composition of chalk, clay and straw – essentially unbaked brick. This was mixed up into a sort of dough-pudding close to where the cottage was to be built. The mixing was performed by treading and shovelling – women some-times being called in to tread – and the straw was added to bind the mass together . . . It was then thrown by pitch-forks on to the wall, where . . . it was left to settle for a day or two.' When the fabric had dried and hardened in the sun, the roof was built of thatch. This was the method used by the Britons before the coming of Rome. It was used by the English during the reign of Victoria.

The dimensions of a modest thirteenth-century house are given in a Worcestershire court roll of 1281; it was of one storey, 30 feet long (9 metres) and 14 feet broad (4.25 metres), with three doors and two windows. The windows were on each side, to be left open when a cool breeze blew, but stuffed with straw or fern in inclement weather. The family would have eaten and slept together within the same room. This was not a period in which the private self can be said to exist. A thirteenth-century cottage excavated in Berkshire consisted of one room, 10 by 12 feet (3 by 3.6 metres), and another in Yorkshire had dimensions of 10 by 20 feet (3 by 6 metres). The room was generally open to the roof, with a central hearth. In the longhouses of the same period the rooms were used for livestock as well as people, together with a store of grain. The inhabitants were living and sleeping side by side with their animals.

Houses were lengthened, or rebuilt, or extended, as time and occasion demanded. Certain improvements, from human industry and human ingenuity, were possible. The houses of the eleventh century were made of clay without timber frames; by the thirteenth century most houses were constructed with timber frames and, less than a century later, the walls were being erected on stone bases to curb damp and decay. The beaten-earth floors were generally strewn with rushes that became so moist and dirty that they were known as 'the marsh'. The first evidence of chimney pots comes from Whitefriars, just south of Fleet Street, in London; in 1278 Ralph de Crockerlane was selling clay chimney pots in that quarter.

Yet the essential structure of the dwelling remained identical for many hundreds of years. The furniture was scanty, household items rudimentary; the spoons and dishes were generally made of wood by members of the family. There might have been a few brass pots and cups. A bed acted in the daytime as a seat. These were bare rooms for bare living. It is surprising, perhaps, that richer and poorer agricultural workers of England tended to live in the same kind of dwelling; whatever their economic circumstances, they reverted to the ancient model. It is another indication of the customary traditions of the countryside. In the larger houses the same identity of purpose can be found, with a central hall flanked by smaller rooms. One gradual change did occur: towards the end of the thirteenth century more provision was made, at least in the larger towns, for adequate drainage and cesspit systems.

Houses from the fourteenth century have survived in far greater numbers than those of any earlier period. They are generally more solid and substantial than their predecessors, and in London they often attained three storeys with a height between 30 and 40 feet (9 and 12 metres). A visitor from the country would have been surprised by these urban 'skyscrapers', quite a new thing in England.

From the middle of fourteenth-century London, too, come fragments of small yellow bricks. The townhouse of a wealthy merchant from that century was highly decorated, with interiors of colour and of costliness; tapestries, curtains and hangings draped the walls. Tiles, rather than rushes, were laid upon the floors; finely glazed pottery was imported from France and Spain, sparkling glass from Venice and silks from Persia. This was still in great contrast to the rudimentary furnishings of the ordinary English house, but the appetite for luxury and colour slowly spread among the wealthier families. In the fifteenth century inventories of the richer households include such items as cushions and tapestries, painted cloths and carpets, basins and screens, wainscoting and coverings for benches and chairs. The colours would by modern standards of taste be considered inharmonious, with strident yellows and purples and greens placed beside each other. The intended effect was one of brilliancy and vivacity. That is why an image of the sun was sometimes embroidered on cloths and tapestries and articles of dress. In a similar spirit men often wore shoes of different colours. Brick and glass became more common. Open hearths were being replaced by fireplaces.

The objects of medieval life are still recovered from the ground. Traces of wooden stools and of other pieces of furniture, undisturbed for many hundreds of years, have been found at Winchester and Beverley. Two locks were smashed with an axe before being discarded; another lock was repaired by its owner. The vast quantity of medieval locks and padlocks, found within the excavated spaces, suggests a life of threat or at least of suspicion and caution. Medieval life was dominated by the key.

Candlesticks, of lead and copper alloy, have been taken from the earth by archaeological teams. By the fifteenth century these candlesticks have become larger, an indication that candles had increased in thickness. This in turn suggests greater wealth. So from small material details we may be able to reach larger conclusions. Hanging lamps of glass began to take the place of hanging lamps of stone or ceramic by the end of the thirteenth century; oil lamps, in which a wick floated upon a small pool of oil, were being replaced by candles at the beginning of the fourteenth century. Vessels of wood (generally of ash) are to be found everywhere, but glass was becoming popular among the wealthier families by the fourteenth century. There are glass flasks, jugs, and of course glasses. Glass urinals, in which urine was examined for the signs of health or disease, are relatively common.

Other archaeological relics of the dead have been found. A balance to weigh coin had been adjusted to give false readings, but at a later date it was deliberately destroyed; perhaps its owner had then been placed in the pillory. Vessels of copper alloy or of ceramic were often patched up, suggesting how in the domestic economy the cheapest items were valued; cracks in the ceramic surface were sealed with lead. An iron helmet was inverted, supplied with a handle, and turned into a cooking vessel. Spindles are found everywhere. So are needles and thimbles, from an age when both men and women were skilled in sewing cloth and leather. It was a common and necessary household occupation. Many spoons and spoon-handles survive, some of them inscribed with a pattern or mark to indicate ownership; this gives a picture of communal dining. Some vessels have been found bearing the legend CUM SIS IN MENSA PRIMO DI PAVPERE PENSO – 'When you are at the table, first think of the poor'. A brooch of the thirteenth century has, as its inscription, 'I am a brooch to guard the breast, that no rascal may put his hand thereon.' A ring of the fourteenth century has the legend 'He who spends more than belongs to him, kills himself without a blow.' Whistles, book clasps, writing implements, hooks, hinges, chests, caskets, leather shoes, are all mute testimony of a forgotten life.

The most commonly found location is naturally that of the 'undercroft' or basement. Many of them are lined with chalk or flint, and in some of them the tiles still cover the floor. There is evidence of steps leading from the street, and of small windows on a level with the ground. The life of the past leaves other marks on the earth. A worn floor will trace the path of a door once swinging to and fro. Go in.

# 9

# Devils and wicked men

To the victor came the spoils. William set about ordering his new kingdom. He confiscated the estates of his English opponents, particularly of those who had fought against him at Hastings. Some of the English thegns had fled, and others had gone into exile. Just as Canute had done before him, he raised a large sum with a sudden tax. He was greedy, with the appetite of a conqueror. Another sign of his strength rose upon his new lands. Wherever he went, he planted a castle. One was soon built in London itself, on the site of the present Tower.

He was helped in his enterprise by many survivors of the old regime. William realized, as other foreign conquerors before him, that he needed the experience and knowledge of English administrators. In the first years of his rule he retained the English sheriffs. The monasteries were still being governed by English abbots, despite the fact that two of their number had fought at Hastings. Regenbald, head of the writing office under Edward the Confessor, became William's chancellor.

Yet others among the English decided to fight. William's power did not really prevail beyond the south-east of the country, and Harold's own immediate family established a base in the south-west at Exeter. They took advantage of William's absence in Normandy to raise the banner of revolt in 1068. The senior protagonist in this affair was Harold's mother, Gytha, with the assistance of the Irish and perhaps even of the Danes. Gytha was the aunt of the king of Denmark. William realized the gravity of a rebellion that might embroil the whole of northern and western England and, immediately on his return, he took his army to the walls of Exeter. He laid siege to the city for eighteen days, and in the end Gytha made her escape down the river Exe; the citizens then surrendered.

This was only a prelude to a much more significant revolt in the northern counties, when in 1069 the English of that region enlisted the help of the Danes to take York. Memories of the Danelaw were still strong. William marched up the country, planting castles wherever he halted. He did not immediately attack York, but employed the tactics he had used against London three years before; he left a trail of destruction across the surrounding lands. This became known as 'the harrowing of the north' and consisted of nothing less than the wholesale destruction of the people and the territory in William's path. He fell upon them as if in a lightning storm. The men and the animals were killed, the crops destroyed, the towns and villages wasted. All the reserves of food were put to the torch, creating widespread famine; 100,000 people were reported to have died. No cultivated land was left between York and Durham, and a century later the ruins of the destruction were still be to be found. The villages of the region were described in the *Domesday Book* as 'waste'. Yet the north would rise against William no more. He had created a desert, and called it peace. William is supposed to have confessed on his deathbed that 'I fell on the English of the northern shires like a ravening lion.'

In the harrowing of the north William had not behaved as an English king. He had behaved like a tyrant. That is why other local insurrections emerged, and many of the English formed what would now be called guerrilla forces to harass the invaders. 10,000 Normans were attempting to control a country of 3 or 4 million natives, and the only weapons they had at their disposal were those of brute power and terror. Spies and collaborators, punishment beatings and secret murders – the whole panoply of occupation and insurgency – were indispensable. An English chronicler of the eleventh and twelfth centuries, Orderic Vitalis, wrote that the English 'were groaning under the yoke of the Normans, and suffering from the oppressions of proud lords who did not obey the king's injunctions'. The Norman lords, in other words, were pushing their power to extremes. So, in the first four or five years of Norman rule, there was talk everywhere of revolt. The English rose against William every year between 1067 and 1070.

One force of rebels has remained notorious because of its association with Hereward. He took refuge in the watery fenland around Ely, from where he launched sporadic but murderous raids against the Normans despatched to capture him. He joined with some Danish forces, who had landed on the coast, to attack Peterborough Abbey ostensibly to save its treasures from the Normans. He and his band were known as *silvatici*, men of the woods. He was joined on Ely by other leaders of the English revolt, who thus posed a distinct and recognizable threat to William's regime. For over a year the Norman forces tried, and failed, to dislodge Hereward from the fastness. Some people say that he was compromised by the treachery of the monks of Ely, who pointed to a secret path. It is certainly true that it was only after a prolonged assault, by forces on land and water, that the stronghold was taken and Hereward chased into exile. From this time forward, William appointed only Norman lords and abbots.

The confiscation of land hitherto held by the English was accelerated. It was an accepted principle that, ultimately, the king possessed the entire land of England. It was his realm. William put this principle into practice. By 1086 only two English barons, Coleswain of Lincoln and Thurkill of Arden, survived; they had retained their position only by enthusiastic collaboration with the new regime. The rest of the great estates went to a small number of Norman magnates, who promised in return to provide knights for the king's service. England had become a militarized state, supporting an army of occupation.

The smaller English landowners may have had a better chance of holding their estates, but only at a high price. Many of them became tenants on land they had previously owned. Some of them were roughly treated. Aelric had been a free tenant in Marsh

Gibbon, Buckinghamshire, but by 1086 he paid rent to a new Norman lord 'harshly and wretchedly'. It was said by one chronicler in the early twelfth century, Simeon of Durham, that 'many men sold themselves into perpetual servitude, provided that they could maintain a certain miserable life'. Other Norman families emigrated to this newfound land of opportunity, and the pattern of colonization persisted well into the twelfth century.

Other changes can be documented. Novel forms of building were brought into the English landscape, most notably with the castles and the churches. By 1100 all the English cathedrals were either being rebuilt or newly constructed. They were larger, and more massive, than their predecessors; the nave was longer, and the side chapels proliferated. The Normans built well; they gloried in the strength and power of stone. The great round arches, borrowed from Roman pomp, were a sign of their triumphalism. The massive walls, and the ranges of pillars and arcades, tell the same story. The immensity of Durham Cathedral engulfs the wanderer within a great wilderness of towering stone.

The Norman castles are square masses of masonry, with extraordinarily thick walls and tiny windows. They crush the land beneath them. They are indomitable. They exude an air of gloom and even despair; according to the English chronicler of 1137, they were 'filled with devils and wicked men'. They were at the same time prisons and fortresses, courthouses and barracks. The English hated them as the strongholds of their oppressors. Yet they are in their own fashion magnificent creations, born out of the will to power and control that the Normans possessed in full measure. It was said in the *Anglo-Saxon Chronicle* that William had provided such security in the land that 'any honest man could travel over his kingdom without injury with his bosom full of gold; and no man dared kill another . . .'.

The English landscape was changed in other ways. Hundreds of monasteries were planted across the country. Deer parks and rabbit warrens were created. Great swathes of land came under the jurisdiction of 'forest law', a Norman invention, whereby all the fruit and the animals of the field became the property of the king. Anyone who hunted a hart, or a hind, was to be blinded; no one was to chase a wild boar or even a hare; no trees were to be felled, and no firewood was to be gathered. The law covered more than forest and eventually one-third of the country became the preserve of the monarch; the whole of Essex, for example, was enclosed. The New Forest, Epping Forest, Windsor Great Park, and the 'forests' of Dartmoor and Exmoor are part of that legacy.

Kings have always loved to hunt. It is an aspect of their power. Alfred hunted wild beasts in the same spirit that he hunted the Danes. Hunting was a way of exercising military skills in a peaceful environment. It created a miniature battleground, where every nerve and sinew was tested. It was, for William, also a form of commerce; venison was expensive meat, and a ready supply from his own lands was highly desirable. Hunting was, and is still in the twenty-first century, a royal duty as well as pastime. Yet 'forest law' was another hated imposition upon the English, who had treated the produce of the woods and fields as their own. As always, the poor suffered most from the indulgence of princes.

A great division was introduced by language. The tongue of the new ruling elite was Norman French, while that of its subjects was of course still English. It used to be believed that for official purposes French entirely displaced the native language; in fact English continued largely to be used as the language of administrative record, together with Latin. But the use of vernacular French by the leaders of the nation did have other consequences. The problems of pronouncing certain English words, for example, turned Snotingham into Nottingham and Dunholm into Durham; Shipton became Skipton and Yarrow became Jarrow.

By 1110 the number of native names in Winchester had fallen from 70 to 40 per cent; the presence of foreign merchants, attracted by the flourishing English economy, may have played a part here. William even attempted to learn English in order to dispense justice, but it proved too difficult for him. In fact, over the centuries, the language of the law was imbued with words derived from the French – among them 'contract', 'agreement' and 'covenant'. The argot that came to be used in the courts was known as 'Law French'. 'Master' and 'servant' come from the French. 'Crime' and 'treason' and 'felony' are French, as are 'money' and 'payment'. The language of courtiers was the language of business and of punishment. There was also a difference of appearance between the invaders and the natives; the English wore their hair long, whereas the Normans were short-shaven. But in this, as in so many other ways, the English custom eventually prevailed.

That is why there are so many continuities throughout the eleventh century, untouched by the events on the surface of the time. English law and administration survived intact. William declared that the laws of Edward the Confessor were to be respected, although he effectively reissued the laws of Canute. The Normans had little, or no, written law. They had everything to learn from the English.

The thegns were now to be called knights, but their essential purpose as masters and judges of the land remained the same. The names changed, but the institutions did not. The hundred, and the shire, and the tithing, were intact. The sheriffs remained, too, although the later Norman incumbents may have been more exacting upon their shires. The county courts were conducted in the familiar way. The various privileges and customs of the towns and cities were maintained. Taxes or 'gelds' were raised in the same way. The system of military service, for general conscripts, was the same. The makers of the coin of the realm were still English; the Normans did not have the skill or expertise. Writs were issued and composed in the familiar manner. The witenagemot, or parliament of principal landholders, retained its ancient form. Wherever we look, we see signs of continuity. That is the essential feature of England. The deep structure of the country remained intact. William was undoubtedly a strong king who imposed his own strength upon the country, but so were Canute and Athelstan.

Many of the developments that have been described as Norman in fact represented only the acceleration of English custom. Much has been written about Norman feudalism, whereby the nation was bound in a military compact, but most of the constituents of that system were present in England before William's arrival. The defining principle of feudalism was the act of homage; a man knelt before his lord with his hands outstretched, and the lord took those hands within his. The supplicant, with bowed head and raised hands, resembled a penitent in the act of prayer. He promised to become 'your man for the tenement I hold of you' and to 'bear faith to you of life and members and earthly honour against all other men' except the king himself. But in England land had always been held in return for military service; the oath may have been different, but the social obligation was unchanged. We know from the English poetry of the eighth century that the lord and his men had always been inseparable. One significant change, however, took place. It had previously been the tradition that, on death, property was inherited by many kinsmen; by the twelfth century, property was bequeathed to a single male heir. All of these things worked together to create the social structure of the country.

An essential part of that structure was the English Church. William introduced a number of Norman reforms, as well as Norman clergy, in order to bring rigour and order to the religious communities of the country. By 1087 only three of twenty-one abbots were English. Not all of the new abbots were sympathetic to their English inferiors. The abbot of Abingdon refused to keep the feasts of certain English saints on the principle that the English were 'rustics'. At Glastonbury the new abbot used an armed retinue of Norman archers to shoot down his own monks, protesting against the imposition of a new liturgy. Others were more concili-atory. The abbot of Selby helped to build the first stone church for his community. He dressed in a workman's cowl, and carried on his shoulders the stone and chalk used for the construction; he received his pay at the end of the week, like the other labourers, and then gave it away to the poor.

William also appointed an Italian, Lanfranc, as archbishop of Canterbury. Lanfranc had resided at the Norman abbey of Bec, and was already well known to the king. He was one of those learned and pious men, like Anselm and Becket after him, who had a deep and lasting influence upon English life. Lanfranc drew up the first principles of canon law, and William conceded that all spiritual matters should be addressed in ecclesiastical courts. It was under the leadership of Lanfranc that the great cathedrals arose. He was also instrumental in bringing monastic discipline to often recalcitrant English monks. In 1076 he decreed that none of the English clergy would be allowed to marry.

The pope had blessed William's invasion, but the new king was not to be in thrall to the pontiff. He was determined to be the master of all his subjects. Was his office not sacred, too? In a divided papal election no victor was to be recognized in England without the king's permission. No papal letter could be sent to any of the king's subjects without his knowledge. No papal legate could enter the country without his approval. It was the king who would sanction the appointment of bishops and abbots. The battles between king and pope, or between king and archbishop, would continue for many centuries with an uncertain outcome; they came to a defining crisis only at the time of the Reformation.

If there is one signal reminder of William's reign, it is that document originally called 'The King's Book' but more popularly known as *Domesday Book* because its evidence could no more be evaded than the day of doom. It was a survey of the resources of the realm, unique in Europe but not unusual in England where various national and regional accounts had already been compiled. According to the *Anglo-Saxon Chronicle* William had 'deep speech' with the men of his council and sent officials into every shire to find out 'what or how much each landholder had in land and livestock, and what it was worth'. The subsequent work was in fact so copious and so detailed, in single columns and double columns of Latin, that it must have made use of earlier records. It comprises two books, one of 475 pages and the other of 413 pages, with some of the capital letters touched with red ink. It describes over 13,000 locations, the vast majority of which survive still. The authors of the *Chronicle* state that there was not 'an ox nor a cow nor a pig that was overlooked and not included in the record'. The level of detail is evident in one entry. In Oakley, Buckinghamshire, it was reported that 'Aelfgyth the maid had half a hide which Godric the sheriff granted her as long as he was sheriff, on condition of her teaching his daughter gold embroidery work. This land Robert FitzWalter holds now.'

The *Domesday Book* was commissioned by William at Christmas 1085, and was completed a year later; such speed was only possible within an existing administrative system. It was not a Norman, but an English, device. William could not have transferred English land to French magnates, after his invasion, without some existing record of English holdings that has long since been lost. It was in part compiled as documentation and evidence of that transfer, but it was also used as an instrument both for the more efficient raising of taxes and for the more accurate imposition of military service. It seems also to have been instrumental in a fairer distribution of the financial burdens William was placing on the country. He summoned his chief landholders to Salisbury where they swore loyalty to him once more; but now he knew both the extent of their possessions and their annual income. They were reminded that they held their lands directly or indirectly from the sovereign. He was their master. *Domesday Book* can now be seen in a glass case at the National Archives in Kew.

We learn from its pages that England consisted of arable land (35 per cent), woodland (15 per cent), pasture (30 per cent), and meadow (1 per cent); the rest was mountain and fen and heath and waste and wild. We learn also that the manor, inherited from the Danes and the Saxons, was the foundation of agrarian and economic life. In its essence it meant a dwelling, and in *Domesday* several manors are often listed in one village; but by this period it had generally come to mean an estate of land or lands in which the tenants were bound by fealty to one lord. The lord's land was known as 'demesne' land; it might be adjacent to the manor house, or it might be scattered in strips among the fields.

The free tenants paid him rent for their acreage, and were obliged to help him at the busy times of harvest; the unfree tenants or villeins performed weekly labour service in work such as thresh-ing and winnowing. The terms of this labour were maintained by tradition. Approximately 10 per cent of the population were deemed to be held in slavery, while 14 per cent were described as 'free men'; the rest of the population were part of a variable range between the two.

The manor was itself established upon the ancient customs and obligations that bound together a small community. A manor might consist of a village with scattered hamlets, all the inhabit-ants of which did service to the lord. It might consist of several villages. Whatever its form, it was the linchpin of the social order of England. The local court of justice was the manor court, where every aspect of life was ordered and scrutinized. The paths and hedges had to be maintained, and the rights of cultivation or inheritance supported.

The origins of the manor are still a matter of debate. Was a manorial system imposed upon what was once a freer communal system of agriculture? It is more likely that there were always lords, and that their control over the centuries became more rigorous. Yet no certainty is possible. We must accustom our eyes to the twilight.

*Domesday* did not of course describe the conditions of actual life in late eleventh-century England. The summer of 1086 was the worst in living memory; the harvest failed and some malignant fever affected half of the English population. 'The wretched victims had nearly perished by the fever,' the *Chronicle* wrote of that year, 'then came the sharp hunger, and destroyed them outright.'

William himself died in the autumn of 1087. He had been campaigning on the borders of Normandy, during one of his frequent visits to his duchy, where he became gravely ill from heat and exhaustion; when his horse jumped a ditch, his internal organs were in some way ruptured. He was carried to a priory at Rouen, where he lingered for three weeks. When his body was taken to the monastery of St Stephen at Caen for burial the body burst, exuding a foul stench that sent the mourners running from the building. It was, perhaps, a fitting end for one who was already swollen with greed and cruelty. He had a cold heart and a bloody hand.

He bestowed the duchy of Normandy upon his eldest son, Robert; Robert had asked him for it before, but William had replied that it was not his custom to take off his clothes until he went to bed. The dying king left England to God's mercy and to the care of his second son, William Rufus. To his youngest son, Henry, William left £5,000 of silver as a consolation; Henry carefully weighed it before taking it away. The threefold disposition was a source of much strife and disquiet in subsequent years; the three brothers quarrelled over Normandy, in particular, like children fighting over a piece of pie.

William Rufus held England. William the Red, of red face, of red beard and of red temper, was almost a comic-book version of his father. He was short and thickset, with a protruding stomach; he was very strong but, unlike his father, he was not of forceful address. A medieval proverb might suit some of William's characteristics. Who ever knew a tall man who was clever, a red-head who was faithful, or a short man who was humble?

When in a passion or in a rage, he stammered or spoke in short sentences. But he possessed more attractive characteristics. He soothed difficult situations with a joke, and liked to outrage the more serious-minded of his clerical advisers with a scandalous or blasphemous remark. This amused his courtiers. His most famous oath was 'by the face of Lucca'; this was the face of a wooden image of Christ in the church of St Martin in Lucca. He was boastful and ebullient, extravagant and bold; he always appeared to be greater than he was.

In his youth William had been devoted to the interests of his father, believing that this was where his own advantage lay. He stayed in Normandy until he was in his twenties, and so it is very unlikely that he was fluent in English. We may prefer to call him Guillaume le Rouge. He had left his dying father's side at Rouen, and crossed the Channel in order to claim his kingdom. At the age of thirty-one he was crowned in Westminster Abbey by Archbishop Lanfranc as William II, apparently on Lanfranc's own initiative; the archbishop was the most powerful man in England and, as it were, was standing in for God. The coronation liturgy was Anglo-Saxon, but the languages of the service were French and Latin.

The king's skills were soon tested. He put down a rebellion by some of the Norman magnates of England in favour of his older brother, Robert, by using what was essentially an English army; one chronicler suggests that 30,000 men flocked to his standard, but that may just be a device to convey a large number. Nevertheless Englishmen fought against the rebellious Norman magnates on behalf of their king. National feeling was coming forward once more, and this resurgence of national consciousness is plain in the soldiers' call on William to win the whole 'Empire of Albion'.

He answered this call by marching north. In the spring of 1091 Malcolm of Scotland had invaded northern England, hoping to advance his claims to a large part of that territory. As the leader of the southern part of Scotland, Malcolm Canmore, or Malcolm Big Head, had already provoked William I with raids and alarms; eventually he had submitted to the stronger power. Now he was testing his son.

William Rufus moved against him by taking Cumbria, then under the overlordship of Scotland. He captured and refounded Carlisle, settling it with English farming families, and effectively redrew the north-western frontier of England. It remains the frontier to this day. He found the English settlers among the workers on the royal lands in the south and, unfree as they undoubtedly were, they could only obey the summons. Yet they represent the beginning of English colonialism. In pursuit of the 'Empire of Albion', William Rufus had invoked the spirit of English imperialism. He also began the work of conquering Wales that until this time was comprised of warring principalities. That land was planted with castles, as the English moved slowly forward. But they were beset by Welsh rebellion, and in the end William held only Glamorgan and one castle in Pembroke. On the battlefield he never completely failed and never wholly succeeded; but his bravado kept him going.

The king always needed more money, too. He was constantly battling against his enemies – in Scotland, in Wales, in Northumberland and in Normandy. He was most alive in the preparation and prosecution of wars. That was what a king did. When he was about to set sail for Normandy, for another assault upon Duke Robert, a great tempest threatened. But he jumped upon his boat. 'I never heard of a king being drowned,' he cried. 'Make haste. Loose your cables. You will see the elements join to obey me.'

He fell dangerously ill in the early months of 1093 and, in peril of his life, his thoughts turned to God. His religious advisers urged him to repent of, and amend, his sins; it must have been difficult for him to know where to start. He could at least rectify one grave fault at once. After the death of Lanfranc, three years before, he had left vacant the archbishopric of Canterbury so that he himself could enjoy its revenues. With the prospect of hellfire before him, he acted. One outstanding candidate was, fortunately, close to hand. The abbot of Bec, Anselm, was in England on a fraternal visit. He was known throughout Normandy for his piety and learning, albeit disguised by genuine humility.

William summoned him to his bed of illness, and offered Canterbury to him. Anselm refused, on the very good grounds that he did not trust the king and foresaw great difficulties in working with him. William then cried out, according to a monk in the surrounding company, 'Oh Anselm what are you doing? Why are you delivering me to crucifixion and eternal punishment?' More was said in that vein. Anselm was still unmoved, and so the king ordered everyone in the chamber to prostrate themselves before the holy man. Anselm in turn fell upon his knees, and begged them to find another candidate for the office.

It was time to resort to force, in a thoroughly medieval way. The courtiers pulled him to the bedside, and gave the king the pastoral staff that was the symbol of office. When Anselm refused to take it, they tried to prise open his fingers. They managed to bend the forefinger, at which he cried out in pain. They placed the staff against his clenched hand, and the office of investiture was read out in haste. Then they all cried out, 'Long live the bishop!' Anselm was carried protesting to the nearest church, where what the monk called the 'appropriate ceremonies' were performed. It was an unedifying start to what proved to be an unpleasant relationship between the king and the archbishop. As Anselm said at the time, an old sheep was being yoked to an unbroken bull. The king recovered from his illness, and promptly reneged on all the sacred pledges he had made on what he had believed to be his deathbed. What man, he asked, can keep all of his promises?

Anselm had a deep respect for the office of archbishop, which he deemed to be equal in authority to that of the sovereign. Where Lanfranc had believed it to be prudent to avoid antagonizing the king, Anselm had a more delicate conscience. He was also a trained logician, with the habit of rigour and persistence. He lectured the king on his duties, to which William replied in his usual forceful and impetuous manner. 'I will see to this matter when I think good,' the king once said to him. 'I will act, not after your pleasure, but my own.' On being told that he must rid the nation of sin the king asked him, with a sneer, 'And what may come of this matter for you?'

'For me, nothing,' Anselm replied. 'For you and for God I hope much.'

'That's enough of that.' The king had spoken.

When the archbishop implored him to fill the vacancies among the abbots, he became very angry. 'Are not the abbeys mine? You do as you choose with your manors. Shall I not do as I choose with my abbeys?' When the final parting came, and Anselm was about to leave England as a virtual exile and retire to Rome, the king was still vengeful. 'Tell the archbishop,' he said, 'that I hated him yesterday and that I hate him even more today. Tell him that I will hate him more and more tomorrow and every day. As for his prayers and benedictions, I spit them back in his face.'

The problem was that William would have no rival authority in his kingdom. He spoke disparagingly of the pope as well as the archbishop. It was the endless dilemma of church and state. Clerical rights and royal authority were on occasion opposed one to another. The decrees of the pope were sometimes at variance with the customs of the realm. Did the king have the right to nominate bishops and abbots? Could he dispose of church property if he so wished? Could he refuse a papal legate entry into the country? A further difficulty arose. The archbishop, technically, was a vassal of the king to whom he pledged loyalty; but he was also a servant of the pope. It is sometimes impossible to serve two masters, as the later career of Thomas Becket will reveal.

William Rufus was continually on the move, taking his court with him. The equipment of the larder, the pantry and the buttery was packed into carts and transported wherever the king wished; the hounds were leashed and led forward; the members of the court rode on horseback, followed by 'parasites' and prostitutes. It resembled a small army on the march, and was as much feared as an army. The courtiers took, or stole, whatever they needed. They devastated small towns and villages with their exactions. This was the real nature of power in England at this time. It was based on violence and greed.

That court itself was an object of scandal in another sense since it was rumoured that the king's closest companions were sodomites. It is a practice not altogether unknown among warrior elites; the Spartans are a prime example. So it was not wholly against the

Norman ethos. William never married, and had no illegitimate children; it seems likely, in fact, that he was a practising homosexual. He was surrounded by what the chroniclers called 'effeminates' with mincing step and extravagant costume; they wore their hair long like women, letting it tumble down in ringlets that had been curled by crisping-irons; the lamps of the court were put out at night so that unnatural sins might be committed under cover of darkness.

William II died in 1100, in as swift and sudden a fashion as he had lived. The story goes that, on the night before his death, he had a dream in which he was being bled by his leeches; his blood surged upwards and covered the sky, turning day into night. He woke up in great fear, and called out to the Virgin Mary; then he ordered lights to be brought into his chamber. There is another story of his last night on earth. The account of a dream or vision, granted to a monk from the abbey at Gloucester, was brought to him. In the monk's dream the king was seen to attack the crucifix, and gnaw at the arm of Christ; but Christ kicked out at him, and left him sprawling on the ground. It is a vivid image, but not so vivid as to overawe William Rufus. He is reported to have laughed, and ordered that the monk be given 100 shillings.

Another source records that it was the abbot of Gloucester who sent news of the monk's vision in a letter to the king. William's response is interesting. 'Does he think that I act like the English,' the king is supposed to have asked, 'postponing their travels and business because of the snores and dreams of little old women?' The English were indeed noted for their superstitious credulity as well as their piety; William might very well have made a remark of that kind, with its implicit contempt for his subjects.

He had decided to spend the day of 2 August 1100 hunting in the New Forest, one of the large stretches of land devoted to the king's sport. As he prepared himself for the hunt, a blacksmith presented him with six arrows; the king kept two for himself and gave four to a companion, by the name of Walter Tirel. He sat down to eat before riding out, and drank more than was good for him. Then he and Tirel set off, separating from the others so that they could shoot at the deer that were being driven towards them. The king shot first, and wounded a stag. Walter Tirel then aimed at a second stag, but by accident hit the king in the chest. William staggered forward, and then fell on the arrow. Tirel, in panic fear, fled from the scene of the king's death.

That is the accepted version of William's end. In truth there is no reason to question it. None of the chroniclers seems to doubt that the death was accidental. Hunting accidents happen. Many of the great events of history are simply accidents. But the death of a king arouses suspicions. His younger brother, Henry, was a member of the hunting party. Could he have hoped to succeed to the throne? Or could a foreign court have been at work, using a Norman accomplice? Or was there perhaps some private enemy, taking advantage of the king's presence in the forest? The ancient philosophers have said that truth lies at the bottom of a well.

There is another, kinder, story about his death. It has been reported that in his final agony he called out for the Eucharist to be administered to him. No cleric, or communion bread, could be found in the forest. So one of the hunting party put flowers and herbs into his mouth, as a form of natural communion.

William's end forcibly impressed his contemporaries. It made such a deep impression, in fact, that his death is the only event of his reign that has stayed in the consciousness of the English. He had come and gone like the lightning flash. He had behaved as a king. He had exploited the realm entirely for his own benefit, and had attempted to extend it as a measure of his own power. He pushed the boundaries further back. He had achieved very little else but, in a period of factional violence, it was perhaps enough that he had kept the country united – even if it was only united in suffering.

His body, bleeding profusely, was taken in a horse-drawn wagon to Winchester, where the canons of the Old Minster took charge of the proceedings. It was said that his corpse resembled that of a wild boar pierced by a hunter. William Rufus was buried, without much ostentation or show of grief, under the tower. The tower crumbled and collapsed a few years later. A black pillar, known as the Rufus Stone, marked the place in the New Forest where he fell. It still stands.

Some of William's own monuments also survive him. He completed the White Tower and built Westminster Hall, largely with gangs of pressed labour groaning under the exaction. He rebuilt London Bridge, but a flood washed away much of its structure. Westminster Hall survives, albeit in altered form, as the most appropriate token of William's might. This dark and solemn building, of thick walls and huge pillars, was unimaginably large to the people of the time. But it was not vast enough for William. When it was finished, he declared that it was not half as great as he had intended. 'It is', he said, 'big enough to be one of my bedchambers.' Listen to the indomitable arrogance of the Norman kings of England.

The last of them, Henry, came down quickly like a wolf on the fold. As soon as he heard the news of his elder brother's death, he rode to Winchester and seized the treasury there. Three days later, on 5 August 1100 at the age of thirty-two, he was crowned as Henry I at Westminster. He had been alternately bribed and bullied by his two elder brothers, as they all fought over lordship of Normandy, but the possession of England was a greater benefit. He was more reserved and cautious than William Rufus, and proceeded to handle his prize with circumspection. He was called 'Beauclerc' or 'the good scholar'; he was literate, and spoke Latin. But he also had other accomplishments; he fathered over twenty bastards.

In his coronation charter he promised to undo the wrongs committed by his predecessor. He invited Anselm to return to Canterbury, a polite request that the cleric accepted. He gained the loyalty of the principal magnates by the judicious use of patronage. He extinguished private wars between barons. And he married Edith, the niece of the new king of Scotland; more importantly, perhaps, she was linked by blood with the line of Anglo-Saxon kings and was a direct descendant of Alfred the Great. The Norman dynasty was thereby sanctified in the eyes of the English. She did, however, abandon her English name and was known as Matilda; this was the name of Henry's mother.

Henry was intent upon consolidating his dominion. Forty years after the Norman invasion and conquest of England, the English invaded and conquered Normandy. Henry led his troops into the duchy and, at the battle of Tinchebray, captured his elder brother; Duke Robert was taken to England, and spent the rest of his life in prison. It was a signal victory for the new king, having reunited the lands of his father. For all but the first two of his thirty-five years as monarch, the country was at peace. He set up a ferry service between Southampton and Dieppe. One other innovation of the realm deserves to be mentioned. At the beginning of the twelfth century, the rabbit was introduced to England.

Henry maintained the borders with Scotland, but did not choose to enlarge them. He built upon his brother's conquests in Wales by a policy of encouraging Anglo-Norman settlement and of conciliating various Welsh princes; a Welsh chronicler declared that Henry 'had subdued under his authority all the island of Britain and its mighty ones'. That was not entirely true. The eastern and southern parts of Wales had come under the control of Norman lords, with their panoply of castles and of courts and of burgeoning towns, but the central and northern areas of the country were still governed by the native princes. When many Flemings migrated to the east coast of England, on account of the floods in their own region, the king settled them in Pembrokeshire, where they maintained their own language and culture until the end of the eighteenth century.

He was a strong sovereign, then, but not necessarily a benevolent one. He was concerned only with his own immediate interest, and the government of England became a form of estate management in which all of the available assets of the land were exploited. That was the Norman way. Throughout his reign the monks from Peterborough Abbey lamented 'manifold oppressions and taxations'. An extraordinary series of bad harvests also undermined the ability of the people to withstand his exactions. 'God knows', an Anglo-Saxon chronicler wrote, 'how unjustly this miserable people is dealt with. First they are deprived of their property, and then they are put to death. If a man possesses anything, it is taken from him. If he has nothing, he is left to perish by famine.' The king did take care to protect his supporters. When the coinage was debased with tin, Henry's soldiers complained that their pay was nearly worthless; he ordered that all of the coiners should be castrated and lose their right hands. He cultivated the interests of the magnates, too, by royal gifts and allowances; eulogists duly celebrated the harmony and loyalty of England. The aristocracy, in other words, could always be bribed and bought.

He of course also fostered the interests of his immediate family. He strengthened his authority by an intricate series of marital arrangements whereby his illegitimate daughters became aligned with the various ruling families of Europe. He married his legitimate daughter, Matilda, to the prince of Anjou; from this union a new race of kings would spring.

It was said that he was endlessly inquisitive about the lives of his magnates, and knew of the existence of plots against him before the plotters themselves. He was a man of great natural curiosity, too, and was nicknamed by one of his kinsmen 'stag foot'; he could determine, from the track of a stag, how many antlers the creature had.

There was one significant event, however, that he could not foresee. It occurred on the evening of 25 November 1120. His sixteen-year-old son and heir, William Adelin, was about to sail from Normandy to England. His party went aboard the *White Ship* in a festive atmosphere; the presence of an heir apparent always gives rise to gaiety. The crew, as well as the passengers, were drunk. The rowers kept up a frantic pace, but the helmsman was inattentive. The ship rushed on to its fate, and crashed against a large rock hidden just below the waterline. The heir to the throne was drowned, as well as many younger members of the nobility. Only one person, a butcher from Rouen, survived.

A survivor, in another sense, was left alive. The king's nephew, Stephen, count of Blois, was suffering from a severe bout of diarrhoea and declined to join the revelry aboard the *White Ship*. Since he would be crowned as king of England fifteen years later, it can plausibly be maintained that an attack of diarrhoea determined the fate of the nation. Statesmen may plot and plan. Learned men may calculate and conclude. Diplomats may debate and prevaricate. But chance rules the immediate affairs of human-kind.

It was said that, after the disaster, Henry never smiled again. But that is a line from a fairy tale. More realistic consequences ensued. The problem of succession, for example, soon became acute. Henry had only one legitimate child, Matilda, and he fathered no other children in the latter years of his reign. No woman had ever sat on the throne of England before, but Henry was not deterred. He gathered the principal barons of the land in Westminster Hall, and ordered them to swear an oath that they would uphold the succession of his daughter. Henry had a voice like thunder, and they quailed before the blast. They duly swore. Yet what was unintended and unforeseen once more came to pass. The perilous consequence of the succession was a long civil war.

While hunting in one of the royal forests of Normandy, the king contracted a violent fever. It was reported that his death was hastened by 'a surfeit of lampreys', and indeed he had always liked marine delicacies. In one charter he allowed the bishop of London to take porpoises from the Thames 'except the tongue which I reserve for myself'. He lay for some days in weakness and confusion; but he confessed his sins, in front of many witnesses, and was given absolution. His body was embalmed but the unfortunate and unskilful embalmer died from the infectious stench that rose from the cadaver; one chronicler, Henry of Huntingdon, remarked that 'he was the last of many whom King Henry had put to death'. The corpse, leaking what was described as black fluid, was eventually taken to Reading Abbey. This was the abbey that Henry had established as a memorial to his son. Its ruins can still be seen.

It is hard to speak of his achievement in any very positive way. He kept the peace in England. He was a good manager of business, and helped to maintain the administration of the country by appointing what were called 'new men'. These were Norman or Breton clerks 'of base stock', according to Orderic Vitalis, whom the king had raised 'from the dust' and 'stationed above earls and owners of castles'. He worked them hard but rewarded them accordingly. They represented a new class of professional administrators or *curiales* who stayed in one place and who were not part of the itinerant royal household. They were a sign of central administration.

The king always needed to make money, and the intensification of the royal government was essentially another way of increasing his income. Goods, and land, were forfeited to the king. Plaintiffs of every kind could negotiate a fine, by which they purchased royal favour. This is sometimes described by historians as legal reform. One judge from Henry's own court was very stern with his contemporaries. 'From the desire of money we become tyrants', he wrote. 'Legal process is involved in so many anxieties and deceits that men avoid these exactions and the uncertain outcome of pleas.' So much for the description of Henry as 'the Lion of Justice'. The lion's law was the law of the jungle.

Other means could be found of making money. The exchequer, with abacus beads for calculation and a court for the audit of accounts, became more prominent during Henry's reign. The money came from taxes and tolls. A rich orphan could be sold to the highest bidder, who then became his or her guardian; a wealthy heiress could be purchased as a bride. It was just a question of seizing the opportunity. 'The king enquired into everything,' Orderic Vitalis wrote, 'and what he learned he held in his tenacious memory.'

As the king, so the age. In the early twelfth century there was a steady increase in what would now be known as bureaucracy, the word coming from the writing desk or bureau. Written documentation now became an essential element in the calculation of revenue and expenditure. The laws, and other formal rules, were written down. The essential movement of the age was towards systematization and centralization. In this period the two central departments of the court, the chancery and the exchequer, emerged in recognizable form. The chancery, staffed by clerics, dealt with manifold aspects of government business from the writing of treaties to the granting of charters. The exchequer was the department in which all of the king's revenue and expenditure were controlled. So by slow and almost imperceptible means the English 'state' was created. No one was interested in creating a 'state'. No one would have known what it meant. Yet it was the direct consequence of all these disparate activities.

Henry had never really liked or trusted the English. He did not appoint any of them to high office, but relied instead upon his French clerics and courtiers. 'No virtue or merit could advance an Englishman', one contemporary wrote. Henry's son, William, had said that if he ever ruled England he would yoke the English to the plough like oxen. It was perhaps better that he drowned in the

Channel. Yet the English had survived, and the slow process of assimilation had already begun. The Norman settlers had indeed settled, and were beginning to refer to England as their true home. A whole world of English song existed. The English monks wrote histories of their foundations and the lives of their local saints.

Another force for the cultivation of England can also be traced. In the early decades of the twelfth century a new order of monks came from France into England. These were the white monks, originally from the abbey of Cîteaux, who were known as the Cistercians. It was part of their unique mission to live far apart from the ordinary habitations of men, and to survive by tilling the soil; the land was supposed to be their sole source of income, and they eschewed all forms of luxury. They were soon established over vast swathes of northern England, where they employed lay brothers as their farm workers. So large tracts of undeveloped country came under the plough. The fens were drained and the forests were cleared; more controversially, however, villages were sometimes destroyed to make way for fruitful fields. The Cistercians soon proved themselves to be excellent sheep farmers, too, and the local economy flourished under their supervision. They became the most significant group of woolgrowers in the country and, despite their profession, they grew rich. That is the story of the Church itself.

1. The building of Stonehenge, from an illuminated manuscript. It was the largest programme of public works in English history.

2. A silver relief of Cernunnos, the horned god of Iron Age worship. It may have been a god of fertility.

3. A mosaic from the Roman villa at Bignor in West Sussex; the residence itself dates from the third century AD.

4. A stylized depiction of some protagonists in the Roman conquest of Britain, from a late eighteenth-century history.

Engraved for Russel's History of England.

A ROMAN.    An ANCIENT BRITON.    A PICT.    A DRUID.

5. The helmet of a great Germanic overlord, presumed to be Redwald, buried at Sutton Hoo in the early seventh century.

6. A nineteenth-century print of a Saxon manor. In reality it was a wooden halled residence with several outbuildings, forming a small community.

7. Saxon soldiers about to engage in battle. A Roman chronicler of the fifth century declared that 'the Saxon surpasses all others in brutality'.

8. 'Alfred in the Danish Camp.' In legend, the king infiltrated the Danish camp in the disguise of a minstrel, where he sang to Guthrum.

9. Aethelbert, the great king of Kent, is here depicted at his baptism by Saint Augustine in AD 597. It was the beginning of the saint's mission to convert the Germanic settlers.

10. The Venerable Bede in his scriptorium. His most famous work, *The Ecclesiastical History of the English People*, earned him the title of 'The Father of English History'.

11. The *incipit* of the Gospel of Saint Matthew from the Lindisfarne Gospels. The richly illuminated manuscript was fashioned at Lindisfarne, in Northumbria, in the late seventh or early eighth century.

12. A Viking ship, suitably stylized as an engine of the invasion that began in AD 790. 'Never before', one chronicler wrote, 'has such a terror appeared in Britain.'

13. An image of Ethelred, commonly known as 'the unready' or 'the ill-advised', who was king of England in the late tenth and early eleventh centuries. The great sword is no doubt intended to emphasize his prowess or masculinity.

14. Edward the Confessor, king of England from 1042 to 1066. He was known as 'the Confessor' because he was deemed to have borne witness to the Christian faith, but in truth he was not especially pious.

15. The Normans crossing the Channel for the invasion of 1066. Fourteen thousand men were summoned by William for the onslaught against England.

16. The death of Harold in battle, from the Bayeux Tapestry. Once the king had been slain, all was lost.

long the high roads since the time of the Saxons; the word 'inn' is itself of Saxon origin and takes its place beside 'gest-hus' and 'cumena-hus' as a lodging for tired and dusty patrons. Alehouses were to be recognized by a long projecting pole beside the door, from which a bush was hung. That tradition has continued into the twenty-first century, with hanging baskets of flowers commonly suspended outside public houses.

The most common form of travel was by horse, although the native breeds were not considered to be as sturdy as those from the continent; a white horse was the most prized, followed by a dapple-grey and a chestnut. The roads were not safe from thieves and outlaws, so the travellers would form groups or 'caravans' for mutual protection. Even the knights and landowners of the neighbourhood might engage in highway robbery, and it was not uncommon for travellers to be obliged to pay exorbitant rates to cross a bridge or a ford. The members of the group would carry with them flint and steel, in order to prepare a fire, and also the rudiments of bedding in case they could not find accommodation; they also brought with them bread, meat and beer.

A long tradition of hospitality made it shameful to turn a wayfarer from the door. It was the custom that a traveller might stay two nights with a household, sharing its food and its beds, before taking his or her leave. After that time the host became responsible for the stranger's conduct. It was also customary, on first arrival, for the traveller's hands and feet to be washed. But there were benefits for the host in the arrangement. Where are you from? What news? What have you seen? In a nation where communication was often slow or non-existent, the arrival of a stranger was a matter of consequence.

Sometimes only slow progress could be made. The Canterbury pilgrims rode for three or four days before they could cover the 54$\frac{1}{2}$ miles (88 kilometres) from London. But there were also 'pilgrim roads'. One route, from Winchester to Canterbury, has even become known as the Pilgrims Way or what Hilaire Belloc called the Old Road. Pilgrims were the largest and most recognizable of all bodies of wayfarers. They walked or rode to Durham in order to visit the tomb of St Cuthbert; they came to the shrine of Edward the Confessor at Westminster; they travelled to Glaston-

# 10

# The road

The ancient roads, the witnesses of prehistoric life and travel, still persisted in the medieval landscape. But they were joined by other highways in the historical period. Many winding lanes between farmstead and farmstead, many sunken hollow-ways leading to the village, deep-set and drowsy on a summer afternoon, were constructed in the twelfth century. It was a great age of building stone bridges that needed roads on either bank, and the growth of towns required the more intensive use of the cart and the packhorse as a means of trade and transport. The 'Gough' map, dating approximately from 1360, reveals a network of major roads linking London with the other regions of the country. More small roads and tracks could be found in the thirteenth than in the twenty-first century.

The width for the king's highways was fixed in the early part of the twelfth century as that which would allow two wagons to pass each other, or for sixteen knights to ride abreast. We might calculate this to be 30 feet (9 metres). They were not all necessarily in good condition, however, and there is evidence of ditches, potholes and even wells dug into the surface. The people were urged as a religious duty to give funds for the mending of 'wikked wayes'; townspeople and landowners en route were obliged to maintain and preserve the roads of their immediate neighbourhood.

The travellers made use of the inns that had been established bury to marvel at the thorn tree miraculously planted there by Joseph of Arimathea; they went to worship the vial of holy blood, a relic of the crucifixion, at Hailes Abbey in Gloucestershire; they visited Winchester to pray at the shrine of St Swithin. The woods beside the road to St Albans had to be cleared to accommodate the throng of pilgrims making their way to the shrine of the martyred saint.

The two most prominent sites of pilgrimage were those of Our Lady at Walsingham and of Thomas Becket at Canterbury. The road from Newmarket to Walsingham is still known as 'the Palmers Way', palmer being another term for pilgrim. It was often crowded with worshippers, and its route was lined with inns and chapels; the town itself was filled to bursting with wayfarers. Many cases of healing were recorded at Canterbury. The diseased limb of a sufferer would be measured with a piece of thread, and a wax replica made of it; this was then brought to the tomb. Many invalids were carried in carts to pray before Becket's remains, but the saint was also known to cure hawks and horses. The noise in the cathedral was deafening.

The pilgrims of England are long gone, but something of that world persists. Buxton Water is still bottled and purchased in large quantities; those who drink it are part of the same tradition as those pilgrims who in the medieval period bathed in the waters of the holy well of St Anne in Buxton that were deemed to be a sovereign curative.

# 11

# The law is lost

On the death of a king, law was lost. When the king died, the peace died with him. Only on the accession of a new sovereign did law return. Knights fled back to their castles in fear of losing them. It was a question of saving what you could at a time when order was suspended. On receiving the news of King Henry's death his nephew, Stephen, count of Blois, left France and sailed to England quickly. He rode to London with his knightly followers, and the citizens acclaimed him as their king according to ancient custom. Whereupon he rode to Winchester and claimed the treasury.

As the son of Henry's sister, Stephen had for a long time been associated with the royal court. He was, after all, the grandson of William the Conqueror. Clearly he considered himself to be Henry's protégé and, in the absence of any legitimate royal sons, perhaps his natural heir. He persuaded many of the leaders of the kingdom that this was so. One person needed no persuasion. His brother, Henry, was bishop of Winchester. It may even have been he who prompted Stephen's decision to claim the throne. He entrusted his brother with the keys of the treasury and, three weeks after the death of the king, on 22 December 1135, Stephen was crowned in Westminster Abbey.

The magnates had sworn fealty to the king's daughter, Matilda, but in truth many of them had no wish to be governed by a woman. No queen had ever ruled in England, and in any case Matilda was known to be of imperious temperament. It was reported with much relief that, on his deathbed, Henry had disinherited his daughter in favour of his nephew. The report may not have been true, but it was highly convenient.

So Stephen was set for a fair start. He was not treated as a usurper, but as an anointed king. He also had the immense advantage of a well-stocked treasury, amassed through Henry I's prudence in years of peace. The money allowed him to recruit large numbers of mercenary troops with which to defend his lands in France and the northern frontier with Scotland. The king of Scotland, David, claimed the counties of Northumberland, Cumberland and Westmorland as part of his sovereign territory; he was inclined to demonstrate the fact by marching south. At the battle of the Standard in 1138, named after the fact that the banners of three English saints were carried to the scene of combat, Stephen's army under the leadership of northern lords defeated the Scots. A chronicler, John of Worcester, rejoiced that 'we were victorious'; the use of the first person plural here is significant. The English were coming together.

But the money began to run out. Stephen had been too generous for his own good. A poor king is a luckless king. He debased the currency, to pay for his troops, but of course the price of goods rose ever higher as a result. Then, in the autumn of 1139, Matilda arrived to claim her country. In her company was her bastard half-brother, Robert, whom the late king had ennobled as earl of Gloucester. This was a war between cousins that became also a civil war. Matilda was strong in the west, particularly around Gloucester and Bristol, while Stephen was dominant in the south-east. In the midlands and in the north, neither party was pre-eminent. In those regions the local magnates were the natural rulers.

The instinct of the Anglo-Norman lords was for battle; like the salamander, they lived in fire. William I had realized that, and had ruled them like a tyrant. He had said that his lords were 'eager for rebellion, ready for tumults and for every kind of crime'. They needed to be yoked and held down. Norman kings had to be strong in order to survive. But Stephen was not strong. By all accounts he was affable and amiable, easy to approach and easier to persuade. More damning still, he was lenient towards his enemies. There could be no greater contrast with the kings who had preceded him. He surrendered to the pope the power of appointing abbots and bishops; he also agreed that the bishops should wield power 'over ecclesiastical persons'. At a stroke the prerogative of kings was diminished. He struck bargains with his great lords that rendered him merely the first among equals.

The barons knew well enough that loyalty and discipline had been undermined by the arrival of Matilda. Here was a welcome opportunity to extend their power. Their castles were further strengthened, and became the centres of marauding soldiers. For the next sixteen years, neither peace nor justice was enjoyed. Private wars were conducted between magnates under the pretence of attachment to Stephen or Matilda. Skirmishes and sieges, raids and ambushes, were perpetrated by the armies of the two rivals. Churches were ransacked, and farms were pillaged. Battles between towns, as well as between barons, took place. The men of Gloucester, supporting Matilda, marched upon Worcester and attempted to put the town to the torch. They also took prisoners, leashing them together like dogs, while most of the people of Worcester took refuge with their belongings in the cathedral.

A brief chronology of warfare can be given. The arrival of Matilda in England had not created any overwhelming enthusiasm for her rule; the barons of the west largely supported her, but her principal ally was still her bastard half-brother. Robert of Gloucester became the leader of her army of mercenaries. Her second husband, Geoffrey of Anjou, was detained by wars of his own.

After her landing at Arundel in 1139 numerous small battles erupted in the western counties, such as Somerset and Cornwall, with castles being taken and recaptured. Sporadic fighting continued in the following year, with incidents occurring in regions as various as Bristol and the Isle of Ely, but without any definite victory or defeat. The great lords of England were confronted with a situation of insidious civil war without precedent in English history; some took advantage of the chaos, while others were no doubt anxious and dispirited. Stephen was widely regarded as the consecrated king, and there seems to have been no great popular support for Matilda's title; even her supporters were instructed to style her by the essentially feudal name of *domina*, or 'lady', rather than queen. Stephen himself was possessed of remarkable stamina, moving across the country almost continually, but his progress was abruptly curtailed when he was captured at Lincoln in the beginning of February 1141.

He was taken prisoner and confined to a dungeon in Bristol; a few weeks later, Matilda was hailed as 'lady of England'. She was never crowned. Nevertheless this was a disturbing moment for those who believed in the sacral role of kingship. No king of England had ever before been imprisoned in his own country. Matilda herself became more vociferous and imperious in her triumph, demanding money and tribute from those whom she believed to be her defeated adversaries. She was admitted into London reluctantly, its citizens having been enthusiastic supporters of Stephen, but she proceeded to alienate the Londoners still further by angrily asking for money. A few days after her arrival in the city, the bells of the churches were rung and a mob descended on a banquet at Westminster where she was about to dine. She took horse and rode precipitately to Oxford. It was one of her many fortunate escapes. On one occasion she retreated from the castle at Devizes in the guise of a corpse; she was wrapped in linen cerecloth, and tied by ropes to a bier. Subsequently she was besieged in the castle at Oxford on a winter's night; she dressed in white, and was thus camouflaged against the snow as she made her way down the frozen Thames to Wallingford.

Despite Stephen's capture his army, under the nominal command of his wife, took the field. Matilda retreated further and further west. Many of her supporters fled for their lives. But Robert of Gloucester was captured in the same year as Stephen. He was the unofficial leader of Matilda's forces, and it seemed only natural that he should be freed in exchange for the king. So Stephen was released and reunited with his kingdom. There resumed the deadly game of chess, with knights and castles being lost or regained. War continued for twelve more years.

Some parts of the country suffered more than others. A monk of Winchester describes the effects of famine, with villagers eating the flesh of dogs and horses. Another monk, from the abbey at

Peterborough, reports in some detail the depredations of the lords of the castles; they taxed the villages in their domains to such an extent that the villagers all fled leaving their fields and cottages behind. Yet the actual incidents of violence were local and specific.

This short period has been called 'the Anarchy', when Christ and his saints slept, but that is to underestimate or altogether ignore the underlying strength of the country. The administrative order of the nation, built over many hundreds of years, remained broadly intact. The walls of most of the towns were fortified in this period, but urban activity continued as before. It is even more surprising, perhaps, that in the years of Stephen's rule more abbeys were built and founded than at any other period in English history. The Cistercians continued to flourish. The tower of Tewkesbury Abbey and the choir of Peterborough Cathedral were completed in the years of warfare.

War itself was not incessant. All hostilities were suspended in the penitential seasons of Lent and Advent. While Matilda's mercenaries and the Anglo-Norman barons fought one another, the English people for the most part went about their business. Of course there were casualties and victims of civil war, adumbrated by the monks of Peterborough and Winchester, but there is no need to draw a picture of universal woe and desolation. It is perhaps worth recording that in the years of 'the Anarchy', the umbrella was introduced into England. It has outlived cathedrals and palaces.

One singular change was wrought by the intermittent warfare. The king no longer trusted the centralized bureaucracy established by Henry I, and he arrested its leading members in the persons of the bishops of Salisbury, Ely and Lincoln. He may have believed that they had secretly taken the side of Matilda and Robert of Gloucester. He also captured their castles; in this world bishops owned castles, too. Then in difficult and unusual circumstances, by instinct or design, he reversed the policy of the former king and devolved much of his power. He created earls as leaders for most of the counties; they were charged with political and military administration of their territories, and represented the king in all but name. There is in other words nothing inevitable in the growth of the English state; what can be proposed can also be reversed. That is why, on his accession, Henry II determined that he would return to the principles of his grandfather. He was a strong king, and therefore a centralist.

In 1147, at the age of fourteen, he had come to England as Henry of Anjou. He commanded a small army of mercenaries, ready to fight for Matilda's claim, but he did not materially benefit his mother. He was defeated at Cricklade, by the Thames, and in a characteristic act of generosity Stephen himself helped him to return to Normandy. In the final years of the conflict it was apparent to everyone that Stephen was the victor, but it was also agreed that Henry of Anjou was his natural and inevitable successor. The magnates of the land were now largely supporting his claims.

So with the aid and entreaty of prominent churchmen, an agreement was drawn up at Winchester in 1153; it was settled that Stephen would reign, but that he would recognize Henry as his heir. Henry gave homage to Stephen, and Stephen swore an oath to maintain Henry as son and successor. The custody of the important castles – Wallingford, Oxford, Windsor, Winchester and the Tower – was secured, and the pact was witnessed by the leading barons on both sides of the dispute. Matilda retired to Rouen, where she devoted her remaining years to charitable works. Sixteen years of largely futile struggle had finally been resolved. The fighting was worse than useless. It had solved nothing. It had proved nothing. In that sense, it is emblematic of most medieval conflict. It is hard to resist the suspicion that kings and princes engaged in warfare for its own sake. That was what they were supposed to do.

Stephen had sworn that he would never be a dethroned king, and indeed that fate was averted. Yet he did not enjoy his unchallenged royalty for very long. He began the process of restoring social order but, less than a year after the signing of the treaty at Winchester, he succumbed to some intestinal infection; he died in the Augustinian priory at Dover on 25 October 1154. It is possible that he was carried off by poison. There would have been many longing for his death and the rule of a young king, including the young king himself. The life and death of monarchs can be stark and dangerous.

# 12

# The names

The names of the English have changed. Before the invasion of William I the common names were those such as Leofwine, Aelfwine, Siward and Morcar. After the Norman arrival these were slowly replaced by Robert, Walter, Henry and of course William. A feast was held in 1171, celebrated by 110 knights with the name of William; no one with another name was allowed to join them.

When Henry I married Edith of Scotland, she was called 'Godgiva' as a joke by his compatriots. It was a parody of an English name, both awkward and archaic. A boy from Whitby, at the beginning of the twelfth century, changed his name from Tostig to William because he was being bullied at school. The serfs and villains kept their ancient names for longer, and a record from 1114 reveals the workers on an estate as Soen, Rainald, Ailwin, Lemar, Godwin, Ordric, Alric, Saroi, Ulviet and Ulfac; the manor was leased by Orm. All these names were soon to be gone. By the first quarter of the thirteenth century the majority of the people of England had new names, many of them taken from the Christian saints of Europe whose cults were spreading through the land. So we have Thomas and Stephen, Elizabeth and Agnes.

The Normans also gave to the English the concept of the inherited surname that came to define a unified family and its property. It generally invoked a place, or piece of territory, owned by that family. Yet there was no very strong tradition of inherited surnames before the fourteenth century. Only very distinguished families had a distinctive name. Instead a person would be given a tag by which he or she would be identified – Roger the Cook, Roger of Derby, Roger son of William. Names were also often used to describe the peculiarities of the individual, such as Roger with the Big Nose or Roger the Effeminate. Mabbs was the daughter of Mabel, and Norris was the female child of a nurse.

Even the occupational names might be changed. In 1455 Matthew Oxe, on gaining his freedom from servile work, changed his name to Matthew Groom. Some ancient names survive still. So we have Cooks and Barbers and Sawyers and Millers and Smiths and Brewers and Carpenters in all of the directories.

# 13

# The turbulent priest

So the son of Matilda, Henry of Anjou, was crowned as Henry II on 19 December 1154. He was the first Angevin king of England. His father, Geoffrey of Anjou, was also known as Geoffrey Plantagenet; this was because he wore a sprig of yellow broom, or *planta genesta*, when he went riding. From this little sprig grew a great dynasty that endured for more than 300 years; all of the kings of England, from Henry II to Richard III, were Plantagenet until they were supplanted by the Tudors. It was said that the family was the scion of Satan himself, and that one of the early countesses of Anjou was a daughter of the devil who fled shrieking from the sight of the consecrated host. When St Bernard of Clairvaux first saw the young Henry, he is reported to have been filled with dismay and to have said that 'from the devil they came, and to the devil they will return'. There is much in English history that might confirm the suspicion.

Henry II was twenty-one when he was crowned. His early life had been one of battle and mastery. He became duke of Normandy at the age of sixteen and two years later, on the death of his father, he also became count of Anjou. He then married Eleanor, duchess of Aquitaine, and thereby became the duke of that province. He now owned a large part of France, even though he was technically subject to its king. When he ascended the throne of England, he boasted mistakenly that he had acquired an empire greater than that of Charlemagne three centuries before.

Yet he had inherited a troubled country, recovering its political balance after sixteen years of intermittent civil warfare. He was only one quarter Norman, but he had a Norman sense of authority. He wished to manifest his will by imposing order. He demanded obedience. He forced many of the great magnates to give up castles and estates that he deemed to be his property; he drove the earl of Nottingham out of the kingdom; he levelled all of the castles that had belonged to Stephen's brother, the bishop of Winchester. In curtailing or arresting the power of individual barons, he tilted the balance of the country towards a strong central monarchy. He ordered out of the kingdom the mercenaries who had been hired by both parties during the civil wars; if they did not leave by a certain date, they were to be arrested and executed. They disappeared swiftly and suddenly.

In 1157 King Malcolm IV of Scotland came to terms with the resurgent king; he did homage for his southern lands, bordering on England, and he surrendered Northumberland, Westmorland and Cumberland that he had dominated in the uncertain reign of Stephen. Malcolm was sixteen, and Henry still just twenty-four. This was a world for young men. Henry then proceeded against Wales, and its princes tendered their homage to him. He also devised grand plans for the invasion of Ireland. He managed all this without ever fighting a formal battle. His genius, instead, lay in the siege and capture of castles.

He was restless by temperament, and impatient of any restraint; he never could sit still, and even when attending Mass he fidgeted and conversed with his courtiers. He always had to be in movement or in activity, even if the activity consisted of gambling or disputation. He often ate his food standing up, so that he might be more quickly done with it. He was stocky and strong, with the look of a huntsman or of a soldier. He had a florid complexion that burned brighter when he was vexed. Yet he was readily approachable, and there are accounts of his modest and benign demeanour when surrounded by throngs of his beseeching subjects. Some of them caught him by the sleeve, in their urge to speak to him, but he never lost his good humour. His jester was known as 'Roland the Farter', and 'every Christmas he used to leap, whistle and fart before the king'.

There is one story that illuminates the happier side of his character. Bishop Hugh of Lincoln had been summoned by the king to explain why he had excommunicated a royal forester. Henry was so incensed that he ordered his courtiers not to notice or greet the bishop on his arrival. Hugh of Lincoln was therefore met with silence and indifference. Nevertheless he eased himself into a position close to the king. Hugh watched his sovereign as he took up a needle and thread to stitch a leather bandage on a finger he had injured; Henry was always careless of his person. Then Hugh suddenly remarked, in French, 'How like your cousins of Falaise you look'. At which remark the king collapsed in laughter, and started rolling on the ground. The 'cousins of Falaise' were related to the illegitimate William the Conqueror; they were well known as lowly leather-workers in that Norman town. The king had seen the joke about his bastard great-grandfather.

In matters of state he was always cautious and circumspect; contemporaries relate that he was a very good manager of business, and that he had an excellent memory for facts and for faces. These were now necessary qualities for any sovereign. His principal purpose was to maintain and organize his empire, and for that it was necessary to be a master of calculation. That is also why he took care never to reveal his feelings, except to those most intimate with him; he needed to remain inscrutable to achieve his ends. Yet, in matters of high policy, he often broke his word.

The year after he had reduced the magnates to submission, he sailed to Normandy where in similarly determined spirit he seized control of his dominion. He took with him his young chancellor. Thomas Becket was a close companion, a friend as well as a counsellor. One of the king's secretaries, Peter de Blois, wrote that 'if the king once forms an attachment to a man, he seldom gives him up'; yet that admirable fidelity was tested to breaking point with Becket. It would need a muse of fire adequately to describe their relationship.

Becket was a Londoner, of Norman blood, who was quickly singled out for royal service. He was witty and fluent, serious without being scholarly. More importantly, perhaps, he had a very firm sense of his own dignity and importance. He had come to the attention of the king through the agency of the archbishop of Canterbury, Theobald, who had already learned to appreciate the young archdeacon's formidable skills as clerk and adviser. Becket soon found himself in the sun of the king's favour, and as chancellor quickly became indispensable. He was one of those men, like Wolsey after him, who resolve the cares of the sovereign while never encroaching on his majesty. Henry disliked the formal and ritual panoply of kingship, preferring instead sudden judgment and quick action; so Becket became the orator and the ambassador, gladly embracing all the matters of state that the king found unpalatable.

When Becket travelled, he travelled in procession. On a diplomatic visit to Paris, in 1158, he was preceded by 250 foot soldiers and surrounded by an escort of 200 knights and squires. His private wardrobe contained twenty-four changes of silk robes. When three years later Henry mounted an expedition to take the city and region of Toulouse, close to his lands of Gascony and Aquitaine, Becket led his own force of 700 knights.

Shortly afterward, the king proposed that he become archbishop of Canterbury in succession to Theobald. The king himself was not especially pious. He wanted a compliant churchman, effectively just an extension of his own power, and he considered Becket still to be a royal servant and adviser. In this, however, he was mistaken.

The character of Thomas Becket has always been the subject of controversy. His reputation as saint and martyr has, as it were, preceded him. He was a man always willing to play the part. Like a later English saint and martyr, Thomas More, he was always on stage. He took off the twenty-four changes of silk robes, and put on a shirt of sackcloth filled with lice. He lived on bread and water muddied with dirt. In that respect, opposites yoked violently together within one man, he was profoundly medieval. He was also proud, and stubborn, and excessively self-righteous.

As soon as he became archbishop, in 1162, he confronted the king. He refused to allow the sheriffs of Canterbury to send money to the royal treasury; then he challenged the king's decision that churchmen, found guilty in the clerical courts, should be handed over to the secular authorities for punishment. 'You do not', he said, 'have the power to command bishops.' But that was precisely what the king wished to do. He was resolved to restore royal authority over the English Church in the style of the Norman kings. They had withstood papal intervention in the affairs of England, and a papal legate could only enter the country at the king's invitation. The behaviour of Becket, as the agent of the see of Peter, incensed him. Henry did not contest the sacred authority of the Church, but he was determined that it would not encroach upon the rights and duties of the throne.

His anger, once roused, was formidable. Anger was a speciality of the Angevin dynasty, a black and ferocious force that could destroy anything in its path. One courtier recorded an incident when 'the king, flying into his usual temper, flung his cap from his head, pulled off his belt, threw off his cloak and clothes, grabbed the silken coverlet off the couch, and sitting as it might be on some dungheap started chewing pieces of straw'. This was the man who became the mortal enemy of Thomas Becket. The king was determined to ruin him.

At the beginning of 1164 the king and his advisers drew up a statement of sixteen clauses, known as the Constitutions of Clarendon, in which royal power was asserted against the interests and demands of the pope. Becket first agreed to the proposals, thus seeming 'to perjure myself', but then retracted his consent; he refused to sign the document. In the autumn of this year the king called a council at Northampton, with the bishops and great lords of the realm in attendance. Becket was now charged with contempt of court and fined, but the king had prepared further measures. Becket was ordered to account for all the revenue that had passed through his hands as chancellor as well as other sums of money for which he was deemed to be responsible. Henry allowed him no room for manoeuvre. Becket then made an entrance. He rode into the courtyard of the council chamber at Northampton, wearing his robes of office and bearing a large cross in his hands.

The story has become well known, and may have been elaborated in the telling. Some of the bishops came up to him as he dismounted from his horse, and tried to take the cross from him. 'If the king were to brandish his sword,' one of them said, 'as you now brandish the cross, what hope can there be of making peace between you?' 'I know what I am doing,' Becket replied. 'I bear it for the protection of the peace of God upon my person and the English Church.' Then he walked into the chamber, where he forbade the bishops to deliver any judgment against him. The king asked the lords alone to pronounce sentence against the archbishop. Becket refused to listen. 'Such as I am,' he told them, 'I am your father, while you are magnates of the household, lay powers, secular persons. I will not hear your judgment.' He swept out of the chamber, cross in hand, with loud cries of 'Traitor!' following him. Soon after, he fled the country in disguise.

He made his way to Sens, where Pope Alexander III held his court in exile, and flung himself at the feet of the pontiff. In the course of a long address, in which he denounced the arrogance and impiety of the king in attempting to destroy the powers of the Church, he adverted to his own role as archbishop. 'Though I accepted this burden unwillingly nevertheless it was human will and not divine will that induced me to do so.' He was blaming Henry. 'What wonder, then, it has brought me into such straits?' Weeping, he took the ring of office from his finger. 'I resign into your hands, Father, the archbishopric of Canterbury.' Some of the cardinals present hoped that the pope would put the ring in his pocket; they did not want to be at odds with the king of England. But Alexander III returned the ring. 'Receive anew at our hands,' he told Becket, 'the cure of the episcopal office.'

Henry, cheated of his prey, reacted with predictable fury. Unable to touch Becket, he reached for his men in Canterbury. Their lands were seized and their relatives were laid 'under safe pledges'; they were evicted from their houses and made hostage to the royal will. The first act of the drama was over.

Henry II did not speak English, employing only French or Latin. That is perhaps appropriate for a sovereign who spent only one third of his reign in England; the rest of the time was passed in Normandy or in other parts of France. He was born at Le Mans and died at Chinon; both towns were part of his original patrimony, and he was most deeply attached to the land of his father. He wore the short coat of Anjou rather than the long robe of Normandy. The Angevin Empire was in essence a private fief. Henry had no 'foreign policy' except the pursuit of his own interest and advantage. In this he was not unlike every other sovereign of the period.

It is a tribute to the skills of his administrators that England remained without turbulence in the long periods of his absence in France; it is yet another manifestation of the deep strength of the governance of the country. The key lay in efficient management or, rather, in efficient exploitation. Various taxes and impositions were variously raised; but these scutages and tallages and carucages are now the domain of the lexicographer rather than the economist. It is sufficient to say that the king's power was not in doubt. In 1170 he dismissed all of the twenty-three sheriffs of the kingdom, made them submit to an inquest, and reappointed only six of them. That could not have happened in the reign of Stephen.

In fact the prosperity of the country, insofar as it can be estimated, increased during Henry's reign. By the end of the twelfth century 150 fairs, as well as 350 markets, took place throughout the country. The first windmill was constructed in Yorkshire in 1185. The first church spires, now so familiar a feature of the English landscape, were rising in the limestone belt of Northamptonshire and Lincolnshire. The use of horses, rather than oxen, quickened the pace of agricultural activity. English wool and tin were much in demand.

The English village was also thriving. It was, as we have seen, a very ancient construct, but it was also susceptible to change. By the eleventh century the essential structure was that of church and manor house, with a row of small dwellings for the dependent population who worked on the manor farm in exchange for land of their own. Around the village lay the open fields. In the twelfth century, however, new villages were planned and laid out by the lords of great estates. New labour was introduced onto the land; markets and trading areas were created. The houses of the labourers were often planned around a small rectangular green, where livestock might graze; each dwelling had its own garden.

The records of the manorial courts of the twelfth century are filled with the daily life of the village. A shoemaker, Philip Noseles, is arrested because of his persistent habit of eavesdropping on the conversations of neighbours; a woman named Matilda is taken to court for breaking down hedges; Andrew Noteman dragged the daughter of Roger the thatcher out of her cottage by her ears; Matilda Crane has the habit of stealing chickens and is to be barred from the village; a couple accused of fornication were told that they must marry if they repeated the offence.

The origins of many villages lie in prehistory, and their life was deeply imbued with custom and the tenacious observance of tradition. In one document a young man is described as being 'of the blood of the village', emphasizing the presence of distinct kinship ties. Collective rituals also persisted for many hundreds, if not thousands, of years. Until quite recent times, in the village of Polperro in Cornwall, it was customary to wheel a 'mock mayor' down to the sea and there dip him into the water. At the village of Holne, in Devonshire, a ram was tied to a great stone pillar in the middle of a field where its throat was cut by a band of young men.

The villagers sowed wheat and rye, barley and oats; they reared horses and pigs and cattle; they brewed ale. Some of the freeholders fell into debt, and were forced to sell land; some of them exchanged lands. Village officials were elected every year, either by the lord or the villagers themselves, to take care of such duties as the collection of fines. A common shepherd was employed for the flocks of all the families. It was a stratified but highly cohesive society that depended upon communal agreement in all the principal areas of agricultural life. It was also a society partly established upon mutual help. Yet how much of the material wealth of the nation reached the lowest classes of farmers and labourers cannot be known. History has always ignored the poor.

The number of new towns was growing very rapidly, in the same period, as the economic life of the country quickened; in the forty years between 1191 and 1230 some forty-nine new towns were planted. These were generally planned by a great lord who wished to create a market for the surrounding countryside. He then collected rents and taxes, making money far in excess of the amount to be gained from land devoted to agriculture. The bishop of Lincoln, for example, laid out a street of shops and houses beside a small village; he then diverted the principal road towards it. So was created the market town of Thame in Oxfordshire. Leeds was conjured into being in 1207 when the lord of the manor of Leeds, comprising a small village, planned thirty building plots on either side of a new street just beside a crossing of the river Aire. These were profitable investments, and a measure of their success can be found in the fact that after 900 years they still flourish. Somewhere beneath the modern foundations lie the bake-houses, the latrines, the taverns and the prisons of the early thirteenth century.

Many of these new towns were built by the command or recommendation of the king, and were known as royal boroughs. The same imperative of profit applied. Thus in 1155 the king decreed that at Scarborough 'they shall pay me yearly for each house whose gable is turned towards the street fourpence, and for those houses whose sides are turned towards the street, sixpence'.

The older towns, with their foundations in the first century and perhaps even before, continued to expand. They were becoming more self-aware. Their walls were strengthened and dignified; Hull, for example, built the first surrounding wall made entirely out of brick. The association of the leading townspeople, with the mayor as their chief officer, became known as *communia* or *communa*. In 1191 the system of mayor and aldermen was established in London. The leaders of the towns began to resent external interference; the aldermen of London, for example, were quite capable of defying the royal court at Westminster.

The leaders of the towns built walls and gates, with main streets leading directly to the market area. The same trades, such as shoemaking and bread-baking, had a tendency to congregate together. Certain towns were already identified by their principal commodity, so that we hear of the russet cloths of Colchester and the soap of Coventry. The Knights Templar established a town in Buckinghamshire which they named as Baghdad, hoping to create in imitation a great market there; it is now known more prosaically as Baldock. 'Fairs' were instituted at Boston and Bishop's Lynn, Winchester and St Ives. In the larger towns, an entire street might be devoted to a single trade. The population was growing along with everything else. By the late twelfth century London numbered 80,000, while Norwich and Coventry each harboured 20,000 inhabitants.

The original outline of Stratford-upon-Avon, planned by the

bishop of Worcester in 1196, is still visible in the modern streets; houses still stand on the plots where they were sited by the bishop; many of the names of the streets have also survived. A female huckster of the thirteenth century would still be able to navigate the roads of the town. Even a great city such as London still bears the traces of its origin.

The traders of these towns, old or new, helped to develop guilds that enforced standards; these guilds merchant, as they were called, prospered to such an extent that eventually they took over the administration of most of the towns. The guilds had a long existence, dating back to the ninth and tenth centuries, but in their original incarnation they were 'friendly societies' of a pious nature; they prayed for the souls of their dead brethren, and supported their members in case of dire need.

Members of the same trade naturally tended to join the same guild; so economic, as well as spiritual, interests played a part. They became organized. They laid down standards of business and manufacture. They refused to allow outsiders to participate in their 'mysteries' and instead set up a rigid system of apprenticeship. They had once met in the churchyard or in the town hall, but by the end of the twelfth century many of them had acquired imposing premises of their own commonly known as the guildhall.

Yet they retained their pious endeavours, collecting for charity and for the expenses of death; many of them maintained a chapel, or at least an altar light, at their nearest church. They built bridges and roads, although the improvement of transport was perhaps a matter of self-interest. The craft guilds were also responsible for the sequences known as miracle or mystery plays that were the most important aspect of English drama in the age before Shakespeare. This concatenation of religious, social and economic power is thoroughly medieval.

So the long period in which towns prospered, in the twelfth and thirteenth centuries, was also one in which the sense of urban community was most highly developed. In some respects the notion of a community is specious, however, since the richer townspeople known as 'the better sort' created an oligarchy of power concentrated in a small network of families. In Norwich 60 per cent of the wealth had devolved into the hands of 6 per cent of the population. These were the men who would serve as jurors in the town court and who took up the offices of the local administration. Nevertheless a feeling of common interest was aroused in the maintenance of newly acquired privileges and traditions. In the Commune of London, forged at a time when mutual antagonism between merchants and craftsmen was intense, the voices of the citizens could still be heard shouting 'Ya Ya!' or 'Nay Nay!' in their assemblies.

This sense of corporate identity was strengthened by the belief that towns were areas of relative freedom. The people who gathered there were drawn together in a commercial pact, and were not subject to the rules of labour service that obtained in the countryside. By the early twelfth century it was established that if a villein resided in a town for a year and a day, he acquired his freedom. The air of the town was different.

We may envisage wooden houses and wooden shops, with vacant plots between them where the hens scratched and where the small horses of the period were tethered. Many of the wooden houses were of two storeys, with the shop on the ground floor and the living quarters above it. Permanent shops were erected, but stalls could be set up and taken down from day to day. In any town perhaps two or three stone houses were owned by the richer merchants.

In Chester a wooden footway was raised above the street of beaten earth so that it became a 'first floor' sheltered by the houses above; from there, the pedestrians could 'window-shop'. In the towns of England dirt and refuse were scattered everywhere, partly scavenged by pigs and kites. The streams running above ground were often filthy with industrial waste and excrement. The noise of bargaining, and of argument, was intense. It was busy, always busy, with the particular stridency and excitability of the medieval period in England.


How much the king's advisers revised the administration of justice, and how much was Henry II's own contribution, is a nice question. It is reported that he spent many sleepless nights debating with his advisers over points of law, but that may be a pious fiction. It is undoubtedly true that in the course of his reign the rule of law was amplified in England; one of his contemporaries, Walter Map, noted that the king was 'a subtle deviser of novel judicial processes'. He decreed, for example, that royal justices should make regular visits to the shires and take over legal business previously reserved for the sheriff or the county justice. Six groups of three judges each toured between four and eight counties so that the whole country came under their purview. They were based at Westminster, but the central administration was reaching out.

Their activities were of course designed principally for the king's own profit, as he gathered up fines and other payments; it was well known that the royal courts loved money more than justice, and the king expected 'presents' at every stage of the judicial proceedings. A wealthy man, accused of a crime, would offer a large sum 'for having the king's love'. In a rough and violent society, it was considered to be perfectly natural. You paid money to see a doctor. You paid money to see a judge. Law was another form of power. It was just becoming swifter and more efficient.

But acts of expediency sometimes have unintended consequences. The imposition of uniform royal justice over the country laid the conditions for the development of common law. National law took precedence over local custom. When law became uniform, it could indeed eventually become 'common' to all. Phrases were employed that emphasized this theory of *ius commune*; 'as the custom is in England' or 'according to the custom of the land' became standard formulas. Men could reduce it to order, and to the claims of precedent; it could be codified and standardized. One of the most important legal works in English history, Ranulph de Glanville's *On the Laws and Customs of England*, was composed in the reign of Henry II. It is no accident that 'legal memory' was deemed to have begun at the time of the accession of Richard I, the king's oldest surviving son, in 1189. Henry was acting out of self-interest but his measures, more than any other, promoted obedience to the law and assured the coherent administration of justice. He had no interest in reform, and no scheme for it. He acted out of private and selfish interests only, and was motivated solely by the force of circumstances. He did not have any idea where his actions might lead, except to the extent that they afforded him more and more money. These are the foundations of the mighty edifice of English law. Henry had stumbled upon a system that has endured ever since.

One other unanticipated result issued from the new legal procedures. One of the functions of the judges was to rule on disputes over property. Had anyone been violently dispossessed of his or her land? This was a common problem of the twelfth century where lords, great or small, were always trying to increase their dominion. The judges were inclined to call together twelve local men who would be able to tender advice on the matter. The origin of the English jury is still in dispute, with some authorities placing it within the Anglo-Saxon period, but in the twelfth century we witness at least its systematic use. Within fifty years juries were also employed in criminal cases. Trial by jury replaced trial by battle and the ordeal. The parties involved in these disputes were summoned to the court by writs, which from this period took on a standard form. Writs cost sixpence. The legal system of the country was being created by haphazard and unpredictable means.

Yet all things move together. The creation of royal law, otherwise known as national law, called for a group of skilled adherents to interpret and amend the principles of legislation. There had been no professional lawyers in the eleventh century, and the judges were simply the servants of the king. In the reign of Henry II that happy vacancy ended forever. By the end of the twelfth century the 'learned laws' were being taught at Oxford. Around the law courts of Westminster there clustered ad hoc 'schools' of law. A group known as 'men of law' soon emerged. They organized themselves into a profession of various roles and grades. They ate and drank together, in the various hostels or inns that were at a later date transformed into Lincoln's Inn, Gray's Inn, and the others.

One of the paradoxes of medieval society lies in the presence of extreme violence and disorder alongside an appetite for great formality and hierarchy; England was in many respects a lawless society, but it was also a litigious one. The people loved law, just as they disregarded it; they could not get enough of it. It was consoling. It represented authority and tradition, even as they were being flouted. It was like listening to the king's voice even though, if you had come to Westminster Hall on a law day, you would have found yourself amid a babble of voices.

'Furthermore I marvel that you have not come to the point.'

'The point, sir, is like a quintain. Hard to hit.'

'Do not argue with me about the statute. I was the one who made it.'

'It is lex talionis! Like for like!'

'A great friend is Aristotle. But a greater friend is truth.'

The floor of the hall was covered with rushes containing sweet herbs, to curb the odours of the people and of the prisoners. The judges carried with them a ball of linen soaked in aniseed and camomile.

The King's Bench, the Court of Common Pleas and the Court of the Exchequer had their own panels of judges; the special pleaders were known as sergeants and can be seen as the ancestors of the barrister. It is only to be expected that, in time, the sergeants would be promoted to judges. The professionalization of the law thereby became complete. Pleadings became more technical, and tended to rely upon precedent. We may talk of legalism rather than law. The judges wore scarlet robes and caps of gold silk. The sergeants wore gowns with vertical stripes of mulberry and blue, together with round caps of white silk.

The clarification and standardization of the law meant also that society itself took on a more defined shape. One of the new procedures was known as *mort d'ancestor*, allowing freemen to claim by right their inheritance. Free tenants, in particular, could not be ejected from their land by their lord. But some men were not allowed to plead in the royal courts. The men who were not free, the villeins who held land in exchange for labour services to their lord, were excluded. They had to rely on the smaller local courts for their rights. They were, in other words, still at the mercy of their masters.

It was stated that 'earls, barons and free tenants may lawfully ... sell their serfs [*rusticos*] like oxen or cows'. Unfree men were defined as those who 'do not know in the evening what service they will do in the morning. The lords may put them in fetters and in the stocks, may imprison, beat, and chastise them at will, saving their life and limbs.' This is a presentation of the extreme case and, in practice, traditional custom would have preserved many of the rights of these *rusticos*. The lord also had to prove that his man was unfree; as a legal writer said at the time, 'you must catch the deer before you can skin it'.

The contrast between the free man and the villein had become the single most important social division in the country, underlying the elaborate and intricate hierarchy of roles and functions that already existed. It became the theme of the chivalric romances, with the distinction between *vilain* and *courtois*. The status of the knight was also changed, with the emphasis now on ownership of property rather than military skill or availability for service. In the process the knights adopted a different role. They took up a position in local rather than national society. They became in time the 'gentry', a word first used by the Wife of Bath in the *Canterbury Tales*. 'Gentlewoman' had appeared by 1230. 'Gentleman' emerged forty-five years later. So we have John Ball's rhyme:

> When Adam delved and Eve span,
> Who was then a gentleman?

By slow degrees the class system of England, based on property, was being erected.

Those who lived in towns were by definition free, and so the difference between free town life and unfree country life became ever more marked. The myth of the uncultivated rustic as opposed to the urbane townsman, so much a feature of Elizabethan pamphleteers and Restoration dramatists, can fairly be said to have begun at this time.

Thomas Becket and Henry II were in conflict for six years, with the pope and various other interested parties acting as intermediaries. The antagonists met in France on two occasions, but their meetings became futile confrontations. The dignity and honour of both men seemed to be too great, too sensitive, for any compromise. But in the late spring of 1170 Henry watched the coronation of his son, Henry the Younger, at the hands of the archbishop of

York in Westminster Abbey. He was crowned as 'joint king' in his father's lifetime as a token of dynastic security.

This was a serious blow against Becket. The two sees of England, York and Canterbury, had always been at odds over their respective powers and dominions. It was the established right of Canterbury to crown monarchs and princes, but that privilege had been snatched from Becket by the king. In this age the importance of status, and of precedent, cannot be overrated; they were the pattern of the world. Henry insinuated that the prince might be recrowned by Canterbury, if and when the archbishop returned to England. Becket was so concerned to defend the pre-eminence of his see that the offer was persuasive. A third meeting took place on French soil between Henry and Becket where the terms of a settlement were agreed. On 1 December 1170 the archbishop returned to England.

It was said that he received a hostile reception when he landed at Sandwich. It was also reported that he was soon riding across England at the head of a body of knights. Neither story can be substantiated. One event, however, is certain. On the eve of crossing the Channel he excommunicated the archbishop of York and other bishops who had been present at the coronation in Westminster Abbey eight months before.

There was a Latin proverb, '*ira principis mors est*', to the effect that the anger of the king means death. Becket was to prove the truth of this. When the news of the excommunications reached Henry, he was told that there would be neither peace nor quiet in England while the archbishop lived. The dramatic and vindictive way in which he had dealt with the archbishop of York seemed to be proof of that. Becket was a man who bristled with pride and self-righteousness.

The king may never have used the words attributed to him: 'Will no one rid me of this turbulent priest?' The phrase, however, is sufficiently close to something Henry did say. He himself admitted this at a later date. Four of his knights took him at his word. They left Henry's court in northern France and, riding along separate routes, made their way to the Channel. They met by prearranged agreement at Saltwood Castle in Kent, not far from Canterbury. From there they rode to the cathedral.

Becket was conducting business in an inner chamber and, when they entered, he greeted them calmly enough. Their intentions were not clear, however, perhaps not even to themselves. There are some indications that they planned to arrest him, or to oblige him to leave the country once again. But then the red mist descended. They began to insult and threaten the archbishop; he argued with them and refused to be cowed by their hostile demeanour. He proceeded into the cathedral to hear vespers. The monks wished to bar the doors, but he would not permit it. One of the monks with him at the time, William Fitzstephen, reports that he could have escaped at any moment. Dark passages and winding stairs of stone were all around him; he might have concealed himself in the crypt. But he stayed in the church, and prepared himself for the service.

The four knights burst open the doors and went after him with their weapons. One of them struck Becket on the shoulder with the flat of his sword, saying, 'Fly! You are a dead man.' They tried to drag him out of the cathedral, but he forcibly resisted them. He was wounded in the head, and fell to his knees. Another stroke cut off the upper part of his skull. They butchered him where he lay.

In death, Becket was triumphant. The leaders of Christendom were genuinely appalled by the slaughter of an archbishop in his own cathedral; only the murder of the pope would have been comparable. The king knew that the obloquy of the world would now be turned upon him. He retired to his chamber for three days, refusing food and drink. His enemies were, in turn, contemplating a very satisfying revenge. The king of France, Louis VII, declared that 'the man who commits violence against his mother [the Church] revolts against humanity . . . Such unprecedented cruelty demands unprecedented retribution. Let the sword of St Peter be unleashed to avenge the martyr of Canterbury'. Becket was already wearing the martyr's crown, although he was not canonized for three years.

Very quickly there grew up a cult around the site of the killing. Immediately after the death certain members of his household, and perhaps also some of the people of Canterbury, rushed into the cathedral and cut off pieces of their clothes before dipping them in the archbishop's blood; they anointed their eyes with the precious fluid. It is reported that others also brought vessels to capture the blood as it flowed from the prone body. This was the tactile and instinctive aspect of medieval piety. At a later date the monks of Canterbury developed a thriving trade in the miraculous properties of 'Becket water' that contained a tincture of the blood. Small vessels of tin alloy were manufactured on a large scale, each one bearing the inscription (in Latin), 'All weakness and pain is removed, the healed man eats and drinks, and evil and death pass away'. If this miraculous healing did not take place, it was agreed that the afflicted man or woman lacked sufficient piety. After Becket's tomb was constructed, and a shrine erected, the pilgrims began to arrive in multitudes. Chaucer's *Canterbury Tales* is devoted to them.

One of those pilgrims was the king himself. In the summer of 1174 Henry, beset by enemies invading from Scotland and from Flanders, made a formal and ritual penance for the death of Becket. He dismounted from his horse a mile (1.6 kilometres) from Canterbury and took off his silken robes; then he walked barefoot to the cathedral, badly lacerating his feet on the way. As soon as he entered the church he prostrated himself, weeping, before the shrine. The bells of the cathedral had been ringing to summon as many spectators as possible for this act of piety. The king was led into the crypt where he stripped off his shirt. The assembled bishops inflicted 'correction' on his body with a whip of several lashes; they were no doubt gentle with their royal lord. The king then spent the whole of the next day and night in fervent prayer, taking no nourishment, and finished his pilgrimage by drinking some of the water blessed by Becket's blood. He had been cleansed. The effect was immediate, and almost miraculous. His Scottish enemies were defeated.

Yet his return to papal favour came at a price. He was forced to concede that churchmen would only be tried in church courts. So was established the practice known as 'benefit of clergy', which was slowly extended to cover literacy as well; anyone who could read a short passage from the Bible, generally the beginning of the fifty-first psalm, known as the 'neck verse', was spared the death penalty. 'Benefit of clergy' was in fact not removed from the provisions of the criminal law until the 1820s.

God may have blessed him against his enemies, but He cursed

him with his children. The remaining years of Henry's reign were dominated by the struggles with his four sons who, like their Angevin forebears, were violent and rapacious. Henry had, in theory, divided his empire. His eldest son, Henry, was destined to inherit the kingdom of England together with Anjou and Normandy; the second son, Richard, was granted the dukedom of Aquitaine. The third son, Geoffrey, became by marriage duke or count of Brittany. The youngest son, John, had nothing at all; hence arose his nickname 'John Lackland'.

It was a most quarrelsome family from the vicissitudes of which Shakespeare could have profited greatly. The play of these warring parties would have out-Leared *Lear*. The brothers were united only by self-interest; selfishness was in their blood. They were concerned only with their honour and with their power; they fought one another over the extent of their respective territories; they built castles in each other's lands, and they refused to allow the king to mediate between them.

In some spasm of dynastic madness, the two eldest sons rose in rebellion against their father. In this act of subversion they were aided and abetted by their mother who had, for all practical purposes, severed herself from her husband. When the king marched up to Limoges, the headquarters of the young Henry, he encountered a storm of arrows. Yet the king's army prevailed and, in fear of his liberty, the prince escaped from the city. He wandered through his dominion, picking up very little support, and in the process succumbed to dysentery. The young Henry had lacked the resolution and competence of his father; he was at the time considered to be a perfect prince, courteous and debonair, but he would have made a wholly disappointing king. He seemed to be capable of rule, but only as long as he never ruled. He died in the summer of 1183, unreconciled to the father who had become his enemy.

And then there were three. It was supposed that Richard, now the eldest son, would come into Henry's patrimony. In return the king demanded that he transfer the sovereignty of Aquitaine to Prince John; Richard, standing on the principle of natural right, refused to do this. He fled from the court and returned to Aquitaine. The king advised John to recruit an army and march against his elder brother. But John had no army of his own and instead allied himself with his other brother, Geoffrey, who had command of a large army of mercenaries in Brittany. Together the two younger sons marched against their elder brother. They achieved very little, apart from some vainglorious victories in skirmishes, and in retaliation Richard invaded Brittany itself.

It seemed to Henry II that his empire was in an advanced state of upheaval, and that it might fall apart under the combined strains of these internecine wars. He summoned his three sons to England. Here it was agreed that John should become king of Ireland, effectively cancelling his claim to Aquitaine. Richard returned to his dukedom. But he was not to rest easy in this apparent success. It seems likely that the king had now decided to reverse the order of inheritance and to bequeath England and Normandy to Geoffrey; these Anglo-Norman territories fitted well with Geoffrey's fiefdom of Brittany. It was a neat territorial redaction, but it was soon undone. Geoffrey was killed while jousting at a tournament in Paris.

And then there were two, Richard and John, known to the more romantic nineteenth-century historians as Richard the Lionheart and Evil King John. In truth very little separated them, both of them rapacious and arrogant with no interest in their English kingdom except for the purpose of enrichment. Henry kept his sons at bay for five years, principally by refusing to name his successor, but as he grew older the issue became more and more important. In 1188 Richard agreed to submit his duchy to French jurisdiction, much to the displeasure of his father.

At a subsequent conference of the interested parties – Richard together with the king of England and the king of France – the matter of succession was explicitly raised. Richard demanded his father's assurance that he would be named as his heir. Henry refused to comply. 'Then,' Richard said, 'I can only take as true what previously seemed incredible.' He unbuckled his sword and, kneeling before the king of France, did homage for Normandy and Aquitaine. He was, in other words, denying his father's claims over a large part of the Angevin Empire. Father and son walked off in different directions.

It seems unlikely, in retrospect, that Henry would have

disinherited the elder son; it would have struck at the very heart of the medieval principle of rightful inheritance. But of course Richard could not be sure. He pressed the matter into open warfare against his father, fought among the towns and castles of northern France. The summer of 1189 was hot, and the English king was ailing. The tide of war turned against him. Who would wish to defend the old king of England against a young prince and the king of France?

Henry was forced to come to terms with the enemy. He made a promise that Richard would succeed him. When he gave the ritual kiss of peace to his son, according to Richard himself, he whispered in his ear, 'May the Lord spare me until I have taken vengeance on you.' But he was already dying. He was carried in a litter to Chinon, in the valley of the Loire, where he asked for a list of those men who had already pledged allegiance to his son. The first name was that of John. He turned his face to the wall, and would listen no more. His last words, apparently, were 'Shame, shame on a conquered king'. But last words are often invented by moralists. Henry II lies buried in the abbey church of Fontevrault.

Henry is remembered, if at all, because of his association with Thomas Becket. Yet he has a more significant claim to our attention in his imposition of a system of national justice and of common law. He may have engineered these changes for reasons of profit rather than policy, but the origin of the most worthy institutions can hardly bear examination. All is muddled and uncertain. The writing of history is often another way of defining chaos.

# 14

# The lost village

The deserted village of Wharram Percy lies on the side of a valley, by the edge of the Yorkshire Wolds. Its church, of St Martin, lies in ruins; earthworks mark the lines of habitation, rectangular mounds where the small houses once stood and sunken hollows in the grass where lanes and roads once ran. Remains of the manor house, and of a longhouse, survive together with the outlines of smaller houses of chalk. Most of the stonework has gone under the earth, however, covered by grass and weed. The life of the village has departed, but it has left traces of its existence that have survived for hundreds of years.

There are more than 3,000 deserted villages in England, mute testimony of a communal past. An old market cross stands alone among the trees of Stapleford Park in Leicestershire; the market, and the village, are long gone. A line of buttercups, springing from the moist soil beside a wall, will outline a forgotten boundary. The inhabitants of these villages left for a variety of reasons. Fire, famine and disease did their work through the centuries; successive stages of depopulation also crept over the countryside. Some villages were razed to make way for sheep pasture, and the villagers forcibly evicted by the lord of the land. Thus in the village of Thorpe, Norfolk, 100 people 'left their houses weeping and became unemployed and finally, as we suppose, died in poverty and so ended their days'. The Cistercian monks were known for their practice of eviction.

The excavation of Wharram Percy, over a period of fifty years, has discovered evidence of successive rebuilding of walls and parts of walls. The pattern of settlement seems to have been formalized in the tenth century, with the individual houses erected in rows along the two principal streets. A manor house was built at this time, with a second manor house following three centuries later. This second manor is known to have contained a hall-house, a dovecote and a barn. Throughout the entire period the surrounding land was being farmed for wheat and for barley; sheep and cattle were being raised; flax and hemp were grown.

Some of the original houses were long, approximately 15 by 50 feet (4.5 by 15 metres), with animals living at one end and people at the other. These longhouses were inhabited in the same period as simple two-room cottages that were of variable size according to the resources of the particular owner. The cottages were originally made of timber, but the wood was replaced with stone in the late thirteenth century. A continuous process of building and rebuilding took place, so that the village seems to breathe and move. The cottages had 'back gardens' that led down to a 'back-lane', which divided the village from the adjacent farmland. There were two millponds, and a triangular green. On the green were two stock pounds. One of these circular pounds, however, might have been used as an arena for cock-fighting or for bull-baiting.

Yet this utterly medieval landscape is deceptive. Since the site of the village is determined by the presence of six springs in the immediate neighbourhood, it is clear that the territory would have invited earlier English settlers. The archaeology of field-walking has found a Mesolithic site in the immediate vicinity of the village, as well as evidence of wood clearance in the Neolithic and Bronze ages. The presence of stone axes and flints suggests continuous human occupation of the area. In a hollow, just to the south of the church, successive levels of earth or 'hill-slip' were found that can be dated continuously from the Neolithic to the late medieval period. Beside the church of St Martin, on a natural terrace, were found the remains of a grand burial of the Iron Age. It must always have been a sacred place. Under the first manor house was found evidence of a Romano-British building. Under the village itself have been uncovered traces of three Romano-British farms with trackways running beside them. There are also the remains of two buildings from the sixth century in the Saxon style.

The continuity of human life at Wharram Percy can still be seen, therefore, persisting for many thousands of years from the time when the first scattered settlers made a camp in this place. Indeed it is likely that the shape of the village itself was determined by the layout of the prehistoric fields. Its life persisted until the need for pasture declined or disease intervened. The population of Wharram Percy began to fall in the fifteenth century, and the village was finally deserted at the very beginning of the sixteenth century.

Wharram Percy is not an isolated example. It just happens to be the only village in England that has been so exhaustively documented. This suggests, although it does not prove, that there are many other English villages with prehistoric origins. No one can dig to find them because the ground is still inhabited. The history of the oldest settlements in the country lies buried in the silent earth. It is possible to conclude, however, that the sites of Mesolithic and Neolithic settlements still flourish.

# 15

# The great charter

It was said of King Richard I that he cared only for the success he
carved out with his own sword, and that he was happy only when
that royal sword was covered with the blood of his enemies. He
had the ferocity, rather than the heart, of a lion. As a whelp, too,
he had his fair share of fighting; as we have seen, his adversaries
were often the members of his own family.

Although he was born in Oxford, in the autumn of 1157, his
ancestry was thoroughly French. As duke of Aquitaine he ruled
over a vast dominion that may be compared to England in terms
of wealth and prestige; it was in no sense an appendage of the
Angevin Empire but, rather, at the centre of it. Yet in France
he was only a duke; in England, he was king. That made all the
difference. He had no interest in, or care for, the country itself;
he just wanted to be known as sovereign by divine right. At his
coronation in the autumn of 1189, he was stripped down to his
breeches with his chest bare; the archbishop of Canterbury anointed
him with chrism or holy oil on the breast, head and hands. This
was the sign or token of sacral kingship. He then donned the
ceremonial robes, and was crowned. It was usual for the archbishop to take the crown and lay it on the king's head. Richard
pre-empted the gesture by handing the crown to the cleric. It
was a characteristic act of self-sufficiency. Certainly he looked the

part. He was tall, at an estimated height of 6 feet and 5 inches (1.9 metres); in the twelfth century, that made him a giant; he had strong limbs, a good figure and piercing blue eyes.

It would be anachronistic, at best, to condemn Richard's passion for warfare. Kings were supposed to fight, and a warlike ruler was considered to be a good ruler. If God looked kindly upon a monarch, he would bequeath him success in battle. It was one of the essential prerogatives, or duties, of sovereignty reflecting a period in which warfare was endemic. The two least militant kings of medieval England, Richard II and Henry VI, were widely considered to be failures; both of them were deposed and murdered. So military valour was crucially important.

One of the clues to understanding Richard's not necessarily complex character lies in the code of chivalry with its accompanying concern for 'courtly love'. Chivalry can on one level be understood as the practice whereby the laws of honour supersede those of right or justice. Thus in warfare knights would spare the lives and privileges of other knights, while happily massacring the women and children among the local population. Elaborate laws of warfare also governed the conduct of sieges. The cult of chivalry had as little connection with real warfare as scholastic theology had to do with daily worship in the parish church.

Richard liked to participate in tournaments. These were not the stage-managed jousts of the fifteenth century; these were real conflicts, staged over a large area of ground, between trained bands of knights. They closely resembled actual battle, with the provision that a dismounted knight had to retire from the field and give horse and armour to his opponent. Nevertheless fatalities and serious injuries were not uncommon. Tournaments were in fact so dangerous, and so disruptive, that Henry II forbade them in England. But they remained very popular in Aquitaine.

In that French region, too, the cult of courtly love flourished. It was an impulse celebrated by the troubadours of Provence and Aquitaine who in song and story celebrated the love of the female as the source of all virtue and pleasure. A knight fought for his lady; his love for her rendered him stronger and more courageous. Love was appreciative rather than covetous. Like the Platonic love of an earlier civilization – then generally between male and male –

it was a shadow or echo of heavenly harmony. A knight, in theory, was meant to be chaste and pious; the model of knighthood then became Sir Galahad. The two creeds of chivalry and courtly love are alike in being quite remote from the experience of life, but they did represent a pietistic attempt to place warfare and adultery in the context of a sacred world. All this directly impinged upon Richard I's sense of himself and of his kingship. It was believed at the time that he possessed Arthur's sword, Excalibur. And it ought to be remembered that Thomas Malory's *Le Morte Darthur* was translated from a French romance.

The crown was no sooner warm upon the young king's head than he began to prepare himself for a crusade against Saladin and for the recapture of Jerusalem. Crusades were very much part of the spirit of chivalry, for they had of course an ostensibly religious purpose. The crusading knight would be expected to prepare himself with vigils, fasts and prayers. The forces of Christ were meant to be pilgrims as much as soldiers. There grew up cults of military saints, such as St George and St Martin, and the roles of knight and monk were combined in the religious orders of Templars and the Hospitallers. For Richard, the third crusade could not have come at a more convenient time. The holy city had fallen two years before his coronation, and Richard had immediately 'taken the Cross'. His opportunity had now come to bear it into combat. He is in fact the only English king ever to become a crusader.

For this purpose he needed money. He was in England for three months after the coronation, and in that short period he tried to sell everything he possessed – lands, lordships, bishoprics, castles, towns and court offices. He said that he would sell London itself if he could find a purchaser for it. The country was for him only an engine for the making of money. He seized all of his father's treasure; he exacted loans; he increased the burden of taxes. The imposition he placed upon the kingdom in fact played a large part in the rebellion that led to the Magna Carta. The great lords were not rebelling against the rule of King John alone; they were fighting against the very idea of exacting Angevin kingship, made all the worse by the growth of a strong central administration.

The course of Richard I's crusade does not directly impinge upon the history of England, except the extent to which the finances of the country suffered for it. Richard proved himself to be an excellent soldier, and a competent administrator, in the difficult terrain of the Holy Land. He was able to take a fleet and an army to the eastern side of the Mediterranean, in the process capturing the valuable prize of the island of Cyprus; he had promised the leader of the island that he would not be put in irons. He kept his word, as any true knight would, and had silver shackles made for the restraint of the unfortunate man. More importantly he managed to stand his ground against Saladin, the most resourceful and capable military leader of the age. His angry will may be measured by the fact that he ordered 3,000 prisoners, whom he had captured at Acre, to be beheaded. He maintained the discipline, if not the affection, of his men. Usamah ibn Munqidh, a Syrian nobleman and soldier of the twelfth century, described the European crusaders as animals possessing the virtues of courage and fighting, but nothing else. That might be a description of the English king.

One of the chroniclers of this crusade remarks that Richard became known as 'the Lion' because he never pardoned an offence. He was quick to anger and he could be ferocious. If monarchs are judged on the criterion of military prowess alone, however, Richard I would qualify as one of the greatest kings of England. He did not manage to recapture Jerusalem, but the legend of Richard in the Holy Land endured for long after his death. It was said that, for hundreds of years, Turkish mothers would quieten recalcitrant children by threatening them with 'Malik Ric' or 'King Richard'.

When he was not in front of an army, however, he was not so fortunate. On his way back from the crusade, at the beginning of winter, he found the seaways blocked. So he decided to return by land, disguised as a pilgrim, through the territories of his enemies and rivals. It is clear that he was being watched, or that his presence was eagerly awaited. At the end of 1192 he was arrested by officers working for Duke Leopold of Austria.

The English king was a prize to be savoured. He was despatched to a castle on a rocky slope overlooking the Danube; he languished here while the important parties of Europe haggled over his fate. The duke of Austria sold him on to his overlord, Henry

VI, the king of Germany, while Philip of France proceeded to derive as much advantage from the situation as he could. He summoned Richard's brother, John, to the French court. The two men came to an agreement. John would swear fealty to the French king, and in exchange Philip would support John's usurpation of the throne. John came back to England and declared that his brother was dead. No one believed him.

John was thrown back on the defensive. The clerics whom Richard had left in authority, principally the bishop of Salisbury, raised an army and confined him to the area of two of his largest castles. The bishops were the true lords of government. Then there came news that the king of Germany was ready to release the English king for the sum of 70,000 marks. The amount was later raised to 150,000 marks. He was not dead; he had arisen to demand a large sum from his subjects. In order to pay for his ransom the authorities imposed a tax of 25 per cent on all income and moveable property; gold and plate were taken from the churches, and the annual income of the Cistercian wool crop was appropriated. The country was indeed being fleeced.

The king of France and John offered a larger sum to Henry VI, simply to keep Richard in custody, but after much negotiation the offer was finally rejected. That does not, however, minimize the perfidy of John in seeking to prolong his brother's imprisonment. In February 1194, after the ransom had been paid to the king of Germany, Richard was released. The king of France sent a message to John. 'Look to yourself. The devil is loose.' The devil landed at Sandwich, a month after his liberation. It is said that a local lord, holding a castle in favour of John, died in fright at the news. It is an indication of the period itself that a handful of people, most of whom were related, controlled the destinies of many countries. A family feud could cost thousands of lives.

Richard had not been unduly alarmed by his brother's rebellion. He is reported to have said, while still held in captivity, that 'John is not the man to conquer a country if there is a single person prepared to resist his attempt'. In this he was proved to be right. And, on his return, he showed himself to be remarkably magnanimous to his sibling. John had remained in Normandy, fearful of returning to England, and when the king himself sailed across the

Channel John paid obeisance to him in tears. 'You are a child,' Richard told him. 'You have had bad companions.' He knew well enough that John might himself one day assume the throne, and did not wish to alienate him entirely. He had in any case taken the precaution of proclaiming his nephew, Arthur of Brittany (son of his brother, Geoffrey, killed at the Parisian tournament), as his heir; but who knew better than he the vicissitudes of fortune? Richard himself had married while on his way to the Holy Land, but had no children. It has often been assumed, on no evidence at all, that like other martial heroes he was homosexual.

The king performed a solemn ritual of 'crown-wearing' in Winchester Cathedral after his return from imprisonment. It was a way of impressing his subjects with the undiminished majesty of his sovereignty. He did not stay in England for very long. Less than two months later he crossed the Channel in order to reclaim the territories of Normandy that had been conquered by the king of France and to reduce to obedience some rebellious lords of Aquitaine. His sojourn in prison, from which it was always possible that he would not escape alive, had encouraged revolt. He stayed in France for the next five years, burning towns and besieging castles, subduing the surrounding country with sword and flame. His demands upon his English subjects, for money and for men, were prodigious; the country, according to a contemporary writer, was reduced to poverty from sea to sea.

In the last summer of his life the king was visited by Hugh, bishop of Lincoln, who had come to the grand castle of Château-Gaillard in Normandy to seek an audience; he wished to plead for the return of the confiscated estates of his see. He found Richard in the chapel, attending Mass, seated on his royal throne with the bishops of Durham and Ely standing on each side. Hugh greeted the king, but Richard turned his face away. 'Lord king, kiss me,' Hugh said. Richard still looked away. Then the bishop took hold of the king's tunic. 'You owe me a kiss,' he said, 'because I have come a long way to see you.' 'You deserve no kiss from me,' the king replied. The bishop shook the king's cloak. 'I have every right to one. Kiss me.' Then Richard, with a smile, concurred. He said later that 'if the other bishops were like him, no king or ruler would dare raise his hand against them'.

Another sign of restlessness and upheaval became evident as a result of the king's exactions. The citizens of London believed that they were being unfairly and even perniciously taxed, and their complaints were taken up by William Fitz-Osbert or William the Beard. He grew his hair and beard long in token of his Saxon ancestry. He was styled the 'advocate of the people', and at St Paul's Cross argued that the rich should bear the burden of war finance. 52,000 Londoners were said to have supported him, but the authorities in the city hunted him down. He killed the officer sent to arrest him and fled to sanctuary in the church of St Mary-le-Bow, where after four days a providential fire forced him out. He was stabbed by the son of the officer whom he had killed but, while wounded, he was arrested and dragged at the tail of a horse to the gallows at Tyburn. His associates then proclaimed him to be a martyr and the chain that bound him to the gallows was the source of miraculous cures. The gallows itself was venerated, and so great was the press of people taking the bloody earth from the spot where he had died that a large pit was created.

Richard I never did come back to the land he ruled but did not love. He died from a gangrenous wound while fighting in Limousin, and on his deathbed he decreed that his heart should be interred in the cathedral at Rouen and that his body should be lowered into the tomb of his father within the abbey church of Fontevrault. So much for England.

And then there was one. John, the youngest of the sons of Henry II, had survived. He is one of the most interesting kings in English history, primarily because of his infamous reputation. He rivals Richard III in being considered the most 'evil' of the nation's kings. In truth John and Richard were no more vicious or cunning than many other more lauded sovereigns; they were perhaps unfortunate, however, in the chroniclers who chose to write about them. The two monastic chroniclers of John's reign, successively Roger of Wendover and Matthew Paris, were uniformly hostile. Shakespeare of course, more than any other, defined the image of John to posterity; his were wholly dramatic, but wildly exaggerated, versions of the events to be related here. Enter King John, breathing stage fire.

The early life of John has already been glimpsed, disloyal to his father and to his brothers. Yet he was still a Plantagenet, and the sacred blood of the family mattered. Henry II appointed him to be 'Lord of Ireland', but he proved himself to be unequal to the task; his youthful pride and folly alienated him from the native leaders of that country. He was given manors and castles all over the Angevin Empire, and he was in charge of the administration of six English counties that paid their taxes directly to his own exchequer. In Richard I's absence he created a court of his own, in England and in Normandy, which the more devious or ambitious magnates attended. He was the rising son.

Yet he was not the only claimant to the throne. Richard I had nominated Arthur of Brittany as his successor, as we have seen, and the twelve-year-old nephew was a real threat to John's inheritance. The barons of Anjou, one element of the Angevin Empire, already supported the boy. Aquitaine was in the balance. The English and Norman magnates, cautiously and suspiciously, supported John. Although he could not be considered English, he was at least more English than the Breton Arthur. On hearing of his brother's death John hurried to Normandy, therefore, where he was consecrated duke in the cathedral of Rouen; then he sailed to England where he was crowned king at Westminster in the spring of 1199. It had taken him just a month to assert his power.

He was some 12 inches (30 centimetres) shorter than Richard, and he may have suffered in implicit comparison with his brother and with his father. Certainly he grew up in a court filled with rivalries and suspicions of a more than usually bitter nature, with brother pitted against brother and brothers rising against their father. It is not surprising, therefore, that he gives the impression of being a wary and distrustful king. He went about armed and with a bodyguard.

He was not without humour, albeit often of a perverse kind. When he and his horse floundered in a marsh near Alnwick in Northumberland, he devised a suitable punishment for the men of that town who had not maintained the highway; he ordered that every newly created townsman should, on St Mark's Day, pass through that slough on foot. The custom was still being observed in the early nineteenth century. When the pope placed the country under excommunication, the king ordered that the mistresses of all the priests should be held in captivity until their clerical lovers ransomed them. It was an interesting punishment. There is another intriguing memorial of his reign. Among the legal rolls, then being composed in unprecedented numbers, is one stating that 'the wife of Hugh de Neville gives the lord king two hundred chickens that she may lie one night with her husband'. The import of this is unclear, but it may mean that the lady was one of the king's paramours and that she was asking to return briefly to her marital bed. The three incidents reveal that side of medieval life where jocosity and cruelty are allied.

King John was capable of violent anger, like his Plantagenet antecedents. When some monks at Faversham occupied their church, to prevent him from installing the superior he had chosen for them, he ordered the entire monastery to be burned down; nobody obeyed him, and he relented. Monarchs, male and female, have always had bad tempers; it is an aspect of their power.

An element of cruelty, or of ruthlessness, is evident in the first years of his reign. Arthur of Brittany had fled to the court of the king of France in order to shield himself from his uncle's far from avuncular intentions. In 1202, however, John found him. Both of them were on military campaign in France, fighting over the Angevin lands. The king of France had allotted them to Arthur, whereas John considered them to be his proper inheritance. Arthur, now fifteen, had been besieging his grandmother – Eleanor of Aquitaine – in the ancient castle of Mirebeau, near Poitiers in west-central France. The spectacle of grandson threatening grandmother throws further light on the behaviour of the Plantagenet family.

John, on receiving the news of the siege, marched with part of his army day and night; they covered 80 miles (130 kilometres) in forty-eight hours. Taken by surprise, Arthur and his forces were surrounded. The boy was delivered into the custody of John, and taken to a dungeon in Normandy; in an interview with his uncle, he was defiant. He demanded England, and all the lands bequeathed to him by Richard, apparently adding that he would not give him a moment's peace until the end of his life. This was, perhaps, unwise. He was moved to a dungeon in Rouen, the capital of the duchy, and was never seen again.

The more picturesque accounts suggest that John, in a fit of Plantagenet fury, ran a sword through his nephew's body and then dumped him into the river Seine. Or perhaps he hired an assassin. No one is quite clear. The evident fact, however, is that Arthur was dead within a few months. By the spring of 1203 it was widely believed that the king was instrumental in the murder of his nephew. This event has often been interpreted in the same light as the murder in the Tower of the two princes by their uncle, Richard III; but there is really no comparison. Pope Innocent III, for example, is reported as saying that Arthur was 'captured at Mirebeau, a traitor to his lord and uncle to whom he had sworn homage and allegiance, and he could rightly be condemned without judgment to die even the most shameful of deaths'. A fifteen-year-old was considered to be an adult.

Although the death may have been a necessary and inevitable response by John, it helped to alienate his natural supporters in Normandy and elsewhere. Even more serious charges were levelled against him. He was severely criticized for his indolence or inactivity in the pursuit of war against the king of France. He was not acting like a king. One chronicler declared that he was sluggish, where his elder brother had proved himself to be vigorous and powerful. He became known as 'John Softsword'. It was said that he had been enchanted by the sorcery of his wife, Isabella of Angoulême. It is more likely that he was infatuated by the power and majesty of kingship and refused to believe the worst. But the worst was happening. King Philip advanced further and further into Normandy, and the majority of John's barons in that duchy defected to him. They no longer trusted the English king enough to remain loyal to him. There was soon very little left in France for John to defend. As the Angevin Empire collapsed around him, John sailed back to England. By June 1204 Philip had taken Normandy; all that remained of the duchy, in the possession of John, were the Channel Islands. Of the empire itself, only Gascony was preserved. It was the largest single blow to John during the whole of his reign.

The severance of England from Normandy, after 150 years of union, was at a later date deemed to be a natural and inevitable development by which France steadily became aware of its national identity. It heralded the rise of a national consciousness exploited by the Capetian kings. At the time, however, it was considered to be nothing less than a calamity for the king of England. He lost much of his income, from the taxation of Normandy and Anjou and Maine, and of course he forfeited a great deal of his prestige. Yet other consequences followed. The Anglo-Norman lords lost half of their identity. Once they had lost their lands in Normandy, it became clear that they would have to concentrate on those closer to what was now 'home'. They steadily became more English. The Channel had become the border, as it had been in the tenth century, and King John began the construction of a proper navy to defend the English shores. The king no longer possessed Normandy, and as a result he paid more considered attention to England.

He kept the administrators from the last reign, knowing very well that the machinery of government depended upon them. It is from the beginning of the thirteenth century, for example, that we can trace the widespread use of written records as an instrument of state. Licences for imports and exports had to be drawn up; the regulations of trade had to be furnished in writing; a system of taxation had to be standardized; currency and credit had to be maintained in strict order. All this relied upon ink rather than upon custom or oral tradition. The various departments of the king's court began the habit of creating archives. Letters began to be sent over the country, where before written communication had been confined to writs. Diaries of daily expenditure were kept and preserved. New and faster forms of handwriting developed, as monastic calligraphy gave way to what is known as 'cursive' script; the word comes from *cursivus*, the Latin for 'flowing'. The world was going faster.

Wars, and preparations for wars, took their toll upon the nation's wealth in the same period. King John still entertained hopes of winning back his Angevin Empire, but for that he needed money. He was perhaps no more exacting than his brother and his father, but he was more ingenious. He discovered new ways of extracting revenue, and in 1207 levied a thirteenth part on incomes and moveable property to be paid by all classes of people; it was the first move towards general taxation. The clamour of complaint, however, was so loud that he never repeated the exercise.

For ten years he travelled throughout his kingdom in search of money; he was restless; he was always in a hurry, generally staying in any one place for no more than two or three days. In 1205 he spent only twenty-four days in London and in Westminster. For the rest of the time he was on the road. He penetrated the far north at the end of a bitter winter; he fined York and Newcastle for not affording him an appropriately grand reception. He was looking for money everywhere. He was told, during a visit to Hexham in Northumberland, that Roman treasure was buried at Corbridge nearby; he ordered his men to dig for it, but nothing was unearthed.

During the course of his rapid journeys, sometimes covering 30 miles (48 kilometres) a day, he evinced a particular interest in imposing justice upon his subjects. This again was largely because of his desire for revenue, but as a boy his tutor had been Ranulph de Glanville whose legal treatise has already been mentioned. There may be some connection. John declared once that 'our peace should be inviolably preserved, even if it were only granted to a dog'.

So John paid much attention to the details of administration and of justice, with a diligence quite different from the insouciance of his elder brother. If he was suspicious, he was also vigilant and curious. Most of the people had never seen their king before. Yet here he was, in the robes of state, questioning and charging and judging. His own voice was the voice of law. He loved fine gems and he glittered with jewellery. He bathed regularly and often, a practice almost without precedent in the thirteenth century. The body of the king – the flesh and blood – was sacred. Here is the essence of medieval governance.

This was also a time of rising prices; a rapidly increasing population meant that the common resources of life became scarcer and more expensive. Financial, as well as demographic, explanations can be found. The importation of silver from the mines of eastern Germany increased the amount of money in circulation; as a result, prices rose between 100 and 200 per cent in the last two decades of the twelfth century. This is the proper context in which to see baronial rebellion and the sealing of the Magna Carta. The consequent 'inflation', to use a contemporary term, affected the king as much as the lords and the commons. War, in particular, had become much more expensive. The problem was then compounded by recession as the king took more and more money out of circulation in order to pay for his military ambitions. So the king was constrained at every hand; it might seem that the forces of nature were against him.

After the collapse of the Angevin Empire in 1204 King John began to assert himself on the island of Britain. He waged campaigns in Wales, Scotland and Ireland. In Ireland he managed to impose royal government upon the feuding Anglo-Norman barons who had divided the rule of southern and eastern Ireland among themselves; John also gained the fealty of the native Gaelic kings who recognized his power. In 1209 he launched an expedition against Scotland, and forced its king to recognize him as overlord. He subdued, temporarily, the Welsh principalities; he cowed them by violence, in other words, and before the start of hostilities he hanged at Nottingham some twenty-eight Welsh boys, the sons of chieftains who had been surrendered as hostages. It was not the least, or the last, of his acts of cruelty. But the cruelty of kings worked. At the end of these campaigns a contemporary chronicler stated that 'there is now no one in Ireland, Scotland and Wales who does not obey the command of the King of England; that, as is well known, is more than any of his ancestors had achieved'.

Yet he struggled to control his magnates. They were not eager to fight for the restoration of the Angevin Empire, and they resented the manifold exactions he imposed upon them. He demanded huge fees for the granting of inheritances, or for the selling of wealthy heiresses in marriage. On occasions he raised his own claims to estates that had long been the property of wealthy families. A tax called 'scutage' was paid to avoid military service; John levied it eleven times in sixteen years. Payments in kind were also exacted. One magnate, William de Braose, paid the sum of 300 cows, 30 bulls and 10 horses for the approval of a plea. A further twist can be added to what seems to have been the king's unremitting hatred of the Braose family. William's failure to pay further debts led to his being driven into exile. But another fate remained for his wife and son. Matilda de Braose was one of the few people who knew what had happened to Prince Arthur nine years before, and it seems that she was talking too much; John ordered her to be arrested with her son. Mother and son were starved to death in prison.

It was said that the king was as rapacious of wives and daughters as he was of money. They were not safe in their castles when John paid a visit. Yet, on a larger scale, the whole force of Angevin monarchy was opposed to the feudal privileges of the mighty lords. The growth of a bureaucracy, and of a central administration, curtailed their own powers to make money out of the resident population. Business was being diverted from the local honorial courts, for example, to the royal courts. They were losing money as a result. Historians look back in admiration at the increasing growth and complexity of 'royal government'; all it meant at the time was royal exploitation. The emergence of an army of mercenaries also restricted the role of the magnates as the martial leaders of the country. Many of them still had an image of their role derived from chivalric romance. They were the knights of the Round Table gathered beside their king who acted as *primus inter pares*. King John was not King Arthur, however, and the only Holy Grail for which he cared was gold.

To sacred affairs, in general, he was indifferent. When the archbishopric of Canterbury became vacant in 1205, the king refused to fill it. He wanted the money from the wealthy see to be diverted to his own treasury. This was a device he had used in the past with other bishoprics. Pope Innocent III prevaricated, understanding royal sensibilities, but his patience was not inexhaustible. In 1207 he appointed Stephen Langton to the vacant archbishopric. Langton could not have been a better choice; he was an Englishman, out of Lincolnshire, but had been a superb professor of theology at the University of Paris. He was also cardinal priest of the basilica church of St Chrysogonus in Rome, and a canon of York Minster.

John characteristically fell into a carefully staged fury. What had the pope to do with the affairs of his kingdom? He would, like his predecessors, appoint the bishops and archbishops whom he believed to be loyal. He refused to allow the pope any right to appoint an archbishop of Canterbury without royal assent. He banished from England the monks of Canterbury who had acceded to the pope's request. He seized all the English offices held by Italian bishops. He refused to allow any papal legates to enter the country. In the spring of 1208 the pope placed the country under an interdict, forbidding any church services to be held; no sacraments, except those of baptism for the newborn and absolution for the dying, were to be performed. Matthew Paris, in his account of the interdict, illustrated the scene with a drawing of bell-ropes tied up. Sacred time was suspended.

The king retaliated by confiscating all churches and church lands, on the principle that a non-functioning Church does not need property. John was then formally excommunicated, in 1209, which in theory meant that his clerical administrators could no longer serve or obey him. Some clerics fled the king's court and travelled overseas, but there were more than enough ecclesiastical lawyers and administrators to make sure that the machinery of Church and government remained stable; it has been estimated that the majority of the bishops stayed in England during the interdict. The country itself remained relatively unmoved by papal displeasure. It had never paid much attention to the decrees of the see of Peter. The deep continuity of the country, and the secular customs of the nation, remained unbroken. Long negotiations, between the English court and the see of Peter, of course ensued. The king eventually seemed willing to accept Stephen Langton into his kingdom, on the clear and stated agreement that this was not to be seen as a precedent. No future pope would be allowed to appoint the archbishop of Canterbury without royal approval. The pope held out for better terms. This was war.

It is said that the cares of kings come in flocks, and that the sight of dark skies brings further storms. The first signs of internal rebellion emerged in 1209, when some of the northern barons were in communication with the king of France over the possibility of an invasion. It is no coincidence that in this year John went on military expedition to the north in order to cow King William of Scotland. He also took care to assert his authority over his own northern lands. The conspiracy faded away. Three years later the king felt obliged to refortify his castles, particularly in the border regions, where the magnates had always been more independent. Rumour spread that the barons were planning to depose the king. In turn John demanded hostages from the more recalcitrant of them. In 1213 he razed the castles of one who was believed to be planning to lead the revolt, Robert Fitzwalter, until a fragile peace was restored between them.

The king was surrounded by too many enemies, and it became necessary to placate the most important of them. It was widely rumoured, in the early months of 1213, that Pope Innocent III had sent an open letter deposing John and urging King Philip of France to invade England. Yet in spring John surrendered. On 15 May he agreed to accept all of the pope's claims and demands. He went further. He agreed to yield his country to the pope and receive it back as a fief; he was, in effect, about to become the pope's feudal vassal. Several sound reasons could be advanced for what seems on the face of it abject surrender. King Philip, even as he was organizing a force to sail across the Channel, was forced to cancel his invasion. He could not attack the pope's new realm. The king's status as the pope's vassal might also deter his rebellious barons. Pope Innocent III himself, as subsequent events would testify, became a formidable ally and defender of royal power against insurgent subjects. King John was also a newly blessed representative of God. As the papal legate in England put it, 'the lord king is another man by God's grace'.

So the lord king decided to press home his advantage and make one more attempt to recover his Angevin Empire from the French king. In the following year he created a coalition of princes – among them the Holy Roman Emperor, Otto IV, and the count of Flanders – who were intent upon acquiring French land. The count and the emperor would proceed against the French army from the north-east, while King John would advance from Poitou in the west. The strategy was excellent, but its execution was misjudged. Many confused skirmishes and sieges took place, and on 27 July 1214 the forces of John and Otto were decisively defeated by King Philip outside the village of Bouvines. It was the final battle for the Angevin Empire. John had lost everything for which he most cared.

The failure at the battle of Bouvines was in effect the harbinger of baronial rebellion. The magnates may not have been greatly exercised by the loss of empire, but they were enraged at the amount of money wasted on a failed cause. It was the crowning point of their belief in the king's misjudgment and military ineptitude. In the aftermath of the defeat there emerged what has since become known as a 'baronial party', brought together by the manifold causes and complaints that have already been outlined. The imposition of fines and taxes, the predominant advice of 'evil counsellors', the decay in their social and military pre-eminence, were all part of baronial rebellion against authoritarian and ruthless Angevin rule.

The principal centres of revolt were the north, the west and East Anglia; but the barons did not necessarily form distinct or coherent groups. Family was divided against family; district was opposed to district. A group of 39 barons, out of a total baronage of 197, were in open revolt against the Crown; approximately the same number were its faithful supporters. The remainder were uncertain, and probably fearful of the future.

The rebels did find an unexpected champion in the new archbishop, however; on his return to England Stephen Langton restated the old principles enshrined in the document known as *Leges Henrici Primi* that nothing can be taken or demanded by the king except 'by right and reason, by law of the land and justice and by a court's judgment'. That, clearly, had not been King John's manner of proceeding.

The king and the rebellious barons met on various occasions, making little if any progress. The pope was persuaded to write to the rebels, forbidding the use of force or violence against their anointed king. He also wrote to Stephen Langton, accusing the archbishop of taking the side of the barons. The king then engineered what he must have considered a master stroke. On 4 March 1215, he assumed the cross of the crusader. Who could ride against a knight of Christ?

The manoeuvre did not succeed. On 5 May the barons renounced their fealty to the king and, under the leadership of Robert Fitzwalter, opened hostilities. They besieged Northampton Castle, a royal stronghold, and on 17 May occupied London.

This was in itself a notable achievement, and tilted the balance of military power clearly in favour of the barons. More of them declared against the king.

John decided to procrastinate in the well-known form of conducting negotiations. He asked Stephen Langton to arrange a truce, so that some form of settlement might be reached. It is clear enough, however, that he never had any intention of honouring any such agreement. He believed himself to be upholding the rights of a sovereign king against rebellious subjects. In this belief, he was joined by the pope. The barons, however, accepted his invitation. Let the day be the fifteenth of June, they replied. Let the place be Runnemead. Runnemede, or Runnymede, is a meadow on the Surrey side of the river Thames near Windsor; there is a small island or eyot in the middle of the river, where the bargain was supposed to be sealed. A yew tree that was growing there in 1215 still stands.

Some informal notes survive that appear to have been taken down at the time of preliminary negotiations; they may reflect the words the king actually used. Early on it is declared that 'King John concedes that he will not take a man without judgment nor accept anything for justice, nor do injustice'. The barons wished to readjust the balance of power in their favour. They wanted to be secure in their lands and castles, unmolested by the king or the king's men. They also wished to be freed from the financial exactions imposed by John.

Various meetings were held between the opposing parties, with Stephen Langton acting as mediator. A preliminary document was then drawn up, by a chancery clerk, known as the 'Articles of the Barons'. The Magna Carta, or Great Charter, emerged from the baronial articles. It was called great because of its length, not because of its importance. Yet it was the work of highly intelligent and experienced administrators who in an almost literal sense stood at the king's side to urge compromise and restraint. They were also instrumental in persuading the barons to come to terms wider than their own private interests. By 19 June the agreement had been reached. The barons gave their king the kiss of peace, and then he granted the charter.

Over the next five days several copies were made and sent over the kingdom; four of them can still be seen. One of those, preserved in the Cottonian Library of the British Library, contains some eighty-six lines (with additions) written on a skin of parchment, measuring 14½ inches (36.8 centimetres) in breadth by 20½ inches (52 centimetres) in length. It is much shrivelled and mutilated, and has survived at least one fire that reduced the seal to pulp. It is said to have been purchased by Sir Robert Cotton at the beginning of the seventeenth century, for the sum of fourpence, from a tailor who was about to cut it up for his own purposes. Once the copies had been completed by the clerks, they were proclaimed by the sheriffs in their various county courts.

But this was not a new code of law. It was not even a summary of the great principles of legislation. It was essentially an attempt by the barons to return to the state of affairs before the dominance of the Angevin kings. It did not represent some spirit of 'progress' or 'development' in human affairs. None of the participants would have known what those words meant. It was in part a reactionary document. Villeins and slaves, the most numerous portion of the kingdom, were never mentioned. The unfree were of no consequence. Their 'progress' over the centuries was slow and uncertain. This was a charter for the *liber homo* or free man.

Many specific measures were adopted within its sixty-three clauses. The old liberties of the Church were to be respected. Taxes, known as scutages or aids, should not be levied on the nation without the approval of the common council; some have seen this as the emergence of the principle of 'no taxation without representation', but the common council consisted only of archbishops, bishops, earls, barons and tenants-in-chief. They were not 'the people' of a self-governing kingdom.

The charter also stipulated that no man should be made a judge or sheriff without adequate knowledge of the law. The courts of law should be convened in one place, rather than follow the king. The towns and cities of the kingdom were to be granted their ancient liberties. Free men were to be allowed to travel freely. Forest law was to be alleviated, and all the forests created in the king's reign were to be opened. The thirty-ninth clause states that 'no free man shall be taken or imprisoned, except by the lawful judgement of his peers or the law of the land'. The fortieth clause declares that 'To no one will we sell, to no one will we deny or delay right or justice.' Three declarations of the Magna Carta still remain on the statute book of England.

Edward Coke, Lord Chief Justice at the beginning of the seventeenth century, wrote that 'as the gold refiner will not out of the dust or shreds of gold, let pass the least crumb, in respect to the excellence of the metal; so ought not the reader to pass any syllable of this law, in respect of the excellency of the matter'. Since Coke forced the Petition of Right upon a reluctant Charles I, later enshrined in the Bill of Rights of 1689, and since his writings were instrumental in the drawing-up of the American Constitution, we may take seriously his alleged claim that 'Magna Carta is such a fellow that he will have no sovereign'.

Yet he was writing 400 years after the event. The thirty-ninth and fortieth clauses of the charter may have been the most pertinent and significant, but at the time they were simply part of a miscellaneous and haphazard collection of principles taken from canon law and common law and custom equally. It is not at all clear that the negotiators knew precisely what they were doing. They were more concerned with correcting manifest wrongs than proclaiming evident rights. They made a heap of all they found. Not for the first time have great events and doctrines emerged from ambiguous and adventitious circumstances. The charter had no central doctrine. It was piecemeal. Therefore it was adaptable. Its meaning or meanings could be reinterpreted. Its underlying consequences were understood only gradually and slowly. It was reissued three times, with various amendments, and only the final version of 1225 became law. It was ratified thirty-eight times by various kings, the last of them being Henry VI.

Yet even before the moment he sealed it, King John had determined to ignore it. The sixty-three clauses meant nothing to him. He had hoped that by apparently coming to agreement with the barons, he would be able to divide his opponents and purchase a breathing space in which he could reassert his sovereignty. No sooner had he affixed his seal to the document than he sent an emissary to the pope, claiming that every concession won from him was an insult to the pontiff himself whose unworthy vassal he was. He ordered that all of his castles should be provisioned and fortified. He sent commanders to Flanders, Poitou and elsewhere to hire mercenary soldiers. War against his barons could be renewed. On 24 August 1215, Pope Innocent III sent letters annulling the provisions of the Magna Carta as an insult to his authority over England. 'With the advice of our brethren,' he wrote, 'we altogether reprove and condemn this charter, prohibiting the king under pain of anathema from observing it, the barons from exacting its obligations.'

It came too late. The king and the barons were already at war. The Cornish lands of Robert Fitzwalter, the leading rebel, were seized. At this juncture the military advantage lay decidedly with the king; he possessed by far the largest number of fortified castles and he had at his command a professional mercenary army. A party of rebels took refuge in the castle at Rochester; John besieged it, and helped to undermine it by strapping burning torches to a number of pigs. The animals were herded into wooden galleries built beneath the stronghold and set it ablaze. This was one of the less formal techniques of medieval warfare.

Many of the rebel barons took refuge in London. It might have been possible for the king to lay siege to the capital, but London was not Rochester. The undertaking was filled with risk. Instead John decided to destroy the castles of the rebels one by one. He marched to the north, from where many of the barons came, and laid waste the land from Nottingham to Berwick; he left a trail of blood and ruins wherever he ventured. Only one rebel castle, that of Helmsley in Yorkshire, was left standing.

From their stronghold of London the barons called upon the aid of King Philip of France. They resolved to offer the crown to his son, Louis, whose wife was connected in blood to the Plantagenets. In the spring of 1216 Louis landed at Dover and marched unopposed to Rochester. His success was followed by his capture of Guildford, of Farnham, and, most importantly, of Winchester. It must have seemed that God, or good fortune, was on his side. The great earls of the kingdom, many of them hitherto supporters of the king, submitted to him. John retreated to the west, and spent the summer months of 1216 in various sorties throughout Dorset and Devon. In the early days of September he broke out and led his army to the east; he went into Norfolk and Lincolnshire, without achieving any great success. From this last expedition comes the now accepted legend that he lost his treasure in the Wash, when the tide rose too rapidly. It was reported that the crown itself was engulfed by the swirling waters. It was a very convenient story for those of his immediate entourage, who would have been happy to enrich themselves on the principle of *sauve qui peut*. The truth is also lost in the shifting tide.

He must in any case have known that he was reaching the end of his days. Kings die when they feel that their power is fading. He became ill of a fever, and of dysentery; he died in the fortress of the bishop of Lincoln at the age of forty-nine. 'Hell', wrote one chronicler, 'felt herself defiled by his admission.' John had another destination in mind. He was interred in the cathedral at Worcester and at his own request his tomb lay in the shadow of the shrine of the eleventh-century English saint, Bishop Wulfstan. In 1797 the king's sepulchre was opened by curious antiquaries. It was reported that 'the remains of the Illustrious Personage appear entire'. His height was 5 feet and 5 inches (1.65 metres). On one side of him lay his sword, in knightly fashion, with 'the bones of his left arm lying on his breast, his teeth quite perfect'. He was the first king, since the time of the Normans, both to be born and to die in England.

What can be said of a king whose memory has been universally execrated by the chroniclers of his own time and of subsequent centuries? In his rapacity and greed he did not materially differ from his predecessors. He was characterized by the harshness and inflexibility of all previous Norman and Angevin rulers. Yet it was his misfortune to aspire to royal domination in singularly unhappy circumstances – his loss of the Angevin Empire at the hands of a wealthier and mightier king, the havoc of steeply rising prices, and the alienation of his barons, all darkened the picture of his reign. It needed only a few vignettes of his rapacity or cruelty to complete the chroniclers' description of an utterly unfit king.

Yet out of his rule emerged a new or at least an intensified sense of the nation. That is the meaning of the Magna Carta. The English people of the early thirteenth century were already familiar with the notion of *ius commune* or common law; they were accustomed to the role of guilds and fraternities. John himself, in pursuit of the throne, had in 1191 accepted the right of London to form its own commune as a self-governing and self-elected body of the richer citizens. From this time forward communal archives and records were placed in the guildhall. The momentum of the age was behind this new form of identity. Many other towns asserted their own *communitas* during the reign of John, with the election of mayors and the creation of municipal seals. The members of the commune swore an oath to preserve the town and its liberties.

So it was perhaps inevitable that the barons, in rebellion against the king, would assert the values of the *communa* of England and would introduce the concept of the *communa totius terra* with its attendant liberties. It became known, in the thirteenth century, as 'the community of the realm'. There even grew, at the end of that century, a recognition of 'the community of the vill' or village. These were all stages in the growing self-consciousness of England. This is the meaning of the 'field full of folk' that William Langland invokes at the beginning of *Piers Plowman*. He saw, in vision, a community.

# 16

# Crime and punishment

A 'scotale' or drinking party took place at Ashley, near Cirencester, on 7 September 1208; it was in honour of the birthday of Our Lady, and the local officer of the forest sold drinks at his alehouse to celebrate the occasion. It was essentially a form of local tax, because the inhabitants felt obliged to attend in fear of incurring his displeasure. John Scot was riding back from the alehouse when he invited Richard of Crudwell to sit behind him on his horse. Richard thought that he was offering him a lift, but John took up a knife and stabbed him in the shoulder; the wound was 4½ inches (10.12 centimetres) deep. Richard fell from the horse, and John dismounted. He stabbed Richard once more, and proceeded to rob his purse of forty-three shillings. Somehow Richard crawled home, on all fours, and on the next day informed the king's sergeant. This seems to have provoked John Scot who, five nights later, broke into the house of Richard's mother and beat her so badly that it was believed she would not live.

At a convent, near Watton in the East Riding of Yorkshire, in the 1160s, one nun had lost her virginity to a young priest; when her condition became obvious, the nuns interrogated her about the offending man. When she revealed his identity, the nuns captured him. They took him to the cell of the pregnant nun. She was given a knife and forced to castrate her lover; whereupon the nuns stuffed his genitals into her mouth. She was then flogged, and bound with chains in a prison cell. In an age when the call of heaven was direct and unequivocal – and when the spiritual world was pre-eminent – a general indifference was maintained to the fate or the sufferings of the physical body. When one English king was asked if he regretted the thousands of soldiers he sent into slaughter, he remarked that they would thank him when they were in heaven. The chronicler, after telling the story of the savage nuns, exclaimed, 'What zeal was burning in these champions of chastity, these per-secutors of uncleanness, who loved Christ above all things!'

These stories of physical cruelty would have been familiar to all the people of England in a period when violence was tolerated to a surprising degree. Village justice could be savage and peremptory, largely going unreported. The violence of lord against villein does not often appear in the historical record. In this society men and women took weapons with them; even small children possessed knives. William Palfrey, aged eleven, stabbed and killed the nine-year-old William Geyser outside the village of Whittlesford in Cambridgeshire. There was in any case what would now be called a culture of violence. Children were educated with severe physi-cal discipline. Corporal punishment was familiar and usual in all elements of society. Public whipping, for a variety of offences from adultery to slander, was commonplace.

A genuine pleasure was also derived from bitter disputation, denunciation and vilification. This was a culture of rhetoric and the spoken word. A wide vocabulary of scatological abuse could be employed, while sexual misdemeanours were commonly and loudly publicized. In a society of intense hierarchy, a preoccupation with good name and standing is only to be expected. Disputes were sometimes settled by ritualized fights in the churchyard. Slights and insults were the occasion of bloody disputes. The smallest incident could provoke a violent fracas. One man came into a hostelry, where strangers were drinking. 'Who are these people?' he enquired, for which question he was stabbed to death. An element of gratuitous cruelty could also be introduced, as in the case of one man who was dragged to a local tavern and there obliged to drink a cocktail of beer and his own blood.

So the incidence of criminality was great. The justices who

travelled to Lincoln in 1202 were confronted with 114 cases of murder and 49 of rape; this is not to mention the scores of incidents of theft and assault. When the body of a murdered man was found the men of the neighbourhood were summoned, while the corpse was raised upon a wooden hurdle and exhibited for seven days with logs burning around it to provide recognition at night. All males over the age of twelve, from the four nearest villages, were summoned to an inquest.

There was a popular phrase for a felon – 'to become a wolf's head that anyone may cut down'. He could be killed on sight by anyone who encountered him. Real wolves did in fact still inhabit thirteenth-century England. They were not exterminated until 1290. In that year Richard de Loveraz was noted as holding land by the service of hunting the wolf in Hampshire 'if one can be found'. The wolf was deemed to be vermin, fit for nothing except death. So his fate was transferred to the unfortunate offender.

If the life of the nation was harsh, so was the system of punishment and death. The stocks, and the gibbet, were the common properties of English life. 'Let him see a priest' were the last words of the judge in a hanging matter. If you were convicted in Wakefield, you would be hanged; if you were found guilty in Halifax, your head would be cut off. Thieves, apprehended in Dover, were thrown over the cliffs. At Sandwich they were buried alive, in a place known as Thiefdown at Sandown. At Winchelsea they were hanged in the salt marsh there. At Halifax the axe would be drawn up on a pulley, and then fastened with a pin to the side of the scaffold. If the prisoner had been caught in false possession of a horse or an ox, the animal was led to the scaffold with him; the beast was then tied to a cord that held the pin and, at the moment of judgment, the beast was whipped and the pin came out. The proceedings were accompanied by the plaint of a bagpipe. It was a very ancient practice, perhaps pre-dating even the time of the Saxons. The ancient privilege of the private gallows was also in demand; by the old law of *infangtheof*, a lord had the right to string up a thief caught on his property. In the early thirteenth century sixty-five private gallows were set up in Devon alone.

But thieves were not always put to death. A young offender was often blinded and castrated instead. When in 1221 Thomas of

Eldersfield, of Worcester, was accused of malicious wounding he was sentenced to the same punishment; the judges decreed that the relatives of the victim could perform the blinding and castration. They threw the eyeballs to the ground, and used the testicles as little footballs. The apparent severity of the penalties was necessary in a violent society where relatively few offenders were caught. In the absence of a police force or a standing army, condign punishment was one of the few ways of upholding social obligations. That is why the local people were generally compelled to witness the performance of the sentence. The objective was to maintain order.

The trial by water and the trial by ordeal were also considered to be acceptable punishments in criminal cases. Trial by ordeal was conducted under the auspices of the Church. The accused spent three days in fasting and in prayer. On the third day, in a secluded part of the church, a cauldron of water was brought to boiling point by fire; a stone or piece of iron was then placed in the water. The accuser and the accused, each one accompanied by twelve friends, were arranged in two lines opposite one other, with the cauldron in the middle. The participants were sprinkled with holy water by the priest. Some litanies were recited, and the water was once more checked to see that it was at boiling point; the accused then plunged his hand and arm into the water, and took out the weight. The scalded flesh was then wrapped in a linen cloth; if the flesh had healed after the third day the accused was pronounced to be innocent. If the flesh was burned or ulcerous, the prisoner suffered the penalty for his offence.

Another form of divination by water was practised. A man or woman was bound and then lowered into a pit of cold water; the pit was 20 feet (6 metres) wide, and 12 feet (3.6 metres) deep. The priest blessed the water and then called upon God 'to judge what is just and your right judgment'. If the man began to sink, he was deemed to be innocent; if he was guilty, he floated. The blessed water had rejected him.

The trial by fire was slightly more ingenious. The ceremony once more took place in a church. At the beginning of Mass a fire was made, and a bar of iron placed upon it. At the end of the Mass, the red-hot metal was taken to a small stone pillar. The accused then had to pick up the glowing metal and walk with it for three steps before throwing it down. The treatment was then the same as that of the trial by boiling water.

A strange mode of punishment, known as the ordeal of the morsel, was reserved for priests. A piece of cheese, 1 ounce (28 grams) in weight, was placed on a consecrated host; it was then given to the accused cleric on the solemn understanding that it would stick in his throat if he were guilty. The angel Gabriel was supposed to come down and stop the man's throat. It is not clear how this worked in practice.

The concept of sanctuary was clearer. A felon who fled to one of a number of specified churches might remain inviolate for forty days; no person might hinder anyone bringing food and drink to him. The church was watched closely during this period, in case the man tried secretly to escape. After forty days the thief or murderer could formally be expelled by the archdeacon, but he could be permitted to stay. He could choose to abjure the realm, however, in which case he was taken to the church porch and assigned a port from which to sail. He was obliged to walk along the king's highway, deviating neither to the left nor the right, carrying a cross in his hand. When he reached the port he would seek passage within the time of one tide and one ebb; if that were not possible he was to walk every day into the sea, up to his knees, until he found a ship.

Violent crime was of course closely associated with the incidence of drunkenness. The English were well known throughout Europe for their addiction to ale and wine and cider. The French were proud, the Germans were obscene, and the English were drunkards. In English monasteries the daily allowance was a gallon (4.5 litres) of strong ale and a gallon (4.5 litres) of weak ale. Every village had its alehouse. Twelfth-century London was castigated by the chronicler William Fitzstephen for 'the immoderate drinking of fools'. There was private, as well as public, drinking. The most flourishing trade among the women of an English village was that of brewing. It is one of the essential continuities of national life. 'The whole land', Roger of Hoveden wrote, 'is filled with drink and drinkers.'

The court rolls contain many stories of people who fell out of windows, slipped into cauldrons, tumbled from horses, or plunged into rivers, as a consequence of drink. In 1250 Benedict Lithere had been drinking in a tavern in Henstead in Suffolk, and by the end of the session 'he could neither walk nor ride, nor barely even stand up'. His brother, Roger, put him on his horse; he fell off. Roger hauled him up a second time, and again Benedict fell off. Then Roger decided on a more drastic measure. He put him back on the horse, and tied him onto the animal. Benedict slipped and fell off once more, killing himself in the process.

John de Markeby, goldsmith, 'was drunk and leaping about' in the house of a friend when he wounded himself fatally with his own knife. Alice Quernbetere, extremely drunk, called two work-men by the insulting name of 'tredekeiles'; she was then murdered by them. Richard le Brewer, carrying a bag of malt home while drunk, stumbled and ruptured himself. William Bonefaunte, skin-ner, stood 'drunk, naked and alone at the top of a stair . . . for the purpose of relieving nature, when by accident he fell head-down to the ground and died'.

The records of madness evince some of the general qualities of the medieval mind. Robert de Bramwyk took his sister, deformed and hunchbacked from the time of her birth, and plunged her into a cauldron of hot water; then he took her out and began stamping on her limbs in order to straighten them. When Agnes Fuller refused to have sex with Geoffrey Riche, he cut off her head with a sword; he informed his neighbours that he was a pig, and hid beneath a trough. Eventually he went home, found a needle and thread, and tried to sew Agnes's severed head back to the body.

# 17

# A simple king

With the death of King John, the civil war was suspended. Prince Louis was still in England, pursuing his claim to the throne, but his progress met an impediment. John's nine-year-old son, Henry, was in the south-west. The young boy's supporters quickly declared him to be king, and he was crowned as Henry III at Gloucester Abbey in the autumn of 1216; Westminster Abbey was not available, because Louis was in control of London. Another unfortunate circumstance was reported. Since the royal crown had been 'lost' in the Wash, the young king wore a circlet of gold borrowed from his mother. Henry swore an oath of allegiance to the papacy, and the pope duly extended his blessing. Prince Louis and the rebel barons were no longer opposed to a ruthless and violent king; they were the enemies of a young boy in the protection of the see of Peter. They were not liberators, but irreligious usurpers. Even the prince's father urged him to desist. He fought on, for a time, since the instinct for power is a strong one. He held London and much of the south-east, but the sentiment of the realm was against him; he also had a fair share of misfortune, his supporters being overwhelmed at Lincoln and a French fleet sending reinforcements beaten back at Sandwich. Finally he agreed to a truce, and was given £7,000 to leave England.

The young king had been asked by his barons to confirm 'the

liberties and free customs' enshrined in the Magna Carta, so that even those who had remained loyal to King John realized the value of that document as a curb on sovereign power. It had already become an outline of shared principles that could unite the feuding barons. A council was held in St Paul's Cathedral, where the Great Charter was published in slightly modified form. It had become in essence a new coronation charter. Henry III's reign had effectively begun. It endured for fifty-six years. There was hardly a moment when he could recall not being a king. This gave him, perhaps, a certain laxity or lack of wariness. He never had to fight for his rule, or fight for land.

There had not been a boy king since the reign of Ethelred the Unready. So in this difficult situation Henry's most prominent supporters established a regency council. Henry came under the tutelage of three men – the bishop of Winchester, the papal legate and the earl of Pembroke known as the earl marshal. As regents they effectively controlled the administration of the country. They acted quickly and effectively; within a matter of months the exchequer was open for business and the judges had been despatched on their legal peregrinations.

But the consequences of the civil war were plain. Would the barons loyal to John be allowed to retain the castles or lands they had captured from the rebels? Would the various factions within the baronage once more oppose each other? The death of the earl marshal, in 1219, proved the instability of the realm under the boy king. Certain mighty lords declined to hand over royal castles. They were also refusing to pay the taxes levied on them. Small-scale wars sprang up over disputed territory.

A new regency council had been established under the leadership of the papal legate, Pandulf. The head of the judicial system, the judiciar, was Hubert de Burgh. The king's tutor and guardian, the bishop of Winchester, was Peter des Roches. These three men would play a major role in the vicissitudes of the early reign. They fought among themselves for primacy, and of course provoked hostility in all quarters. It cannot be said that they had any real conception of national well-being; with the possible exception of Pandulf, they were concerned to promote the interests of themselves and their families. That was what rule was all about. De

Burgh and des Roches, for example, were engaged in a violent feud. At one meeting the two men broke out in argument against one another; de Burgh accused des Roches of being the instigator of all the troubles in the realm, whereupon des Roches said that he would bring his opponent 'to his knees'. Then he stormed out of the meeting. These were the men who were supposed to tutor the king in good government.

It is evident enough that, in the period of the king's minority, the rule was given to the strongest party or parties; by threat or violence, for example, Hubert de Burgh eventually gained control of the administration and began to deal with recalcitrant barons as well as over-mighty subjects. An approximation to order was maintained, but on de Burgh's terms. Henry does not seem to have been particularly restive or uneasy during de Burgh's ascendancy, but the time came when he was obliged to assert himself. At the beginning of 1227, at the age of nineteen, he declared himself to be of the age when he should assume all the duties of sovereignty.

This is the occasion, perhaps, to take a closer look at the young king. He was of modest height, and seems to have had no remarkable physical characteristic – except perhaps for his left eyelid, which was inclined to droop. He was amiable, but not perhaps docile. He tried to evict his younger brother, known as Richard of Cornwall, from some lands; the combined fury of the other barons prevented him from doing so. It was an early lesson in the limitations of power.

His personality has been variously described, no doubt because it was compounded of various parts. Some people considered him to be a simpleton, while others believed him to be a fool. He was described as *vir simplex*, an adjective that might mean without guile or without sense. He was criticized as weak and credulous, submissive and impulsive. He was very impressionable, and tended to favour the opinions of the last person to whom he had spoken. His resentments, and his affections, did not last for very long. It can safely be argued then, that he was not a strong and ruthless king in the manner of his father and grandfather. Unlike them, he had never been schooled in adversity. He had a temper and he could be sharp-tongued, but was not wantonly cruel.

He was pious, perhaps excessively so for a king who must

sometimes assert his own rights over the Church. Every day he used to hear three masses. When he journeyed to Paris he could not pass a church where Mass was being said, without participating in the sacred ceremony. When the priest raised the eucharist at the solemn moment of elevation, Henry would hold the priest's hand and kiss it. King Louis of France once told him that he preferred to hear sermons than to attend Mass. Henry replied that he would rather see his friend than hear one speak of him.

God was his immediate lord. No one on earth was closer to Him than the king. Henry revived the cult of Edward the Confessor, and considered the old king to be his spiritual protector. He rebuilt Westminster Abbey in veneration of his memory, and he now lies buried close to the shrine of the saint. In one sense he was English. He was born in England, at least, and his nickname was 'Henry of Winchester'; he gave his sons the names of Anglo-Saxon saints.

When a relic of the holy blood of Jesus was sent to him by the patriarch of Jerusalem and the master of the Templars, it was kept in closely guarded secrecy at the church of the Holy Sepulchre in London. The young king carried the phial in solemn procession from St Paul's Cathedral to Westminster Abbey, his gaze fixed upon the relic at all times. He wore a simple robe of humility, but this ceremony was in part designed to re-emphasize the theory of sacred kingship. When after the service in Westminster Abbey he put on his crown and cloth of gold, he became an icon with his finger pointing upward to the heavens. Henry's concept of kingship was one of ritual and spectacle. He crossed himself in the manner of ecclesiastics, and ensured that the words of 'Christus Vincit' were chanted before him on holy days. His father had spent his days on the road but Henry, less driven by his furies, preferred to settle down in comfort and splendour.

Above all he desired, and wished to be remembered for, a reign of peace. He did not like wars. He was no soldier, in any case. In one declaration he commended his reign for the absence of 'hostility and general war' and stated that he had never ceased to labour 'for the peace and tranquillity of one and all'. He might even be considered a 'good' man, but good men rarely make good kings. No quality of greatness could be found in him. Two other shafts of light may help to illuminate him. He liked fresh air and insisted that the windows opposite his bed should be made to open. And he liked images of smiling faces. He ordered a row of smiling angels to be sculpted on either side of a rood screen for the church of St Martin le Grand.

He was in fact the most lavish patron of religious art in the history of England. He built chapels and churches; he was the patron of monkish historians and monkish illuminators; the great development of Gothic art occurred in the course of his long reign when the stones themselves cried out 'Holy! Holy! Holy!' Under the gaze of the king the High Gothic of Westminster Abbey emerged, to be seen at its grandest in the octagonal chapter house. Irresolute as he may sometimes have been, he was responsible for the creation of many of the architectural glories of England. In his reign 157 abbeys, priories and other religious houses were established; there was an efflorescence of Lady chapels.

It so happened that, at the beginning of his reign, the first friars came to England; the Dominicans arrived in 1221, and the Franciscans three years later. Their significance has long since been eroded, but at the time of their first presence in the country they materially affected the cultural and spiritual life of the people. They established themselves in the major towns, where they found favour with the leading merchants who had long fallen out of love with the parochial clergy; they preached, literally, in the marketplace.

They did not live in the cloister in the manner of Benedictine monks; they were in the world. They were mendicants, beggars, who roamed the streets seeking clothes and food. They were not, at least in the beginning, supposed to ask for money. Some of the first Franciscans in London lodged in a street known as Stinking Lane. They preached as poor men, therefore, and as a result helped to change the sentiments and perceptions of the townspeople. They told stories and jokes; they described miracles and marvels. They turned English preaching into a folk art. Before their arrival, there had been few sermons in England. It was a new experience for most of their auditors. The first pulpits were in fact not erected until the middle of the fourteenth century.

Of course the friars went the way of all flesh; they became successful and popular; they attracted patrons who endowed them richly; they built friaries and priories that rivalled the monasteries in comfort and prosperity. They became confessors to the great. Anyone who has read the *Canterbury Tales* will know that, 150 years after their arrival, they had become a byword for worldliness and even licentiousness. Their decline is a measure of the decay of all human institutions, sacred and secular.

On 29 July 1232, Hubert de Burgh was dismissed from the court and the king's presence. He was accused of stirring up attacks on Italian clergy and expropriating their property. The pope had been making enquiries into the baron's third marriage, and de Burgh wanted revenge. He miscalculated the depth of the young king's devotion to the papacy. So the king, on the advice of 'certain men of good faith', dismissed him. One of those men of good faith was of course, Peter des Roches; as de Burgh fell, des Roches rose. Within a short time the bishop of Winchester brought in his nephew – or perhaps it was his son, no one was quite sure – as treasurer and head of the royal household. Peter des Rivaux was, like Peter des Roches, from Poitou. This was the king's maternal homeland. Other Poitevins joined them. A strong affinity existed between them all and it was generally believed at the time that the king preferred their company – and their abilities – over his compatriots.

Yet England was an intrinsic part of a larger European order. Henry's sister Isabella had married Frederick, the Holy Roman Emperor, known as *stupor mundi*, or the astonishment of the world. Henry himself married Eleanor of Provence in 1236, and her relatives played a large role in the king's court. Eleanor's sister had married King Louis IX of France. Those happy few who had inherited royal blood married one another, so that a network of relatives controlled the fates of kingdoms. But this extended family was not necessarily a happy one, and almost by default Henry became engaged in the endless broils of France and Italy. Europe was a nest of warring principalities, none of which had the internal coherence of England. The king of France, the pope and the emperor were ever vigilant and ever suspicious, ready to take advantage of one another at any opportunity.

Henry's relationship with France was in any case strained and uncertain. His father had effectively lost the Angevin Empire and, despite his preference for peace, he was determined to retrieve it. But he had a formidable enemy. King Louis had taken over the whole of Poitou. Another part of the erstwhile empire, Gascony, was threatened by Louis and the kings of Castile, Navarre and Avignon. An expedition under the command of the king's brother, Richard of Cornwall, saved the duchy – if 'saved' is the word for precarious Angevin authority over self-assertive local lords. Very little else was achieved. Henry sailed to Normandy, hoping that it would rise in his favour. This did not happen. The king marched about a bit, but there were no battles. Then Henry sailed back. It had been a most ineffectual invasion. It was said that the commanders of the king's forces had behaved as if they were taking part in a Christmas game.

The king returned to France twelve years later, but his army was routed; Henry was forced to retreat into Bordeaux, the administrative centre of Gascony, and arrange a truce. This second expedition is remarkable for one reason, apart from its failure. The English barons were most unwilling to trust their money, or their men, to Henry's campaign. They considered that an English king should no longer fight for supposed ancestral lands in France. Normandy or Poitou or Gascony were no longer to be viewed as an extension of England. The island was pre-eminently an island. That is why Henry's son, Edward I, was more intent upon the conquest of Scotland and of Wales

It was also clear that the Angevin Empire, once broken, could not be put back together again. Only Gascony remained, to provide England with much of its wine. The vintages of Bordeaux are still very popular, and so the Angevin Empire can be said to remain in the wine racks of England. But Gascony provided more forbidding fruit: as the price of his title to the duchy Henry pledged fealty to the king of France. But how can one king be the vassal of another? The uncertain status of the area, poised between France and England, was to become an occasion for the Hundred Years War.

It is a commonplace of English history that Henry III was an ineffectual king. When the royal seal was changed, in the middle of the reign, he was portrayed as bearing a sceptre rather than the original sword. But in the course of his life the economy of the country improved, with the absence of war playing some part in this general prosperity. The lords and tenants of the land were not removed to fight in foreign territories, and were allowed to concentrate upon the condition of their estates. The surviving documents suggest that there was increased traffic in the sale and purchase of land. A vogue for manuals of estate management soon followed, with advice on matters from dung to dairy production. 14 gallons (63.6 litres) of cow's milk should produce 14 pounds (6.3 kilos) of cheese and 2 pounds (0.9 kilo) of butter. There had not been such a profitable farming industry since the days of Roman England.

The king exacted fewer taxes from his subjects than any of his predecessors and so encouraged the flow of wealth about the realm. Henry relied upon the exploitation of his royal lands, and on the profits to be gained from justice. Richard and John had open mouths, swallowing England's silver; Henry, partly under the strictures of the Magna Carta, was obliged to hold back.

Other reasons for prosperity can be found. The uncertain relations of England with both France and Flanders were eased by the late 1230s, allowing a great increase in the export of wool to those countries. A threefold increase in overseas trade took place in the course of the thirteenth century; this was the age of road-building, easing the routes of commerce. The silver poured in, much to the advantage of the merchants in the towns and ports. The 'marble of Corfe' and the 'scarlet of Lincoln', the 'iron of Gloucester' and the 'cod of Grimsby', were celebrated in doggerel rhyme. They provide the context in which we may best understand the king's programme of church- and chapel-building.

Some unknowable bond exists between the economic and physical health of the nation, marked by the fact that in the period of Henry's rule the population began to rise ever more rapidly. As a result demand at home grew for corn, cheese and wool; the economy expanded together with the number of people who took part in it. There were 5 million inhabitants and 8 million sheep. Yet growth is not always or necessarily benign. Prices were rising as a result of increased demand; the consequence of a larger working population was that wages could be kept low. While the more efficient or prosperous farmers flourished, and enlarged their properties, their poorer neighbours were generally left with smaller and smaller plots of land.

The king once remarked that there were no more than 200 men in England who mattered, and that he was familiar with all of them. Many of them were bound together by ties of marriage or of tenure; many of them were associated in local administration and local justice. They were all in kinship and alliance, one with another. They were bound within regional as well as courtly groupings; and there were times, as Henry soon learned to his cost, when they could act together.

The problem was that the majority of these significant lords were distrustful of a king who surrounded himself with his advisers from Poitou, the greatest of whom were Peter des Roches and Peter des Rivaux. The issue was, in part, their foreignness. The English lords were by the thirteenth century all native-born, and in written documents professed their affection for 'native ground' or 'native soil'. In the sixth year of Henry's reign the feast of St George had been turned into a national holiday. The monkish chronicler of St Albans recorded that those people who did not speak English were 'held in contempt'.

The foreignness of the Poitevins was compounded by their greed. They came to the court to receive annual stipends. They were eager for lands and for money, but these could only be granted at the expense of the native lords. In the spring of 1233 these magnates let it be known that they would refuse to attend the king's council if 'the aliens' were present; the king's representative replied that he had every right to choose foreign counsellors and that he would find the force necessary to quell this baronial mutiny. In June 1233 the lords were summoned to the king's presence in Oxford; they refused to obey. They also delivered a message to the effect that they would throw Henry and the foreigners out of the country before electing a new king. The barons were declared contumacious; they were exiles and outlaws, their lands nominally granted to the Poitevin courtiers.

In this lay a cause for war. The barons went on the offensive, and within six months the king's forces were defeated. The lands and properties of 'aliens' were despoiled. The bishops of the land enforced a truce, in which the king effectively surrendered. The rebel lords were pardoned, and certain of the Poitevins were banished from court. Yet Henry could not separate himself from his instinctive partiality for his extended family of Frenchmen. He was himself half-French, the son of Isabella of Angoulême.

His marriage to Eleanor of Provence in 1236 only compounded the problem. According to Matthew Paris, 'he took a stranger to wife without the advice of his own friends and natural subjects'. The twelve-year-old girl had brought in her entourage her uncle, William of Savoy. He was half-brother to the king himself, sharing a mother in Isabella. He knew that Henry was impressionable and pliable. He had come to stay. The Savoyards were soon everywhere. Peter of Savoy was given the territory in Yorkshire known as the honour of Richmond. It was he who built the Savoy Palace between the Strand and the Thames, now the site of the Savoy hotel. Boniface of Savoy was granted the archbishopric of Canterbury. Henry had not learned the simple lesson. He believed that the country was his alone. Why should he not distribute it to half-brothers or second cousins or great-nephews if he so wished? He was king.

The opposition to Henry, over succeeding years, took various forms and the expressions of grievance were variously couched. The Poitevins and Savoyards were still too much favoured. The queen was playing too dominant a role. The king was being given ill, or indifferent, advice. He was irresolute and inconstant in policy. He was too much in thrall to the pope. When one of his English barons remonstrated with him for ignoring the clauses of the Magna Carta he is said to have replied, 'Why should I observe this charter, which is neglected by all my grandees, both prelates and nobility?' The answer came, that he ought as king to set an example. The general impression is of weak or bad government on a sufficiently large scale to merit some intervention.

In 1244 he demanded a large sum from parliament. In return the lords insisted that they be given authority to elect the justiciar and the chancellor, thus taking command of the law and the exchequer. The king agreed only to renew his vow to accept the provisions of the Magna Carta. Four years later, when he asked parliament to grant him more money, the lords refused. They told him the revenue was wasted on wax candles and on useless processions; they also informed him that the food and drink he consumed, even the clothes he wore, were snatched from their lawful owners. Five years later Henry again demanded money, on the ground that he was about to lead a crusade to the Holy Land. No one really believed him. Once more he only exacted the sum by a solemn vow to obey the precepts of the Magna Carta. Once more he reneged on his promises. We see here the unsettled reign of the first king of England struggling in the restraints of law.

Then there came what was called at the time 'a new and sudden change'. On 7 April 1258 a parliament was called, since the king again needed money. He had promised the pope the vast sum of 135,541 marks, in return for his son Edmund being installed as king of Sicily; the Sicilian adventure was a fiasco, but the debt remained.

The king's demands were all the more onerous because this was a time of famine. The harvest of 1257 had failed, and by the spring of the following year the price of wheat had increased two and a half times. We may survey the activities of kings and lords, but another life sometimes escapes observation: the life of the wretched. Matthew Paris reports, in this year of dearth, 'an innumerable multitude of poor people, swollen and rotting, lying by fives and sixes in pigsties, on dunghills, and in the dirt of the streets'. The resources of the country were confined to relatively few people. Approximately 60 per cent of the agricultural population was deemed to be too poor to pay taxes. They were not on anyone's list to be saved or protected. No 'state' was in place to succour them, and so they went to the wall. The king was in any case only concerned with his own financial problems.

The barons of England were not inclined to honour his debts. At the end of April 1258, after much fruitless debate, a party of barons made their way to the court at Westminster. They deliberately put their swords beside the entrance to the king's hall before saluting Henry in the expected manner. But he was unnerved by the sight of their weapons. An eyewitness report, placed in the Tewkesbury chronicles, describes the scene. 'What is this, my lords?' he asked them. 'Am I, wretched fellow, your captive?'

Roger Bigod, the earl of Norfolk, replied for them all. 'No, my lord, no! But let the wretched and intolerable Poitevins and all aliens flee from your face and ours as from the face of a lion, and there will be glory to God in the heavens and in your land peace to men of good will.'

This affords a glimpse of the colourful and spirited speech of the thirteenth century. Bigod then asked the king to accept 'our counsels'. Henry, naturally enough, asked what they might entail. The barons had already agreed among themselves on their demands. The king was to be guided and advised by a group of twenty-four councillors, twelve to be chosen by the king and twelve chosen by the barons. If the king had refused these terms, he faced a real prospect of civil war. He knew as much himself, and so after deliberation he accepted the terms offered to him. He must also have been swayed by the fact that the barons agreed to grant him 'aid' in his financial embarrassments.

A committee of twenty-four was chosen and, in the summer of 1258, published what amounts to a manifesto on domestic and international affairs. The major proposal was a simple one. The king was to be directed by the advice of a council of fifteen men nominated by the barons, and parliament itself would choose the justiciar, chancellor and treasurer. The king's acceptance of what became known as the Provisions of Oxford was issued in English as well as in Latin and French, testimony to the manifest identity of the realm. In practice the council was soon ruling the country. It took possession of the great seal. It settled all the matters of state without the king's presence. If he remonstrated with them, they replied that 'this is how we wish it'. Henry had become a minor again. This was no longer the government of a king.

That was the reason it did not, and could not, work. How could the power of the country, exercised by one man for thirty-one years, now be dispersed between fifteen people? Quarrels broke out between the barons over the nature and purpose of their control of the king, and they found it difficult to deal with international affairs without the direct intervention of the king with his fellow monarchs. The barons themselves had their own local interests – they were, after all, primarily regional magnates – which were not necessarily compatible with national administration. It was said that they were concerned only with self-aggrandizement.

The baronial government collapsed within two years. A papal bull was published, releasing Henry from any promises made under duress to his lords; the bull stated that when a king was distrained by his subjects it was as if a woodman was assaulted by his own axe. Henry also declared that the barons had stripped the king of 'his power and dignity'. He moved into the Tower, both as a defence against his enemies and as a potent symbol of that power.

Not greatly chastened by events, he resumed the exercise of sovereignty. It lasted for only two years. The 'aliens', the Savoyards in particular, were once more blamed for being 'over-mighty'. Henry had also introduced a body of foreign mercenaries, provoking rumours that the country was about to suffer an invasion. So in 1263 a group of dissident barons found themselves a new leader to press their claims, and in particular their demand that they should be governed only 'per indigenas' or by native-born men.

Simon de Montfort, summoned by the barons, sailed to England. It has been said that he was the first ever leader of an English political party. He was perhaps an odd representative of the English cause. He was born in France and was part of a noble French family. Yet he had native connections. He had inherited the earldom of Leicester, by virtue of the fact that his grandfather had married the sister of the previous earl; it was a circuitous route, but it was a proper one. He had also married the king's sister Eleanor. So, as one chronicler put it, he became 'the shield and defender of the English, the enemy and expeller of aliens, although he himself was one of them by nation'. The barons summoned the representatives of the shires to an assembly at St Albans, while the king called them to Windsor.

The confrontation between Henry III and Simon de Montfort could not be contained. De Montfort himself was an obstinate and intolerant man, with an obsessive hatred for Jews and heretics. He was something of an isolated figure in England, with a disdain for the compromises and irresolution of his English supporters whom he had once described as 'fickle and deceitful'. He was impatient of fools, and could be high-handed both in his manner and in his methods. He was, in other words, a bully. He knew what was right. He knew, or thought he knew, what had to be done. He had in the past commanded a crusading army, and Henry himself had once despatched him to Gascony as his seneschal or viceroy. The king was notoriously fearful of storms. It was an aspect of his simplicity. But on one occasion he told de Montfort that 'by God's head, I fear you more than all the thunder and lightning in the world'.

A large element of self-righteousness existed in de Montfort's nature that may have helped to conceal, even from himself, his true purpose. Like the rest of his family he wanted to extend his power and lordship. That was where proper honour lay. He preferred strong rule as a moral and theoretical imperative, but surely it would be all the stronger if it were wielded by him? Further questions arose. If he were able to gain the victory, would he allow the king to resume his rule under baronial restraint? Or would he himself take on the role of sovereign?

The members of both parties engaged in intermittent conflict after his arrival in England. They were also involved in what would now be called a propaganda war, with open letters to the shire courts and sermons in the churchyards. The political ballad also emerges in this period. In the early months of 1264 the struggle turned into open and intensive warfare, on a scale not seen in England since the battles of King John with his barons. The peace that the king craved was snatched from him. He had an uneasy relationship with his elder son, Edward, since Edward had the stronger and more valiant character. At his instigation the king marched on the rebel town of Northampton, bearing the royal standard of a red dragon with fiery tongue; this bloody flag was a sign that no quarter would be given to those who surrendered. The king took the town. Edward then pillaged rebel lands in Staffordshire and Derbyshire. De Montfort himself was using London, where the citizens had turned decidedly against the king, as the centre of operations. Here he was impregnable. But Henry had the larger army.

A decisive confrontation could not be avoided. Otherwise the administration of the country would perish with a thousand cuts.

On 11 May Henry and his entourage arrived at the Cluniac priory of Lewes in Sussex. The baronial army took up its position 10 miles (16 kilometres) to the north. Two days passed in inconclusive negotiations, but then de Montfort moved forward to the high downs overlooking Lewes. The armies faced one another and, as battle began, Edward led a furious attack upon the contingent of Londoners; he broke them, and pursued the scattered bands for several hours. That was the mistake. By the time he returned the rebels had won a signal victory, with the king himself immured in the priory. De Montfort had not flown the red dragon on his standard, so an armistice was quickly arranged. The Lord Edward, as he was known, was confined in Dover Castle as a hostage for the king's good intent.

A Latin poem of 968 lines, entitled *The Song of Lewes*, was written soon after the event. Its intent was to celebrate what de Montfort had called 'the common enterprise', and it justified the armed rebellion of the barons as the only means of ensuring that they played their proper role in the administration of the country. 'Commonly it is said, as the king wishes, so goes the law; the truth is quite otherwise, for the law stands, though the king falls.' It would not be wholly fanciful to suggest the presence of something like a communal sentiment of the realm in the face of manifest injustice. Strong evidence also exists that the working population of the countryside took matters into their own hands and sided with the barons. Some Leicestershire villagers, for example, surrounded a captain and his men who were fighting in the king's army; they attempted to arrest them on the grounds that they were 'against the welfare of the community of the realm and against the barons'. These were not idle or theoretical concepts; they were part of living reality.

Many hundreds of villagers were also fighting as foot soldiers beside the mounted knights. The poorest of them had knives and scythes, the more prosperous were obliged by law to possess an iron cap and a lance. They were fighting against the king's exactions. At the beginning of the nineteenth century three pits were uncovered in Lewes; each one contained approximately 500 bodies. They had just been piled one on top of another, the unmourned and unremembered casualties of war. They are described by one chronicle as ordinary people bred '*de vulgo*', from the masses. Very few knights were killed in the battle.

Henry III was returned to London after his defeat, where he was placed for safekeeping in St Paul's Cathedral. A small body of nine barons, under the leadership of de Montfort, assumed power while all the departments of state continued to operate in the name of the king. But it was only a name. De Montfort was now the strong man of the state. It is the first instance in English history of a subject seizing rule from an anointed sovereign. He confiscated the lands of eighteen barons who had fought on the wrong side, and took the lion's share of ransom money. He even turned on his fellow barons, and consigned one of them to prison; another fled the realm. De Montfort was becoming a tyrant. That is what happens within oligarchies; one climbs over the others. As a result his support was soon fatally weakened. Who would not prefer a king to a tyrant?

Yet in the search for support he summoned two parliaments, at one of which the representatives of the towns as well as the knights and lords were present. From a period of authoritarian rule emerged an instrument of liberty; it can be said that the growing identity of the nation itself was shaped in opposition to the king. Out of contrast comes growth; out of opposition emerge principles. The exploitations of Richard and John had helped to foster a sense of *communitas* in towns and villages; the weakness of Henry now led to a more general recognition of the 'community of the realm'.

The growth and development of parliament were part of the same process. There had always been parliaments of a kind. The structure itself existed before the moment it reached self-consciousness, thereby acquiring an identity. We cannot look back into the darkness of prehistory, but we can be sure that the tribal leaders had their own councils of wise or noble men. The Saxon invaders had brought with them the idea of the witan, which means literally 'the knowing', or witenagemot (the word itself is not recorded before 1035); this was an assembly, made up of bishops and nobles, that met once or twice a year. They were consulted by the king, and deliberated upon the making of new laws or the raising of new taxes. They may have had the power of electing, and even deposing, a king.

The Norman council, established after the successful invasion of England, was a smaller body of perhaps thirty-five ecclesiastical and secular lords. In 1095 William Rufus called together a larger assembly, comprising all the abbots, bishops and *principes* or chief men of the land. This became the template for the councils of later reigns; with the absence of the Norman and Angevin kings in France and elsewhere, the assembly of magnates learned how to act collectively to enforce its will. They also assumed a collective identity. In the reign of Henry II the abbot of Battle declared that the king could not change the laws of the country without 'the counsel and consent' of the barons. That was still debatable.

The first parliamentary summons came from King John who, in the summer of 1212, demanded that the sheriff of each county should come to him with 'six of the more lawful and discreet knights who are to do what we shall tell them'. The knights were not present to advise the king. They were there to communicate the royal will to their regions. Yet the provisions of the Magna Carta, three years later, were designed to curtail the powers of the king; in particular it was ordained that no monarch could levy extraordinary taxation without the 'common counsel' of the realm. The realm, at this juncture, of course meant only the barons and the bishops.

In 1236 Henry III called a parliament at Westminster. This represents the first official use of the term, but the actual assembly consisted only of lay magnates and bishops. There were no representatives from the shires or the towns. But the king needed money from various and different sources. He could no longer rely on the feudal tax paid by his barons, or on taxes collected from their tenants. So in 1254 the sheriffs were ordered to send two knights from each county chosen by the county court. The lower clergy were also graciously admitted to the parliamentary assembly.

Simon de Montfort, after his victory, summoned two representatives from each town. Knights and the leaders of the towns, known as burgesses, then became as much part of parliament as the bishops and lords. We have here the rudimentary beginnings of the House of Commons. No one seems to have noticed this at the time, however, and there is no extant commentary upon the change. It was not in any case a great exercise in democracy. De

Montfort's immediate purpose was simply to have more supporters in place against the great lords who were antagonistic to him; a large gathering would also help to disguise the enforced absence of his enemies. So he brought in the knights and the townsmen.

Unintended and unforeseen consequences followed the appearance of the parliament. Its growing importance, for example, elevated the role of knights as well as the richer townsmen. A knight can be defined as one who possessed one or several manors and who was generally involved in the government of his local area in such posts as sheriff or forest official. He took on the royal work of his shire, administrative and judicial.

The knights were known as *buzones* or 'big men'. They were approximately 1,100 or 1,200 in number. They are the men whose images are seen, in wood and stone, in the old churches of England. They wear body armour, and some of them are about to draw the sword; some carry shields; others are shown with their hands folded in prayer; they are often cross-legged; double images of husband and wife are sometimes preferred. This was the period when coats of arms were recorded, and the science of heraldry emerged in all its fancifulness. Early in the fourteenth century, knights' burials were commemorated with full-figure brasses.

Their pre-eminence led to a general stratification in the various ranks and classes below them. By the middle of the fourteenth century, at the latest, there had emerged the outlines of what has become known as the gentry, including knights, esquires and gentlemen. An esquire was a prosperous landowner who for various reasons had surrendered the status of knighthood. A gentleman was of lower standing, simply the head of a landed family. By 1400 this difference was stated in monetary terms. An esquire earned between £20 and £40 a year, while a gentleman would earn between £10 and £20. Knights and esquires might serve as sheriffs or as Justices of the Peace, while gentlemen took on such lesser roles as undersheriffs and coroners. Gentlemen were often parish gentry, while knights were always county gentry. It is a matter of some interest that this social structure survived, with modifications, until the latter part of the nineteenth century. It held together the country for more than 500 years.

Wherever we look in the thirteenth century, we see evidence of greater formality and control. In the towns of England an oligarchy of the richer merchants was strictly organized, in consort with royal officialdom; the crafts and merchants were now gathered into guilds and trade associations. The bureaucracy of the king's court was becoming ever more complex and methodical. Administrative historians have noticed the huge proliferation of documents in the reign of Henry III. Even the crusaders setting out from England to the Holy Land were given written contracts that stipulated certain common terms of service. Every right, or verdict, was defined in writing. A royal bailiff, approaching a small farmer for taxes, tells him that 'thou art writen yn my writ'. It is a paradox, perhaps, that in the reign of a weak or indecisive king the apparatus of the Crown had never been more efficient or adaptable. But how else are we to explain the fact that, despite the disasters of his government, Henry III continued to rule for so long? By degrees the nation was fixed and rendered stable, despite the manifest tempests upon its surface.

One of the tempests gathered at the end of May 1265. The Lord Edward, still in custody, was allowed to go riding; he was a prince of the royal blood, after all. But on this spring morning he tried one horse after another, going further and further out; then he chose one particular horse and, on the signal of a gentleman rider in the distance, he galloped off. Before long, he reached the safety of Ludlow Castle. Edward was at liberty. He was free to raise his father's standard against de Montfort and the other rebels.

The threat was immediate, and the result not long in coming. The two armies met on 4 August at Evesham in Worcestershire. When de Montfort saw the royalist forces approaching him in well-ordered array he remarked that 'they learned how to do that from me'. At their head was the Lord Edward; now, at twenty-six years old, he was de facto leader of the realm. De Montfort had taken Henry with him as hostage and, as the battle grew more fierce, he and his knights fought in a circle around the king; one of the royalists, Roger Leyburn, managed to rescue Henry from the mêlée. Edward had already appointed twelve men in what might be called a death squad, whose only task was to kill de Montfort. They were successful. His head was cut off, and his testicles dangled on each side of his nose; the trophy was then sent to the wife of the man who had beheaded him. A general slaughter ensued, the first of its kind in medieval England where lords and knights were ordinarily spared for ransom or for the sake of honour. Edward would not be the same kind of king as his father.

Simon de Montfort's body was given to the monks of Evesham, in whose abbey it was buried. His tomb lies now in the ruins, beneath the high altar, marked by a granite cross. In his death he was by some considered to be a martyr and his burial place became an object of pilgrimage. Here was the grave of a rebel in the cause of righteousness, and failure only added lustre to his reputation. Rumours spread of miracles in the abbey.

But they were not enough to save his supporters. Those who were not slaughtered on the field at Evesham were scattered. Some fled to Kenilworth, the castle of the de Montforts, while others took refuge in the Isle of Ely. Some escaped to the wild woods, and it is possible that the saga of Robin Hood emerged from the life of one such wandering lord. They were known as the 'disinherited', and they only found their way back into the king's grace with massive payments.

Henry resumed his reign. The great seal was returned to him, and he sat as before with his council. The imposition of order was swift enough, although in truth the country had not been much affected by the wars between its lords. Local difficulties had occurred in the immediate neighbourhood of the fighting, but the business of the realm continued as before. Henry's son and heir, Edward, felt able to leave the country and take the part of a crusader in the Holy Land. He prepared himself to ascend the throne in the service of Christ.

The king himself was free to press ahead with the rebuilding of Westminster Abbey, where he was impatient to remove the relics of Edward the Confessor to a new shrine. The abbey itself was another example of the community of the realm. For twenty-five years 800 men had worked upon the glorious fabric with its new presbytery, new chapter house, new crossing and a slowly rising north front. It was a work for the generations. The stonemasons of Purbeck, the craftsmen of all England, the sailors and wagoners, had all played their part in this mighty enterprise. The tilemakers, the mosaicists and the workers in metal had collaborated in the service of the king's passion for curiously crafted things. He lavished so much money on the building that it has become a permanent memorial of his reign. He expired in the fifty-sixth year of that reign, on 16 November 1272; at the age of sixty-five, he is likely to have died simply of old age. The tomb of Henry III, with a gilt-bronze effigy of the king, is still to be seen in the abbey that he built.

# 18

# The seasonal year

Of the ways of marking time in England, the calendar of the years of the king's reign was the least significant; the sacred calendar and the seasonal calendar were pre-eminent. They represented the habitual and unchanging nature of the world; they expressed a deep sense of belonging to the land and to the everlasting that are the true horizons of the medieval period. Seasonal and sacred time were intermingled.

Winter, lasting from Michaelmas on 29 September to Christmas, was the season for sowing; wheat and rye were known as winter seed. Some of the cattle were removed from their summer pastures to the relative warmth of the stalls, while the rest were slaughtered; the pigs were hustled to their sties. November was known as the blood month. What was not eaten was salted. The twelve days of the Christmas celebration were the only long holiday that the farmers and labourers enjoyed; it was a time of feasts and drinking, and of the mysterious rituals of the mummers' plays.

In spring, from Epiphany on 6 January to the Holy Week of Easter, the men set the vineyards and made the ditches; they hewed wood for fences and planted the vegetable garden. The world of work had begun again. The first Monday after Epiphany was known by the women as Distaff Monday and by the men as Plough

Monday, thus neatly describing their two occupations. One spun and the other delved.

On Plough Monday, a 'fool plough' or 'white plough' was dragged about the village by young ploughmen covered in ribbons and other gay ornaments; they asked for pennies at every door and, if refused, they ploughed the ground before the cottage. The leader of the ploughmen, or 'plough-bullocks', was a young man dressed up as an old woman and known as Bessy. Another participant would wear a foxskin as a hood, with the tail hanging behind his back. This ancient ceremony was still being performed in the nineteenth and early twentieth centuries, perhaps testifying to the customary nature of English rural life. It is still practised in certain areas of eastern England, where its origins in the Danelaw are assumed to lie. The feast of Candlemas on 2 February, commemorating the Purification of the Virgin, was the time for tillage to be resumed; it was the moment for the 'lenten seed' of oats and barley and beans to be sown. This was also the time for the pruning of trees.

From Hocktide, the second Monday and Tuesday after Easter, to Lammas, on the first day of August, came the summer. That is why the May queen or Flora was known as the summer queen rather than the spring queen. On the day before Hockday the females of the village captured and bound as many men as they could find, and kept them until a fee or ransom had been paid. On Hockday itself the males of the village engaged in the same sport. Days of festival were always celebrated before the resumption of serious agricultural work. This was the time when the husbandman must lay down the manure, cut the wood, shear the sheep, clear the land of weeds, repair fences, rebuild the fish-weirs and the mills. The fallow fields were ploughed. Midsummer occurred on the feast of the nativity of St John the Baptist. On St John's Eve, 23 June, as a thirteenth-century monk from Winchcombe observed, 'the boys collect bones and certain other rubbish, and burn them, and therefrom a smoke is produced on the air. They also make brands and go about the fields with the brands. Thirdly, the wheel which they roll.' The wheel was the wheel of fire, set aflame and sent rolling down the hills of the region. In this way the pagan rituals and the Christian calendar were united in one celebration.

On St John's Day itself the harvest of hay was brought in. When all the hay had been stacked a sheep was let loose in the field; it became the prize of the mower who caught it. Only after St John's Day were the thistles in the fields cut down; it was said that if they were removed earlier, they would increase threefold.

From Lammas to Michaelmas, at the end of September, came the harvest time of corn known as *autumpnus*. The name Lammas came from the Anglo-Saxon *hlaf-Mass* or loaf-Mass; in a good year it was a time of fruitfulness. When the last sheaf had been ceremonially cut, a supper known as harvest home was served. As Thomas Tusser wrote in the sixteenth century,

> In harvest time, harvest folk, servants and all
> Should make altogether good cheer in the hall.

In their laughter and in their dancing they were keeping time with the seasons and at the same time celebrating the continuities of the earth; they were part of a universal rhythm which they experienced but did not necessarily understand.

After the harvest had been taken in, the cattle would be allowed to graze on the stubble. At the same time rye and wheat would be sown in the fallow fields after they had been ploughed and harrowed. After the sowing was over there was customarily a feast with seed cake, pasties and a dish of milk, wheat, raisins and spices known as furmenty or frumenty. Then came a time when the sheaves of the harvest were threshed, separating the ears from the straw; this was followed by the winnowing, when the grain was divided from the chaff. Also at this period the labourers were obliged to prepare the sheep-pens and the pigsties.

So the agricultural year was embedded in the ritual year. That is why, in the churches and cathedrals of England, the capitals and pillars were decorated with images of the months; the mowers are carved to celebrate the month of July, while a husbandman with sickle is the stone emblem of September. In Southwell Minster the pigs snuffle among the great stone oak leaves for the acorns of November. The natural world is familiar and immutable. The ease of summer and the woe of winter are part of the eternal order in which the humblest labourer participated; in medieval poetry, the ploughman was often considered to be holy. On sacred days the worshippers in the parish church, and the labourers in the field, were participating in complementary rituals. On the three rogation days preceding the Ascension Day, the parishioners would walk around the boundaries and bless the fields.

Murrain, the infectious disease that blighted sheep and cattle, was considered to be susceptible to prayer. A Mass in celebration of the Holy Spirit was sung, each parishioner offering up a penny. The sheep were then gathered in the field, and passages from the gospels were read out to them; then they were sprinkled with holy water while a hymn was chanted. This was followed by the recital of the *Pater Noster* and *Ave Maria*. Nevertheless animal mortality remained very high.

The nature of agriculture, month by month, hardly changed over the centuries. Open-field systems were common in the midlands, where large and unfenced fields were divided into strips which were owned by individual families; small enclosed fields were ubiquitous in Kent and in Essex; in the north and west rectangular fields were aligned one with another. From the thirteenth century there emerged the device of enclosure, whereby individual farmers exchanged their strips of land with one another; they could then create a larger portion that could be enclosed by hedges or fences.

Hamlets and small fields were typical of the north of England, while villages and large fields spread across the midlands. Considerable variety, however, existed within the counties. East Somerset was the home of open fields, while the west of that county was enclosed. East Suffolk was enclosed, and West Suffolk was open. The standard tenement of land was known in the south as yardland, and in the north as oxgang, and its location is ascertained in documents by the position of the sun. The south and the east were considered to be the brighter part of the earth. The lie of the land, the nature of the soil, the patterns of the climate, all played their part in shaping the farming system of each small territory. Parts of Wiltshire were clay land and other parts were chalk; the soil of Hampshire was basin gravel.

An infinite variety of agricultural practice existed in every part of the country, enforced or determined by custom and tradition. The families of each village or hamlet could have been tending the same parcel of land for many centuries, living in intimate relationship with it. They were part of the soil. In an early book of law we find that a hamlet is defined as possessing 'nine buildings, and one plough, and one kiln, and one churn, and one cat, and one cock, and one bull, and one herdsman'. The different kinds of field and pasture may also reflect the persistent influence of tribal customs that cannot be assigned a definite date. The communal history that allowed the partition into small fields or strips is also now irrecoverable; it is merely present as far back as we can look. Every portion of land had over the centuries acquired its own character of uses, rights and duties; it was a living thing, created out of custom and habit.

It was through land that a man gained honour and prestige as well as wealth; the extent of his lands measured the size of his military obligations. It was a commonplace that if you did not own a parcel of land you could not marry or raise a family. The landless man in the countryside was a nonentity. The law was essentially the will of the majority of those who owned land. Social life was dominated by the sale or purchase of land, in which 90 per cent of the population were involved one way or another. Castles were at the centre of military campaigns, from the eleventh century onwards, precisely because they dominated the surrounding land. The most severe form of punishment was the ravaging of the land. The pattern of landholding, rather than any administrative division, determined the nature and policy of each district and each shire.

Land was in fact the single most important cause of violence and social dissension. When one knight named only as Edward refused to do services to the prior of St Frideswide in exchange for a hide of land at Headington, the matter was resolved by judicial combat. 'After many blows between the champions, and although the champion of Edward had been blinded in the fight, they both sat down and as neither dared attack the other, peace was established as follows . . .' Less forceful means of justice could be tried. A farmer from Evesham claimed land from the abbey there; he took the precaution of filling his shoes with earth from his own estate so that he could swear in front of the monks that he was standing upon his own land.

Ploughing time, and the season for mowing, were earlier in some parts of the country than in others. Yet the rewards of labour were the same. The scythe and the sickle, the flail and the winnowing fan and the plough, were part of the common inheritance. A medieval folk song celebrated the appearance of 'oats, peas, beans and barley' that in *The Tempest* became 'wheat, rye, barley, fetches, oats and peas'. In the great fields we would see fifty or sixty men working on the land, scattered over the strips, bent over with toil. Many illustrations of them can be found in calendars and books of hours, dressed in tight breeches with a smock or blouse made of cloth and tied at the waist by a belt; in cold weather they wore a hooded mantle of wool that covered the upper part of the body. Sometimes they wore woollen caps.

'First thing in the morning,' the peasant recites in a tenth-century treatise, 'I drive my sheep to pasture and stand over them in heat and cold with dogs lest wolves should devour them, and I lead them back to their sheds and milk them twice a day and move their folds besides, and I make cheese and butter . . .' On the common land of the village, the cattle would be watched by a boy.

The farm animals of the medieval period were smaller and weaker than their modern counterparts, and the productivity of the soil was far inferior. It was a continuing and earnest business of survival for the farmer and the labourer, who often lived in conditions of rank squalor. The world was not progressing; it was believed to be in a state of steady deterioration from the age of gold to the age of iron. This portrait of the seasonal year must not be taken as an advertisement for a 'merry England'. Even the entertainments, those sports and games and rituals that are at the heart of the ritual calendar, were often brutal and violent. It was a life of sweat and dirt, but one that was quickly over.

# 19

# The emperor of Britain

At the time of Henry's death the Lord Edward was in Sicily, recovering from an attempted assassination. He had been in the Holy Land, where he had achieved nothing. He had been attacked in the city of Acre by a man wielding a dagger dipped in poison and almost died from the wound; the blackened flesh, corroded by the poison, had to be cut away in an operation almost as deadly as the original assault. But he survived, and sailed to safe harbour in Sicily. It was here that he learned of the death of his father.

He did not hurry back for his coronation. He had already been declared king in his absence, but he did not arrive in London for another eighteen months. He lingered in France until the summer of 1274. He had been born at Westminster, but he was by inheritance still essentially French; more pertinently, he was a member of the royal family of Europe. One of the reasons for the delay in his coronation had been his desire to put the affairs of Gascony in order. Gascony was, for him, just as important as England.

In his absence a parliament had been held, suggesting the solid continuity of the country's administration. But there had been instances of disorder, and of rivalries between magnates, that the new king would be obliged to quell. He was one who in truth demanded submission; unlike his father, he was a good soldier. He came back with his crusading knights who would in large part make up his royal household; they were in effect a private body-guard for the king, descended from the warrior bands of an earlier period. It is evidence of the militaristic nature of his reign that, at his coronation in the new abbey (not yet entirely built), his retainers rode into the transepts on their horses. The new reign opened with the clatter of hooves upon stone.

Edward I looked the part. He was of 'great stature', according to Nicholas Trevet, a Dominican scholar who knew him well. His long legs caused him to be known as 'Edward Longshanks'; when he hunted, he galloped after the stag with his drawn sword. He was considered to be 'the best lance in the world', which meant that he embodied all of the chivalric virtues of pride and honour. He was quick to anger, and quick to forgive. Trevet stated that the king was guided by '*animo magnifico*', or what might be described as magnanimity, but this may merely be a truism applied to a warrior king. He had a slight lisp, or stammer, and his left eyelid drooped in the same manner as that of his father. He could be very fierce. When the dean of St Paul's Cathedral approached him in order to complain about the taxation of the clergy, the unfortunate cleric expired on the spot. The archbishop of York, after being rebuked by Edward, died of depression. The aura or presence of the king was very powerful.

As soon as the great golden crown of state had been placed upon Edward's head at his coronation, he removed it with a dramatic gesture. He then made a statement that deviated from the set procedures of the ceremony. 'I will never take up this crown again,' he declared, 'until I have recovered the lands given away by my father to the earls, barons and knights of England and to the aliens.' He was as good as his word. Over the next twenty years he established commissions that looked into the supposed rights and claims of the landowners of the country. The phrase used was *quo warranto?*, 'by what right or title' do you hold these lands? Which of course might mean – surely they are mine? The whole process created a nest of lawyers. As a piece of contemporary verse put it:

And the Quo Warranto
Will give us all enough to do.

One old nobleman, when asked by what right, simply bran-dished his sword. That was the ancient and instinctive response. Come and fight me for it. But no lord, however mighty, could fight Edward. He had learned the lessons of his father's long and confused rule.

In the first parliament of his reign, convened at Westminster in the spring of 1275, Edward further strengthened his hold upon the kingdom. With some 800 representatives, it was the largest parliament ever assembled. Edward can in fact be considered the first king to use that body in a constructive manner. He invited its members to submit complaints about malfeasance or maladminis-tration, some of them no doubt designed to trim the power of over-mighty lords. These complaints were known as 'petitions' and from this time forward parliament was held to be in part a judicial tribunal. Petitions soon arose from all over the kingdom. There were too many of them, and they impeded the work of the parliament, but they had one valuable function. They allowed the king to see what was going on in the various regions of the realm.

At the same time the demand of the king for more taxes turned the knights and burgesses into a definite group; they were the ones, after all, who would have to levy the money from their shires and their towns. So they began to deliberate together, in the chapter house of Westminster Abbey, and came to be distinguished from the prelates and barons. They were not a 'House' of Commons, but they had common interests. They were essentially a parliamentary committee, duly subservient to the full parliament of their betters. They were not always summoned by the king, but steadily they grew in importance. The bishops and magnates still determined the great matters of state, but the knights and burgesses were the voices of those who were being taxed. There would soon come a time when their assent, and oversight, became vital. It should be stressed, however, that there was no general demand from the towns and the shires for representation. It was the king who called forth the knights and townsmen; he imposed upon his subjects the duty of coming to parliament, where he might command them and tax them. When they had obeyed his will, he dismissed them.

In the parliament of 1275 Edward extracted from the assembled lords and knights and townsmen a tax upon the export of wool;

from this time forward the king received 6 shillings and 8 pence upon every sack shipped out of the country. At one stroke, his finances were improved. He handed over their care to the Riccardi bankers of Lucca. In other legislation he bore down heavily upon the Jews, but this is matter for Chapter 20. In the same parliament a long and complicated Act, known as 'the statute of Westminster the First', was passed by which the king intended 'to revive neglected laws that had long been sleeping because of his predecessors' weakness'; these neglected laws, of course, were those that implied or required strong royal control. In a similar move towards royal dominance he replaced most of the sheriffs of the counties with men whom he knew and trusted.

Edward I, unlike his ancestors, had no great empire. Instead he had a kingdom, which he determined to strengthen and consolidate. He first marched into Wales, where he set up the line of castles that still endures. Edward's castles are magnificent creations, in part conceived as the edifices of chivalric romance. The king had a very strong attraction to the mythical history of Arthur and the Round Table; by claiming kinship with his fabulous predecessor, he could also claim sovereignty over the whole island. Arthur was known as 'the last emperor of Britain'. Yet he had been considered by many to have been a Welsh or British king fighting against a Saxon enemy. It was rumoured that he was not dead, only resting, and that he would come again to destroy the enemies of the Welsh. This was not comforting news for Edward's English soldiers.

So his death, and permanent removal from the arena of combat, had in some way to be confirmed. It was fortunate that the bodies of Arthur and Guinevere had been discovered by miracle, in the grounds of Glastonbury Abbey, during the reign of Henry II. Now Edward decreed that the bodies should be dug up, and then reinterred in a magnificent sarcophagus. The corpses of Arthur and Guinevere, if such they were, were wrapped in silk by Edward and his queen before being placed in a tomb of black marble. Their skulls were retained for public display. They were definitely dead. Such was the pious belief in the efficacy of the past, however, that elaborate rituals were considered to be necessary.

The Welsh castles of Edward I, like the stone edifices of imperial Rome and of Norman England, are tokens of brute power.

The walls of the castle at Conway are 10 feet (3 metres) thick. Fifteen hundred workmen and craftsmen laboured on its construction for four years. The towers and masonry of Caernarfon Castle are based upon the double line of walls built around Constantinople by the emperor Theodosius in the fifth century; it was written in legend that the father of the emperor Constantine was buried at Caernarfon, so the historical allusions are clear. The new building also retains the motte of the Norman castle, originally built upon the site, as an emblem of previous English sovereignty. The supervisor of the works at Caernarfon, Conway, Criccieth, Harlech and Beaumaris – Master James of St George – was one of the great spirits of the age through whom the genius of a warrior aristocracy was embodied.

Edward believed that, in the conquest of Wales, he was pursuing his own regal rights in the same spirit that inspired the '*quo warranto?*' investigations. This was his land. Or so he declared. The Atlantic folk, who had lived in the territory for many thousands of years, may not have agreed with him. With a cavalry force of approximately 1,000 men Edward chased the Welsh from mountain to mountain, and from hill to hill, until the native princes finally submitted to his authority. English law, and the English system of shires, were then imposed upon them. In the safety of the shadow of the castle walls, settlements of English colonists were introduced. Towns sprang up from markets. The life of the country was being quickened. Subsequent revolts and rebellions disturbed the peace, but the settlement itself has never since been overturned. When all was complete the king held an Arthurian tournament at Nefyn, a small coastal town from where the *Prophecies of Merlin* were supposed to emanate.

The costs of this war of conquest had been huge. That is why Edward called so large a parliament early in his reign; the wider the net, the larger the catch. The whole country was soon enmeshed in a general system of taxation that heralded the rise of a fiscal state. It was a necessity of war that became, almost by accident, a principal element of the English administration.

The taxation on wool, also passed by the parliament, materially assisted the king's treasury. But it had further consequences.

Edward set up the system of customs that, for better or worse, has been a feature of English economic life ever since. For the first time the king was seen to be acting in concert with the merchants, to whom he now offered his protection. Foreign traders were granted certain privileges. They were allowed to come and go as they wished, were made free from interference by local officials and were immune from local taxes. The merchants of Gascony and elsewhere were given the status of citizens in all dealings with Londoners.

The king's connection with the bankers of Lucca meant that he was now involved in questions of international finance; that is why he took great care to preserve the standard of the money supply. Debased coinage would not bolster his prestige with the brokers of Europe. A more elaborate system of credit, borrowed from the financiers of Venice and Genoa, was introduced to England. The necessities of war once more created the context for innovation.

Edward also found ingenious ways of making money. The law stated that those with property worth more than £20 a year were obliged to adopt the status of knights; but knighthood was an expensive business, with the cost of equipment alone, and many landowners were ready to pay a relatively large sum to avoid the honour. By an order known as 'distraint of knighthood' Edward ordered that all eligible men should bear arms, and then proceeded to collect the money from those who wished to remain exempt. It was a legal form of extortion.


Edward I was once known as the 'English Justinian' on the grounds that he gave shape and purpose to English law. The great jurist of the seventeenth century, Edward Coke, remarked that he enacted 'more constant, standing, and durable laws than have been made ever since'. The 'Statute of Westminster the First', passed in the earliest parliament of his reign, was followed by nine other statutes ranging from matters of law and order to the debts of merchants. They were practical and specific measures to confront immediate problems. In the Statute of Winchester, for example, it was decreed that all hedges and underwood should be cleared from the sides of the highways to a distance of 200 feet (61 metres); they could not then be used to provide shelter for thieves.

The measure was timely and necessary. Parts of the countryside were beset by marauding gangs, many of them drawn from the soldiers who had fought in Edward's wars. There were no other rewards for old soldiers. Other groups of ruffians were hired by members of the local gentry in order to pursue private feuds or to terrify their tenants. So special courts known as 'trailbaston', which meant the act of clenching a club or staff, were set up to deal with acts of felony and trespass. The name originally described the ruffians themselves, and then became applied to the judges who sentenced them.

The king took his share of the proceeds of justice, of course, and the judges themselves grew rich. They were despised as much as they were feared. In some of the popular verses of the period the judges are compared unfavourably to those outlaws who sought refuge in the woods. What difference between the thieves in hiding and the thieves in office? In one song the usher of the court addresses a defendant. 'Poor man, why do you trouble yourself? Why do you wait here? Unless you give money to everybody in this court, you labour in vain. If you have brought nothing, you will stand altogether out of doors.' We have here a medieval paradox. Even as the law was being shaped and refined, the exponents of the law were mocked and vilified. Royal law was being condemned even as it was being extended.

Nevertheless forms and procedures had to be followed; there had developed a legal routine. In the period of Edward's reign the number of attorneys rose from approximately 10 to 200. They became a new elite. Where there is money to be made, there are people who will wish to create privileged access to it. The phenomenon itself is of a piece with other developments of the early fourteenth century. The households of the great were being run by staffs of trained managers, and farms were organized by estate managers. War itself was being professionalized. The king no longer summoned a national host from the shires; instead he came more and more to rely upon paid troops led by full-time commanders. As the business of the realm became more complex, it became the province of full-time officers whom we might describe as a civil service; the chancery alone employed more than 100 clerks, and had a secure home at Westminster. The first proper parliamentary record, giving an account of proceedings, dates from 1316.

Yet the force of the royal will was still paramount. Two judges were once arguing a case in the king's presence. Edward was beginning to lose patience with their lengthy deliberations. Eventually he interrupted them, saying, 'I have nothing to do with your disputations, but God's blood, you shall give me a good writ before you arise hence!' He did not mean good in the sense of meritorious; he meant one that worked in his favour. The monkish author of *The Song of Lewes* had written of Edward, when he was a prince, that 'whatever he wants he holds to be lawful, and he thinks that there are no legal bounds to his power'.

Edward had remained in Gascony from 1286 to 1289, seeking to control the affairs of the land that mattered as much to him as England. On his return he discovered, according to one chronicler, 'a very real oppression hanging over the country'. One of his clerical servants, Adam de Stratton, had acquired an unsavoury reputation for various financial malpractices. He was part of a system of bribery and corruption that had flourished more than ever in the king's absence of three years. The rage of the king was wonderful to behold. He stormed into the chambers of the man, exclaiming, 'Adam! Adam! Where art thou?' In Adam's house, at Smalelane near the Fleet Prison, was found a hoard of £13,000.

Edward could trust only the advisers whom he had taken with him to Gascony, and he ordered them to find out the truth about all accusations. As a result of their enquiries many judges were found to be manifestly corrupt. One of them, the chief justice on the Bench of Common Pleas, fled for sanctuary to a Franciscan friary. From there he was forced to abjure the realm, walking barefoot to Dover with a cross in his hand. The king had returned from abroad, and had become an avenging angel. Once more he had proved his strength.

In November 1290, his queen died. Eleanor of Castile is not well known to history. She is supposed to have been devout, but her principal devotion was to her family's interests; she speculated in land, for example, and took financial advantage of those who were heavily in debt to the Jews. One contemporary reveals that 'day by day the said lady continues to acquire plunder and the possessions of others by these means. There is public outcry and gossip about this in every part of England.' In this she was not very different from other members of the family who, travelling in the wake of Edward, were inclined to be rapacious and mercenary; it was one of the settled policies of his realm that his kinsmen should be granted the great earldoms of the realm. Four of his daughters were safely married to the richest magnates and were given extensive lands.

The king was much affected by his wife's death, and along the route of her burial procession from her deathbed in Nottinghamshire to her sepulchre in Westminster he caused to be erected a series of crosses. These are the 'Eleanor crosses', three of which still stand at Geddington, Northampton and Waltham Cross. Another of them, at Charing Cross, is a replica and is in the wrong place. After the funeral the king went into a religious retreat for more than a month.

By March 1291, however, he was on the border with Scotland. He had travelled there to arbitrate between the claimants to the Scottish throne, on the assumption that he was somehow overlord of the kingdom. He chose one of them, John Balliol, and then proceeded to treat him as a vassal. The Scots would not endure this situation for long. Four years later Balliol was persuaded by his barons to renounce his homage to the English king, ally himself with the French monarch, and declare for independence. Edward then marched north and, within a matter of weeks, had subdued the Scottish army. Dunbar opened its gates to him; Edinburgh made a token resistance; Perth and St Andrews submitted unconditionally. He destroyed Berwick and butchered the people savagely; according to a chronicler thousands of the inhabitants 'fell like autumn leaves'. He seemed to have a thirst for blood.

Edward now believed himself in truth to be the proper king of Scotland. Lia Fáil, 'the speaking stone' otherwise known as 'the stone of destiny', was taken from Scone Palace and removed to Westminster Abbey where it remained until 1996. According to legend it formed the pillow on which Jacob's head rested when he was vouchsafed the vision of the angels ascending the ladder. It is in truth an oblong rectangular block of limestone, pitted and fretted with age. But it was a token of Scottish destiny. When Edward handed the seal of Scotland to its new English governor, he remarked that 'a man does good business when he rids himself of a turd'. One Scottish patriot was determined to cure him of this complacency. William Wallace had fled to the safety of the woods, having been convicted of murder, and there he gathered together a band of disaffected men.

Curiously enough Edward had placed Balliol in an invidious situation similar to his own; as lord of Gascony and duke of Aquitaine, Edward was theoretically the vassal of the king of France. This meant that, in practice, he was continually colliding with the interests of the court at Paris. It took only a small spark to light a modest flame. Some rowdy fights between English and Norman sailors led to reprisals and confrontations; the French king then summoned the English king to his court and, when he refused, he declared Edward's lands in France to be confiscated.

Edward sailed with his army across the Channel in 1297, although many of the participants were quite unwilling to join this continental endeavour. Why should they fight for Edward's lands in France when they derived no benefit from them? The earl of Norfolk and marshal of England, Roger Bigod, had refused to take command of the army. 'Bigod,' the king said in a rage, 'you shall go or hang.' 'By God, sir,' the earl replied, 'I shall neither go nor hang.' He did not go. In fact Edward never actually engaged his opponents in battle. He sailed to Flanders to attack the French king from the north, but he did no more than bluster. In the end he signed a treaty, by which he retained Gascony, and then he sealed it with a kiss. He married the French king's sister, Margaret, making sure that European power stayed within the family.

The news nearer home was more disquieting. Reports of a Scottish invasion were widespread and, in the autumn of 1297, William Wallace and his men defeated an English army at Stirling Bridge. More significantly, a domestic rebellion was growing in the face of royal extortions. The taxation for the French expedition had been immense. The king had taken one fifth of the income of the clergy; the clerics had at first refused to grant as much, and the king promptly outlawed them on the grounds that a body which did not support the country did not deserve to be protected by it. The goods of the clergy were seized, and the courts of law were closed to them. Their tenants refused to pay rent, and often physically attacked them. They were in the end compelled to surrender to the force of a powerful and ruthless king.

They were not the only ones to suffer from his depredations. The citizens of London were compelled to part with a sixth of their moveable wealth. Edward had increased the customs on exports of wool, and as a result the merchants had cut payments to their suppliers. The wool tax became known as the 'bad tax' or 'maltote'. The plight of those in the countryside who suffered from excessive taxation is captured in a vernacular poem written in 1300, *Song of the Husbandman*:

> Yet cometh budeles [beadles] with ful muche bost [pride]:
> 'Greythe me selver [silver] to the grene wax [official
>     document].
> Thou art writen yn my writ, that thou wel wost [know]!'

Every fourth penny went to the king; seed-corn, and immature corn, had to be sold in order to raise money for taxes; the king's bailiffs seized oxen and cattle; bribes were paid to the royal officials; some people were forced to flee their lands because they could not afford to be taxed. Royal officials had taken grain from the farmers in order to feed the troops in France. Edward also levied fines and taxes on the great magnates, with whom he never enjoyed satisfactory relations.

Whereupon some of the earls – Roger Bigod among them – decided that it was time to confront the king. Another round of warfare between king and barons seemed to be inevitable. The regency council that governed the nation during the king's absence, under the nominal command of the king's young son, retreated for safety within the walls of London. A baronial army was assembled at Northampton. At this point the royal party gave in. With the news of the defeat at Stirling Bridge before them, they could not risk a war on two fronts. The earls demanded a reissue of the Magna Carta with important new provisions, such as the removal of the 'maltote'. This was granted to them. It was now solemnly sworn that there would never be taxation without the consent of those being taxed. The king returned a month later from his inconclusive overseas adventures, and reluctantly agreed. The Magna Carta had, by slow degrees, now become the guardian of English liberty – or at least the English economy – against royal aggression.

The earls then for the most part turned their attention towards the threat from Scotland. Edward convened a parliament in York, a sure sign that he was now intent upon subduing the northern regions. He gathered a great army of more than 28,000 men, including the soldiers previously posted to Flanders and Gascony. Yet a major victory for the English at Falkirk in 1298 over the army of William Wallace did not prove decisive, and the next six years of the Scottish wars consisted of seasonal campaigns in which the English forces were matched by fierce native resistance. The Scots eventually came to terms in 1304, and a year later William Wallace was captured; he was dragged on a pallet from Westminster to Smithfield, where he was ritually hanged, disembowelled while still alive, and quartered. A plaque is still fixed to the wall close to the point where he was killed. Yet all the butchery did not work against a determined people. A year after Wallace's execution, Robert Bruce was crowned king of Scotland at Scone. The old war continued.

As long as the war was being prosecuted successfully, the magnates took the side of the king; but in periods of failure or indecision the huge sums of taxation that the wars incurred became a matter of considerable concern. The king was, as always, untrustworthy; he tried various means of evading the provisions of the Magna Carta to which he had assented. He was so convinced of his rectitude that any means of attaining his ends was considered acceptable. That is the point – in all his demands and exactions, the king never thought that he was doing anything wrong. He was behaving only as a king ought to behave. He was raising *his* money from *his* country in order to wage war against those who threatened him. That was his duty. The magnates were suspicious and resentful, but they did not rebel. They harried him, and chided him, but they did not seek to overthrow him. He was now growing old as well as stubborn and irate. They waited for his death, and the reign of his son. An unfinished war, combined with a rapidly growing debt, were the two stones against which the last ten years of Edward were ground. The king's finances were in disorder, with all the prudent measures of previous years discarded or ignored. Edward had been made by war, and would be broken by war.

In 1307 Robert Bruce appeared at the head of an army, ready to claim his rights as the crowned king of Scotland, and at Loudoun Hill in Ayrshire defeated an English force that had been ordered to hunt him down. Edward decided to march north, with the settled purpose of destroying Scottish royal ambitions for good, but even the best-laid plans are never perfect. In the summer of 1307, at the age of sixty-eight, Edward I died at Burgh-by-Sands on the Solway.

We may grow weary of the life and death of kings but in truth, for an historical account of medieval England, there is no other sure or certain touchstone. The general current of the nation persists beneath the surface of action and event but, as a result, it is not susceptible to chronology. The institutions of the state are similarly outside the historical record. They can be inferred and described, at rough intervals, but there is really no appropriate timescale. Administrative history has no proper narrative. This is also the case with the life and development of the English towns. As for the English people themselves, they can be glimpsed fleetingly in political ballads and in court records. Of their suffering, and of their pleasures, little is known. They are largely absent from the written record simply because they were not considered important; they were not worthy of representation.

They emerge, however, in certain manorial accounts. We may read for example, in the accounts of the manor of Sutton, of Stephen Puttock. He was a *nativus* who, at the end of the thirteenth century, lived and worked on the prior of Ely's land in that manor. He owed labour services to his lord and was obliged to pay certain fines or taxes at the ritual moments of his family's life. He had to pay a fine, for example, when he married each of his two wives; his sister was similarly taxed when she was married. He was also fined when he failed to carry out his labour services; he may have been negligent in planting or harvesting his lord's crops. Yet he was a significant man in his own village. He had a large holding of his own land, and was appointed both as reeve and as ale-taster in his community; he was also frequently selected as a juryman. He was an acquisitive purchaser of land, buying it in parcels of several acres at a time. Stephen Puttock was a man of his time, taking part in an unconscious life of custom and tradition. He was unfree, but he was prosperous; he was a labourer, but he was also a landowner. He was part of a nexus of duties and obligations, but he was also a prominent part of his community. He has now returned to the soil of England.

Another means of access to the general life of the period comes in the now voluminous court reports. They provide of course a haphazard account, based upon civic or criminal offences, but they are suggestive. The fowler, Robert, spends a great deal of money but no one knows how he earns it; he wanders abroad at night, so he is suspected. John Voxe was fined fourpence for cutting down two ash trees on his land. Another man was fined for fishing in his lord's pool. Ranulph, the fishmonger, goes out to the oyster boats in order to buy up their catch before it reaches the market. Three men were arrested as 'common breakers of hedges to the common harm'. The butchers of Sprowston bought infirm pigs cheaply, and then sold sausages unfit for human consumption. John Foxe, a chaplain, was fined one penny for attacking William Pounchon with a knife. Walter of Maidstone, a carpenter, brought together an assembly or parliament of carpenters at Mile End in order to agree on a policy to defy the mayor. The butchers of Peterborough were reminded that they must cleanse the churchyard of all filth and bones that their dogs brought into it. Certain people made 'a great roistering with unknown minstrels, tabor-players and trumpeters' to the grave disquiet of the entire neighbourhood.

Here is another vignette of medieval England. John and Agnes Page, from a village in Kent, took John Pistor to the manor court. Agnes Page had purchased John Pistor's wife in exchange for a pig worth 3 shillings; John Pistor was happy with the arrangement for a while, but eventually he asked that his wife be returned to him on payment of 2 shillings. The bargain was agreed, but Pistor did not pay the sum. The jury found against him.

We may sense here a life more intense and more arduous than our own; it was at once more sensitive and more irritable. The contrasts of life were more violent, and the insecurities more palpable. This evidence is all of a piece with a strident and often violent society where the growing number of people provoked collision and unrest.

It has been estimated that by the beginning of the fourteenth century the population had reached in excess of 6 million. The figure, in isolation, means nothing at all. But it is salutary to realize that it was not matched again until the latter part of the eighteenth century. The England of Edward I was more populous than that of Elizabeth I or of George II. So in the relatively crowded conditions of the early fourteenth century, land was at a premium. The woods and underwoods were cleared. Farming land was often divided and subdivided into smaller and smaller parcels, owned by men who also earned their living as carpenters or shoemakers. But many landless men were also available for hire; wages, therefore, were not ordinarily very high. Great pressure, and competition, existed within all sectors of the economy. The first 'strike fund', to support workers who refused to do mowing services, was organized in 1300.

The condition of England was made infinitely worse by a series of harvest failures from 1315. The price of bread, and other essential commodities, rose and rose. 'Alas, poor England!' one chronicler of the time wrote. 'You who once helped other lands from your abundance, now poor and needy are forced to beg.' This was one of the worst periods of English social history, and may act as a suitably troubled context for the last years of the reign of Edward I as well as the unhappy reign of Edward II. It might have been said at the time – the kings of England do nothing but harm.

# 20

# The hammer

Edward was known as 'the hammer of the Scots' but he could more pertinently be known as the hammer of the Jews. He exploited them and harassed them; finally he expelled them. Their crime was to become superfluous to his requirements. The history of the Jews in medieval England is an unhappy and even bloody one. They had arrived, from Rouen, in the last decades of the eleventh century; they were first only settled in London across a broad band of nine parishes but in the course of the next few decades they also removed to York, Winchester, Bristol and other market towns. The previous rulers of England, in the ninth and tenth centuries, had not welcomed them; Jewish merchants would have provided too much competition for Anglo-Saxon traders.

William the Conqueror brought them to England because he had found that in Normandy they had been good for business; in particular they provided access to the silver of the Rhineland. The Jews of Rouen may also have helped to finance his invasion of England, in return for the chance to work in a country from which they had previously been barred. Another reason can be given for the favour they found with the king. Since Christians were not allowed to lend money at interest, some other group of merchants had to be created. The Jews became moneylenders by default, as it were, and as a result they were abused and despised in equal measure. But they did not only lend money; they were also moneychangers and goldsmiths. They exchanged plate for coin. They provided ready money, a commodity often in short supply.

The Norman kings of England, therefore, found them to be very useful. They could borrow from them but, more profitably, they could tax them. They could levy what were known as 'tallages', and succeeding kings were able to take between a third and a quarter of the Jews' total wealth at any one time. As a result the Jews, in the twelfth century, were afforded royal protection. No Jew was allowed to become a citizen, or to hold land, but the neighbourhood of the Jewry was like the royal forests exempt from common law; the Jews were simply the king's chattels, who owed their life and property wholly to him. They were granted the protection of the royal courts, and their bonds were placed in a special chamber of the royal palace at Westminster. A Jewish exchequer was established there, with its own clerks and justices.

In return for royal favour the Jews brought energy and prosperity to the business of the realm; their loans helped to make possible the great feats of Norman architecture, and the unique stone houses of Lincoln and Bury St Edmunds are credited to them. Jacob le Toruk had a grand stone house in Cannon Street, in the London parish of St Nicholas Acon. The Jews also introduced the more advanced forms of medical learning, and were able to serve as doctors even to the native community. Roger Bacon himself studied under rabbis at Oxford.

More dubious legal tactics were also enforced. William Rufus decreed, for example, that Jews could not be converted to Christianity; he did not want their number to fall. That may not have been a very Christian act, but William Rufus was never a very good Christian. He supported the Jews partly because it offended the bishops; he enjoyed causing affront to his churchmen.

That royal protection did not necessarily extend very far. At the time of the coronation of Richard I, in 1189, some Jews were beaten back from the front row of spectators; the crowd turned on them, and a riotous assault began upon the London quarters of Jewry. The incident became the cause of fresh outrages as the news of the attack spread; it emboldened native hostility, and gave an excuse for further carnage. 500 Jews, with their families, took refuge in the castle at York where they were besieged by the citizens; in desperation the men killed their wives and children before killing themselves. Richard was even then making preparations for his crusade to the Holy Land; violence and religious bigotry were in the air. His successor, John, renewed his protection in exchange for large sums of money. In 1201 a formal charter was drawn up, giving the Jews their own court. They were allowed to live 'freely and honourably' in England, which meant that they were here to make money for the king. Nine years later John took over all the debts of the Jews, living or dead, and tried to extract the money from the debtors for his own benefit. It was another reason for the barons' revolt that led to the sealing of the Magna Carta.

Anti-Semitism was part of the Christian condition throughout Europe. The Jewish people were abused for being the 'killers of Christ', with convenient forgetfulness of the fact that Jesus himself was a Jew, but other more material reasons accounted for the racial hatred. By the middle of the twelfth century several prominent Jewish moneylenders had extended very large loans to some of the noblest men in the kingdom; men like the famous Aaron of Lincoln were the only ones with resources large enough to meet the obligations of the magnates. If they could be attacked or killed, and their bonds destroyed, then the great ones of the land would benefit. The myth that they were engaged in the 'ritual murder' of Christian infants became common at times of financial crisis, when the populace could be incited to take sanguinary vengeance. It is a matter of historical record that England took the lead in the execration of the Jews. The first rumour of a ritual crucifixion emerged in 1144, with the story of the death of William of Norwich, and thereafter the tales of ritual murder spread through Europe. England was also the first country to condemn all Jews as criminal 'coin-clippers', and the iconography of anti-Semitism is to be found on the west front of Lincoln Cathedral.

In 1239, during the reign of Henry III, a great census of the Jews and their debts was carried out. The representatives of all the Jews in England were then obliged to convene at Worcester and agree to pay over 20,000 marks to the king's treasury. This measure effectively bankrupted some of them, which meant that their usefulness had come to an end. Fourteen years later, Henry III ordained a Statute of Jewry that enforced a number of disciplinary measures, including the compulsory badge of identification. This was a token or *tabula* of yellow felt, 3 inches by 6 inches (7.5 by 15 centimetres), to be worn on an outer garment; it was to be carried by every Jew over the age of seven years. Two years later Henry investigated the death of a boy, Hugh, in Lincoln; he believed or professed to believe that this was a crime of ritual murder and, as a result, 19 Jews from that city were executed and 100 despatched to prison in the castle.

Edward I was even more ferocious. He ordered that certain Jews, who had been acquitted of the charge of ritual murder, be retried. In November 1278, 600 Jews were imprisoned in the Tower of London on charges of tampering with the currency; 269 of them were hanged six months later. In 1290 he expelled all of the remaining Jews from his kingdom; they were now approximately 2,000. He did not take this step out of misplaced religious zeal; it was the measure demanded by the parliament house before they would agree to fresh taxation. In fact the expulsion was seen by many chroniclers as one of the most important and enlightened acts of his reign. The anti-Semitism of the medieval English people is clear enough. Some have argued that, in subtly modified forms, it has continued to this day.

# 21

# The favourites of a king

The new king, Edward II, had been born in 1284 on the site of his father's new castle at Caernarfon; Eleanor's labour came to an end in temporary accommodation beside the castle that had only been begun in the previous year. She may have been brought to the spot in a deliberate move by the king to lay claim to this part of the island. In later life the new king was known as 'Edward of Caernarfon' and in 1301 he was acclaimed as 'prince of Wales', the first heir of the throne to be thus designated.

He did not care much for his principality. In 1305 he sent a letter to his cousin, Louis, count of Evreux, in which he promised to send 'some misshapen greyhounds of Wales, which can catch a hare well if they find it asleep, and running dogs which can follow at an amble. And, dear cousin, if you would care for anything else from our land of Wales, we will send you some wild men, if you like, who will know well how to give young sprigs of noblemen their education.' If nothing else, he had a sense of humour.

He was brought up in a military household, and was engaged in his father's last Scottish wars. After the defeat of the English army by Robert Bruce at Loudoun, he vowed that he would not spend two nights in the same place until he had exacted revenge. He never kept the promise. He was not in any case as bellicose or as overbearing as his father. He always disliked taking part in tournaments. The writer of a contemporary life of the king, Ranulf Higden, remarked that 'he did not care for the company of lords, but preferred to mingle with harlots, with singers and jesters'. He also was most at ease with 'carters and delvers and ditchers, with shipmen and boatmen, and with other craftsmen'. It is hard to interpret this last remark, except as a general indication that the young prince was not particularly interested in royal pursuits. This was the rebuke that followed him in succeeding years. He did not behave like a king.

The coronation of 1307 did not go quite according to plan. The crown was carried, much to the scandal of the great lords, by a close companion of the king with the name of Piers or Peter Gaveston. The number of people at the ceremony was so large that a plaster wall collapsed, bringing down the high altar and the royal scaffolding for the service. One knight was killed. The service was then quickly and even summarily completed. There was an indication that the new king was not altogether trusted. A new provision had been added to the coronation oath. The king now declared that he would 'uphold and defend the laws and righteous customs that the community of the realm shall choose'. The 'community of the realm', in this instance, meant the magnates and prelates. It was an ominous beginning.

The royal banquet, after the ceremony, was also badly managed. Piers Gaveston seemed inclined to outshine even the king with a costume of imperial purple and pearls. When Edward preferred the couch of Gaveston to that of his queen, Isabella of France, his wife's relatives returned indignant to their homeland. We have here the makings of a royal disaster.

Gaveston was the same age as Edward. The old king had placed him in the prince's household to provide a fitting military example to his heir, but they may have had other interests in common. There quickly grew up an attachment between the two young men that some have considered to be sexual, but which others have believed to be simply fraternal. He has been described as Edward II's 'minion' but that is a courtly and chivalric term which does not imply homosexuality; Henry VIII had his minions. It was considered proper that the king, at court, should lean upon the shoulder of his minion. It was an accepted posture. Modern sexual terms have no meaning in fourteenth-century England, where in any case they would not have been understood. Edward did have a bastard son, Adam, even before he became king. Isabella herself would subsequently give birth to two sons and two daughters.

It is certain only that the young king preferred the company of Gaveston to that of his new bride. He had married the twelve-year-old Isabella, daughter of the king of France, on the orders of his father intent upon creating yet another grand and prosperous territorial alliance. The wedding had taken place in France a month before the coronation and, in his absence, Edward had appointed Gaveston as the keeper of the realm. This in itself was enough to arouse the envy and wrath of the English magnates. One of Edward's first acts as king was then to honour Gaveston with the earldom of Cornwall, a title generally kept within the royal family. This was a serious blow to courtly protocol, and was more than a problem of etiquette. It was a question of land and money as well as title; if they were not properly distributed by the king, was then anyone safe? It was even believed that Gaveston himself had been given charge of patronage at court, granting goods and benefits without consultation with the barons. There could be no more important office in the fourteenth-century royal court, and it raised immediate problems about the king's judgment.

Gaveston did not help matters with a waspish wit and a strong sense of his own importance. He was reported to be 'haughty and arrogant' with a pride 'intolerable to the barons'. He invented nicknames for the leading magnates, such as 'black dog' for the earl of Warwick and 'burst belly' for the earl of Lincoln. He revelled in the king's grace.

A parliament was held in the spring of 1308, at which the earl of Lincoln invoked the new provision of the coronation oath and demanded that Gaveston be dismissed from court. Edward refused but two months later, cowed by the presence of the magnates with their armed knights, he agreed to exile his favourite to Ireland. He wrote to the pope admitting that there had been 'disturbance and dissension' and that he had not yet 'fully enforced unity'. This was the period, too, when his cousin abruptly left the court. Thomas of Lancaster was another grandson of Henry III, and was perhaps the richest as well as the best-connected noble in the land. He had also become disaffected, with fatal consequences for Piers Gaveston.

A year after his exile in Ireland, the favourite was back. The king had recalled him for assistance in his campaign against Robert Bruce. The Scots refused a set battle, however, and so the king was reduced to a number of sorties and skirmishes that still left the northern part of his kingdom unprotected against attack. Unlike his father, he had not kept the peace.

He had not kept his promises, either. The likely shape of his reign had already become clear. He was considered by the magnates to be weak and ineffectual. He slept late. He prevaricated. None of this would necessarily disqualify a modern monarch but, in fourteenth-century England, it was inexcusable. A king was supposed to embody the prowess and vigour of the country. The failure of the Scottish campaign was a specific sign of the king's general incapacity. It was further stated that he had so badly managed his resources that his entire household was in decay; as a result he had extorted money unfairly. Numerous complaints were also made concerning specific infringements of Magna Carta, such as the unjust seizure of lands and the misuse of writs.

The parliament of 1311 issued a set of twenty-four ordinances by which the king was supposed to govern. It was declared that the country was on the point of open revolt 'on account of oppressions, prises and destructions'; 'prises' were the confiscations made by royal officials. One contemporary chronicler wrote that the threat of deposition was made against Edward if he failed to comply; if that is correct, then the forces against the king rivalled those against King John a hundred years before. The rebel lords called themselves 'the community of the realm' but they were no abstract or objective force; they were not a constitutional 'party'. It was a world in which the force of individual personality was the cause and spring of action; personal rivalries and affections made up the politics of the period.

The ordinances themselves were designed to produce what might be called baronial rule. The king was not permitted to make war, or leave the kingdom, without the consent of the barons; the king's justice and the king's treasury must come under their supervision. A parliament, naturally under their control, would meet once a year. One other stipulation was made. Gaveston, once more, had to go. He was to be banished from the realm before All Saints' Day, 1 November.

The king refused to countenance these demands and prepared himself for civil war. Gaveston did sail from Dover, two days after the stipulated date, but he returned a month later. Edward and his favourite then moved to the north, and began recruiting an army. It was at this point that the king's cousin, Thomas of Lancaster, became his most prominent challenger; Lancaster wrote to the queen, promising to rid the court of Piers Gaveston forever. And this was what he proceeded to do. Gaveston was taken at Scarborough, when the forces of the barons besieged the castle there, and a month later he was beheaded in the presence of Lancaster. Two sayings of the period have survived as an apt accompaniment to these events. 'There is no one who is sorry for me,' the king is supposed to have complained, 'no one fights for my rights against the barons.' The other is a more generalized statement: 'The love of magnates is as a game of dice, and the desires of the rich like feathers.'

The execution of Gaveston was according to precedent unlawful, since as earl of Cornwall he should have been judged by his peers, but it had the effect of bringing to a summary end the threat of civil war. The gratuitousness of the deed seems to have surprised everyone. Some of the rebel barons returned to the king. If there were a civil war, only the Scots would benefit. The prospect of further hostilities, and the threat of an enemy on the border, concentrated the minds of the lords. Negotiations, in and out of parliament, took place for the best part of two years. In October 1313 the rebel lords made a public apology in Westminster Hall, and the king resumed his powers very little affected by the ordinances of 1311. He had won a marginal, and provisional, victory that was compounded by the birth of a son that guaranteed the continuation of his dynasty. His hatred, for the murderers of his 'minion', smouldered.

But his power soon fell apart once more. He took an army into the north, finally to dispose of Robert Bruce, but at Bannockburn he suffered a mighty defeat. The battle was fought in what was called 'an evil, deep and wet marsh' wholly unsuited to the English

cavalry but more amenable to the Scottish infantry; the earl of
Gloucester led a charge into the Scottish ranks, but was cut down.
The army of the Scots then attacked the horsemen, crying out 'On
them! On them! On them! They fail!' The English were massacred,
their bodies lying in the marsh or in the river Bannock. The king
fled for his life and, with a few followers, sailed to Berwick where
he hoped to find safety. He had lost Scotland. The battle of
Bannockburn ensured the independence of that country, and was
perhaps the worst military disaster of any medieval English king.

It is difficult for a sovereign to survive the shame of defeat.
It implies the forfeiture of his single most important duty, that
of protecting his realm. Edward I had been known as 'the most
victorious king' and 'the conqueror of lands and the flower of
chivalry'. His son bore no such titles. When Edward eventually
arrived in York he was in disgrace. Thomas of Lancaster insisted
that once again he should be bound to the ordinances of 1311.
A contemporary chronicle reports that 'the king granted their
execution, and denied the earls nothing'.

Lancaster at this juncture took effective control of the kingdom,
but he proved no more popular or effective than his cousin; he
was considered to be arrogant and overbearing. He stayed on his
estates, and was loath to attend councils or parliaments. He did
not take advice. It was also rumoured that he was in secret contact
with Robert Bruce on the principle that the king's enemies might
become his own friends. The king stirred himself out of his
weakness or incapacity, and began to gather his supporters. Two
centres of power and of patronage existed, with the retainers of
the king and the earl vying for mastery. There cannot be two suns
in the sky.

A weak king seems always to presage, or to represent, a weak
country. In the medieval period there is some strange alchemy
between the state of the nation and the state of the monarch. The
harvests of three successive years from 1314 failed, as a result of
prolonged and torrential rain, and according to one chronicler there
ensued misery 'such as our age has never seen'. It became known
as the 'Great Famine', and from that period we can date the continual fall in the English population throughout the fourteenth
and fifteenth centuries. In the summer of 1315 the archbishop of

Canterbury ordered that every parish perform solemn processions; the clergy were to walk barefoot, surrounded by the sound of bells and by chanting, in order to implore mercy from God.

But God was not listening. The cost of wheat rose from 5 shillings to 40 shillings a quarter (28 pounds or 12.7 kilograms). Often there was no bread to buy. The prices of the basic commodities rose to a level higher than any previously recorded. The cattle and the sheep were destroyed by outbreaks of murrain. The population itself, laid low by starvation, was attacked by various forms of enteric fever that often proved fatal. Rumours of cannibalism abounded, but they were plausible rather than probable. The situation of the English garrison at Berwick, however, is instructive; as the horses began to die the cavalrymen boiled their carcases in order to eat the meat, and then left the bones to the infantry.

In northern England as a whole the situation was rendered increasingly desperate by the raids of Scottish gangs. The incidence of violent crime also increased, as the hungry and the dispossessed looked for relief. There are records of gangs of 'vagabonds' perpetrating robberies and assaults. Reports of 'corrupted air', and of strange alterations in the atmosphere, were frequent. Human beings were, as always, powerless in the face of great natural disasters. The bodies of the dead were lying in the streets. According to the *Brut* chronicle, 'so miche and so faste folc deiden, that unnethes [scarcely] men might ham bury'. Life for the majority of the English people was nasty, brutish and short.

Yet this was the period when, for two years, direct taxes were levied upon the people to pay for the Scottish wars and the royal household. Twelve thousand quarters (336,000 pounds or 152,480 kilograms) of corn and malt were needed to feed the armies, further depriving the people of their necessary food. The king and the noble lords were not particularly interested in the sufferings of the English, despite their claims to represent 'the community of the realm'; they were concerned only with their own wealth and power. The citizens of Bristol rose up in their despair and occupied the castle. It was written that 'to seek silver for the king, I sold my seed'.

By 1318 the worst of the famine was over, the spectre of starvation banished by a bountiful harvest. Prices steadied, and then fell. But signs of overall decline were still in evidence, with the spread of disease among cattle and a general contraction of agricultural production. There would be really no sustained recovery for a hundred years.


The king always relied upon a strong confidant to deal with the business of the realm; he could not of course put his faith in Thomas of Lancaster, because his cousin was implacably opposed to him. So he placed his trust in a new favourite. The successor to Gaveston was Hugh le Despenser who, together with his father of the same name, gained a considerable hold over the irresolute king. Despenser soon acquired lands and castles, particularly in Wales where the family was already strong, and as a result he alienated all the other lords of the principality. His officers assaulted or threatened anyone who stood in their way; they burned down barns, and laid false charges against prominent landowners.

Despenser, as the king's chamberlain, tried to conceal his thefts and extortions under the guise of constitutional propriety; it was his duty and responsibility to bring order to Wales. But everyone knew that his case was fraudulent. The king's favourite had once more become arrogant and over-mighty at the expense of the barons. Thomas of Lancaster then stepped forward, and announced that no reliance could be placed in the king or his courtiers. In the spring of 1321 the land and property of the Despensers were attacked by those whom they had disinherited; it was a form of revenge that came perilously close to civil war. One chronicler, Robert of Reading, wrote that now the king's 'infamy began to be notorious, his torpor, his cowardice, his indifference to his great inheritance'.

At the beginning of August in the same year the great lords of the north and the west came to London with their armed retinues, and insisted that the Despensers be expelled from the realm. They were accused of 'encroaching' upon royal power, and of controlling access to the king's presence. They had perverted the law and illegally gained custody of lands. Edward, faced with the solid phalanx of their enemies, yielded. The Despensers were banished from England.

Yet this was only the beginning of what turned into a general civil war. The king had decided that it was better to remove his opponents one by one. He besieged Leeds Castle, the home of one malcontent, and executed its garrison. These executions were not part of the chivalric code, and were met with widespread disapproval. They demonstrated, however, that the king was in earnest. He then recalled the Despensers, and began to organize a military campaign to defeat those whom he considered to be rebels against his power. Having mustered his forces at the beginning of March 1322, he defeated Thomas of Lancaster in battle. He had cornered his old enemy at last and, after a summary trial, he executed him. It was the first time that a sentence of death, on the charge of treason, had ever been directed at a member of the royal family. Lancaster had cut off the head of Piers Gaveston; Edward, long meditating his revenge, beheaded Lancaster.

Other members of noble families, who had taken Lancaster's part, were now at the king's mercy. 'Oh calamity,' the anonymous author of a life of Edward II wrote, 'to see men recently adorned in purple and fine linen now dressed in rags and imprisoned in chains.'

Many of these lords were hanged on the lands that they had once owned. The king ordered altogether twenty-five executions. No English sovereign had ever punished his enemies among the barons so mercilessly.

A curious sequel to Lancaster's execution can be recorded. He was conceived by many to be the noble opponent of a vicious enemy. As such, his memory was revered. At the site of his execution, and at his tomb in Pontefract Priory, there grew a sacred cult in which miracles were attested. A drowned child returned to life beside the tomb itself; a blind priest recovered his sight at the place of Lancaster's death. A servant of Hugh Despenser decided to shit on the same spot, as a gesture of contumely, but a little later his bowels were parted from his body. Another centre of piety was established at St Paul's Cathedral, in London, when a stone table commemorating Thomas of Lancaster became the site of further miracles. The king issued ordinances to dissuade the people from making pilgrimages to Pontefract or St Paul's, but he could not thwart the piety of the populace.

In this uncertain and disordered period sporadic outbreaks of violence arose throughout the country. In 1326 the chief baron of the exchequer, Robert Belers, was ambushed outside Melton Mowbray and murdered; the gang, led by Eustace de Folville, was well known. Five sons of a lord of the manor, John de Folville, had turned themselves into a criminal fraternity; they terrorized their home county of Leicestershire, with numerous murders and robberies. They hired themselves out as mercenaries, and kidnapped prominent local people in return for large ransoms. They even fought in foreign wars as part of the retinue of lordly patrons.

One of the brothers, Richard de Folville, had been appointed as rector of Teigh by his eldest brother. It was a convenient cover. When he and his followers were one day pursued by various officers of the peace, they took refuge in his church. From that vantage they shot many arrows, killing at least one of their pursuers. But then the local people took the law, literally, into their own hands; they dragged Richard from the church and beheaded him on the spot. The other brothers managed to escape justice.

Other criminal bands were to be found in the early decades of the fourteenth century. One leader called himself 'Lionel, king of the rout of raveners', and he wrote threatening letters from 'our castle of the wind in the Greenwood Tower'. So violence at the centre rippled through a country already troubled by famine and disease.

Smaller incidents of disorder are recorded. Robert Sutton insulted Roger of Portland, clerk of the sheriff of London, in open court; he put his thumb to his nose and exclaimed, 'Tprhurt! Tprhurt!'

John Ashburnham rode up to the sheriff's court, held in the open air, and so threatened the sheriff that he fled; at which point Ashburnham whistled on his fingers, as a signal that his men should rise up in ambush.

When a writ was served on Agnes Motte, she appealed to her neighbours; with drawn weapons they compelled the servers of the writ to eat it, wax and parchment.

When the mayor of Lynn tried to change the rules of trade, a crowd of tradesmen, under the leadership of the prior, dragged him from his house, placed him on a stall in the marketplace, and forced him to swear on the host that he would make no changes. It is interesting here that the prior of Lynn led the charge. But other clerics were involved in lawlessness. A gang of six monks from Rufford Priory attacked, and held to ransom, a local gentleman.

The rector of Manchester invited a local couple, with their daughter, to dinner. The rector's servants seized the daughter, broke two of her ribs, and then deposited her in the rector's bed; he had sex with her that night, but the unfortunate girl died from her injuries a month later.

The king's court at Westminster was not immune from lawlessness. An attorney was sitting on a table in the great hall – 'close to the sellers of jewels' – when the other party to his suit threatened to kill him if he did not abandon it; he was then dragged off the table and struck on the head. Someone else pulled a knife on him. The attorney extricated himself from his attackers and ran to the bar of the court calling for help; the men followed him, their swords drawn, but the officials of the court somehow managed to bar the doors against them. They were then disarmed and taken to the Tower.

In the summer of 1322 the king called a parliament at York, in the course of which a statute was passed that allowed him complete and independent rule. The ordinances of 1311 were once more abandoned. Contemporaries were in no doubt about the situation. The magnates were now too frightened to thwart the will of the king. Parliaments were of no account. Reason had given way to threats and penalties. Whatever pleased Edward, now had the force of law. He sought out the rebels in every shire, confiscating their lands or fining them heavily. His treasury grew and grew on the proceeds. 'Serve us in such a way that we will become rich', he wrote to the officials of his exchequer.

He was not to find riches in conquest. He led a campaign in Scotland against Robert Bruce, but achieved nothing except the detention of six Scottish prisoners; with the absence of provisions severely affecting his troops, he marched southwards across the border. But the Scottish army pursued him, and almost caught him near Bridlington in East Yorkshire; he fled in panic to York, a singularly unfortunate end to a futile expedition. He was forced to sign a treaty with Robert Bruce at the beginning of 1323, the principles of which he broke almost immediately. The king's bastard son, Adam, was killed in the course of the campaign.

The difficulties with France, over the disputed territory of Gascony, had not been resolved. The French had even planted a *bastide* or fortified town in the middle of the duchy. So the king sent his wife, Isabella, to negotiate with the French king, Charles IV; since she was that king's sister, some hope of success could be conjectured. But there was a problem. Edward did not trust Isabella, and Isabella had no affection for Edward. Once they were separated by the Channel, anything might happen. The king made another fateful decision; he sent his eldest son, Edward, to the French court to do fealty for the land of Gascony. Both wife and son were now in France.

The king did not travel there himself because he was too concerned about the stability of his own kingdom. It was said at the time that the Despensers advised him to stay at home, because they feared the wrath of the other barons descending upon them in his absence. There were reasons to be fearful. Edward's rule had become a form of covert tyranny. He became according to one chronicler 'as wood [mad] as a lion'. He disinherited many magnates so that the Despensers could have their lands; as a result, no landowner felt secure. When a king of England disregards the rights to property, he cannot long endure. For four years, however, Edward lavished earldoms and other titles on his favourites; he harried and persecuted all those who opposed his will. It was so arranged that revenue went into the king's own chamber rather than to the general exchequer, and the king demanded absolute secrecy from his officials. He resembled a later king in his counting-house, counting out his money. In truth his opponents could do nothing. After the execution of Lancaster, and the imprisonment of other prominent nobles, he was pre-eminent.

Yet he still had enemies in exile, particularly in France. One of them, Roger Mortimer, had been part of the rising against the Despensers; he had submitted to the king and had been imprisoned in the Tower of London. From that place, with a little help from his friends, he managed to escape; it is reported that he drugged his captors and then climbed down from his chamber on a rope. It sounds apocryphal, but it may be accurate. There were very few other paths out of the Tower, except of course by way of the gallows. He sailed to France and offered his services to the French king. It was at Charles IV's court that he began an intrigue, in every sense, with Queen Isabella. Around the queen there now gathered a cluster of exiled or disaffected barons and bishops. When her son arrived to offer fealty to her brother, she had found the perfect weapon. The king ordered her to return to England, but she refused to do so; she declared that she would come back only if the Despensers were banished. In any case she preferred the more benign atmosphere of the French court.

Throughout 1325 rumours and fears of invasion circulated through the kingdom. It was believed that Isabella would sail with the French king, but she was more immediately concerned to increase her support among the interlinked royal families of north-western Europe. She travelled north to Hainault (a Flemish province now in south-western Belgium) where the count of that region was amenable to the proposition that his daughter, Philippa, should marry the lord Edward; this young man of fourteen would, in all likelihood, be the next king of England. With Philippa's dowry Isabella and Mortimer then raised troops for the coming invasion.

Fifteen hundred men took to their ships from the port of Dordrecht in Holland and, having endured storms at sea, landed at the haven of Orwell in Suffolk on 24 September 1326. There had been no attempt to harry or prevent them, and it is likely that Edward still believed that the invading force was to come from Normandy. The commander of the royal fleet along the eastern coast, in any case, allowed her to land without obstruction. He had in the past been an opponent of the king, and once more turned against him. It is also reported that English sailors refused to fight Isabella because of the hatred they felt for the Despensers.

Her progress was swift. Her supporters flocked to her, and the king's secret enemies now rose in defiance of his rule. The queen moved on to Dunstable, her troops ransacking the lands of the Despensers on their way, where she learned that the king and the Despensers had in their panic fled from London and marched to the west; it is a measure of their confusion that they left most of their treasure behind. The king's supporters now changed sides; one who remained loyal, the elder Despenser, the earl of Winchester, was executed in Bristol under the distraint of martial law. His son, Hugh, was captured and awaited trial.

Edward fled into Wales, with only a handful of supporters, and the last surviving record of his reign is an account book found at Caerphilly. He had nowhere to turn. He was pursued by Isabella's men, and taken somewhere near Neath in the middle of November. From there he was escorted under armed guard to the royal castle of Kenilworth.

Hugh Despenser had refused food and drink since his capture, hoping perhaps to die before he was painfully killed. He was taken to Reading, where he was crowned with a ring of nettles; words of execration were cut into his skin. To the sound of drum and trumpets, and to the shrieks of the crowd, he was hanged from a gallows 50 feet (15 metres) high; while still alive he was hacked down and his intestines were burned before his face. Finally, he was beheaded.

Despenser had been executed in Reading rather than in London because the capital was in a feverish state. The citizens, having long been under the financial constraint of the king, exulted in their liberty and turned on any of the officials of the old regime they could find. Bishop Stapledon, once the royal treasurer, was dragged from his horse and butchered. Merchants and bankers, who had financed the king, were murdered.

Yet how were the victors to depose a lawful king? It was illegal and unprecedented. The king was supposed to be protected by the majesty of God. It would be difficult to lay hands on God's anointed. At the beginning of 1327 a parliament was held – although, without the requisite presence of the king himself, it should more properly be called an assembly, or convention – in the name of the king's son, the prince of Wales. He had been appointed as keeper of the realm for the duration of the king's absence 'abroad', although of course Edward had got no further than Kenilworth Castle. Various acclamations and proclamations were made in favour of Isabella and Prince Edward, so that the power of London could be shown to be firmly with them. Two bishops were despatched to Kenilworth, but no record of their interview with the king survives; it is reported that he cursed them, and refused to return with them to London.

A second meeting of the assembly was then convened, under the control of Mortimer, at Westminster. In careful words he declared that the magnates of the land had deposed Edward, on the grounds that he had not followed his coronation oath and had fallen under the control of evil advisers; he had been bent on the destruction of the Church and of the magnates of the realm. Adam Orleton, bishop of Hereford, then delivered a sermon with the theme that 'where there is no true ruler, the people will be destroyed'. There seems to have been a general assent.

Another delegation visited the king at Kenilworth, where they gave him an ultimatum. Adam Orleton lectured him once more on the evils of his arrogant and unworthy reign before declaring that 'his son should be substituted for him if he should give his assent'. The assent was crucial for lending at least a veneer of legality to the proceedings. It is claimed that the king, wearing a black gown, was consumed with tears and sighs; when he saw the delegation, he swooned in fear. On recovering he first refused to surrender his crown but then, after further argument, reluctantly assented. The threat, of course, was that he could be forcibly removed and someone else put in his place. The truth of the proceedings will never be known, but it can be assumed that the whole affair was messy, unpredictable and uncertain. Too many interests were at stake to make it otherwise. Some magnates and bishops, for example, must have doubted the legality of the whole exercise.

Yet it had come to pass. The dethroned king was taken from Kenilworth and consigned to Berkeley Castle in Gloucestershire. He seems to have been treated well at first, but an uncrowned king can never be safe. Two attempts at rescue were made, one of them partially successful, and with the possibility of escape his fate was determined. It has been said that 'between the prison and the grave of a king there is little space'. His death, in September 1327, has a quality of barbarity that has scarcely been equalled in the annals of England. It was said that he was slain with a poker, red-hot, inserted into his fundament. Or as Ranulf Higden put it in his *Polychronicon*, 'he was sleyne with a hoote broche putte thro the secrete place posterialle'. Yet this may simply be a poetical touch, an allusion to his supposed sodomitical tendencies. His heart was taken from his body and placed in a silver vase, which was put later in Isabella's own coffin. His body was viewed, at a distance, by the knights and magnates of Gloucestershire. At his funeral, in Gloucester Abbey, large oak barricades were built to hold back the crowds. None of his gaolers were ever convicted of his death; two were found innocent, one entered the service of Edward III, and the fourth was murdered in strange circumstances.

There is a stranger epilogue still. In the archives of the French province of Languedoc was found a letter addressed to Edward III, from an important papal official named Manuel di Fieschi. He repeats the confession of a hermit, whom he calls 'your father'. In specific and circumstantial detail the hermit gives an account of his flight, arrest and detention in Kenilworth and Berkeley castles. He describes how his guard in Berkeley warned him that two knights, Lord Thomas de Gornay and Lord Simon d'Esberfort [Beresford], were coming to kill him. The specific details, again, are given. The king put on different clothes, and made his way out of the castle. He killed the porter, sleeping, at the last door and then took his keys before escaping into the night.

It is recorded that the two knights, thwarted of their victim and terrified of the wrath of the queen, cut out the heart of the porter and put his corpse into a wooden chest. They then pretended that the organ and the body were those of Edward II. In this account, therefore, the queen was buried with the porter's heart, and the porter's body still rests beneath the canopied shrine of Edward II in what is now Gloucester Cathedral.

The hermit goes on to recount a period of concealment in Corfe Castle before he began his wanderings through Ireland and France. He was received by Pope John in Avignon, where he remained for two weeks. In the habit of a hermit he crossed into Germany and then into Lombardy, in which region he wrote down his confession. The letter ends with a sentence from Manuel di Fieschi to the king. 'In testimony of these things I have appended a seal for your lordship's consideration.' This was, perhaps, the privy seal that accompanied the king's person. It all sounds the merest melodrama, unworthy of serious consideration, but the writer of the letter was a papal official of repute. He would not have written to the king of England on a mere whim. The details of the account, too, are accurate as far as they can be checked in the historical record. So it remains a surmise and a mystery. It is possible, to put it no higher, that Edward II ended his life as a hermit in Italy. It would have been an edifying end to a not very edifying life.

The brief supremacy of Queen Isabella and Roger Mortimer, lasting from the autumn of 1326 to the autumn of 1330, was not itself a glorious one. The lands and treasures of the deposed king, and of the Despensers, were seized by the victors; the queen and her consort took the greater share, of course, and the rest was distributed among their followers. They also had to reward the mercenaries they had brought with them from Hainault. So the financial reserves of the Crown were severely depleted; the sum of £61,921 left by Edward in 1326 had been reduced by 1330 to £41. Taxation, and loans from Florentine bankers, were the only expedients.

The young king was crowned in 1327, but his power was nominal rather than real. He was governed by a council of barons and bishops, while Roger Mortimer was at the head of affairs. Robert Bruce could not let slip this opportunity of a minority and so invaded the northern territories of England; Mortimer and the young king led armies to oppose him, but achieved nothing. It is said that Edward III wept at the failure of the campaign, which was followed by a treaty in which the title of Bruce to the throne of Scotland was recognized. The capitulation did not bode well for his future reign.

Yet the new king was of a quite different stamp from his father. At the age of eighteen, he was becoming restless and resentful. Like his grandfather, Edward I, he longed for martial glory as the prerogative of sovereignty. He may have blamed Mortimer for the fiasco in Scotland, and have held him responsible for the decline of his revenues. Mortimer had become another 'over-mighty' subject at odds with the king.

Isabella was also now carrying Mortimer's child, and Edward

feared a forced change in succession. He was told that it was better to eat the dog than allow the dog to eat him. So an assassination was planned. Mortimer and Isabella had travelled to Nottingham Castle, where a party of knights under the command of Edward had concealed themselves in the undergrowth outside the walls. An official of the castle had revealed to them a secret passage that led directly into the private quarters; there they surprised Mortimer, and arrested him. Isabella ran out of the chamber, shrieking, 'Good son, have pity on noble Mortimer!' But, in that period, pity was in short supply. He was tried, and summarily executed, in London. Isabella was sent to one of her private houses. Edward III had obtained his kingdom.

17. A man wielding an axe, taken from *Topographia Hibernica*. The work was written by Gerald of Wales in 1188, and includes the remark that the native Irish allow 'their hair and beards to grow enormously in an uncouth manner'.

18. An image of man and dogs from the Luttrell Psalter, an illuminated manuscript that was written and illustrated at Lincoln at some point in the decade after 1325.

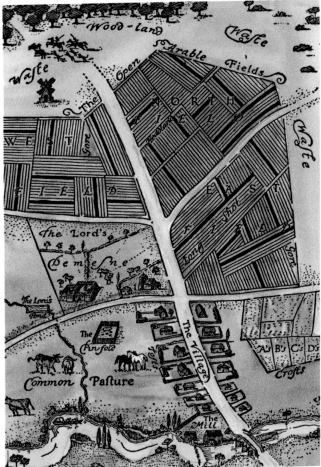

19. A nineteenth-century woodcut of a medieval manor, with the lord's demesne, the village and the church all neatly outlined. Note the areas of 'waste' just beyond the fields.

20. An image of Matilda, de facto queen of England from March to November 1141, holding a charter. The illumination comes from *The Golden Book of Saint Albans* by Thomas Walsingham, circa 1380.

21. Henry II confronting Thomas Becket. The soldiers beside them are an apt reminder of those who killed the archbishop on 29 December 1170.

22. Richard I, more commonly known as 'Richard the Lionheart', watching the execution of the 3,000 prisoners, whom he had captured at the siege of Acre in the Gulf of Haifa during the Third Crusade.

23. 'John Lackland' (otherwise known as King John) on horseback. He is here seen riding out against a castle with sword in hand. He was also known as 'John Softsword'.

24. The season of March as seen in The Bedford Book of Hours, an exquisite and lavish manuscript dating from the early fifteenth century. The farm animals of the medieval period were smaller, and the productivity of the soil inferior, to their modern counterparts.

25. The varied labours of the agricultural year. The scythe and the sickle, the flail and the winnowing fan and the plough, are to be seen in many medieval illuminations.

26. The abbots, and monks, of a medieval monastery. The monks of England were the historians and illuminators who helped to preserve the continuities of the country.

27. The building of a monastery, taken from a miniature of the fourteenth century.

Alexander Rex Scotore. leẅellin princeps ẅallie

PARLIAMENT

28. Edward I addressing one of his parliaments. The first parliament of his reign, assembled in 1275, had some 800 representatives. Once they had obeyed his will, he dismissed them.

29. A view of Harlech Castle, one of the Welsh castles created for Edward I by Master James of St George; he was the master-builder of the age. The castle itself might seem to have been fashioned out of the rock on which it sits.

Charles le bel recevant la Reine d'Angleterre

Ronjat pinxt.      Imp. Fraillery      Prelon. chromolith.

30. Queen Isabella, errant wife of Edward II, being received by her brother
Charles le Bel in France.

31. The Black Death, reaching England in the autumn of 1348, killed approximately 2 million people. There had never been mortality on such a scale, nor has there been since.

32. A woman who has contracted leprosy. The leper would carry a clapper and bell to warn of her approach.

33. A blood-letting. The doctor would taste the blood of his patient. Healthy blood was slightly sweet.

# 22

# Birth and death

The infant mortality rates of the medieval period were high, with over a third of boys and a quarter of girls dying at or soon after birth. That is why baptism was of overwhelming importance to the family of the child; if not baptized, the infant would go into the indeterminate eternal world of limbo and be denied the bliss of heaven. In the event of imminent death the midwife was permitted to sprinkle water over the child and pronounce 'I baptize you in the name of the Father, Son and Holy Ghost.' If the mother died in labour, the midwife was obliged to cut the child from the womb in order to save its soul. In extreme cases the infant was baptized even before birth, given a name such as 'Vitalis' or 'Creature' or 'Child of God'.

The room of birth was supposed to be warm and dark, with a scent of rose petals somewhere in the air, but of course not all births could be performed in ideal conditions. That accounts for a large number of the deaths. Men were not allowed to witness the birth. The husband was permitted to mimic a symbolic act of release at that moment, however, by firing an arrow into the air or opening a box.

The infant survivors came into what was for some a world of pain and suffering. There is widespread evidence of anaemia, sinusitis, leprosy and tuberculosis; osteoarthritis and diabetes were common, but essentially for no larger a proportion of the population than in the twenty-first century. Eye complaints such as sore eyes, red eyes, watering eyes, running eyes and 'boiling eyes' were ubiquitous.

Doctors or 'leeches' could be summoned for a relatively large fee. Their medical skills were not remarkable. One of the more famous of them in the fourteenth century, John of Arderne, wrote in a treatise that a young doctor should learn 'good proverbs pertaining to his craft in comforting of patients. Also it speedeth that a leech can talk of good and honest tales that may make the patients to laugh, as well as of the Bible and other tragedies.'

Laughter was perhaps, under the circumstances, the best medicine. The cure for toothache was to burn a piece of mutton fat under the affected tooth, so that the 'worms' would fall out. A remedy for the stone was a mash made out of the bodies of beetles and crickets applied to the sick part of the body. The cure for tonsillitis was inspired. 'Take a fat cat, skin it, draw out the guts and take the grease of a hedgehog and the fat of a bear . . . All this crumble small and stuff the cat, roast it whole and gather the grease and anoint the patient therewith.' The lice of hogs was a sovereign curative of consumption. If you combed your hair with an ivory comb, your memory would be improved. For a condition known as 'web in the eye' the marrow from the great bone of a goose wing was to be mingled with the juice of the red honeysuckle, but the flower had to be plucked 'with the saying of nine paternosters, nine aves and a creed'.

It is easy to mock what seem to be absurd provisions, but they belonged to a tradition that viewed the human and natural world as part of the same unity. That is why doctors prescribed the flesh of tame beasts rather than of wild ones; a carp from the pond was better than a shrimp from the seashore. It calmed, rather than excited, the patient. Melancholy men must avoid eating venison; the deer is a beast that lives in fear, and fear only augments the melancholy humour. If a man was sick of the jaundice and saw a yellow thrush, the man would be cured and the bird would die. The power of suggestion was also very great, judging by the extraordinary number of miraculous cures that took place at the shrines of the saints. The majority of people never saw a 'leech' in the whole course of their lives; they relied upon the herbs and potions of the local wise woman.

Buildings known as hospitals did exist, but they were essentially large chapels in which invalids were lodged; prayer was as good a remedy as medicine. No medical attendants were employed in the hospitals, only monks and chaplains. If illness was a punishment sent by God, then it might be impious to seek to cure it. The soul's health was in any case more important than that of the body. Yet the hospitals played their part. An interval of rest and care was probably more efficacious than many of the available remedies.

The medical treatment of the period, where available, was based on folklore or the instructions of Galen from the second century AD which were based on the doctrine of the four 'humours'. Just as the universe was made of four elements – earth, water, air and fire – so the human body was comprised of phlegmatic, choleric, sanguine and melancholy humours in various proportions. The house of melancholy, for example, lay in the spleen. Good health was the result of the balance between them. The doctor would taste the blood of his patient, after one of the frequent bloodlettings considered to be necessary. Healthy blood was slightly sweet.

The inspection of urine, in special glass vessels or urinals, was also an important part of the doctor's regimen; it bears a resemblance to the modern blood test. Urine is in fact still inspected as part of a general health precaution. Twenty types of urine could be found, with certain broad divisions based upon the humours. If the urine was white and thin, for example, it signified melancholy; melancholy was considered to be cold and dry. The doctor would observe, smell and taste the urine to discover the governing condition of the patient and the part of the body most in danger. A good doctor also had to be an astrologer. When the moon was in Aries, a fiery and moderately dry sign, it was proper to operate upon the head and the neck. The leaves of henbane, good for the gout, could only be picked on Midsummer Eve.

The possibility of saintly intervention was also at hand. St Blaise was the patron saint of throat disease, St Hubert of hydrophobia and St Martin of the itch. The top joint of the second finger of the right hand was dedicated to St Simon Cleophas, while the second joint of the third finger of the left hand was under the protection of St Bartholomew. By various means, sacred and secular, the good doctor was thus able to prepare a diet and a routine of life to suit the particular temperament of each patient; if the body was in tune with the stars and the elements, then it would not suffer.

Bathing was a luxury of the upper classes and those who liked to imitate them; bathhouses were established in the larger towns, and the magnates possessed their own wooden bathtubs which were shaped like vats and bound with hoops. Soap was readily available, as well as instruments for cleaning the teeth and ears. Bathwater was supposed to be tepid, the same temperature as that which ran from the side of Christ at the time of his crucifixion. The prayer 'Anima Christi' has the invocation, 'Water from the side of Christ, cleanse me.'

Only four English kings of the medieval period lived beyond the age of sixty, which can be considered as the gateway to old age. It was once widely supposed that men and women over the age of forty were considered to be old, but that is not the case; only after sixty was that attribute used. In the century and a half after 1350, 30 per cent of the members of the House of Lords were over sixty, and 10 per cent over seventy. It would still be considered a respectable proportion of that parliamentary chamber. Life expectancy was of course a different matter; throughout our period it has been variously estimated at forty or fifty years. In some regions it might have been as low as thirty.

When death arrived, the body was wrapped in a shroud tied at head and neck. Coffins were not used for the ordinary dead. The favoured part of the churchyard was the south, the north part being considered damp and mossy. The corpse was met at the principal gate of the churchyard by the priest, who led the mourners in procession to the site of the grave where the burial service was held. Only the rich dead deserved a stone memorial, which was to be found within the church. So the cemetery itself was free of gravestones, except for a few wooden markers and small carved stones. The churchyard itself was considered to be part of the common space of the parish, used for sports and markets; it could also be used as a pigsty and as pasture for cattle. As the dead multiplied, so did the surface of the churchyard rise.

# 23

# The sense of a nation

The new king, Edward III, was compared to the Israelites taken out of the house of bondage; he was free at last from the schemes and wiles of his mother who had sometimes been known as 'the she-wolf of France'. After the capture of Mortimer in Nottingham Castle a public proclamation was issued, to be read by the sheriffs in churchyards, courts and marketplaces. It stated in part that 'the king's affairs and the affairs of his realm have been directed to the damage and dishonour of him and his realm, and to the impoverishment of his people'; it went on to promise that the new king 'will henceforth govern his people according to right and reason, as befits his royal dignity'.

He could not have made a stronger contrast with his unfortunate father. He is generally reported to have been convivial and engaging. One of the mottoes woven into his jacket stated simply 'It is as it is.' Another, worn by the courtiers as well as the king, read 'Hey, hey, the white swan, by God's soul I am thy man.' He also spoke English much better than his predecessor.

He had personal courage, too, and identified himself with all the chivalric virtues. As a result he inspired loyalty among the magnates. He restored lands that had been rendered forfeit by his father, and actively helped to enlarge the membership of the nobility; four of the senior members of his household, for example, were granted earldoms. He had to rely at first upon the councillors and courtiers he had inherited, but over a few years he gathered together a group of knights and nobles who would remain with him for the rest of his reign.

Yet the token of a righteous sovereign was still success in war. The new king realized that his father's military incapacity was the single most important reason for his failure, and he strove very hard to reverse the image of weakness. That is why his first enterprise was against Scotland. The tears he had shed, at his earlier humiliation by the Scots, had not been forgotten. An opportunity soon arose for action. The death of Robert Bruce in 1329 put his infant son upon the throne of Scotland, but Edward III espoused the cause of a rival claimant, Edward Balliol; he was eager to undo the damage of the previous campaign, and in 1333 he won a notable victory at Halidon Hill two miles outside Berwick. Balliol then became the client king; Berwick and the surrounding area were returned to English rule. This was only the beginning of further raids and campaigns in the area of the border, but Halidon Hill was in fact the only battle Edward himself fought on English soil. The field of his other military endeavours lay across the Channel.

The kings of France and of England were, at the time, the two most powerful sovereigns in Europe; much of the continent was divided into dukedoms and principalities that fought only against each other. So it was perhaps inevitable that France and England should vie for mastery. That is the law of life.

The particular source of conflict was, once again, the duchy of Gascony that represented the last piece of the Plantagenet Empire still in English hands. In the Treaty of Paris, signed more than eighty-three years before, Henry III had given up his old French empire in exchange for its possession. Yet Gascony was still considered to be part of France, and therefore the new king of England on his succession was obliged to do fealty (or 'liege homage' as it was known) as a vassal of the French king. But how could an English sovereign owe loyalty to a foreign sovereign? He would be obliged to supply the French king with arms and soldiers. He was not allowed to enter an alliance with the enemies of France. If he did so, Gascony might be confiscated.

It was unthinkable. It was also an anomaly, a structural imbalance, that could only end in discord. Edward III refused to accept that he was a feudal subject of Philip of Valois and instead declared himself to be the king of France as well as of England. He claimed that through his mother, Isabella, he was in the direct line of royal succession – despite the fact that the French crown could not by law be transmitted through the female line. His declaration was inspired in part by bravado and in part by pride. He declared that he was fighting 'to recover his rights overseas and to save and defend his realm of England'. He was looking for an excuse to attack the enemy.

In the largest perspective it might be said that he was helping to break down the old European feudal order and to supplant it with the new recognition of the power of nation-states; in this period England and France became more centralized and bureaucratized. Edward III himself, however, is most unlikely to have seen it in those terms. He just wanted to preserve his honour and perhaps win some spoils. Of arms and the man, I sing. His fighting spirit had the unfortunate consequence, however, of beginning a conflict that became known as the Hundred Years War. The controversy lasted for a much longer period. Only in the nineteenth century did the English throne renounce its claim to the French crown.

The war, costing so many lives and so much money, had little permanent consequence. The English gained Calais, but that town became a burden rather than a glory. The real interests of England were not involved in the conflict, except perhaps for the consumption of wines from Gascony. But the appetite of the king for power and glory took precedence over the claims of the nation.

It is true to say that when war was first declared in 1337 some enthusiasm might be found, at least among the magnates, for a campaign against France. The indolence and indignity of the previous reign were supplanted by something approaching martial fervour. War might be said to animate the leaders of the nation, and bring together its disparate and sometimes feuding parts. There would be no need for the magnates to fight each other if they could reap the spoils of battle in an enemy country.

This newly found unity of purpose was dramatized when, in 1348, Edward III instituted the Order of the Garter. The celebrated motto, *Honi soit qui mal y pense* or 'Shame on him who thinks ill of it', refers to Edward's claim upon the throne of France. Almost all of the original twenty-six knights, divided into two groups for the sake of jousting competitions, had taken part in the French campaigns. It was a military brotherhood.

The king had in any case a strong sense of the dramatic, and loved ceremonial occasions; he engaged in all the panoply of chivalry and, more than a century before Sir Thomas Malory wrote *Le Morte Darthur*, he tried to restore an Arthurian sense of kingship. The king was therefore popular among the grandees of the realm. They were once more part of a great adventure, and Edward had become their warrior king. The king's eldest son, Edward – dressed as Lionel, cousin of Lancelot – took part in a grand tournament. The contemporary chronicler, Jean Froissart, wrote that 'the English will never love or honour a king who is not a victor and a lover of war'. Other kings of Europe might be celebrated for their piety, or for their learning, but in England those criteria did not apply.

The king's lavish architectural patronage was part of the chivalric programme. He had been born in Windsor Castle, but he proceeded to demolish the existing castle and build an even grander edifice in its place. It was his way of advertising his own glory and of proclaiming his superiority over the French king. It was here, in 1344, that the Round Table was recreated; the king and queen, clothed in red gowns, led a procession of knights and barons into the castle chapel where their quest for valour and virtue was consecrated. In the circular Round Table building, larger than the Pantheon of Rome, lavish feasts and dances were held in which the participants dressed as characters out of Arthurian romance. The foundations of this early theatre, or centre of ritual activity, were uncovered in the summer of 2006.

As the knights sat on a stone bench running around the wall, and watched jousts as well as tournaments, the real conflict of the period was proceeding slowly enough. The first two of the hundred years of war (in fact 116) were spent in posturing; Edward sailed over to the Low Countries for the purpose of launching an invasion from Flanders, and for purchasing new allies. It was said that he was spending his time, and the money of the country, idly. The complaints against heavy taxation were mounting all the time. The poems and chronicles of the period are filled with complaints about oppression and shortages; no farmers or merchants were safe from the king's depredations. It had become a familiar refrain of the fourteenth century. 'He who takes money from the needy without just cause', one versifier wrote, 'commits sin.' The wool merchants, in particular, were forced to pay for the king's armies; the proceeds of 30,000 sacks of wool were to be lent to the king, accompanied by a temporary ban on exports to keep the prices high. Since wool was the single most important aspect of the English economy, the king's demands led directly to unemployment and consequent poverty. The country had become essentially a cash cow for Edward's military needs.

Yet his plans for a rapid campaign were frustrated; the scheme for financing the war through wool proved disastrous; problems arose both with the merchants and the collectors of the customs. The king's financiers were growing restless, and threatened to cut off supplies. With the king out of the country, too, rumours spread of invasions from France and from Scotland. The members of the council that Edward had set up to rule England in his absence were growing fractious; the king accused them of withholding money from him, while they in turn complained that they had many expensive duties to perform including the defence of the realm. It was said that the king was growing as reckless and as extravagant as his father. 'I counsel that ye begin no war in trust of your riches,' Dame Prudence declared in Chaucer's 'Tale of Melibee', 'for they . . . suffice not wars to maintain.'

In 1340, three years after the declaration of war with France, a taxpayers' revolt was organized in the parliament house. It was said that 'a king ought not to go forth from his kingdom in manner of war unless the commune of his realm agree to it'. The parliament had become the institution that, according to the injunctions of Magna Carta, gave the consent of the realm to fresh taxation. Successive kings, under force of circumstance, had accepted its role.

The knights and townsmen had already begun humbly to submit petitions from their various neighbourhoods, to which appropriate royal legislation came in response. It was a system of quid pro quo.

The parliament had already granted heavy taxation for the first three years of the conflict. In the summer of 1339 the king asked for a further grant of £300,000. The Commons, made up of the townsmen and the knights of the shires, prevaricated; they asked leave to return to their own districts, and consult the people. When they assembled again, in the early months of 1340, they offered a grant in return for certain concessions from the king. They had in effect distinguished themselves from the Lords. They were beginning to feel their power.

Their principal submission was that the finances of the nation should be ordered and controlled by a council of magnates answerable to parliament. It was to be directed by John Stratford, the archbishop of Canterbury. The king, in desperate need for the means to wage war, conceded this demand. As long as he was fighting, he was happy. His agreement also marks the moment when the Commons became a coherent political assembly that gradually began to formulate its own rules of procedure. War, and taxation, had brought them together. The parliament itself was now supposed to meet on a regular basis; it was also the assembly in which the council of the nation, and the custodians of taxation, were chosen. Thirty-five years later, it would be strong enough to impeach the king's principal councillors. The idea of an independent parliament, then, was part of the consequence of the Hundred Years War.

On 22 June 1340, Edward returned to the Low Countries in the full expectation that hostilities would soon be resumed. Stratford would ensure that the money reached him. Yet the fresh exactions of the king provoked hostility and violence throughout the country; the collectors were supposed to take up 20,000 sacks of wool, from the nine most productive sheep-rearing counties, and sell them to the local merchants. But the people successfully resisted this extortion. As a result the king was not receiving the aid he had expected; he could not pay his debts, or his troops, and his active campaign came to an end.

In his fury he turned upon Archbishop Stratford. He sailed

back to England and, in the middle of the night of 30 November, he suddenly arrived at the Tower of London. He asked for the constable, but the absence of that official confirmed the king's sense that his realm was not being properly administered. Edward accused the archbishop of wilfully withholding money; he believed, or professed to believe, that Stratford had wished to sabotage the French campaign of which the cleric disapproved. The senior members of the council were dismissed. Stratford fled back to Canterbury, where he was in theory safe from the king's wrath.

Then Edward, in defiance of his previous pledge to parliament, took control of the country without consultation. He embarked upon a reassessment of the whole administration, and in particular of its financial resources; he appointed new collectors of the wool supplies; he levied fines on individuals, and communities, that had evaded the tax. On 29 December Stratford entered the pulpit of Canterbury Cathedral, and delivered a sermon in English defending his actions. He declared that he was only enforcing the collective will of the parliament and that the king had been swayed by evil councillors. He alluded to the Magna Carta, with the clear implication that the king had broken its provisions. He knew that the nation was supporting him, and he demanded a trial by his peers. He was effectively defying the king to do his worst.

The king then called a parliament, to which he reluctantly admitted Stratford himself. The archbishop was formally reconciled to the king – he was received 'into the king's grace' – and the work of parliamentary negotiation began. In return for an extra 10,000 sacks of wool, Edward agreed that his chief ministers would in future be approved by the magnates and the council. Accommodations and compromises were agreed on every side; the king was reconciled to the Lords on the condition that he would be their good lord, and he eventually reached a settlement with the Commons on the understanding that he would 'rule them by leniency and gentleness'. He had a more astute understanding of political realities than his father had ever shown. He knew when to turn his cheek. It was only to be expected that, five months later, he reversed his concessions on the grounds that he had granted them unwillingly. Within two years he had regained most of his power. In his duel with parliament he had survived.

The war with France continued like a piece of vast background music. In the summer of 1340 the English fleet surprised and destroyed French ships on the Flanders coast at Sluys. It was the first notable victory of the conflict and after the battle the king issued a gold coin, called the noble, in which he was portrayed standing on board a warship. Here was the image of the master of the seas. His reign had become identified with the pursuit of war. No French minister had dared to inform Philip VI of the English victory, and it was decided that only his Fool could break the news with impunity. So the Fool declared to his master that the English were arrant cowards; when asked the reason he replied that they, unlike the French, had not leapt into the sea.

The defeat of the French fleet meant that the English were at liberty to invade by means of the Channel. Yet Edward's squabbles with his allies, and with the Flemish in particular, meant that no immediate successes were achieved. The French forces ducked and wove, refusing to be drawn into battle. This was in fact to become the pattern of the French defence. In the autumn of 1340 a truce was agreed. But it could not last. There were inconclusive hostilities in Brittany, and in Gascony, over the succeeding few years and then in 1346 Edward made the decisive move of invading Normandy; he hoped to join his Flemish allies in an assault upon Paris or perhaps a march into Gascony. He kept the French king guessing.

On 11 July 1346, 8,000 men (half of them archers) sailed south from Portsmouth to northern France. They marched through Normandy on their way to Paris, plundering and wasting everything in their path. They advanced as far as the suburbs of the capital, where they turned north towards Calais in order to join forces with the Flemish allies. Philip VI marched rapidly across the great northern plain of the Somme in an effort to divert or destroy them; on the afternoon of 26 August, he attacked them as they assembled near the wood of Crécy-en-Ponthieu. An impetuous army of Genoese crossbowmen and French cavalry were beaten back by the English forces and, in the ensuing mêlée, the French army was effectively crushed.

Gunpowder cannon were for the first time used in battle,

causing more panic than death; but the palm of victory must be awarded to Edward's archers who, wielding longbows, defeated the knights of feudal chivalry. It had been a day of partial eclipse, of thunder and of lightning; at its close the French knights lay on the field, many of them despatched by the use of long and slender daggers known as 'misericords' or mercy killers that ripped open the body from the armpit to the heart. One among the 30,000 dead was John, the blind king of Bohemia, whose motto of *Ich dien* or 'I serve' was adopted by subsequent princes of Wales.

The battle of Crécy was a signal victory, of which Edward took immediate opportunity; he marched north and, nine days later, he was waiting beneath the walls of Calais. This town would be an excellent base for further incursions into French territory; it was also a convenient port for raids against French pirates. The townsmen of Calais endured almost a year of famine. The commander of the French garrison wrote to Philip VI that 'we can find no more food in the town unless we eat men's flesh . . . this is the last letter that you will receive from me, for the town will be lost and all of us that are within it'. The letter was intercepted before it reached the French king and was delivered to Edward; he read it, applied his personal seal and sent it on to its destination.

In the eleventh month the women, children and old people of Calais came out from the gates as 'useless mouths' to be removed. The English would not allow them to pass through their lines, and they were hounded back to the town ditch where they expired from want. So the town was forced to submit. The story of the six burghers of Calais, coming out with nooses around their necks and submitting to the clemency of a gracious king, may well be authentic. It is a type of political theatre at which Edward excelled.

He had already vanquished another ancient enemy. In the year of Crécy, David Bruce, or David II of Scotland, had invaded England; he had inherited the 'old alliance' with France, and hoped that the absence of Edward would demoralize the English forces. But at Neville's Cross, close to Durham, the Scottish forces were overwhelmed and David Bruce himself was escorted to the Tower of London where he remained for eleven years. The Black Rood of Scotland, a piece of Christ's cross kept in a black case, was taken in triumph to Durham Cathedral. So Edward III was victorious over all his foes. The knights and lords now clustered around him in amity. He had become their ideal of a monarch.

Whether it meant as much to the English people is open to doubt. The war against the French represented a quarrel between two monarchs, who were members of the same family and who both spoke French as their native language. What had the affairs of princes to do with the condition of England? The people had in any case far more serious matters with which to deal when, in 1348, all the forces of infection and death were unleashed in an epidemic without parallel.

It was named as 'the pestilence time'. The disease itself was called 'the plague' or 'the Black Death'. It may not have been bubonic plague, however; it has been variously described as anthrax or influenza or a form of haemorrhagic fever. It may have been a disease that no longer exists. Contrary to popular superstition it is unlikely to have been carried by rats.

It came out of Central Asia in the early 1330s and then spread throughout the known world by means of the trade routes. It had reached Italy by 1347 and, in the summer of the following year, touched Bristol and other ports. By the autumn of 1348 it had reached London before travelling north. It manifested itself in buboes, ulcerated swellings in the groin or armpit; a contemporary described a bubo as in 'the form of an apple, or the head of an onion . . . it seethes like a burning cinder, and is of the colour of ash'. In some cases the body erupted in abscesses filled with pus. This was accompanied by aching limbs, vomiting and diarrhoea; the victims were generally dead within three days.

They were buried in mass graves, laid side by side in long trenches, the adults carrying their dead children on their shoulders. An old belief still persists that the parts of certain graveyards must never be disturbed for fear of 'letting out the plague'. It is not completely without justification; the spores of anthrax can survive for hundreds of years. The cemeteries of London were soon filled, and 13 acres (5.2 hectares) of land were purchased on the borders of Smithfield to be converted into a vast graveyard. One third, or even perhaps one half, of the population died. There had never been mortality on this scale, nor has there been since. At the best estimation a population of approximately 6 million was reduced to 3 million or 4 million. It remained at this level until the early sixteenth century.

It is likely that, before the plague, the country had been overpopulated; it may even be that malnutrition actively hastened the fatalities. So on some form of Malthusian calculation the distemper freed the energies of the surviving population and increased the availability of resources. It did not seem like this at the time. According to Henry Knighton, a chronicler of the period, 'many buildings, great and small, fell into ruins in every city, borough, and village for lack of people; likewise many villages and hamlets became desolate, not a house being left in them, all having died who dwelt there; and it was probable that many such villages would never be inhabited'. Men could not be found to work the land, so women and children were obliged to drive the plough. In a school textbook of the next generation there is a set sentence, 'The roof of an old house had almost fallen on me yesterday.' Ruined buildings were a familiar hazard.

A Franciscan friar, John Clyn, left an account of the period. 'Lest things worthy of remembrance should perish with time', he wrote,

> and fall away from the memory of those who are to come after us, I, seeing these many evils, and the whole world lying, as it were, in the grasp of the wicked one – myself awaiting death among the dead [*inter mortuos mortem expectans*] as I have truly heard and examined, so I have reduced these things to writing; and lest the writing should perish with the writer, and the work fail together with the workman, I leave parchment for continuing the work, if haply any man may survive, and any of the race of Adam escape this pestilence.

He added, some time later, two words – '*magna karistia*' or 'great dearth'. Then another hand followed. 'Here it seems that the author died.'

The plague was generally considered to be an act of God, punishing sinners for their pride and presumption, their vanity and faithlessness. It represented an evil so great that, according to William Langland in *Piers Plowman*, 'prayers have no power to prevent this pestilence'. Langland also stated that the south-west wind, blowing in the evening, was a baleful sign. It was the breath of the devil. It was said that all those born after the arrival of the pestilence had two fewer teeth than those born before. In 1361 the pestilence time returned. It was known as 'the mortality of children'. A third epidemic followed in 1369, and a fourth in 1374. It was noticed at the time that the wealthier classes were not so severely affected as the rest of the population; they were not forced into close or intimate contact with the sick.

Despite these grievous blows the society of England held together. The courts of justice were closed, and the meetings of parliament were repeatedly delayed, but no general collapse of order occurred. The records of Church and state reveal a surprising continuity and coherence of administration. The level of wool exports, for example, remained stable. Yet the pestilence had slow but permanent effects on English society. The shortage of labour had the immediate result of increasing both the level of wages and the chances of employment. The phenomenon of the landless or impoverished peasant wholly disappeared. But the rising demands of the working people who had survived, their worth now doubled by the epidemic, provoked a reaction from the landowners and magnates. The knights of the shires, in particular, perceived a threat to good order.

An Ordinance of Labourers was passed by a parliament in 1349, forbidding employers to pay more for labour than they had before the pestilence. The same Act deemed that it was illegal for an unemployed man to refuse work. The measures were not realistic. Many workers and their families could simply move to another district and to a more generous employer who was willing to ignore the law. Some migrated to the towns, for example, where there was a great demand for manual labourers such as masons and carpenters. A ploughman might become a tiler. More than enough work was available. So from a court roll of the period we have the following entries.

Thomas Tygow of Hale is a freelance roofer and he took at Hale from Hugh Skynner of Little Hale on various occasions in 1370 a daily wage of fourpence and his dinner, contrary to statute; excess 3s. 4d . . . William Deye is a freelance plough-man and took from Gilbert Deye at Ingoldsby on 2 December 1370 3d and food, and did this for the rest of the week, and received the same from others in the following year; excess: 12d . . . John Couper, carpenter, refused to work by the day in order to earn excessive money, and he took a lump sum from William Bourton of Sudbrooke; excess estimated to be 2s.

Many younger people now possessed their own holdings of land. And the best land did not remain vacant for very long. There had once been too many farmers and labourers working too little soil, but now they were dispersed over the countryside. Some lords tried to tie down their servile population by enforcing the obligations and duties owed to them, but any success was balanced by the problems of a reluctant and disaffected workforce. As that work-force became more aware of its value, the old tradition of labour service could not hold.

Wealthier peasants were ready to take on more land; they left wills, written in English, to confirm their aspiring position. The relatively low cost of produce, and the incidence of high wages, encouraged many of the larger landlords to give up production and lease their farms to the highest bidder. Or they converted their arable land into pasture; the rearing of sheep required less invest-ment of labour than the growing of crops.

The old manorial and village ties were being dissipated. The pestilence slowly began to dissolve, therefore, the old certainties of status and position; the traditional network of communal relations was being supplanted by the exigencies of private interest. There is evidence that the remaining people, on the land, now worked harder; manor accounts show that output per man increased, and that women often took over jobs previously reserved for men. Their wages increased proportionally higher than those of men.

In this context we can place the various ordinances and meas-ures taken by the Lords and Commons to discipline the thriving peasantry. Legislation was passed to forbid the wearing of costly clothes, and to impose restrictions on the daily diet. Women were to dress according to the social position of their fathers or husbands, and the wives of servants were not allowed to wear veils above 1 shilling in value. The wives of yeoman were not permitted to purchase silk veils, and agricultural labourers were not allowed to wear cloth priced at more than 12 pence a yard (0.91 metre). A worker's gown and coat must 'cover his privy members and buttocks', and the toes of his shoes or boots 'must not pass the length of two inches' (5 centimetres). This was in remonstrance against the fashion for tight-fitting and figure-hugging clothing, as well as the taste for elongated shoes. At dinner or supper the lower classes were to enjoy only two courses. Laws were also passed that prohibited peasants from carrying weapons or indulging in disorderly games. Idleness, if proven, could be punished. Despite these maladroit exercises in social control, the feudal England of the twelfth and thirteenth centuries was coming to an end. The English poet, John Gower, wrote at the close of the fourteenth century that:

> The world is changed and overthrown
> That it is well-nigh upside down
> Compared with days of long ago.

There is no known response of Edward III to the pestilence time. He no doubt regarded it simply as a threat to the supply of soldiers for his army. All his thoughts were of war. An armistice was agreed after the fall of Calais that endured for six years before foundering on claims of bad faith. The king combined in warfare against the French with his eldest son, Edward of Woodstock, prince of Wales. The young man would also become known as the Black Prince, on account of his armour rather than his morals or disposition. Edward of Woodstock embarked upon what was effectively a reign of terror by which contingents of his army were despatched to ravage selected bands of French territory; ordered to pillage, burn or destroy whatever lay in their path, they were dedicated to wiping out the lives and the livelihoods of the people of France. They had not been summoned in a feudal call to arms; they were either forcibly conscripted or they were mercenaries paid by the day. Many of them were common thieves or murderers attracted to the prospects of spoil. In this pursuit they were eminently successful.

The folk memory of English raids lived in the French national consciousness for many hundreds of years. Edward of Woodstock boasted that, in the space of seven weeks, he had laid waste 500 cities, towns and villages in the region of Bordeaux that had never known warfare in its history. It was a policy that had already been successfully deployed in Scotland.

The strategy of the French seems to have been to refrain from open confrontation but, in the autumn of 1356, the two armies came into contact; a French reconnaissance party stumbled upon the forces of the English. Battle could not be honourably delayed. The new king of France, John II, held a vast superiority in numbers with an army of 35,000 against the Black Prince's 7,000; but his position, at Poitiers, was on rising ground covered with hedges and vineyards.

The location itself was not the principal difficulty. The English could always now claim the mastery of the field by the use of the longbow, and the Black Prince followed his father's tactics at Crécy by using the archers as the main fighting force. The French cavalry were flung against the English line, only to be cut to pieces by a hail of arrows; the rest of the French knights then followed on foot, but they were also repulsed by the bows of yew. The average length of the bow was 6 feet (1.9 metres), and the arrows were 3 feet (0.91 metre) in length. The archer drew it to the ear, rather than to the chest, and with that momentum he could send it 250 yards (228 metres); he fired ten volleys each minute. This was a new age of warfare.

The French lines broke and dissolved; a retreat, and a general panic, ensued. In the confusion the French king and his son were captured by the English forces. It was a fresh calamity for the native army. King John was escorted to England by the Black Prince, and a truce of two years was agreed. When John was taken through the streets of London, it became a festive occasion for the citizens as the captive king was led in triumph to Westminster Hall where Edward III was waiting to greet him. It was a thoroughly medieval form of captivity. He was released on the surety of his son but, when his son escaped from England, he voluntarily returned to resume his life as a prisoner. He could not endure the dishonour of violating the terms of the agreement. Four months after his return to London, he died of an unknown disease. The king's body was then sent back to France.

Edward resumed hostilities after the time of truce, but a campaign in the winter of 1359 did not supply the overwhelming victory for which he had prayed. He was, however, still in the ascendant. So in 1360 a treaty was reached in which Edward agreed to renounce his claim to the French throne in return for full sovereignty over Gascony, Calais, Guienne, Poitou and Ponthieu in northern France. The Black Prince set up his own court at Bordeaux, the capital of the duchy of Guienne. All seemed to be set fair for English power across the Channel but in 1369 the new French king, Charles V, known as Charles the Wise, reasserted his feudal rights over all the territories of France.

The Black Prince defied him, but all of his martial vaunts proved useless in the end. The English prince contracted dropsy and grew too weak to lead his forces into the field; there were in any case no set battles, the French king proceeding by raid, sortie and ambush. This reconquest of French land by stealth was eminently successful, and five years later Charles had taken back almost all of the duchies and provinces once claimed by the English. A truce was then formulated that continued until the time of Edward III's death. All of Edward's spoils, acquired at the expense of so much blood and suffering and cost, were one by one stripped from him. Only Calais and parts of Gascony were left. His quest for the French crown was ineffective and ineffectual. This continual see-saw, this claim and counter-claim, demonstrates the futility of the entire conflict. Its major consequences, as we have seen, were wholly domestic in the fashioning of an independent parliament and the formation of a national system of taxation.

Edward of Woodstock came back to England, where he lingered in ever declining health for six years. The morbidity of his symptoms served only to emphasize the sickness at the court itself, where the absence of any military success infected the atmosphere with rancour and suspicion. The ageing king no longer seemed to be wholly in command of affairs and was widely rumoured to be in thrall to his mistress, Alice Perrers; much of the government of the realm, therefore, devolved upon one of his younger sons, the duke of Lancaster known as John of Gaunt. Unlike his older brother, however, John was not widely popular. It was believed that a group of councillors around the king were exploiting the resources of the exchequer for their own ends. When a parliament was called in the spring of 1376, for the purpose of raising fresh taxation, the Commons refused to continue their deliberations until certain 'evil counsellors' had been removed from the king's side.

The Good Parliament, as it became known, wished 'to make correction of the errors and faults of the realm if such are found to exist'. It proclaimed itself to be assembled 'on behalf of the community of the realm', and then moved against corrupt courtiers and merchants who had conspired to defraud the country. They were impeached, and sent to trial before the Lords. One or two of them fled the country; others were dismissed, imprisoned, or forfeited their property. It was an early test for the efficacy of the Commons, which had shown itself to be capable of determined action. It was not representative of some supposed popular freedom, however, since it proved to be equally capable of rebuffing the demands of the peasants and labourers. In the following year it introduced the 'poll tax' which was feared and hated in equal measure. The members of the parliament house were concerned only with the interests of their own particular 'community' of the realm.

The Black Prince died during the sessions of the Good Parliament, and his father followed a year later in 1377. It is said that Alice Perrers took the rings from his fingers as he lay upon his deathbed in the palace of Sheen, but this may be no more than a morality tale. The baubles of glory had already been stripped from him in France. He had achieved nothing much of his own volition, but during his reign of fifty years England itself had acquired a more coherent or at least more organized national life.

Another consequence of his reign is of equal importance. Edward III's early victories at Sluys and Crécy, and his capture of Calais, had augmented the sense of national identity. The people may not have cared a whit about Edward's claim to the throne of France but they understood the force of arms against 'strangers'. The news of battles was issued from market crosses and church pulpits, spreading quickly throughout the entire country. English merchants, rather than Italian or German traders, were now in charge of the country's business. In the port of Hull, for example, English exporters of wool had made up only 4 per cent of the total in 1275. By 1330, it was almost 90 per cent.

'I kan noght construe all this,' a character remarks in *Piers Plowman*, 'ye most kenne me this on Englissh.' It is worth remarking that Chaucer began his poetic career at the court of Edward III. His first verses were written in courtly French but the power of the vernacular overcame his literary conventionality; it is a measure of the strength of spoken and written English that Chaucer now celebrated it as worthy of comparison with the classical tongues. In *Troilus and Criseyde*, and more especially in *Canterbury Tales*, he created or adapted a language that was capable of the highest lyric flights and the most vulgar comic effects. It is already the language of Shakespeare. Within Chaucer's lifetime English replaced French as the language of school-teaching, and in the reign of the next sovereign it became the language of the court.


Human ingenuity is unceasing. The first mechanical clock was introduced to England in the reign of Edward III. It marks the demise of the feudal and seasonal world no less plainly than the advent of the longbow and the decline of the serf. The first reference to a crane, working in a harbour, comes from 1347.

# 24

# The night schools

In the reign of Edward III there arose the greatest disturbance within the Church since the time that Augustine imposed the primacy of Rome upon the English at the end of the sixth century. In the succeeding 800 years the Church had become part of the governance of England, with all the obligations and dangers that implies. It had become rich. It had remained powerful, with its principal servants becoming the chief administrators of the king. The bishops were effectively the king's clerks, chosen and promoted in a complex hierarchy of service; they had their own small armies of knights and retainers, sometimes leading them into battle.

The Church was by far the greatest landowner in the country, and therefore the largest employer. Many saintly and devout clerics could still be found, but the majority of the clergy had gone the way of the world. The bishops and abbots, for the most part, lived in great state and luxury. The lowlier monks also lived in conditions of comfort, with the obligations of prayer and study offset by the more familiar pursuits of hunting or hawking. They gambled and they drank; they often pursued women where they did not lust after boys.

The secular clergy, better known as the parish priests, were often unlearned. They may have had to till the land and gather the harvest together with their parishioners. They were of the earth.

Many no doubt offered spiritual consolation, and administered the sacraments with due care, but others set no such good example. They lived openly with their mistresses, and neglected their duties. They were in the marketplace and the alehouse more often than they were in the church. The people of Saltash in Cornwall, for example, complained about their priest to the dean of Windsor. 'He is deaf,' they wrote, 'and cannot hear confessions except to the scandal of those confessing; he is a discloser of confessions, because he gets drunk and reveals the confessions of parishioners ... he sells the sacramentals to his parishioners, and refused to minister the last rites to those labouring in the final stages when he was asked.'

In times of famine and plague, of course, the piety of the people in such matters as individual prayer and mortification was all the more plaintive and fervent. At a slightly later date, manuals of devotion became more popular among the literate. This did not amount to a rejection of the authority of the Church. The institution was taken for granted, but fresh avenues of access to the divine were required by the pious. Some, however, questioned the wealth of the Church; some knights and London merchants, in particular, were opposed to clerical pretensions in every sphere of social and economic life. In the parliament of 1371 they argued that the lands of the clergy should be taken over for the sake of the public purse.

The life and career of John Wycliffe must be placed in this context. He was himself in holy orders, a Fellow of Merton College in Oxford before becoming Master of Balliol College at the same university. He was a doctor of divinity, and in that profession he had acquired a great reputation both as a teacher and a writer. He became known as 'the flower of Oxford', and was held by many contemporaries to be 'the greatest clerk that they knew then living'. He held two 'benefices', two rural parishes that he did not visit but from which he collected the revenue. He had also come to the attention of the king's court, and was granted a retainer for his services to the Crown.

He was useful to certain members of that court, among them John of Gaunt, because of his avowed disdain for clerical wealth and privilege. He represented a genuine distaste, shared by some of the nobility and many of the gentry, for the temporal possessions of the Church. But he was a scholar who pressed ahead his arguments with a blithe disregard for the consequences in the world around him; he followed the light, or will-o'-the-wisp, of reason wherever it led him. He wrote in university Latin, and in books whose titles may be translated as *On the Eucharist* and *On the Power of the Pope* he denounced the claims and corruptions of the Church. No printing presses were of course then available to disseminate his message, so it was laboriously copied by hand.

In these manuscripts he espoused the power of scripture, and suggested that the holy word of God was more important than the sacramental hierarchy of the Church. He believed in a version of predestinarianism, by which the elect were already known to God. There was no need for an elaborate machinery of Church power, which simply interfered between the individual soul and its maker. He taught that the king, rather than the pope or the bishops, was the fountain of grace in the land. He denounced the pope as the Antichrist. Friars and monks were repellent and superfluous. Wycliffe also condemned the worship of the saints as idolatry.

More significantly, perhaps, he denied the doctrine of transubstantiation by means of which the substance of the bread and wine of the Mass was changed by miracle to the body and blood of Christ. His animus against the clergy was one of the commonplaces of the period, but his argument against the eucharist laid him open to the charge of heresy. It was said that he was a 'wicked worm' sowing the seeds of schism.

It is not clear that one word of the supposed 'Wycliffite Bible', the first English translation of the entire body of Scriptures, was actually composed by Wycliffe himself; it seems to have been the work of his followers at Oxford, but they were undoubtedly moved by the same spirit of change. Wycliffe wanted the word of God to be made known directly to the people without priestly mediation. In particular he wished to deliver the Bible to the labourers in the field. The ploughman should be able to hear the word of God. The ploughman should also be able to interpret it in his own way and for his own purposes. This was where the Church drew the line. St Peter himself had stated that 'no prophecy of the scripture is of any private interpretation' (2 Peter 1:20).

Wycliffe was never charged or tried, and was allowed to retire to the parsonage of Lutterworth where he continued his studies in peace. But he was effectively silenced. In the following century, on the orders of the pope, his bones were dug up and burned. But in the 1370s no formal apparatus existed for the suppression of heresy. It was so little known, in fact, that no defence against it was considered necessary. Heretics were believed to be strange enthusiasts from overseas, like the Cathars of Languedoc or the Waldensians of Lyon and elsewhere. They were not, and never could be, English.

Yet this university doctrine, promulgated by Wycliffe, was soon taken up by popular preachers and sectarians who rejoiced in his attack upon the pope and his stripping the altars of sacredness. His doctrines were discussed in small assemblies or 'night schools'. These enthusiasts came to be known as Lollards, derived from the Low Dutch *lollen* or *lallen* meaning 'to sing'. An informal network of Oxford scholars, grouped around Wycliffe, may have taught their lessons to receptive audiences. The connections can no longer be followed. 'They have nothing more', wrote one hostile contemporary, 'than a certain appearance of humility of posture, in lowering of the head, abandonment of clothing and pretence of fasting; they pretend simplicity in words, affirming themselves to be burning with love of God and neighbour.'

Burning or not, there did emerge a broad Lollard movement that espoused Wycliffe's arguments as well as adding some of its own. The sacraments were dead signs. There was no purgatory, other than life on this earth, so Masses for the dead have no value. Bread could not be made holier by being muttered over by priests. Confession could only be effective if the priest was full of grace, but no such priest has ever been found. Prayers cannot help the dead any more than a man's breath can cause a great ship to sail. Pilgrimages served no heavenly or earthly purpose. What is a bishop without wealth? *Episcopus Nullatensis*: Bishop of Nowhere. St Thomas of Canterbury had already been consigned to hell for endowing the church with material possessions. The pope is an old whore, sitting on many waters, with a cup of poison in his hands. Greater benefit could be derived from a cask of ale than from the four Evangelists. More eccentric propositions were sometimes entertained. One Lollard, William of Wakeham, believed that the land was above the sky.

The Lollards seem to have flourished in the towns, and along the trading routes between towns. It was the faith of the merchant and the artisan rather than the farmer or the agricultural worker. It was strong, therefore, in London and Bristol, Coventry and Leicester. We are talking of hundreds, rather than thousands, of adherents. Yet it was persistent, and provoked royal vengeance in a later reign.

William Smith of Leicester was a 'deformed' man who became one of the new sectarians and set up a school in the chapel of St John the Baptist next to the leper-house in Leicester. He gave up the eating of flesh or fish; he avoided wine and beer; he walked about barefoot. He also taught himself to read and to write. One evening he and some of his disciples, sitting in a local inn close to the chapel, grew hungry. They had a supply of vegetables, taken from the fields, but they had no fuel with which to cook them. Then William Smith remembered a wooden image of St Katherine that lay in a corner of the chapel. 'Look, my friends,' he said, 'God has provided us fuel; this image will be holy fuel. By hatchet and fire she will suffer a new martyrdom and perhaps, by cruel pains, arrive some time in the kingdom of heaven.' He took up the hatchet. 'Let us see if she be a true saint,' he added, 'for, if so, she will bleed; if not she will be good for fire to cook with.' This reflects the true spirit of Lollardism, rejecting the images of saints as nothing but senseless idols. The incident was inconceivably shocking to the ordinary people, however, and Smith's words were reported to the authorities of the town. He was ordered to walk, barefoot and bare-headed, in a procession from the church of St Mary's in Leicester; he was to hold an image of St Katherine in his right hand, and kneel at the beginning, middle and end of the procession. The ceremony was to be repeated during the Saturday market of the town.

Yet not all of the new faith were poor or disadvantaged. Sir Laurence of St Martin, Justice of the Peace, sheriff and MP for Wiltshire, attended Easter Mass in the spring of 1381 and received communion; he did not swallow the host, however, but spat it into his hand. He took it home and divided it into three parts; he ate the first part with some oysters, the second part with onions, and swallowed the remaining piece with his wine. His sin was observed and denounced. He was ordered to do public penance on every Friday for the rest of his life; he was to kneel before a stone cross that was carved with the images of his sin. He was also dismissed as sheriff. There had of course always been a strain of unbelief and as early as 1200 the prior of Holy Trinity, Aldgate, suggested that 'there are many people who do not believe that God exists, nor do they believe that a human soul lives on after the death of the body. They consider that the universe has always been as it is now, and is ruled by chance rather than by providence.'

Others did not travel so far in heresy. Certain knights and grandees favoured only elements of the new teaching. Some of them attended the preachings of the Lollards, armed with sword and buckler to protect the preacher from the insults of bystanders. These men were not necessarily heretics in any real sense; they were more interested in Wycliffe's attack upon the clergy and the general wealth of the Church. Some were genuinely devout, however, and took part in that broad movement of lay piety known as *devotio moderna* which emphasized the inner life of the spirit and the individual's humble love of God.

At the beginning of the fifteenth century the convocation, or general assembly, of the Church asked the parliament to announce some action against the Lollards. They were still a small sect, but they appeared to be growing. They were finding an audience among the disaffected, and the spiritual authorities were worried about any possible consequences. So in 1401 an Act was passed against 'a certain new sect, damnably thinking of the sacraments and usurping the office of preaching'. They were spreading sedition and insurrection. The bishops were granted the power to arrest and imprison any offenders. If they did not renounce their pernicious beliefs, they could in the end be burned 'in an high place' before the populace. This is the first time that the stake was appointed as the ultimate penalty for heresy. In the next century the fire would become one of the notable judicial sights of England.

The first to die was a London chaplain, William Sawtré, who had declared that the bread of the Mass remained merely bread.

On 26 February 1401, he was stuffed inside a wooden barrel at Smithfield and placed upon the flames.

In what sense did Wycliffe and the Lollards presage the general religious reformation of the sixteenth century? An affinity in certain doctrines, later promulgated both by the Lutherans and the Calvinists, no doubt exists. The detestation of the pope and the spiritual hierarchy, the denial of transubstantiation, the rejection of any worship of images and the increasing reliance on a vernacular Bible, are all part of the same general repudiation of the Catholic Church. Yet in the fourteenth century these attitudes were held only by a small minority. They did not spread very far, and were detested by a large proportion of the population. 'I smell a Loller in the wind', is the line given to one of the pilgrims in the *Canterbury Tales*. It needed another set of accidental circumstances, and another cast of characters, before the Christian faith of England could be reformulated.

In the fourteenth century, however, the religion of the vast majority of the English people remained utterly orthodox and familiar. There was no appetite for change, and no sense of an ending. The Church was part of the texture of life, as enveloping and as inescapable as the weather. England was in any case an island of saints, with the cult of English sainthood being encouraged from the twelfth century; seventeen Englishmen and Englishwomen of that century were beatified.

This was the land of the ecclesiastical style known as the Perpendicular, a peculiarly English form of architecture that flourished in the reign of Edward III. Just as Chaucer abandoned French for English, so the great masons of the latter half of the fourteenth century renounced the Rayonnant and Flamboyant styles of France. The greatest of all these English masons, Henry Yevele, died in the same year as Chaucer himself; his early patron, John of Gaunt, was also the poet's patron. So there is a correspondence. Yevele worked at Windsor, Westminster, Canterbury, Durham and St Paul's as well as superintending the building of many castles, chapels and collegiate churches throughout the country.

Perpendicular was a wholly and uniquely national style, first adumbrated in Gloucester Cathedral. The king introduced it in his rebuilding works at Windsor. It became the pattern for a myriad of parish churches, and is the dominant style for the rest of the medieval period in England. Perpendicular is plain and ordered, with soaring shafts of stone; on slender piers and high arcades there rests a vast and stately vault. The emphasis is always upon the vertical line. The effect is simultaneously one of simplicity and magnificence. It is an austere style, perhaps hastened by the more sombre mood of the country in the years succeeding the Black Death. Carving of too elaborate a nature was no longer fashionable; as the nave of Canterbury Cathedral will testify, the emphasis rested upon total effect rather than on curious detail. There was an instinct for unity.

The 9,000 parish churches of England were the centres of all communal activity, where the living were organized and the dead were commemorated. This was the place where the parishioners were baptized, married and buried. Royal proclamations were issued from the church; local elections were held, and local accounts audited, in the nave. The prized possessions of the community were held there in chests, under lock and key. Disputes were settled and negotiations undertaken, within the walls painted with images of the saints and the apostles. The sculpted forms of angels and saints looked down on the throng from the hammerbeam roof. Assignations, and trysts, were kept by the church porch. Each church had its own brewhouse, to make 'church ale'. Many of the parishioners joined religious guilds, by means of which an altar or a side chapel was maintained with voluntary contributions. On the days of procession the members of the parish would walk in harmony around the church, sometimes showered with flowers and unconsecrated hosts known as singing cakes. The churchyard was used for Sunday markets, and for games such as wrestling and football. But it was also a sacred and even fearful place. The key to the church door was prized as a sovereign remedy against mad dogs, and the ringing of church bells exorcized demons riding in thunder and lightning. Church liturgy itself was deemed to be a form of magical incantation, and sometimes the eucharist was preserved by those who had taken communion; the holy bread could be used to cure ailments or to ward off witches.

The Mass was part of village life; as it was performed before the altar in the chancel, behind the rood screen, the people would gossip and yawn and whisper. The chancel was maintained by the priest, while the nave was the responsibility of the parishioners. The rood screen itself, between the nave and the chancel, was a highly decorated wooden panel on which were painted or sculpted images of the Crucifixion or of the Day of Doom. The service was accompanied by a continual murmur of voices, except at the holy time of the consecration of the eucharist, and by occasional laughter. There was little, if any, preaching and very few pulpits.

Dogs and chickens wandered among the people, who stood or kneeled on the rushes or straw strewn over the earth floor. Sometimes the churchgoers just walked around, staring at the statues of the Virgin or the saints. Some attempt was made at seating in the thirteenth century, but pews did not become a familiar aspect of the church interior until the fifteenth century. Disputes over status were frequent. Who should first go forward for communion? Some of the congregation played chess, or even gambled with dice. Women brought in their needlework. Arguments might erupt, and fights might break out, in the course of the Mass. A bargain might be sealed with a handshake. Thus proceeded the vigorous and ebullient religious life of the fourteenth century, in which earth and heaven were inseparable.

# 25

# The commotion

Richard of Bordeaux was ten years old at the time of his coronation as Richard II. He was the son of the Black Prince and thus closest in blood to the dead king. In the summer of 1377 he was led to Westminster Abbey under a canopy of blue silk borne on spears of silver, and he lay prostrate before the altar as the choir sang the litany. By the end of the long ceremony the boy was exhausted, and was taken to a private apartment in Westminster where he might rest. On the following morning the prelates and the magnates met in a great assembly to choose twenty-four of their number to form a minority council. It might have been thought that the young king's eldest surviving uncle, John of Gaunt, would have taken precedence; but, having ensured that some of his supporters were part of the council, he withdrew with his followers to Kenilworth Castle. He may have been awaiting events.

The boy king assumed the crown at a time of murmuring and dissatisfaction. The shortage of labour, as a result of the pestilence, meant that the great landlords were trying to exact as much work as they could from their unfree tenants; the legislation prohibiting any rise in wages, although only intermittently effective, was still the cause of much complaint. General discontent had also been aroused at the heavy burden of taxation; war supplies were always needed as a result of unsettled business with the French. Only a few days before the coronation, the forces of King Charles V had plundered Rye and burnt down Hastings.

Yet the king's first real test came four years later, when he was confronted by the greatest rebellion in English history. At a meeting of parliament in Northampton, in November and December of 1380, 'a great and notorious rumour' spread among the Commons about a 'dreadful thing' that had taken place in York; a group of rebels, armed with swords and axes, had broken their way into the guildhall of that city and driven out the mayor. They were protesting about the level of taxes imposed upon them by the royal court.

Nevertheless, the Northampton parliament decreed a poll tax three times more exacting than the last. It was the third such tax in four years. A poll tax, literally a tax on every 'poll' or head, was a wholly inequitable mode of taxation; rich and poor paid the same alike, with the proviso that the richer people had the means and opportunity of evasion. So the greater burden fell upon the poor. Widespread unrest followed, naturally enough, and judicial officials were sent to the more disobliging areas in order to ensure collection. The commissioners in London declined to carry on their unwelcome work, for the good reason that it had become too dangerous.

The men of Essex were the first who refused to pay; on 30 May 1381, at Brentwood, a royal official was attacked and driven off. The revolt quickly spread to Kent, Suffolk, Norfolk and Hertfordshire, encompassing some 340 villages. It is pertinent that these were the counties most affected by the pestilence; they were the areas most likely to feel the effects of economic instability and insecurity in the wake of the vast mortality. Change, in medieval society, was always unsettling. In Essex and Kent, also, the labour laws were most strictly imposed. Here, if anywhere, are the causes of rebellion.

The Kentish rioters occupied Canterbury and released all the prisoners held in the archbishop's prison, among them a cleric known as John Ball. The rebels went on to burn the rolls of the county on which the estimates for taxation were written. On the following day the crowd broke open Maidstone Prison and freed its inmates. They already had a clarion call. 'John Ball greets you all and gives you to understand, that he has rung your bell.'

The movement grew much more dangerous when, on 11 June, the rebels of the various regions agreed to march or ride upon London. That was the centre of their woes, the home of the lawyers and the royal officials. It has been estimated that some 30,000 men were now on the road. The men of Kent, always the most fierce, went northwards, while the men of Essex came from the east and the rebels of Hertfordshire from the north. The Hertfordshire men made a camp at Highbury, while the men of Essex rested and waited at Mile End. It was at this point that they were informed of risings all over England. Riots erupted in Norwich and in St Albans, in Winchester and in York, in Ipswich and in Scarborough.

The Kentish men, under the leadership of Wat Tyler or Wat the tiler, gathered on Blackheath on 12 June. The king had retreated to the Tower of London for safety, but on 13 June he and his most trusted councillors agreed to meet the main body of protesters on the heath. The royal party sailed in four barges down the Thames in order to land at Rotherhithe, but too many rebels were clustered on the south bank to allow a safe landing. The young king could now quite clearly hear the terrible shrieks and cries that would soon echo through the streets of London. A chronicler reported that the rebels 'made such a great clamour that it really seemed as if the devil himself had joined their company'. The barge returned to the Tower.

The royal retreat inflamed the rebels. Tyler now led his people to the city itself. They stormed the Marshalsea, in Southwark, and freed its prisoners. Another party burned the tax records held at Lambeth Palace. Then they made their way across London Bridge. The people of London refused to allow the city gates to be closed against them; they sympathized with the cause. They, too, were oppressed by royal exactions on behalf of an unpopular war. The crowd surged along Fleet Street, opening the Fleet Prison and pillaging the lawyers' quarter of New Temple. The Londoners, now invigorated by their example, burned down the residence of John of Gaunt, the Savoy Palace, and killed many of his officials. As the leading nobleman of England, during the minority of the king, Gaunt was the most hated.

The young king surveyed the scene of looting and burning

from a window of the Tower, and asked what should be done. No one knew. But at fourteen he was old enough to think for himself; he would ride out to Mile End and address all of the rebels. He hoped that this would draw them from the city into the eastern suburb, and thus allow his court and household to escape from the Tower. In this, he was only partially successful.

On Friday, 14 June, he made the short journey to Mile End on his horse. He was accompanied by the mayor of London, William Walworth, and some of the household knights. He was already showing signs of personal courage worthy of a king. When the royal party approached the rebels knelt upon the ground, and some of their number shouted, 'Welcome, King Richard. We wish for no other king but you.' Richard then asked them what else they wanted. They wanted 'the traitors', by which they meant the officials who had taxed them and harassed them beyond measure. They wanted to remove a government of scoundrels. The king replied that he would surrender to them any men who were convicted of treachery according to the law. It was a convenient answer to turn away wrath. One of their other demands was that all serfs should be given their freedom, and that land should be rented at fourpence per acre (0.4 hectares). Richard agreed to these proposals. Certain 'traitors', however, were already being summarily despatched. A group of rebels had entered the Tower, in the king's absence, and had dragged out the archbishop of Canterbury and other officials who were sheltering there. All of them were beheaded on Tower Hill, the site of public execution.

More blood was to be shed in this fortnight's storm. The people of London and the suburbs were confronted by groups of rebels and asked 'With whom holdest thou?' If they did not reply, 'With King Richard and the commons', they were beaten up or even beheaded. The rebels declared that they would have no king with the name of John, a clear reference to John of Gaunt. All over England the manors of lords were now being pillaged, and their inhabitants killed. Lawyers and justices were seized, and tax records burned. The proceedings of one manorial court are typical; the heading of one page reads *curia prima post rumorem et combustionem rotulorum*: 'this is the first court after the revolt and the burning of the rolls'.

War and plague had done their work. At approximately the same moment of the fourteenth century, popular rebellions emerged in neighbouring nations. In Flanders the commons had rebelled against their count, Louis, and swept him out of the country; the Jacquerie, in France, unleashed a wave of riot and bloodshed in Paris, Rouen and the surrounding countryside. In Florence a popular revolt of the wool carders and other workers, the *ciompi*, destroyed the political structure of the city.

The morning after the young king's ride to Mile End, on 15 June, Richard came to parley with the rebels at Smithfield. Wat Tyler waited for him there at the head of 20,000 insurgents. As soon as Tyler saw Richard, he rode up to him and began to converse with him. There is a hint that at this point he seemed to be threatening the king, or at least treating him disrespectfully. He began to play with his dagger, and then laid his hand on the bridle of the king's horse. At this point, fearing treason, the mayor of London stabbed a short sword into Tyler's throat. Tyler rode a little way, fearfully wounded, and was taken to the hospital of St Bartholomew beside Smithfield.

The rebels were shocked and angered at the event; some of them drew their bows. The young king galloped up to the front line of archers. 'What are you doing?' he called out to them. 'Tyler was a traitor. Come with me, and I will be your leader.' He did literally lead them a little way north into Islington, where 1,000 armed men had been summoned by the mayor. It seems likely that the rebels had walked into a hastily improvised trap. The leaders fell to their knees, and begged for pardon. Some of the court wished to punish them on the spot, but the king wisely desisted. He ordered the rebels to return to their homes, and forbade any stranger from spending the night in the city. Soon afterwards Tyler was taken from the hospital of St Bartholomew and beheaded in Smithfield itself.

A few days later Richard revoked the charter of emancipation he had granted to the crowd at Mile End, on the ground that it had been extorted from him by violence. He travelled to Essex in order to observe the aftermath of the now extinguished revolt. A group of villagers there asked him to remain faithful to the pledges he had made to them a few days before. His retort, as described by one contemporary chronicler, is worth recording for the insight it shows into the temperament of the king. 'You wretches', he said, 'are detestable both on land and on sea. You seek equality with the lords, but you are unworthy to live. Give this message to your fellows: rustics you are, and rustics you will always be. You will remain in bondage, not as before, but incomparably harsher. For as long as we live we will strive to suppress you, and your misery will be an example to posterity.' A parliament was called later in the year, where it was proposed that the state of bondage known as villeinage should be abolished. The Lords and the Commons, their vital interests as landlords at stake, unanimously voted against any such action. This marked the essential conclusion of the rebellion.

In some areas, such as the recalcitrant county of Essex, the punishments were harsh. The leaders of the rebels were beheaded. John Ball was arrested in St Albans, where he was hanged, drawn and quartered. Wat Tyler had gone before him. After their deaths, they were enshrined as heroes in folk memory. Yet in other regions the reaction of the authorities was more moderate than might have been expected. It is clear that they did not wish to inflame a still dangerous situation.

The unsuccessful rebellion has been called in retrospect 'the peasants' revolt', suggesting that the rebels came from the lowest agricultural class. But the court records show that the participants were generally the leaders of village life, and acted as bailiffs, constables and jurors in their neighbourhoods. It can be argued that these men, far from being accidental or opportunistic rebels, were in fact enunciating real and important grievances. They were of course protesting against the judicial commissions set up to claim the poll tax, but they were also objecting to the corruption of justice by the local magnates. The ordinances and statutes concerning labour, after the Black Death, had materially changed the role of law. It was no longer an instrument of communal justice; it had instead become the machinery of exaction designed to control and discipline the lower classes. The rebels were also protesting against an increasingly futile war, for which they had to pay. They were denouncing greedy landlords. They were violently opposed to a noble class that had shown little interest in the condition of the countryside.

And, as their claims and demands came together, a more general sense of protest was being enunciated against the conditions of life in the fourteenth century. 'Ah, good people,' John Ball declared in a sermon to the rebels on Blackheath, 'matters will not go well in England until everything is held in common and there are neither villeins nor gentlemen. These gentlemen dwell in fair houses, and we have the pain and labour, the rain and wind in the fields. Let us go to the king. He is young. Let us show him in what servitude we live.'

Other wandering preachers dwelled on the age-long theme of equality and justice, going from parish to parish and calling to the villagers just as they were leaving church; their theme was that all things under heaven should be held 'in common'. The day of 13 June – the day when the king's barge turned back to the Tower in the face of the rebels – was Corpus Christi, the feast of the body of Christ in which the whole community was deemed to be a token of that holy body. It was a day of village celebrations and processions, in which the eucharist was carried in triumph around the streets and lanes of each community. So the rebels had, in a sense, pronounced themselves to be holy by marching or riding in a host. They were pronouncing the sacredness of fellowship. The holy bread is made up of many grains. Christ is the miller.

It was claimed at the time that Ball was a follower of Wycliffe, and that Lollardy itself was one of the causes of sedition. Since the Lollards were in no sense a popular movement, the connection is in many respects implausible. But ideas of change and renovation were in the air. Wycliffe had taught that the right of property was founded in grace and that no sinful man was entitled to the services of others; the theories of the scholar could easily be translated into the slogans of the people. So Ball, in his sermon at Blackheath, taught that all men were created equal, and that the ranks and stations of the social hierarchy were the inventions of their oppressors. God wished them to recover their original liberty.

Songs and sayings flew out of the rebellion like sparks from a fire. 'Jack Trueman would have you know that falseness and guile have reigned too long. Truth has been put under a lock. Falseness reigns in every flock . . . Sin spreads like the wild flood, true love, that was good, is fled, and the clergy work us woe for gain . . .

Whoever does wrong, in whatever place it fall, does a wrong to us all ... With right and with might, with skill and with will; let might help right, and skill go before will, and right before might, so goes our mill aright ... The commons is the fairest flower that ever God set on an earthly crown.'

The consequence of the revolt was unease and even dread. A chronicler, recording troubles eleven years after the events here related, remarked that 'men all over England were sure that another general insurrection was at hand'. For more than two centuries the fear most expressed by the authorities was that of local rebellion. A revolt of the masses could trigger disaster for the state. Sporadic revolts after 1381 did indeed take place, often in the form of 'rent strikes' against oppressive landlords. In the face of unbearable tensions, however, attempts were made to appease and accommodate the demands of the peasants. No further poll tax was ever exacted, not at least in the medieval period. The slow abolition of serfdom, and the rising prosperity of those in work, created a sense of freedom that had found one manifestation in the revolt. It also encouraged a greater relaxation of the old feudal order.

The living standards of the agricultural workers improved perceptibly over a generation. Real wages grew, despite the attempts at legislation prohibiting any such rise, and a poem such as 'How the Ploughman learned the Paternoster' reveals the profusion of meat, fish and dairy products in the households of the labourers:

> November: At Martinmas I kill my swine
> December: And at Christmas I drink red wine.

Life expectancy also rose. The historians of dress have noted that clothing became brighter, and more luxurious, and jewellery more evident, in the latter years of the fourteenth century.

The king himself had passed a test of fire. He had confronted, and defeated, the first and last popular rebellion in English history. His later behaviour suggests that his belief in himself, and in the essential divinity of kingship, was thereby redoubled. At the age of fifteen he was truly a king whose presence alone was enough to command large crowds of people into obeying his will. He was 6 feet (1.8 metres) in height, with blond hair and a round, somewhat feminine face; he had flared nostrils, prominent cheekbones and heavy eyelids. John Gower, at the beginning of the king's reign, described him as 'the most beautiful of kings' and the 'flower of boys'. He may have been indulging in a little flattery, but the chroniclers of the period were at one in emphasizing Richard's beauty. He looked the part.

His manner, however, was considered to be abrupt. He was inclined to stammer, when he was excited, and he flushed easily. His temper was somewhat uncertain, and he was always quick to assert his royal dignity. His words to the rebels of Essex, whether he actually uttered them or not, are in that sense characteristic. Other accounts of his speech and behaviour tend to corroborate them. 'I am a king,' he said to one earl, 'and your lord. I will continue to be king. I will be a greater lord than ever I was before, in spite of all my enemies.' His anger was terrible, just like that of his Plantagenet ancestors. He once drew his sword on the archbishop of Canterbury, and would have killed him had he not been restrained. One chronicler, known only as 'the monk of Evesham', described him as being extravagant in dress and imperious in temper; he was frightened of war and preferred to spend the night 'carousing with friends' and indulging himself in 'unmentionable' ways. This has often been taken as an allusion to Richard's possible homosexuality, but to a monk many things may be unmentionable.

The emphasis on his royalty meant that he cared deeply for ceremony and for spectacle. He enjoyed dressing up. On one occasion he wore a costume of white satin on which were hung cockle-shells and mussel-shells plated in silver; his doublet was adorned with orange trees embroidered in gold thread. He loved to preside at tournaments, but he was not so enthusiastic about true battles. One of his relatives, Thomas of Lancaster, declared at a later date that 'he is too heavy in the arse, he only asks for drinking and eating, sleeping, dancing and leaping about'. The medieval texts often refer to 'leaping about' without explaining what is meant by it. Thomas of Lancaster went on to say, according to the chronicler Froissart, that 'this is no life for men-at-arms who ought to win honour through deeds of arms and put their bodies to work'.

In 1383 the young king declared that he was now prepared to rule in person, having taken the precaution of marrying Anne, the daughter of the Holy Roman Emperor, at the beginning of the previous year. Both parties were fifteen years old, and Anne was described by a chronicler as 'a tiny scrap of humanity'. Now bolstered by formidable marital relatives, and by his own assumption of power, Richard felt able to choose his advisers beyond the charmed circle of the hereditary lords. This was not to the taste of his uncles, John of Gaunt and Thomas of Woodstock – dukes of Lancaster and Gloucester respectively – who withdrew from the court in protest against what they called 'evil advisers'. Richard feared Gaunt and Woodstock, as possible claimants for the throne, and he filled his household with favourites. The new king was lavish in the grants of lands, castles and titles; he borrowed heavily, and was obliged to give the crown of England as security. The old lords, out of favour and denied gifts, were growing restless. It is the familiar story of jealousy and suspicion, compounded by the king's own secretive and sensitive temperament. The court had become a dangerous place once more.

In the spring of 1383 there had been a botched campaign to relieve Flanders of French control; it had been led by Henry Despenser, bishop of Norwich, but the bishop did not prove to be a good commander. In full martial gear he led his troops into battle against the Flemish towns, but his victims were ordinary Flemish citizens. 'Men, women and children', according to one report, 'were hewed together in one vast massacre.' The bishop may have believed that he was saving their souls. His army was eventually surrounded, and terms were agreed without Despenser ever having attacked the French enemy. It seems likely that the king himself planned an invasion of France in this year, but the prospect of heavy taxation and another popular insurrection deterred him.

Another military failure followed two years later. France and Scotland, old friends in arms, were eager to pursue a joint campaign from the north of England. So in the summer of 1385 Richard II gathered an army to forestall them. He called a feudal summons, the last such summons in English history, and the larger magnates were obliged to respond to the call. The English army met at Newcastle and marched northwards, burning Melrose Abbey and other religious houses on their way to Edinburgh. Once the king arrived in the capital, however, he realized that the Scots had gone; the Scottish soldiers were moving towards the Highlands. Some of his commanders urged him to pursue them, but he declined to do so. Why march into barren countryside without the chance of finding supplies? So he went home. This was an eminently wise decision. Doing nothing is sometimes the best course. But it did not improve the king's reputation for valour. He had been given the opportunity of displaying himself as a sovereign of war, the indisputable qualification for a king, but success eluded him.

The debacle only served to increase the young king's antipathy to war. In the course of his reign he would never again lead his armies against the French or the Scots. There would be no memorable battles, no sieges, no towns or castles conquered. In any case the English treasury could no longer afford the cost of further military adventure.

Further rumours of war were being whispered in the spring and summer of 1386. A French army of 30,000 men was being gathered on the coast of Flanders, and was compared to the Greek army that had overcome ancient Troy. The people of Rye, Sandwich and Dover were commanded to remain within the walls of their towns, and the castles close to the southern coast were strengthened and refurbished. The citizens of London were ordered to stock food supplies that might last for three months. It was reported that some Londoners were leaving the city. Richard himself planned yet another attack upon France, but the Commons refused to supply his coffers. The threat of invasion faded away by the end of the year. The French court, like that of the English, did not have the funds to maintain so large an army for so long. Autumn gave way to winter. The fierce weather of that season was another deterrent. The business of the country could go on unimpeded, in theory, and the English people could enjoy the pleasures of peace.

In October 1386 the parliament met in Westminster Hall, as had become the custom, but Richard had prepared a surprise for its members. The statues of previous monarchs, larger than life-size, adorned the hall; the thirteen kings, from Edward the Confessor to Richard himself, looked down upon the proceedings. It was a signal vision of Richard's concept of kingship. The power of sovereignty was meant to overawe the lowlier subjects of the realm.

It did not work out like that in practice. The Lords sent several petitions to the king, all designed to curb his use or abuse of power. He was accused of flouting the law, and ignoring the advice of his proper councillors. He was condemned for appointing and rewarding unsuitable advisers; he gave out land and offices without advice, and made free use of pardons for rape and murder in order to raise revenue. It was clear, at least, that he was now strong enough to resist the counsels of the senior members of the realm.

A deputation from the parliament visited the king at the palace of Eltham, since Richard himself had refused to travel to Westminster. They demanded the removal of his chancellor, Michael de la Pole, one of the 'new men' whom Richard favoured at the expense of the old nobility. The king raged against the assembled Lords and Commons, accusing them of disloyalty and even of treachery. He told them, in his abrupt and angry manner, that he would not dismiss a servant from his kitchen at the behest of parliament. Rumours of plots and counter-plots were everywhere. Richard was behaving in secret and arbitrary ways, and it was whispered that he wished to behead the most notable of his enemies.

It was time for a more powerful intervention. Thomas of Woodstock, the duke of Gloucester, sought a further interview with Richard at Eltham; he was accompanied by Richard FitzAlan, eleventh earl of Arundel, a powerful and skilful nobleman. These two magnates informed the king that he had been ruling England unwisely and unlawfully. They said that the country had always been governed by the concord between the king and the noble lords; only a sliver of truth can be found in this argument, but they enforced their claim with a barely disguised threat that the king could be deposed. The example of his great-grandfather, Edward II, was laid before him. That unfortunate monarch had been forced to resign in favour of his son before being cruelly murdered. Thomas of Woodstock, one of Richard's uncles, may even have desired the throne for himself.

Richard took the example of Edward II to heart. Nine years later he would plead with the pope to canonize his predecessor as one of the great royal saints of England. There is no doubt that he always felt a strong sense of identification with his unhappy ancestor. But in the winter of 1386 he was obliged to temporize with his enemies. He was still only twenty-one years old, and could not have been entirely sure of himself. He could not yet afford to antagonize them. So he yielded to their demands. The king would come to Westminster. He agreed that his household could be investigated and administered by a commission of nobles and bishops. Michael de la Pole was dismissed, and later imprisoned. Thomas Arundel, bishop of Ely and brother of Richard FitzAlan, took his place as chancellor.

The parliament house had never been so powerful as it was in the last months of 1386, but it would be unwise to praise its members too highly. They were not necessarily good patriots fighting against a tyrant. They were just as preoccupied with their own interests as were the king and his household; a poem of the period describes their conduct as confused and uncertain. Some members sat there 'like a nought in arithmetic that marks a place but has no value in itself'. Some were taking bribes from royal officials or other interested parties, and some were paid dependants who would not say anything without orders. Some stumbled and mumbled; others slept or stammered their way through their speeches, not knowing what they meant to say.

The king chafed under the restrictions imposed upon him by what soon became known as the 'Wonderful Parliament'. The commission was given its powers for a year; Richard decided to wait and watch, while at the same time mustering his resources. He consulted with the aldermen of London and the sheriffs of the counties, but received only ambiguous encouragement. His exactions had hardened their hearts. Then he called upon the judges. The most senior of them met in the summer of 1387, and determined that the king could change or dismiss the ordinances of parliament at his will. This effectively annulled the power of both Lords and Commons. The judges also declared that those who had attempted to curb the power of the king could be punished as traitors even if they were not technically guilty of treason.

This was most serious for the king's opponents. The earls could be beheaded, for example, and their lands held forfeit. Throughout the autumn a tense confrontation was continued, the lords refusing to meet the king after he had summoned them. The earl of Northumberland tried to act as a mediator between the two parties, but it became clear that there was no room for compromise or negotiation. So in November the lords rose up in arms. They called upon their household forces and, at a battle beside the Thames near Radcot on 20 December 1387, they defeated an army sent against them. Then they marched upon London, where Richard was sheltering in the Tower.

It seems likely that the king was deposed for two or three days, effectively stripped of his power, but no clear agreement about the name of his successor could be found. Faced with rival claims, the only real choice was to reinstate the young king suitably chastened and obedient. To be deprived of his throne, even for a few days, was a severe blow to his own regal sense of selfhood. He had in effect been stripped of his identity.

Richard did indeed submit to their demands. The lords took over his household, and dismissed some of the royal servants. Other household officials were arrested. The lords then summoned a parliament to meet on 3 February, where they wished to deal with their other enemies. There is an account of the opening session in which the lords, dressed in gold robes, linked hands and slowly advanced upon the king as he sat upon the throne; then they bowed to him, and filed into their places. It became known as the 'Merciless Parliament'.

Their first victims were the judges who had pronounced them to be traitors. The Chief Justice of the King's Bench, Robert Tresilian, was tried and condemned to death while his judicial colleagues were sentenced to exile in Ireland. Tresilian fled for sanctuary to a chapel of Westminster Abbey, but he was dragged out and carried off to Tyburn. The mob carved images of the devil, and of the zodiac, upon his body before his throat was cut and his corpse hung upon the gallows. Seven of the king's followers were also executed.

Yet the new regime of the lords was not marked by any great success. The Commons had hoped that the removing of the 'evil' counsellors from the king's side would benefit the realm by financial and judicial reform. But the Lords were divided; they pursued their own interests to the detriment of the Commons. The finances of the country did not improve, and factional violence became increasingly common. They also failed in the pursuit of military glory;

a planned invasion of France degenerated into a series of coastal skirmishes. The kingdom could only properly be guided by a king. A gathering of notables was not sufficient.

So Richard struck back. In the winter of 1388 the king offered to act as a mediator between the Lords and the Commons. The great lords were effectively lawless, and were able to escape justice with impunity. They were, to use Langland's word, 'wolveskynnes'. With their bands of followers they were acting like local tyrants oppressing the common people. Richard offered to restrain his own use of retainers, and sweetly asked the lords to follow his example. His was a policy of divide and rule. He represented strength and compromise.

In the spring of 1389 the king declared, to his council at Westminster, that he had decided once more to assume full responsibility for the affairs of the nation. There was little disagreement. He said that for twelve years he and his kingdom had been ruled or overruled by others. What had been the result? The people had been burdened by excessive taxation that had benefited no one. He was now twenty-two, and would rule alone.

Richard's sense of kingship had been threatened and almost destroyed in the last days of 1388; now he projected it more fiercely and defiantly. His nomenclature changed. The petitions of the Commons were addressed to 'your highness and royal majesty' rather than, as before, to 'your rightful and gracious lord'. The royal servants began to describe him as 'highness', 'majesty' and 'your high royal presence'. He told one knight out of Warwickshire, Sir William Bagot, that he wished to be remembered as one who had 'recovered his dignity, regality and honourable estate' and who had ensured that his prerogative was 'humbly obeyed . . . as it had been in any other king's time'.

He believed himself to be the source of all justice and order, the pattern of authority; that is why he was gracious to the Commons as well as to the Lords. They were all equally his subjects. It is a measure of his sense of greatness that his household was three times as large as that of Henry I. In the autumn of 1390 he also began to gather around him a body of followers, known as an 'affinity', who adopted as a badge the image of the white hart. He derived it from the coat of arms of his mother. All is of a piece with his love of pageantry and his taste for magnificent robes. The court became the stage for his splendour. At some banquets, and at the three festal crown-wearings of the year, he would sit in state upon his throne watching everyone but conversing with nobody; he would remain very still, crowned and in full regalia, as if he had become a living statue. 'And if his eye fell upon anyone,' a chronicler reveals, 'that person had to bend his knee to the king.'

His sense of royalty was also an aspect of his piety. God was his only overlord. He frequently visited the shrines of saints, and instituted new cults; he was fascinated by reports and rumours of miracles; he was the patron of the Carthusians, and lavished treasure for the rebuilding of churches and abbeys. There is a panel painting, known as 'the Wilton Diptych'. On the left panel Richard is depicted kneeling, dressed in a red mantle embroidered in gold, with Edward the Confessor (saint), John the Baptist (saint) and King Edmund (saint and martyr) standing around him. On the right-hand panel is painted an image of the Virgin and Child surrounded by eleven angels. One of the angels holds aloft the flag of St George. So here Richard celebrates the continuity of his reign with his saintly Anglo-Saxon forebears, united in the veneration of peace and national renewal. He compounded his attachment to the memory of Edward the Confessor by impaling his own arms with the arms of the dead king. It might almost seem that Richard even considered himself to be worthy of canonization.

Yet triumphalism can turn into tyranny. In the summer of 1397 Richard invited the earl of Warwick to dinner and then, when the meal was over, ordered his arrest. On hearing the news of this, the earl of Arundel was persuaded to surrender himself. The king then rode out to Pleshey Castle in Essex, the home of Thomas of Woodstock, duke of Gloucester, with a party of armed retainers. Woodstock was roused from sleep, and was then personally arrested by his nephew. Richard ordered the immediate arrest of these three great lords on the grounds that they were conspiring against him. He may also have been brooding on old offences, since these were the three men who had led the rebellion against him and had briefly deposed him in the Tower. He now believed himself strong enough to destroy them. He was asserting his manhood by avenging past affronts.

The chronicler, Thomas Walsingham, wrote that the kingdom was 'suddenly and unexpectedly thrown into confusion'. Richard then called a parliament that, in the general atmosphere of suspicion and terror, was notably submissive. It had every reason to be cooperative. Westminster itself was filled with troops, and the king was protected by a bodyguard of 300 archers from his favourite county of Cheshire. The building in which the parliament assembled was surrounded by archers. Richard was relying upon force, and the threat of force, to make his way.

At the beginning of the session he declared, through the mouth of his chancellor, that the king demanded the full plenitude of his power. He had been aware of many illegalities committed in previous years but now, out of his affection for his people, he extended a general pardon – except to fifty individuals, whom he would not explicitly name. This was of course a policy to keep everyone in subjection. He might include anyone he pleased within the category of the unknown fifty. The king was also gracious enough to accept, at the urging of the Commons, the duties levied on leather and wool in perpetuity.

Thomas of Woodstock, after his arrest, was despatched to the English bastion at Calais where on the king's direct orders he was quietly killed. Reports suggest that he was either strangled with a towel or suffocated beneath a featherbed. The result was in any case the same.

Arundel was subjected to what would now be called a show trial, of which a partial transcript survives. John of Gaunt, the duke of Lancaster, presided.

> *Lancaster:* Your pardon is revoked, traitor.
> *Arundel:* Truly you lie. Never was I a traitor.
> *Lancaster:* Why in that case did you seek a pardon?
> *Arundel:* To silence the tongues of my enemies, of whom you are one.
> *Richard:* Answer the appeal.
> *Arundel:* I see it all now. You, who accuse me, are all liars. I claim the benefit of pardon, which you granted when you were of full age.
> *Richard:* I granted it provided it were not to my prejudice.
> *Lancaster:* The pardon is worthless.

It was indeed worthless. On the same day Arundel was led to Tower Hill where he was beheaded. The earl of Warwick suffered a more lenient fate. He was banished for life to the Isle of Man. The extensive lands of the three lords were confiscated, and given to the king's friends and supporters. His enemies appeared to have been scattered.

Yet Richard was despondent. His wife, Anne of Bohemia, had died in 1394 from an outbreak of the plague; they had been married for twelve years, but had produced no children. That was another mark against him. He was, after all, already twenty-seven years old and should have sired a family. In his extravagant grief he ordered that the palace of Sheen should be razed to the ground; this is the place where he and Anne had once been happy. It seems likely that his health was also deteriorating, since the royal accounts show very large sums of money being paid to his physicians. He may have been becoming dangerous.

Many of the lords testified later that they had in fact become frightened of the king. With the invisible list of fifty traitors he could confiscate lands and property as he wished. He could consign anyone to prison. According to a later deposition the king had declared that the law of England resided in his own breast, and that he could make or break laws at his discretion. He levied large fines on the towns and shires that had sided with the rebel lords. He demanded loans from the richer abbeys and monasteries. He was, like most kings, avaricious and acquisitive; but his greed was compounded by violence and disregard of law. 'He is a child of death,' he wrote to the count of Holland, 'who offends the king.' Yet like all tyrants he was fearful. He was defended at all times by the 300 Cheshire archers. 'Sleep securely while we wake, Dick,' the captain of his guard was heard to say to him, 'and dread naught while we live.'

Richard's pre-eminent will became manifest in a quarrel between two lords at the end of 1397. Thomas Mowbray, the duke of Norfolk, and the king's cousin, Henry Bolingbroke, the duke of Hereford, had only recently been ennobled to the highest rank of the peerage. They were rewarded for their support of the king.

Mowbray, for example, had been captain of Calais when the unfortunate Thomas of Woodstock was despatched to that garrison
town; there is no doubt that he played some role in his suffocation.
In the climate of fear and suspicion in which they now lived,
however, even the king's friends began to fear for their lives.

They had a conversation. 'We are on the point of being
undone,' Mowbray told Bolingbroke. 'That cannot be,' Bolingbroke
replied. 'The king has granted us pardon and has declared in
parliament that we behaved as good and loyal servants'. Mowbray
went on to remark that 'it is a marvellous and false world that we
live in', suggesting that Bolingbroke and his father, John of Gaunt,
narrowly escaped being murdered by the king's men; he also
suggested that Richard, with the connivance of other lords, was
planning to disinherit both of them and give their lands to others.
'God forbid', Bolingbroke exclaimed. 'It will be a wonder if the
king assents to such designs. He appears to make me good cheer,
and has promised to be my good lord. Indeed he has sworn by
St Edward [the Confessor] to be a good lord to me and others.'
Mowbray was dismissive. 'So has he often sworn to me by God's
body; but I do not trust him the more for that.' In a world of
whispers and of clandestine plotting, of lies and of secrecy, this was
equivalent to treason.

Rumours spread. Bolingbroke informed his father, John of
Gaunt, of the conversation. Word got back to the king. It seems
likely that he confronted Bolingbroke, and demanded a full account
of what had been said. Having heard his report the king demanded
that he repeat it to the parliament. Mowbray then gave himself up
into the king's custody, and denied everything that Bolingbroke
had revealed. The two dukes were told to appear before a parliamentary committee set up to resolve the dispute. Still the controversy could not be concluded and, in the old judicial fashion, it was
decreed that Thomas Mowbray and Henry Bolingbroke should
fight a duel in which God would confer victory upon the true man.
Yet who was the true man? It is possible that their roles should be
reversed, and that Bolingbroke had been the one who had first
expressed misgivings about the king; when they failed to work
upon Mowbray, he decided to accuse him of treason to cover up
his own guilt. That is one possibility. It is also possible that

Mowbray had whispered treason as a plot to snare Bolingbroke; Bolingbroke, suspecting this, decided to end the conspiracy by denouncing him. The truth cannot now be recovered.

The battle was set for Coventry on 16 September 1398. The tournament was to be held at Gosford, and the field survives still as Gosford Green. Bolingbroke commissioned armour from Milan, and Mowbray from Bohemia. The lords of the kingdom were consumed with excitement; this would be the most famous duel of their lifetimes. The days of Arthur and the Round Table might be said to have returned. The two dukes came forward on the appointed day. The archbishop of Canterbury was among the many thousands of spectators. Henry Bolingbroke arrived at nine in the morning, with six mounted retainers. Challenged about his business he proclaimed in a loud voice, 'I am Henry, duke of Hereford, come to do my duty against the false traitor Thomas, duke of Norfolk'. He crossed himself and rode to his pavilion at one end of the lists. The king entered, surrounded by the Cheshire archers, and proceeded to his chair of state where he might survey the proceedings. Mowbray then appeared and, giving the same challenge as his antagonist, cried out, 'God save the right!'

The two knights were about to proceed against one other. Bolingbroke spurred his horse forward, while Mowbray remained still. But the king rose and called out, 'Hold!' The dukes retired to their respective pavilions, and the king withdrew. Two hours passed, inciting intense speculation among the crowds of spectators. Then the Speaker of the Commons appeared and announced to the multitude the king's decision. Bolingbroke was to be banished from the realm for ten years, and Mowbray would be exiled for life. The sentence on Bolingbroke provoked loud calls of dismay, but the king's will was law.

The king really had little choice in the matter. Victory for either man would cause him considerable difficulty. If Mowbray was triumphant, the king's role in the murder of Gloucester might be subject to scrutiny. If Bolingbroke were the winner, his chance of succeeding or even supplanting the king might be increased. The king had no heir, and he had only recently married a child of seven – Isabella, the daughter of the king of France – from whom no issue could yet be foreseen. It was a most disappointing end to what might have been a great tale of chivalry. But the king prevailed. The two men sailed into exile. Thomas Mowbray died in Venice in the following year, but for Henry Bolingbroke the story was only beginning.

He had sailed to France with a manifest sense of injustice at the hands of the king, and waited there in the hope that favourable events might follow. The king of France, Charles VI, granted him a residence in the centre of Paris. Then, five months after his departure from England, his father died. John of Gaunt, as the first duke of Lancaster, was the progenitor of what became known as the house of Lancaster; he owned vast territories in the north of England, and possessed more than thirty castles throughout the realm. He had been a prominent, but not a notable, commander and administrator. He had in particular earned the hatred of Londoners, and of those who had taken part in the rebellion of 1381, as de facto leader of the realm during the king's minority. He was a man who combined familial greatness with personal mediocrity.

Henry Bolingbroke might in the normal course of events be expected to inherit his father's lands and castles. But he was in exile. And the king was greedy. Richard then took a course that alienated much of the support he had acquired over the years of his rule. He extended Bolingbroke's banishment in perpetuity, and confiscated his father's estates. Such an interference in the laws of inheritance was immensely shocking to a society that relied deeply upon custom and precedent. No landowner, or landowner's family, could feel safe under such a king. Any monarch who unlawfully deprived his subjects of their property, in defiance of the injunctions of the Magna Carta, was at once considered to be a tyrant.

At the beginning of May 1399, in a spectacular act of folly, Richard sailed to Ireland with an expeditionary force. It is difficult to understand why he chose to absent himself from his kingdom at such a difficult time; the only explanation must be that he had lulled himself, or been lulled, into a false sense of security. Certainly he believed that he was under divine guidance, and that no earthly enemy could defeat an anointed king. With God as his guard, what did he have to fear?

Henry took advantage of the king's absence and, in the early summer, sailed from Boulogne; on 4 July he landed at Ravenspur in Yorkshire with no more than 300 soldiers. His courage, and earnestness, cannot be in doubt. From his own old territories in the north, he began his campaign to destroy the tyrant of England. Richard had left the kingdom to the guidance of Edmund, duke of York, his uncle and Henry's. York was neither principled nor courageous. He had no intelligence of Henry's movements, and at first marched west rather than north-east. In the confusion Henry strengthened the castles on his lands, and in the process several thousand men flocked to his service. At Doncaster he met the senior family of the north, the Percys; Henry Percy, earl of Northumberland, was accompanied by his son known as Hotspur.

In their presence Henry swore an oath that he had returned to England only to claim his lands; he had no designs upon the king himself. He may have been lying, but it is more likely that he was not yet sure of his ultimate goal. He would proceed with caution, taking advantage of events as they unfolded. The combined army of the rebel lords and retainers then began the march south, taking control of central and eastern England with only pockets of resistance. It may now have occurred to Henry that the king was too unpopular to be saved.

Richard himself was still in Ireland. He received news of the invasion by 10 July, but did not set sail for England for another two weeks. He could not muster enough ships. In that period his cause was lost. When the Welsh gentry were summoned to support him, they replied that they believed Richard to be already dead. Henry had decided to move west in order to confront the king, if and when he should return, and at a parish church in Gloucester the duke of York surrendered to the invader. York realized that Richard's hopes of retaining the crown were diminishing day by day. He joined Henry's army and went on to Bristol, where three of the king's most prominent officials were executed. It had become a triumphal progress.

Richard landed on the Welsh coast on 24 July. He lingered here for five days, by which time he had received news of both the surrender of his uncle and the events at Bristol. It is reported that he was alternately despondent and defiant. Eventually he decided to attempt to reach one of his supporters, the earl of Salisbury, who was at Conway Castle in North Wales. He put on the garb of a poor priest and, with fifteen supporters, fled in the dead of night. It took him nine days to reach his destination. A contemporary observer reports that he was now utterly downcast and dejected. He frequently broke into tears.

Henry shadowed him along a parallel course. He, too, went north from Bristol towards Chester. So the two cousins were ready for the final encounter. The king and the earl of Salisbury agreed that they would send representatives to Henry, demanding to know his intentions. In return Henry sent his negotiator, the earl of Northumberland, to converse with the king at Conway. Northumberland, prudently, concealed his army before entering the king's presence. It is reported that Northumberland swore to the king that Henry wished only for the return of his own lands and would protect the king's right to rule. It is impossible to judge whether Henry was deceiving the king. After a delay of a few days Richard agreed to leave the castle in the company of Northumberland. Yet his was only a tactical surrender. He told his supporters secretly that Henry 'would be put to bitter death for this outrage that he has done to us'. That prospect must also have occurred to Henry himself.

Richard and Northumberland had only travelled a few miles when the king, on ascending a hill, saw the army that his companion had previously concealed. He fell into a panic, and demanded to be taken back to Conway Castle. Once more Northumberland swore, on the precious host, that Henry had no thought of deposing him. If this was a bluff, it was a sacrilegious bluff. So the party travelled onwards to Flint Castle in north-eastern Wales where, alerted by swift messengers, Henry had agreed to meet Richard. It must have occurred to the king that he had now effectively been taken prisoner. He reached the castle before Henry and, on the morning after his arrival, he climbed up to the battlements; from that vantage he saw Henry's army approaching, and is reported to have said that 'now I can see the end of my days coming'.

He kept Henry waiting, at the great door, while he ate his last meal of freedom in the keep of the castle. Then at Northumberland's request he came down to speak with his enemy. In the play

*Richard II* by William Shakespeare, he uttered at this point the words, 'Down, down, I come like glistering Phaeton'. Henry took off his cap and bowed low to the sovereign. 'My lord,' he said, 'I have come sooner than you sent for me, and I shall tell you why. It is said that you have governed your people too harshly, and they are discontented. If it is pleasing to the Lord, I shall help you to govern them better.' This report has the ring of truth. Henry would have made sure that his words were exactly recorded. It is significant, too, that he spoke in English rather than in French. Now he represented the nation. 'If it pleases you, fair cousin,' Richard replied, 'then it pleases us well.'

On that same day the two men, and the army, rode on to Chester. The king was consigned to a small room in the castle; he was under the control of the sons of Gloucester and Arundel, two men whom he had put to death. Henry now set his mind to the future. He issued a summons, in the king's name, for the assembly of a new parliament at Westminster. On 20 August he and his captive rode to London. Henry took up residence in the bishop of London's palace, while the king was despatched to the Tower.

It may have been only at this point that Henry decided to strike and claim the throne. He had been waiting on events, but now saw his path clear ahead of him. The king was at his mercy, and no body of royal supporters was able to liberate him. There may have been a show of force by the Cheshire archers upon whom the king had relied, but it came to nothing. Henry now decided to consult the histories of the realm for precedents. Two weeks later a committee of dignitaries was established to consider 'the matter of setting aside King Richard, and of choosing the duke of Lancaster in his stead, and how it should be done' (Henry had become duke of Lancaster on the death of his father). The committee came to the conclusion that Richard should be deposed 'by the authority of the clergy and people'.

On 29 September a deputation had gone to the king lodged or imprisoned in the Tower. The official parliamentary report suggests that the members of this deputation 'reminded' the king that at Conway he had volunteered to give up his throne; the king, recalling this promise, agreed that he should abdicate. This is most unlikely and, in any case, a contemporary chronicler provides a wholly different picture of the occasion. The author of the *Chronique de la Trahison et Mort de Richard II* states that the king raged at the nobles who had come to interview him and declared that he would 'flay some of these men alive'. Another chronicler had visited the king eight days before, and described him as bitterly angry at the country that had betrayed him. It seems fair to say that he did not go quietly into the night.

On 30 September a parliament met at Westminster. There are reports that it was packed with Henry's supporters, 'many sorts of folk who were neither noble nor gentle . . . in such great heaps that the officers could scarcely enter the hall'. The king's renunciation of the throne was read out to those assembled. Although the official report asserts that he had agreed to its terms, and that he had signed it in the presence of witnesses, there is still a possibility that the document was faked. It was, at the very least, extorted with threats. Richard may have agreed to it as the only way of saving his life.

Yet by acclamation of all those present, it was accepted. They were asked if Henry had the right to be king. 'Yes!' they cried out. 'Yes! Yes!' Even though parliament had no formal right to deposition, the king was removed in what was essentially a coup d'état. Henry then declared that by virtue of 'the right line of blood coming from the good lord King Henry the Third' he had come to 'recover' a realm on the point of being undone by bad laws. There is no reason to question his sincerity in this. He had a very good claim to the crown. By the complicated processes of genealogy only a boy of eight, Edmund Mortimer, earl of March, had a stronger; but England did not want, or need, another juvenile monarch.

Henry was led towards the throne; he stood for a moment, and then knelt down to pray. Then he rose, made the sign of the cross on the back and the front of the throne, and sat down upon it to general acclamation. He was anointed with the chrism that had come from a miraculous phial given by the Virgin Mary to Thomas Becket; or so it was believed. Richard II had discovered it, two years before, while searching in the Tower for a necklace once worn by King John. It is also reported that, as a result of the anointing, the new king's hair was soon full of lice.

From his earliest youth Henry had been acquainted with the

uses and abuses of power; he was only three months older than Richard, and had carried the sword before him at the coronation in the summer of 1377. Henry had also been with him in the Tower when Richard and his entourage sheltered from the peasants' rebellion. There had never been peace between the two men, however, and Richard also chose to view Henry as a personal enemy. He gave him none of the great offices of state and had chosen his uncle, Edmund of York, to succeed him in a direct rebuff to Henry. Now the whirligig of the world had turned. Lancaster had triumphed over York, but the forcible removal of the king would bring much mischief and bloodshed to the realm.

On the day after the parliament Richard was informed of his deposition. He replied that he 'hoped that his cousin would be a good lord to him'. He was soon disabused. The new king asked the lords for their advice on the deposed monarch; he was told that Richard should be placed in a stronghold under the care of trusted gaolers and that no one else be allowed to see him. So Richard was removed, in disguise, to Leeds Castle. From there he was taken, at the beginning of December, to the more heavily fortified castle at Pontefract in Yorkshire.

Some of Richard's courtiers and supporters rose in rebellion two or three weeks later, but Henry thwarted and defeated them. The rebellion, however, made it clear that the deposed king was still dangerous. At the beginning of February 1400, the king and council met to debate Richard's future. If he was alive, they concluded, he should be heavily guarded; if he was dead, his body should be shown to the people. Death had entered the room. A week or two later the body of Richard lay in his prison cell. The manner of his going is not known. Some say that he was starved by his gaolers; others believe that, in his grief, he refused all food and so killed himself.

His body was taken south, in procession or in pageant; it was displayed at several convenient sites, so that the people of England could be assured that he was truly dead. An illustration of the scene can be found in an illuminated manual of the period. It shows the king lying in a litter covered in black cloth with a black canopy above him; his head is uncovered, lying on a black cushion. Two black horses, and four knights dressed in mourning, complete the picture. On its arrival in London the bier was taken to St Paul's Cathedral where a requiem Mass was held. The coffin was then taken to a Dominican monastery at King's Langley, 21 miles (33.8 kilometres) outside London. A later king, Henry V, ensured that Richard II was reburied in Westminster Abbey; he may have done so in order to expiate the impiety of his father, Henry Bolingbroke, in overthrowing a lawful king.

In the reign of Richard II, a splendid and dangerous sovereign, the handkerchief was introduced to England.

# 26

# Into the woods

Robin Hood is an English native. He and his 'merry men' inhabit the forest, where they live by means of various laudable crimes such as robbing the rich and poaching the king's deer. They always manage to elude the law, generally represented by the sheriff of Nottingham; they dwell in Sherwood Forest, which lies under the sheriff's jurisdiction.

The story was current in the thirteenth century, and may have been fashioned in its early decades from attested events. In 1216 Robin Hood, a servant of the abbot of Cirencester, was accused of murder; but this may be coincidental. In 1225 the sheriff of Yorkshire seized the goods of Robert Hood or Hod, who had fled from the city of York heavily in debt to the church courts. The same sheriff was asked in that year to pursue a notorious outlaw, known as Robert of Wetherby; the fugitive was eventually hanged in chains. Were Robert of Wetherby and Robin Hood the same person? The names of Robert and Robin were more or less interchangeable. The sheriff of Yorkshire had previously been the sheriff of Nottinghamshire. So facts are conflated and reinterpreted until the point when a legend of outlawry and liberty can appear.

Robin Hood is first mentioned as the generic name for an outlaw in the justice rolls of the late thirteenth century, where he appears as 'Robehod' or 'Robinhood'. He was so well known a hundred years later that the idle priest Sloth, in *Piers Plowman*, admits that he does not know his 'pater noster' but he 'kan rymes of Robyn Hood'. Among those rhymes was one still being sung at the beginning of the fifteenth century, 'Robyn hode in scherewode stod'. In this period the outlaw also appears as part of the chronicle of England. One chronicler asserts that he was a follower of Simon de Montfort in his insurrection against the rule of Henry III in 1263; a real outlaw, who supported de Montfort at this time, did indeed live in Sherwood Forest. But his name was Roger Godberd. Nevertheless a monkish hand, in the margins of a copy of *Poly-chronicon*, refers in 1460 to 'a certain outlaw named Robin Hood' who in Sherwood Forest commits innumerable robberies. Andrew of Wynton, compiling his chronicle a few years earlier, places him in Inglewood near Carlisle and then in Barnsdale.

Soon enough Robin Hood begins to appear everywhere as the epitome of the brave and self-reliant Englishman who rejects oppressive authority; he emerges in songs and ballads, in plays and in mummings. In these works he is eventually joined by the most renowned of his forest companions, Little John and Maid Marian and Friar Tuck, who between them comprise a veritable pageant play. These characters did in fact become an integral part of the May Games of the fifteenth and sixteenth centuries, prompting speculation that they may be essentially of pagan origin. They are more interesting, however, as representative of the thirteenth and fourteenth centuries.

The early ballads identify Robin as a sturdy 'yeoman', a man somewhere between small farmer and gentleman; his enemies are the sheriffs, the bishops and the archbishops. He does not wish to harm other yeomen, or even knights and squires; he will 'beat and bind' only the members of the secular and clerical nobility, who can be classed as rapacious landlords. It is the dream of the oppressed. Certainly Robin was not a member of the aristocracy fallen on hard times, as some of his later and more romantic chroniclers insisted. He was always a representative of the ordinary folk of the land, and in that respect the ballads might have been sung in the local tavern as often as in the knight's hall. A roughly hewn justice or sense of morality lay behind the fights and the pursuits, the themes of disguise and revenge; the motifs of lawlessness and greenwood liberty were also part of the English dream in a land that was continually and closely administered, in particular by the strictures of royal 'forest law'.

The woods and forests of England are a token of its ancient life, and as such have been feared and protected in equal measure. The charters of the Anglo-Saxons reveal the presence of woods that still exist. 'Westgraf', mentioned in 703 as part of the topography of Shottery in Warwickshire, is now Westgrove Wood in the parish of Haselor. Wanelund, a word the Vikings used when they came to Norfolk, has become Wayland Wood a little south of Watton. A charter of 682 refers to 'the famous wood known as Cantocwudu'; it is now known as Quantockwood in Somerset. There are many other examples of an ancient presence.

Sire-wode, later known as Sherwood, stretched from Nottingham to the centre of Yorkshire. The present Birklands contains the last remnant of the medieval oak forest that covered this region; the trees are now gnarled and dry. The other forest connected to Robin, Inglewood, was also of great extent and lay between Penrith and Carlisle. These had become the natural refuge of outlaws from the king's justice, those who were deemed to wear 'the wolf's head' and could thus be instantly cut down. Yet the English have always made heroes out of robbers and cutpurses; as a result the outlaws of the forest became representative of national freedom and equality. Robin Hood is supposed in legend to have died at Kirklees in Yorkshire. But in truth he did not die. He became part of England's mythography.

# 27

# The suffering king

Henry Bolingbroke, now distinguished by the title of Henry IV, had obtained the throne by violence and perhaps by fraudulence. The crown on such a head will not sit easily or securely. He himself had proved that kings can be removed at will, and gain legitimacy by popular acclamation. Henry therefore courted the Lords and Commons. He promised that he would not levy taxes, and repealed some of the previous king's more oppressive legislation. He resumed the mantle of the warrior, pledging to lead armies into Scotland and into France, and thus adopted the style of previous martial kings. He also attempted to bring God on his side, by promising the bishops that he would be the hammer of heretics.

Yet many still believed Henry to be a usurper. From the beginning of the reign rumour spread that Richard II still lived – that he was in Scotland, that he was in Wales, that he was everywhere. Dominican and Franciscan friars preached open sedition in marketplaces and taverns, with the news that the deposed king had survived. One Franciscan friar was brought before the king.

> *Henry:* You have heard that King Richard is alive, and you are glad?
> *Friar:* I am glad as a man is glad of the life of his friend, for I

am in his debt, as are all my kin, for he was our patron and
promoter.

*Henry:* You have said openly that he lives, and so you have
excited and stirred the people against me.

*Friar:* No.

*Henry:* Tell the truth as it is in your heart. If you saw King
Richard and me fighting on the battlefield together, with
whom would you fight?

*Friar:* In truth with him. For I am more beholden to him.

*Henry:* Do you wish that I and all the lords of the realm were
dead?

*Friar:* No.

*Henry:* What would you do if you had the victory over me?

*Friar:* I would make you duke of Lancaster.

*Henry:* Then you are not my friend.

Another interesting exchange took place with a friar.

*Henry:* Do you say that King Richard is alive?

*Friar:* I do not say that he is alive, but I say that if he is alive he
is the true king of England.

*Henry:* He resigned.

*Friar:* He resigned against his will, in prison, which is against
the law.

*Henry:* He was deposed.

*Friar:* When he was king, he was taken by force and put into
prison, and despoiled of his realm, and you have usurped the
crown.

At the conclusion of this spirited interview the king lost his temper
and cried out, 'By my head I shall have your head!' So it proved.

The fact that Henry felt it necessary and expedient to confront
these friars in person suggests how seriously he considered any such
rumour or rumours to be. He could not be safe – he could not be
an anointed king – if Richard were believed to be alive.

In the early months of 1400 some Ricardian loyalists attempted
an insurrection by riding on Windsor. They were dispersed and
fled westwards, where eventually they were surrounded and despatched by the citizens of Cirencester and Bristol. The king's
punishment was no more merciful. One of the accused, Sir Thomas

Blount, was hanged at Smithfield for a minute or so before being cut down; he was then ordered to sit in front of a great fire while the executioner came to him with a razor in his hand. After begging the prisoner's pardon he knelt down, opened up his stomach with his razor, and took out the bowels. Blount was asked if he would like a drink. 'No,' he replied, 'for I do not know where I should put it.' The executioner tied the bowels with a string so that, in the words of a contemporary, 'the wind of the heart should not escape'; then he threw them into the fire. One of the bystanders shouted out in derision, 'Go seek a master that can save you'. Blount cried that 'I shall die in the service of my sovereign lord, the noble king Richard!' The executioner cut off his head.

Yet the severity of the punishment did not deter other rebels. In the autumn of 1401 an attempt was made to assassinate Henry, by means of an 'infernal machine' with poisoned spikes placed in his bed. The plan fared no better than the attempt by another assassin to smear his saddle with a deadly poison. Yet Henry was aware that dangerous forces were working against him.

Protests grew of a different kind. Despite the king's early promise to avoid taxation, he was soon obliged to break his word. In the parliament of 1401 the chief justice revealed that the deposed king's 'treasure', if such it was, had disappeared into thin air. The real costs of defending and administering the realm were increasing to such an extent that the king was already heavily in debt. The Commons eventually granted his request for aid by taxation, but in return they submitted various petitions and complaints; only when these appeals were granted was their consent to taxation obtained. This would be the pattern for all of Henry's parliaments. He would receive money only when he satisfied the demands of the Commons. In that sense he was not a strong king. The parliament of 1399, however illegally assembled and constituted, had in effect sanctioned the coronation of a new sovereign. Why should it not now attempt to curb that monarch's power?

In the summer of 1403 his erstwhile allies, the Percy family, rebelled against his rule. They joined a Welsh prince, Owen Glendower, who had formally defied the English king. Henry Percy, the earl of Northumberland, and his son, Hotspur, had been charged with the defence of the north against Scottish raiders.

They had hoped by their early support of Henry's invasion to enjoy the spoils of victory. To their surprise and alarm, however, they found themselves obliged to maintain the defences of their northern lands without any proportionate help from Henry. It had been rumoured in the parliament house that the Percy family had been granted £60,000 from the king. They denied this, claiming that they had received only £20,000. Where had the money gone?

Hotspur had come to Westminster, at the end of 1402, and demanded more money in the presence of the king. The result was a bitter confrontation. One chronicler asserts that the king punched Hotspur in the face, while another reports that he drew a dagger upon him. Whatever the truth of the matter, their alliance was broken. The Percys had another grievance against the king, in theory more serious but in practice a convenient excuse for their rebellion. They accused the king of betraying his oath. He had promised them, on first landing in Yorkshire, that he had no designs on the throne. This was in later weeks found to be a palpable fiction. But from the beginning they must have been at least aware of the possibility of Richard's overthrow.

In the summer of 1403 Hotspur gathered an army at Chester, and proclaimed that King Richard was still alive. This was the familiar rallying cry for all those who opposed the king. Owen Glendower was poised to move from Wales, and Henry Percy was mustering his forces in the north. The king moved rapidly and expeditiously. He sent an army to Shrewsbury, the town where the rebels were supposed to muster. When Hotspur arrived there, he found the gates shut against him. While he paused outside the town, the king's army advanced. The opposing forces met at Berwick Field, 2 miles (3 kilometres) outside Shrewsbury. Hotspur had with him 1,000 archers, and he placed them on top of a ridge from which they would be able to see the king's men approaching. Henry had taken the precaution of asking two of his prominent supporters to wear his livery, since he knew well enough that he was the real target of Hotspur; if three Henries were on the field, it might prove confusing.

The king's men advanced up the slope, and were met by thousands of arrows shot from the longbows of the Cheshire men. The sky grew dark, and the carnage began. The king's men fell, according to one chronicler, 'as fast as autumn leaves fall in autumn after the hoar frost'. On the death of one of the king's commanders, the earl of Stafford, the vanguard of the royal army gave way and began to flee. Henry now had to act promptly to prevent a rout and bloody defeat. So he gave orders for the main body of the army to advance, and he threw himself into the action.

'There was such slaughter', one chronicler wrote, 'that the like had not been seen in England for a long time.' The royal soldiers seemed to prevail, and Hotspur staked everything on a charge against the king. Henry fell back, so that Hotspur and his followers were lost in the general mêlée. When they faltered, they were cut down. Hotspur was among the dead. The king's son, Henry, received a wound to his skull. Yet he lived. He was one of the victors to celebrate the king's triumph. It seemed that Henry IV had truly been anointed by God.

Two years after the battle of Berwick Field, however, another insurrection emerged in the north. The archbishop of York, Richard Scrope, rose up against royal government and issued a manifesto or list of grievances to the effect that Henry was demanding too much taxation; the burden upon his subjects, secular and clerical, had become insupportable.

It was not a successful rebellion, and within a few days the forces of the archbishop forsook him or were taken into custody. The earl of Northumberland, having survived his son's defeat outside Shrewsbury, was again implicated in the uprising and fled to Scotland. Scrope himself was captured and beheaded, part of Henry's crude and brutal attempt to beat off all opposition. Yet the murder of an archbishop was, in the context of the time, an act of blasphemy; it invited comparisons with the murder of Thomas Becket in the thirteenth century. Henry IV avoided much of the public obloquy that fell upon Henry II, but his private character was more severely affected. To the insecurity of his throne was added the impurity of sacrilege.

The death of the archbishop weighed on his conscience. He was riding his horse on the afternoon of 8 June 1405 – the day of Richard Scrope's execution – when he was struck by some force so powerful that 'it seemed to him that he had felt an actual blow'. That night he suffered a nightmare in which he cried out 'Traitors!

Traitors! You have thrown fire over me!' When his attendants reached him, he complained that his skin was burning. This was the time when he became afflicted with a mysterious illness that was rumoured to be leprosy; since the sickness came and went over the next few years, that is unlikely to be the true diagnosis. It is more probable that Henry had contracted syphilis. As a young man he had gone on crusade to the Holy Land, and the crusaders were notorious for carrying back the venereal disease.

Yet he had passed through the fire, and from 1406 onwards there were no serious attempts to take the throne. He remained cautious; he remained stubborn; he was ever vigilant. He realized, unlike his predecessor, that he did not have the power or the resources to confront the great magnates of the land; so he equivocated, and he compromised. He permitted his nobles to enjoy a measure of independence and influence that had been denied to them in Richard's reign. He allowed himself to be in part ruled by a council of notables. He was a good manager of men. The Crown was poor, and the treasury all but exhausted; local law was not kept, and the districts of the country were ruled by local faction. The possibility of riot and robbery was always close. Yet the king did not fall. It might be said that he muddled through, were it not for the fact that his abiding aim was to preserve his own authority and to maintain a new national dynasty. In these respects, he was successful.

His hopes devolved upon his eldest son. Henry of Monmouth, prince of Wales, had been wounded in the skull at the battle of Berwick Field, but this wound did nothing to dampen his martial fervour. He loved battle, and lived for warfare. From the age of fourteen he had served, and succeeded, in various battles and skirmishes against the Welsh insurgents. He joined the king's council in 1406, on his return from Wales, and at once took a leading part in affairs. He was nineteen years old, and of course gathered about him the younger members of the nobility. One chronicler noted 'the great recourse of the people unto him, of whom his court was at all times more abundant than the King his father's'. As such he was seen as the unofficial 'opposition' to the already ageing king and his advisers, inclined to more purposeful and energetic activity both at home and abroad. It was the dynamic of youth against age, hope and optimism against experience and fatigue.

The king himself, beset by illness, steadily withdrew from public affairs. He left his palace at Westminster and retired to the archbishop of Canterbury's residence at Lambeth; then he moved further out to Windsor. In this period, from the beginning of 1410 to the end of 1411, the prince of Wales successfully administered the kingdom on his father's behalf. An expeditionary force was sent to assist the duchy of Burgundy against the depredations of the French. At the same time a determined effort was made to resolve the finances of the king. In September 1411 it is reported that the prince approached his father and advised him to abdicate 'because he could no longer apply himself to the honour and profit of the realm'.

But then Henry IV struck back. He could not permit his royal identity to be put at risk. What else did he have left, after a decade of weary power? While breath lasted in him, he would rule. At the end of the year some of the prince's supporters were arrested. A parliament was called, in the course of which a motion was proposed that the king should abdicate in favour of his son. It was debated, with all due decorum, but then rejected. It seemed that the prince had been outwitted. The rumour then spread that the prince was contemplating open revolt, thus reawakening fears of civil war. The rumour was quashed. It was then whispered that the prince had confiscated money due to the English garrison at Calais. In the summer of 1412, he came to London to deny this and to defy his enemies; but he brought with him an army or what was called 'a huge people'.

The prince was also accompanied by his favourite young lords. He was wearing a peculiar costume of blue satin which, according to the translator of his first biography into English, was punctuated by 'eyelets' or round holes from each of which a needle was hanging upon a thread of silk. The significance of this dress is not immediately clear.

He strode into Westminster Hall, and told his supporters to remain there while he sought the king. He found him in a chamber and asked for a private interview; in the presence of four courtiers Henry asked his son 'to show the effect of his mind'. Whereupon the prince made a long and impassioned speech, at the end of which he went down on his knees and produced a dagger. 'Father,' he is reported to have said, 'I desire you in your honour of God, and for the easing of your heart, here before your knees to slay me with this dagger. My lord and father, my life is not so desirous to me that I would live one day that I should be to your displeasure.' There was more to the same effect, a peroration that reduced the sick king to tears. Father and son were thus reconciled.

This scene is rendered in the second part of Shakespeare's *Henry IV*, a play that with its successor *Henry V* has more than any other preserved the image of this age. Whether it is a faithful image is another matter. Nevertheless the pictures of the young Henry carousing with Falstaff and Bardolf, of Justice Shallow and Mistress Quickly, of Pistol and Doll Tearsheet, are now effectively part of English history. It was said that the prince worshipped at the altars both of Venus and of Mars. Since his youth and early maturity were spent in fighting wars in Scotland and in Wales, Mars must have been in the ascendant.

The mutual respect between father and son was not destined to survive for long. Six months after this affecting interview Henry IV, worn out by guilt and illness, died in the Jerusalem Chamber of Westminster Abbey. In his will, drawn up two years before, he had described himself in English as a 'sinful wretch', a 'sinful soul' and 'never worthy to be a man' whose life had been 'misspent'. These are not the traditional testamentary words and reveal a human being who was suffering a severe sense of spiritual un-worthiness. Henry IV was, after all, unique among English kings in having killed one monarch and one archbishop. Yet he had survived, albeit only to the age of forty-six. He had faced down rebellions and conspiracies; there had been attempts made on his life, and efforts to force him to abdicate. But in the end he confounded his enemies. He had instituted a royal dynasty – the house of Lancaster, part of the Plantagenet legacy – that would endure for three generations.

The king's body was washed, his brain and his bowels were removed; he was then embalmed in a mixture of myrrh, aloes, laurel flower and saffron. He was wound in strips of waxed linen before being dressed in a long robe. His brown beard was smoothed over the throat, and the crown placed upon his head. The right hand clutched his golden orb, while the left hand touched his sceptre. In this state he was taken down to the cathedral at Canterbury where he was buried and where his tomb can still be seen.

# 28

# Old habits

The world was in a condition of decline and decay; there was no 'progress', no 'evolution' and no 'development'. If you needed an image of medieval thought, it would be that of the slow movement of a descending spiral. Everywhere you looked, suffering and violence and corruption held the mastery. That was the state of the earth. The most that could be hoped for was stability and steadiness; the degeneration might therefore be arrested for a moment. The four humours of man must be held in balance; the universe itself was established upon the harmonious union of the four elements, the cold earth for example having an affinity with the cold water. The manifest uncertainties of life, and the anxiety aroused by them, compounded the need for stability.

Order was the first principle, sustaining the great chain of being. That is why so much concern was attested for hierarchy and degree, with all the 'estates' of society carefully designated and maintained. Nothing must get out of balance. The past was revered beyond measure. Historical writing was recognized as a set of lessons or moral illustrations. The great writers were those who most closely imitated previous masters. The philosophers of the past were more acute, the architects more subtle and the rulers more eloquent. The medieval delight in ritual and ceremony was in itself a veneration of custom.

Just as medieval law was based upon precedent, so medieval society was governed by habit. Custom was the great law of life. The earliest written records show its importance. In the sixth century Aethelbert, the king of Kent, described his laws as those which had been long accepted and established; this would mean in practice that a large body of oral tradition was passed from generation to generation by the men of Kent. The witan or Anglo-Saxon assembly was to be made up of the wisest men, namely those who 'knew how all things stood in the land in their forefathers' days'. An eleventh-century treatise in Anglo-Saxon affirms that the landowner should 'always know what the ancient tradition of the land is, and what the custom of the people is'. Surely 'custom' would go back into prehistoric times? This atavism was the expression of a deeply communal society, whereby the ties binding people together were almost unbreakable.

In the feudal society of the Normans the serf or villein was also known as *consuetudinarius* or *custumarius*, meaning 'a man of custom'. His rights and duties were upheld by a body of customary law that would not allow outright oppression or enslavement. It would perhaps be better to say that the people of England lived by custom and not by law. Rights and duties were perpetual. No lord, however great, would willingly violate such a tradition. It would be against nature. At an important trial in 1072 the bishop of Chichester, Aethelric, was brought in a cart to expound and explain 'the old customs of the laws'. So a continuity was maintained even after William the Conqueror's invasion. It could not be otherwise. It was the essential life of the country. The unanswerable complaint of the labourer or the villager was that 'we have never been accustomed to do this!'

Another aspect of this historical piety may be mentioned. Any institutional or administrative change, introduced by the king and council, had to be explained as a return to some long-lost tradition. Any innovation that had endured for twenty or thirty years then in turn became part of ancient custom. Nothing was good because it was new. It was good because it was old. It was closer to the golden age of the world. So the existing structure of things had at all costs to be protected. Any piece of legislation was said to be a 'declaration' of the existing law, the revelation of something previously hidden. In the reign of Henry III the barons of the realm announced '*Nolumus leges Angliae mutari*' – 'we do not wish the laws of England to be changed'. Government itself was established upon habitual forms and institutions. The Black Book or royal household manual of 1478, in the reign of Edward IV, urged the treasurer to seek out 'good, old, sad [serious], worshipful and profitable rules of the court used before time'.

Custom was therefore immemorial. In the words of the period it was 'from time out of mind, about which contrary human memory does not exist'. It was expected that the same practice and habitual activity would go on forever until the day of doom. There was no reason to envisage anything else. That final day might in effect be the day when the customary round grew ragged and creaked to a halt. Who could tell?

Customs could be of inexplicable mystery. If the king passed over Shrivenham Bridge, then in Wiltshire, the owner of the land was supposed to bring to him two white domestic cocks with the words 'Behold, my lord, these two white capons which you shall have another time but not now'. If a whale was stranded on the coast near Chichester, it belonged to the bishop except for the tongue, which was taken to the king; if a whale landed anywhere else along the shores of his diocese, the bishop was permitted to have only the right flipper. There were urban, as well as country, customs. At Kidderminster in Worcestershire, on the day of the election of the bailiff, the town was controlled for one hour by the populace; they spent the time throwing cabbage stalks at one another before pelting the bailiff and his procession with apples. The porters of Billingsgate decreed that any stranger entering their market was obliged to salute a wooden post set up there and pay them sixpence; the man was then adopted by two 'godparents' among the porters. If an unmarried man was condemned to death in London, he was pardoned if a woman applied for his release on condition that he married her.

The nation itself represented the nexus of custom with custom, the shifting patterns of habitual activity. This may not be a particularly exciting philosophy of history but it is important to avoid the shibboleth of some fated or providential movement forward.

# 29

# The warrior

Henry of Monmouth came to the throne, as Henry V, with the determination to restore the foundations of the royal finances and to deal with the old enemy of France. He was set to renew 'bone governaunce' or good government, with an especial intention to redress injustice and corruption. He had youth and vigour. A French visitor to the court remarked that he resembled a priest rather than a soldier; he was lean, and fair complexioned, with an oval face and short cropped brown hair. Certainly he had the look of an ascetic. On the night of his father's death he consulted a recluse at Westminster Abbey, to whom he confessed all his sins.

He was crowned on Passion Sunday, 9 April 1413, a day of hail and snow. The weather was said to presage a reign of cold severity. There can be no doubt that Henry V was driven by a sense of divine right as well as of duty. All was changed. He abandoned his youthful pursuits and almost overnight, according to the chroniclers, became a grave and serious king. He acquired a reputation for piety and for the solemn observance of ceremonies; until his marriage, seven years later, he remained chaste. He established several monastic foundations of an ascetic nature, where the daily exhalation of prayer was meant to support the Lancastrian dynasty. His devotion also had an aesthetic cast. The annalist, John Stowe, recorded that 'he delighted in songs, metres and musical instruments; insomuch that in his chapel, among his private prayers, he used our Lord's prayer, certain psalms of David, with diverse hymns and canticles'. When he went to war in France, he took with him organists and singers.

He spoke English naturally, unlike his father, and in that respect set the standard for the written records of the country. He was something of a martinet, peremptory and commanding. One of his letters to an ambassador, Sir John Tiptoft, opens succinctly with 'Tiptoft, I charge you by the faith that you owe me . . .' 'Tiptoft', that brief salutation, is of the essence. 'A king', Thomas Hoccleve wrote, 'from mochil speche him refreyne.' He was clipped and precise. He was also an efficient administrator, who looked to the details of his policies; he demanded much in taxation from his kingdom, but he never squandered money unwisely. He maintained cordial relations with the most important nobles, and worked well with the parliament house. He proved that, with firm oversight, medieval governance was not inherently unstable or incoherent.

The test of his religious commitment came a few months after his coronation, when he was obliged to confront the forces of heresy. The activity of the Lollards has been examined in earlier pages, but it reached a point of crisis in the early months of 1413. During the king's first parliament a proclamation was pinned to the doors of the London churches stating that, if the brethren were to face persecution and outlawry, 100,000 men would rise up to protect them. In the consequent state of alarm and insecurity one of the king's own friends, Sir John Oldcastle, was accused of harbouring and promoting heretics. It is a matter of some irony, therefore, that the original name of Falstaff in Shakespeare's play of *Henry V*, written almost 200 years after the events related, was Oldcastle. Shakespeare had portrayed him as Henry's boon companion in the years of the alehouse and the brothel.

The proclamations fixed to the church doors were traced back to this now earnest man. One of his chaplains was preaching Lollardy, and Oldcastle himself had been caught in possession of certain heretical tracts. The king tried to argue with him, and to persuade him to recant, but he refused to do so. He was taken to the Tower in the autumn of 1413 and, at his subsequent trial, repeated the Lollard disregard for confession and the doctrine of transubstantiation. He was judged to be a heretic and passed over to the secular arm for burning. The king intervened once more and granted him forty days for the further searching of his conscience, but in this period Oldcastle managed to escape from his confinement.

He spent two months in hiding, somewhere in the purlieus of London, during which period he conceived a plot to kill the king and his brothers before leading a general insurrection of Lollards. Messages were secretly conveyed to the brethren, asking them to meet at St Giles's Fields just outside the city. But the secret was revealed to someone in authority. On the evening of 9 January 1414, the king moved with his forces to the fields. As the Lollards marched towards the city, they were dispersed and consigned to Newgate Prison. Thirty-eight of them were drawn on hurdles from Newgate and hanged in the fields, on gallows newly built for that purpose.

It had not in any case been a popular insurrection, with perhaps no more than a few hundred participants. Yet it did effectively destroy any sympathy with the Lollard movement among the general population; heresy itself was now considered to be equivalent to rebellion.

Oldcastle himself evaded capture for almost four years; he was eventually seized in the neighbourhood of Welshpool and taken to London where he was hanged above a burning fire that consumed the gallows as well as the victim. In his last words before this painful death he declared that he would rise again after three days. In truth his resurrection took a little longer. In the sixteenth century he became celebrated as a proto-martyr of Protestantism; that is one of the reasons why Shakespeare felt obliged to change his name to Falstaff.

In a sense, however, the insurrection was a distraction. The young king's reign was primarily defined by war. He gathered around him a group of young men who saw in battle and victory the foundations of glory. Principal among them were his three brothers, wholly committed to the success of the dynasty. War was considered to be the highest duty, and greatest achievement, of any king. It was this fervour, or lust, that effectively reopened the Hundred Years War after the interval of the previous two reigns.

Almost at once the new king moved against France. He had been made duke of Aquitaine in 1399, as part of his patrimony; now he wished to reclaim the lands of Gascony, Calais, Guienne, Poitou and Ponthieu that had been granted to the English Crown in the treaty of 1360.

By the summer of 1415 all was ready for the French endeavour. The parliament house had furnished the necessary funds without any of the usual misgivings; the troops and the ships were requisitioned efficiently, and it seems that the nation supported this show of strength and determination by the young king. Yet not all of his subjects were ready to pay fealty to him. Some still questioned the legitimacy of the house of Lancaster and, in the days before the launching of the military expedition, certain nobles tried to organize a rebellion. They were forestalled, and swiftly executed. No one else would ever again threaten the reign of Henry V.

He sailed to France with an army of 8,000 men. There were archers, both mounted and on foot; there were 'men-at-arms', knights and esquires in full body armour complete with lance, sword and dagger. There were foot soldiers, fletchers, bowyers, carpenters, priests, surgeons, gunners and engineers. The two latter were needed for the prosecution of siege warfare, a technique for which Henry had trained himself in Wales. A royal officer, known as 'the grand sergeanty', was also on board; his sole job was to hold the king's head in case of seasickness. It has been calculated that approximately 15,000 horses were transported to France. No female followers of the camp were allowed to sail. The punishment for any prostitute found among the soldiers was for all her money to be taken and for one of her arms to be broken before her being driven off with staves.

The expedition left Southampton on 11 August, accompanied by a flock of swans, and set sail for the coast of Normandy; the duchy belonged to Henry's family, or so he claimed, and to land there was itself an act of proprietorship. He laid siege to the town of Harfleur, at the mouth of the river Seine, but it did not prove to be an easy victory; the town held out for five weeks, in which period Henry's men suffered dysentery from the eating of unripe fruit. Yet he prevailed; the leaders of the town surrendered, and Henry promptly laid plans to turn it into an English colony. Since

Harfleur was connected to Rouen and to Paris by the river, it was in a desirable position.

In his campaigns he was a rigid and severe disciplinarian; that is why he was successful. He planned meticulously, while retaining his command over the court administration at Westminster. Above all else he was possessed of great energy; whether in a tournament, or at a hunt, or in the field of battle, he was swift and unrelenting. He gave the impression of always being in a hurry, as if he had some strange presentiment of his early death.

From Harfleur he led his men north-east towards Calais, a distance of some 120 miles (75 kilometres); but then he received the unwelcome news that the French army was waiting for him on the right bank of the Somme. He was obliged to make a detour, marching along the left bank of the Somme until he could find a place of safe passage. The trek to Calais was supposed to have taken eight days, but only two weeks later did the English army cross the river. The king's men were exhausted and hungry but, despite the presence of a French army shadowing them closely, he ordered them to march on to Calais. Everyone knew that he would have to confront the enemy before reaching the town.

On 24 October, he saw them; they were gathered, according to the author of *The Deeds of Henry V*, like a swarm of locusts near the village of Agincourt. One of the English commanders prayed aloud for 10,000 more archers, but the king told him that they had the more certain protection of God. He rested his men that night, and ordained a strict silence; the songs and music of the French could clearly be heard. At dawn he attended three Masses before mounting his horse; he wore a gold crown upon his helmet. Then he ordered his army into position. He had approximately 8,000 men against a French army of 20,000. Another crucial difference was in place; the English combatants included 6,000 archers or longbowmen, while the French had very few. They were relying upon the force of their armour. So the English were placed in a thin line across the field of battle, in the same posture as the shield wall of the Anglo-Saxons or 'the thin red line' at the battle of Balaclava in 1854. The heavy rain of the previous night had rendered the terrain muddy and treacherous. For three hours, from nine in the morning to midday, the two armies faced each other without moving.

Henry then took the initiative, fearing that the enemy were waiting for reinforcements. 'Now is good time, for all England prays for us,' he shouted, 'and therefore be of good cheer, and let us go to our journey!' He continued with an invocation. 'In the name of Almighty God and St George, advance bannerer! And St George, this day your help!' His soldiers prostrated themselves upon the ground, each of them putting a small piece of earth into his mouth to remind him that he was mortal and must one day return to dust; it was a different form of holy communion. The English archers advanced some 700 yards (640 metres), stopped, and rammed sharp pointed stakes into the soft earth as a form of protection from horses and armed knights alike. Then they took aim and fired at the massed French host with a great storm of arrows, causing immediate carnage in its ranks. The French cavalry charged, but the men and horses were wounded or impaled upon the stakes.

The body of the French army moved forward, but their great numbers made them unwieldy and confused. The arrows of the English archers continued to do their deadly work, and the riderless horses created further alarm among the men. The bodies of the dead already lay in piles upon the muddy ground, and the more nimble English soldiers were able to turn in upon the groaning mass of the enemy. Two-thirds of the remaining French army now fled. Henry was not yet certain of the victory; a third part of the army still remained on the field, and many unarmed French prisoners were held in the rear of the action. He ordered these men to be put to death, to avoid any threatening movement on their part. This was in defiance of the rules of chivalry, which forbade the execution of unarmed prisoners, and was also to the detriment of the English who could have been expected to earn sizeable ransoms from their captives. Yet Henry ordered 200 archers to carry out the work of killing. It can only be said that in the blood and heat of battle some pressing reason must have suggested itself to him. What that was, we do not know. His command was not wholly carried out, however, and many hundreds of noble prisoners survived the ordeal of the battle of Agincourt.

The king now marched unimpeded to Calais from where, after a few days' respite, he sailed back to England. His reception in London on 23 November was a great occasion of state. 20,000 citizens met him at Blackheath, where he was hailed as 'lord of England, flower of the world, soldier of Christ'. Two giant figures, of a man and a woman, were erected on London Bridge to welcome him; effigies of the lion and the antelope wearing the royal arms, with a choir of angels singing 'Blessed is he who comes in the name of the lord', greeted his progress. Other giant figures, and pageant wagons, and fanciful castles, decorated the route to St Paul's Cathedral; the king, in a simple gown of purple, was greeted by groups of singers holding garlands. In this year, also, Henry began to wear an arched or imperial crown modelled upon that worn by the Holy Roman Emperor; it was an 'imperial diadem of gold and precious stones', adverting to the fact that he had regained an imperial kingship.

The victory was not immediately followed by an advantageous truce. No overwhelming victory has ever had such tenuous result. The sinews that had been stiffened were now relaxed again, and the blood summoned was permitted to subside. Yet the reputation of the king was greatly strengthened; he did now seem to be one favoured and protected by God, and the right of his dynasty to rule was manifestly confirmed. At a stroke he had become the leading figure in the royal politics of Europe. On a more practical level the parliament house bestowed on him a new grant of taxation, and guaranteed him for life the excise on exports of wool and leather.

The French attempted to recapture Harfleur both by land and by sea, but a decisive naval battle in the summer of 1416 proved their undoing. Henry prided himself on his navy; he was the first king since Alfred to create a national force at sea, and by the end of 1416 he possessed six great ships, eight barges and ten single-masted sailing vessels known as balingers.

With these he launched his second invasion of France in February 1417. He had come to claim the throne of France '*de facto et realiter*'; it was his by right. He undertook a sequence of sieges, beginning with the town of Caen, slowly moving southwards until he arrived at Falaise, best known as the birthplace of William the Conqueror. He was returning to the land of his now remote predecessor, and in the process had effectively seized Normandy. Then he moved on to the capital of the duchy, Rouen; the siege lasted for almost six months, creating intense misery for the citizens. According to a popular verse of the period:

> They ate dogs, they ate cats,
> They ate mice, horses and rats
> For thirty pence went a rat . . .

Rouen surrendered on 19 January 1419. The way to Paris now lay open. Some inconclusive negotiations took place between the two sides; facing Henry was the king of France, Charles VI, together with his son and successor known as the 'dauphin'. These two men were joined by the duke of Burgundy, who had formed an unlikely pact with the dauphin in an effort to repel the English. But the allies fell out; at a meeting arranged upon a bridge, one of the dauphin's retinue killed the duke. It may have been a plot or, as was claimed, an accident; the result was the same. With his enemies in disarray Henry came up to the gates of Paris and demanded the French crown. Who could now deny it to him? The new duke of Burgundy was inexperienced, the dauphin was in disgrace, and the king of France was intermittently insane.

After much debate a treaty was agreed in the spring of 1420 in which it was confirmed that Charles VI would disinherit his son and declare the English king to be his successor. Henry V would marry the king's daughter Katherine, so that any male child would then automatically become king of France as well as of England. It was on the face of it a great victory; Henry had won more than any of his predecessors. Subsequent events, however, would prove that the concord was ultimately unstable. Why should the French agree to be ruled by a king at Westminster? Serious misgivings also existed, in some quarters of the English parliament, about the wisdom of the English domination of France; the costs of war were very large. The price of maintaining power would also be high. It was unwise to tangle with the affairs of the French.

At the early date of 1417 the clergy had ceased to pray for the king's success in foreign warfare; the parliaments of 1420 and 1421 reverted to their former ways and refused to grant money for the enterprise. The chronicler of the period, Adam of Usk, finished his narrative with the exclamation, 'but, woe is me! Mighty men and treasure of the realm will be most miserable foredone about this business.' Some compensations were available, most notably for the great knights and the soldiers of fortune who brought back treasure and booty. Thomas Montague, the earl of Salisbury, wrote to the king that 'we broughten home the fairest and greatest prey of beasts as all those saiden that saw them that ever they saw'. He returned with riches, in other words. Whether this heartened the clergy and the yeomen of England is another matter.

Fears existed about English sovereignty itself. What if one treasurer, for example, were to superintend the revenues of both countries bound in an intricate embrace? What if the king, or his successor, appointed a French noble to that task? These may have been groundless fears, but nonetheless they existed. It had become obvious that the king was already spending more time in France than in England, to the detriment of national interests.

The proof is to be found in the fact that Henry was obliged to consolidate his gains in France with further military campaigns. He possessed, or occupied, the duchy of Normandy together with the area known as Vexin – the region of north-west France on the right bank of the Seine. But there were still provinces ruled by the duke of Burgundy, and others governed by the dauphin. There could be no peace in a divided land.

Henry married Katherine of France, or Katherine of Valois, soon after the treaty with her father; they entered Paris in state and moved into the Louvre Palace. The king of course wished to crown his wife in Westminster, and on 23 February 1421 she was led to the abbey. The Valois and Plantagenet dynasties were united.

Four months later Henry was in France once more, to counter French resistance and insurrection. He was obliged to fight for his gains, but during the siege of the town of Meaux he became ill; he relapsed into a fever and grew steadily weaker. He sensed that death was approaching, and he made a codicil to his will. He now had a son, only eight months old, and the child was given into the protection of one of his brothers. The duke of Gloucester would guide and support the infant Henry. On the last day of August 1422 the king died. The corpse was brought to London, and was buried with due solemnity in the abbey.

No king won such plaudits from his contemporaries as Henry V. The misgivings about his wars in France were forgotten for the sake of celebrating his martial valour. He was devout as well as magnificent, chaste as well as earnest. He was as generous to his friends as he was stern to his enemies; he was prudent and magnanimous, modest and temperate. He was the very model of a medieval king. Yet there are some who have doubted that verdict. Shakespeare's play *Henry V* can be interpreted in quite a different spirit as an account of a military tyrant who staked all on vainglorious conquest in France. What did he finally achieve? Once his French conquests were dissipated, and the dream of a dual monarchy dissolved, very little was left to celebrate. All was done for the pride of princes.

One more elusive and unintended consequence, of the revival of the Hundred Years War by Henry V, can be recorded. The language of England was now spoken by all the king's subjects. The letters of the king were always written in English, and the writer of *The Deeds of Henry V* invoked *Anglia nostra* or 'our England'. The first document of royal administration written in English is dated in 1410. The London Guild of Brewers began to record its proceedings in English from the early 1420s, citing the fact that 'the greater part of the Lords and the trusty Commons have begun to make their matters be noted down in our mother tongue'.

The archbishops of Canterbury now spoke routinely of 'the Church of England' as an identifiable element of the Universal Church, and at a Church council in 1414 it was declared that 'whether a nation be understood as a people marked off from others by blood relationship and habit of unity, or by peculiarities of language . . . England is a real nation'. The fact that the matter had to be asserted suggests that in previous periods this nationhood had not been self-evident. In the fifteenth century, too, there were persistent attempts to contrast the prosperous kingdom of England with the parlous state of France. It was a way of escaping from the inheritance of the French-speaking royalty and a French-speaking court that had shaped the governance of the three previous centuries.

The first surviving letter written in English dates from the winter of 1392. A slightly later epistle, also written in English, is of more human interest. It was 'written at Calais on this side the sea, the first day of June, when every man was gone to his dinner, and the clock smote noon and all our household cried after me and bade me come down. Come down to dinner at once! And what answer I gave them ye know it of old.' You can hear the voices. Come down! Come down!

# 30

# How others saw us

The English were pronounced by other nations to be guilty of the sin of pride; that was their most prominent characteristic. The fourteenth-century French chronicler Jean Froissart described 'the great haughtiness of the English, who are affable to no other nation than their own'. A German knight, Nicholas von Poppelau, visited the country in 1484 and complained that 'the English think they are the wisest people in the world' and that 'the world does not exist apart from England'. Fifteen years later a Venetian traveller stated that 'the English are great lovers of themselves and of everything belonging to them'. Whenever they see a handsome stranger, they say that 'he looks like an Englishman'.

Other nations were sure that the English had tails. The Greeks of Sicily, who were obliged to entertain the presence of English crusaders in 1190, referred to them as 'the tailed Englishmen'. At the end of the thirteenth century the Scottish forces, besieged in Dunbar Castle, shouted from the battlements, 'You English dogs with long tails! We will kill you all and cut off your tails!' It is possible that the offence was originally that of long hair, worn down the back like a tail, and gradually became a term of general opprobrium.

The French accused the English of being drunken and perfidious; the notion of *la perfide Albion*, current in the late eighteenth and the nineteenth centuries, has a long history. They were aloof; they were phlegmatic; they were insensitive to their own suffering, and to the sufferings of others. They were not afraid of death. That is why they quarrelled with so much ferocity; they robbed and murdered one another quite openly. Sometimes they even killed their king. So they were known for their violence.

The English themselves admitted many faults. The author of *Vita Edwardi Secundi*, writing early in the fourteenth century, maintained that his countrymen excelled 'in pride, in craft and in perjury'. Ranulf Higden of Chester, in the same period, described his compatriots as drunken, greedy and dishonest. Their drunkenness was a common cause of complaint, so often described and condemned that it became almost a caricature. A papal envoy to England wrote in 1473 that 'in the morning they are as devout as angels, but after dinner they are like devils'. Certain national characteristics may never change.

# 31

# A simple man

If Henry's son had been declared king immediately on the death of his father, he would have been crowned in his swaddling clothes. It was deemed prudent, therefore, to wait until he had reached the age of understanding before he was anointed. Nothing spells disaster so much as a child king, however, surrounded by magnates who consult no interest but their own. Indeed in the course of his long reign, lasting for almost forty years, the fortunes of the ruling houses of England went through so many bewildering vicissitudes – so many reversals and surprises, so many victories and defeats – that the nineteenth-century critic, William Hazlitt, described the country as a 'perfect beargarden'. This was the era in which were fought the series of battles that have become known as the Wars of the Roses.

Three brothers supervised the minority of the infant king. They can be introduced as the *dramatis personae*. The first of them, the duke of Gloucester, was his younger uncle; it was he to whom Henry V had entrusted the life and safety of his son. His older uncle, the duke of Bedford, had been chosen by the dying king to protect and enlarge the conquered territories of France; the war continued as before. Henry Beaufort, the child of John of Gaunt and therefore the king's great-uncle, was bishop of Winchester; he became chancellor of England and therefore its principal officer.

He had been born illegitimate but the subsequent marriage of John of Gaunt to his mother, Katherine Swynford, rendered him legitimate.

Brothers, legitimate or illegitimate, may fall out. Gloucester wished to be given the title of 'regent', effectively assuming control of the country. Instead at Bedford's request he was only named as 'protector', obliged to yield precedence whenever his elder brother returned from France to England. Gloucester also quarrelled with Beaufort over the direction of the kingdom, and their rivalry reached such a pitch that in 1425 it precipitated them almost into internecine war. Beaufort gathered his army of retainers in Southwark, where his palace lay, and Gloucester ordered the mayor of London to close London Bridge against them. Bedford had to come over from France in order to arrange a compromise between them. They were dogs fighting over the bone of power.

The new king, Henry VI, was formally crowned in the winter of 1429. The eight-year-old boy was carried into the abbey in the arms of his tutor; this suggests that he was a little frail, but he managed to survive the strain of the lengthy ceremony and walked down the aisle unaided at its conclusion. It has been said that he remained a child all his life. At the end of 1431 he was taken to France, according to the treaty agreed by his father, where he was crowned in the cathedral of Notre Dame in Paris. On the head of this young boy the lines of Valois and Plantagenet royalty had come together. At barely the age of ten he was the only male monarch ever to be king both of England and of France.

It is significant however that, in the year before he came to France, the figure of Joan of Arc emerged as the inspiration and hope of the French army. That is one of the reasons why Henry was so prominently displayed in Paris. In May 1429, in a series of brilliantly executed skirmishes, she had lifted the English siege of Orleans and proceeded to recapture other French towns that had submitted to the enemy. Orleans had been the key to the English strategy, its fall meant to anticipate the general defeat of the French army. That victory had been snatched away. In a letter Joan wrote at the end of June to the citizens of Tournai, she declared that 'the Maiden lets you know that here, in eight days, she has chased the English out of all the places they held on the river Loire by attack or other means; they are dead or prisoners or discouraged in battle'. She had begun a process that would end in the complete unravelling of the victories of the previous reign. At Joan's urgent instigation the dauphin rode in triumph to the cathedral in Rheims, where he was crowned as Charles VII. Two kings, Henry VI and Charles VII, were now claiming supremacy over the French people. It would take another twenty years to assign victory to one of them.

The affairs of France, ever since the death of Henry V, had not been well managed. Without the presence of this inspiring king, the enthusiasm for conquest seems slowly to have been dissipated. Disputes over strategy, between Bedford and Gloucester, did not augur well; Bedford was also denied the finances that he needed. It was said in the parliament house and elsewhere that French actions should be subsidized by the taxpayers of France. Among the English themselves the virtues and advantages of a dual monarchy were openly questioned. What was the point of owning or seizing territories in France when there was so much amiss in England? The king of England should reside in England, not in Paris or in Normandy.

Yet the war continued, the French and English possessing neither the will nor the resources effectively to decide the matter. Charles VII entered an alliance with the new duke of Burgundy, formally apologizing for the assassination of the duke's predecessor and promising to punish the guilty parties. Those areas of France under the influence of Burgundy now reverted to their allegiance to the Valois king, and Charles could truly claim to be the king of most if not all of the French. In the process Burgundy had deserted his English allies, in a move that profoundly shocked the infant king; Henry had burst into tears when he read the letter from the duke renouncing fealty. More than twenty years later he still recalled the event. 'He abandoned me in my boyhood,' he said, 'despite all his oaths to me, when I had never done him any wrong.' We might notice here the innate simplicity of the remark.

The story of Joan of Arc is well known. Bedford led the war of words against her, denouncing her as a witch and an unnatural hag in the service of the devil. She had declared that the purpose of her mission was to recapture Orleans and expedite the coronation of the French monarch; after she had completed the latter object she seems to have faltered. She was wounded during a military skirmish in Paris, and was then captured by a force of soldiers led by John of Luxemburg. He sold her to Bedford, claiming a large ransom, and the Maid of Orleans was put on trial for witchcraft. The French king made no attempt to save her, and seems to have regarded her as no more than a casualty of war. In the spring of 1431 she was dragged to the stake in the marketplace of Rouen.

The council of nobles held together for the duration of the young king's minority; they were all men who had served under Henry V, and the shared memory of that king was at least as strong as their individual self-interest. The uneasy triumvirate of the three brothers survived until the death of Bedford in 1435. In 1437, in his sixteenth year, Henry declared that his minority had come to an end and that he would now begin to govern for himself. It is more likely, however, that someone made the decision for him. He relied on the judgment and advice of others, and it was said that he always agreed with the last person who had spoken to him. For two years he had been coached in the rights and duties of a king. It was time now to take the centre of the stage. Beaufort and Gloucester, the pre-eminent nobles after the death of Bedford, would in theory be obliged to incline to his wishes. Beaufort had been raised from bishop to cardinal eleven years before, but his elevation still left him below the rank and power of his sovereign. In the summer of 1437 Henry VI embarked upon a grand tour of his kingdom.

So we may now survey the young king. The extant portraits, albeit somewhat idealized, display a man with a prominent jaw and a faintly pious or innocent expression. Concerning his character and judgment, no general agreement exists. He was of an honest and simple nature, but the virtues of ordinary life may not sit well upon a monarch. For some chroniclers he became the model of the saintly king, 'without any crook of craft or untruth'; he was 'pure and clean', modest in success and patient in adversity. Yet to others he seemed to be a simpleton, an idiot, half-witted, a veritable 'sheep'. Pope Pius II said of this devoted son of the Church that he was 'more timorous than a woman, utterly devoid of wit or spirit'. The English churchmen had been gossiping to him. In truth a fifteenth-century king had to be aggressive and brutal; he had to possess innate authority; he had to be shrewd and courageous. Henry VI seems to have possessed none of these qualities. Those who condemned him as an imbecile and a natural fool were simply registering their disappointment. In any other sphere he would no doubt have passed as a devout and kindly man.

Of his piety itself there can be no doubt. He would never conduct business, or move his court, on a Sunday. He rebuked any of his lords who swore, and his only declamatory language was 'Forsooth, forsooth!' His eminent contemporary, William Caxton, wrote that he 'made a rule that a certain dish, which represented the five wounds of Christ as it were red with blood, should be set on his table by his almoner before any other course, when he was to take refreshment; and contemplating these images with great fervour he thanked God marvellous devoutly'.

After the adhesion of the duke of Burgundy to the French cause, the endless war did not go well for the English. They still held on to Normandy, as well as parts of Gascony and Maine, but their aspirations to French supremacy were now at an end. Bedford, the commanding presence on the English side, proved impossible to replace. All the spirit had gone out of the enterprise of France. Step by step Normandy was being reclaimed by the French. It was perhaps unfortunate that Henry VI himself had no military experience or aptitude. His only visit to France was at the time of his coronation, and never once did he lead his forces into the field. He was emphatically a man of peace, more at home with his studies or his devotions; he was more intent upon his foundations, at Eton and elsewhere, or with his building works at Cambridge. In this he may not have been wholly misguided. Eton College and King's College, Cambridge, remain the most enduring manifestations of his reign.

When Paris fell to Charles VII in the spring of 1436, and the state of Normandy grew more disordered, Henry was inclined ever more favourably towards peace. Negotiations between the two sides accomplished precisely nothing, however, while the French continued their slow conquest of the disputed territories. The English did not have the men or the materials successfully to defend both Gascony and Normandy, while the central market town and garrison of Calais was always under threat from the forces of the duke of Burgundy. The French king offered a truce, and the possibility of England maintaining its control of Gascony and Normandy, on the condition that Henry VI renounced his claim to the French crown. The king and his council prevaricated, and sent out a series of confused responses. Henry's council in Normandy said that they were dismayed and apprehensive like 'a ship tossed about on the sea by many winds, without captain, without steersman, without rudder, without sail'. The king could be construed as the substitute for captain and steersman, rudder and sail.

Plenty of interested parties were of course ready to throw in their opinions. Beaufort and Gloucester were joined by a third such party. Richard, duke of York, had taken the place of Bedford as commander of the English forces; he was in fact Bedford's nephew, and would continue the factional strife that already undermined English policy. In the complicated tangle of primogeniture he was now one of the likely and immediate heirs to the throne, being directly related to the fifth son of Edward III; Henry himself was descended from the fourth son. It may seem excessively obscure to a modern reader, but at the time all the protagonists knew exactly where they stood in relation to sovereignty; it was in their blood, literally, and guided their actions. Henry never trusted York.

There is a further complication. John Beaufort, the nephew of Cardinal Beaufort and already made duke of Somerset, was despatched to France in order to relieve Gascony – much to the fury of York who was already facing great disturbances in Normandy and was desperately in need of fresh resources. It is easy to see how English policy was in disarray. York and Gloucester were part of the council that favoured fresh aggression and determination in the face of French attacks; Cardinal Beaufort preferred a policy of compromise and negotiation. The king, although temperamentally in favour of peace, demurred between the two factions. Somerset set sail for France in the summer of 1443, but achieved nothing in the field; finally he had the humiliation of taking refuge with York in Rouen. His army was disbanded and he sailed home. He died in the spring of the following year, and it was widely rumoured that he had committed suicide. The last great English enterprise had been a fiasco. The members of the 'peace party' at Westminster felt themselves to have been vindicated.

In these unpromising circumstances Henry VI sent a personal envoy to negotiate directly with the French king. William de la Pole, duke of Suffolk, had already served in the French wars and had become one of the king's most favoured councillors. He travelled to the French court at Tours in the spring of 1444 where both sides, exhausted by war and attrition, came to a relatively easy truce for the space of ten months. The treaty was sealed with a kiss. As part of the pact Henry VI was to marry the daughter of the Duke of Anjou, one of the most powerful families at the French court; she was also the niece of the French king. Margaret of Anjou, in the company of Suffolk, sailed to England in the following year.

So there came to England one of its most forceful queens. It was not long before it was widely reported that she ruled her husband; one London chronicler, John Blocking, declared that she was cleverer than Henry and of a more powerful character. She was 'a great and strong and active woman who spares no effort in pursuing her affairs'. She found her favourite in Suffolk, who had arranged her marriage, and together they controlled the general policy of the council. It was Margaret, for example, who played a leading role in the negotiations with the French; she was trying to bring the members of her extended family into happy unison. So it was that her husband secretly agreed to cede the province of Maine to the Valois king, in exchange for the security of a general peace. Maine had been an English possession since it had passed to Henry II in 1154 as part of his Angevin inheritance; that older Henry had been born in its capital, Le Mans. The news of its forfeiture provoked discontent and dismay among many of the king's councillors; even the king's envoys in France were opposed to the surrender they had come to negotiate, and insisted on a signed declaration that they had come only in the higher purpose of peace. The treaty, after much confusion and suspicion as a result of Henry's vacillation, was finally sealed.

Gloucester, the leading figure among those who had once favoured war with France, was now in eclipse. His power and authority had been notably undermined, not least in the prosecution of his wife for witchcraft on the grounds that she had sought the king's death by means of the black arts. It is possible that he now planned to move against Suffolk, or in some way to gain control of the king. In 1447 a parliament was summoned to Bury St Edmunds, an unusual setting for that assembly. Gloucester arrived for the opening of the proceedings but, on the day following his arrival, he was arrested in his lodgings on the charge of high treason. A few days later, he was found dead in his bed. It was widely believed he fell ill immediately after his arrest; he had been struck down by anxiety and dismay. He may have died of natural causes, in a most unnatural world. It may of course have been a case of judicial murder, at a time when such events were not uncommon.

The death of Gloucester did not enhance the king's authority. Henry had not proved himself during his personal rule; he was as negligent in his conduct of English affairs as he had been vacillating in his prosecution of the war. He had given away to his favourites more royal lands than any of his predecessors; his debts rose higher and higher, while it was an open secret that the members of his household were purloining money from the royal income. All the perquisites of royal favour – offices, pensions and wardships among them – were being drained. On certain occasions Henry granted the same office twice to different people.

He was generous, too, in the bestowal of new honours; in the eight years between 1441 and 1449 he created ten barons, five earls, two marquises and five dukes. Even the most impartial observer must have concluded that he was unduly diluting the reserves of patronage. Existing barons and dukes might also have surmised that their rank, at the very least, was not necessarily being exalted. Henry had never known any other position than that of monarch; he took his wealth and power for granted. He did not understand the value or importance of what he bestowed. He was always ready, and even eager, to pardon people; he was following the model of his Saviour. But this generosity did not endear itself to those who believed themselves to have been wronged.

He was too weak to arbitrate between the more powerful nobles of the reign; this encouraged them to take matters into their own hands, and to solve by force or threat the disputes that should have been resolved by a strong king. As a result armed feuds between the powerful families presaged the greater civil conflict of the Wars of the Roses. The king was supposed to guide and to lead his nobles; that was part of their compact with the court. They were the natural supporters of the anointed monarch. They did not wish for a weak king, and they were more secure if a king was strong. But, if they were masterless, then all order was destroyed.

The consequences were obvious to all. With the death of the duke of Gloucester, the duke of York became the direct heir to the throne. Yet Henry still did not trust him and, to lessen his capacity for influence at court, he was despatched to Ireland as lord lieutenant. For two years York refused to take up the appointment, but in the summer of 1449 he sailed across the Irish Sea. The command of the English armies in France was then given to the new duke of Somerset, Edmund Beaufort, brother of the supposed suicide. Suffolk and Somerset were now aligned against York. York and Somerset would soon enough become rivals almost to the death. These were the fruits of Henry's 'personal rule' that would end in the bloodiest dynastic dispute in English history.

A more general sense prevailed that the rule of the law had been left in abeyance. 'The law serves of nothing else in these days,' the men of Kent said in a declaration of 1450, 'but to do wrong.' All was accomplished by 'bribery, dread or favour'. The extant letters of the period, particularly those of the Paston family, are filled with accounts of wrongdoing that went unpunished and of nobles who exercised justice (if that is what it can be called) for their own advantage. Endless stories were told of armed gangs threatening tenants, besieging manors and invading courts of justice.

John Paston wrote of one hired gang that 'no poor man dare displease them, for whatsoever they do with their swords they make it law'. He had direct experience of such violent behaviour. In a petition to the archbishop of York he wrote of 'a great multitude of riotous people, to the number of a thousand persons or more' who 'broke, despoiled, and drew down' his manor house at Gresham; they 'drove out my wife and servants there being, and rifled, took, and bore away all the goods and chattels'. The gang then fortified the manor, and kept out Paston himself as well as the king's Justice of the Peace.

Another gang, commanded by William Tailboys, was under the protection of Suffolk; it will be remembered that Suffolk, with the queen, helped to control the council of the realm. Tailboys and his 'slaughterladdes' were accused of three murders as well as charges of trespass and assault; but Suffolk helped him to escape justice. 'On lordship and friendship', it was said, 'depends all law and profit.' The spirit of misrule prevailed over the land, and the king could do nothing about it.

When Paston's manor house was plundered and taken, his adversary procured a royal letter asking the sheriff of Norfolk to show 'favour'. Paston was powerless in these circumstances, and he was advised to place himself under the protection of the duke of York. In 1454 one of Henry's knights who had done well out of the French wars, Sir John Falstolf, laid aside money to bribe a sheriff; he wanted a jury that would favour his suit in a legal case. It is clear enough that the juries of the period were, on a routine basis, bribed or intimidated.

In an interpolation to his version of *The Game and the Playe of the Chesse* William Caxton castigated 'the advocates, the men of law and the attorneys of the court', describing 'how they turn the laws and statutes at their pleasure, how they eat the people, how they impoverish the community'. We may read for instruction a great juridical text of the period, Sir John Fortescue's *De Laudibus Legum Angliae* – 'In Praise of the Laws of England' – and even applaud the development or 'evolution' of justice; but in practice the law was rotten and worm-eaten. We may say the same of the parliament house and of the court. It is not to be expected that any human institution will be other than rackety and only partially competent; only in histories do they proceed with ease to their ordained end.

All these forces of disorder and injustice came to a head in 1449. In that year Henry's authority had suffered a mortal blow when Charles VII, on the pretext that the English had broken the terms of a formal truce agreed two years earlier, marched into Normandy with the ambition of expelling the English altogether from his territories; his success was evident and immediate. The towns, hitherto occupied by the English, surrendered without a fight to the three French armies who advanced upon them from various directions.

In November 1449 the parliament house met in the face of the grave news from France and at its second session, in early 1450, the duke of Suffolk was accused of treason. It was alleged that he had planned to assist the invasion of England by Charles VII, and that he was willing to place his castle in Wallingford at the French king's disposal. The charge may seem unrealistic, but at a time of failure and suspicion it was believed. Those responsible for the fiasco in France had to be made to pay in one form or another. At the same time the chancellor of England, Archbishop Stafford, resigned his post. Suffolk was placed in the Tower, where a bill of impeachment was drawn up against him; the king now intervened and brought these proceedings to an end. Henry could not countenance the spectacle of his chief minister and adviser being humiliated.

The Commons were not to be diverted, however, from their display of public anger and revenge. They put forward a second set of charges, among them the evident fact that Suffolk had protected William Tailboys from arrest and imprisonment. The king now called the lords to his inner chamber in the palace at Westminster, where he repudiated the jurisdiction of parliament by placing Suffolk under his own 'rule and governance'. It was a peculiarly maladroit manner of proceeding, but there seemed at the time to be no alternative. A few weeks later Henry announced that Suffolk would be banished from the realm for a period of five years. Suffolk set sail from Ipswich at the end of April, bound for the Low Countries; but he did not reach his destination. The ship in which he sailed was detained, and he was taken on board another vessel where he was quickly tried by the sailors. He was decapitated with a rusty sword, and his body dumped on a beach near Dover.

The French king's recapture of Normandy took only a year and six days. By the summer of 1450 the English forces had been expelled from most of the towns and cities of France; only Calais and parts of Gascony remained. In a portrait of the time Charles VII was described as *Le Très victorieux Roi de France*. A French chronicler remarked that 'never had so great a country been conquered in so short a space of time, with such small loss to the populace and to the soldiery'. Henry's marriage to Margaret of Anjou had done less than nothing to consolidate English rule in France, and indeed Margaret was blamed by many for having engineered or expedited the final disaster. A rhyme went around at the time, 'The king's son lost all his father won'. The war of a hundred years was almost over.

It is hard to exaggerate the damage to the king. Not only had he failed in his bid for military conquest, he had actually been forced to surrender territories which the English monarchy had previously held by right. From this time forward Henry effectively lost control of his realm, and in the absence of leadership the confusion turned into chaos. It was also reported, in the parliament of 1450, that the king's debts had more than doubled in sixteen years; at this point the merchants of London, individuals and corporations, withdrew their financial support. That is another reason for the dynastic struggle of the Wars of the Roses; the king did not have the money to administer the country. There were fears that this was becoming what was known as a 'wild world'. A man who called himself 'Queen of the Faery' preached in the towns and villages of Kent. In Canterbury a fuller by the name of 'Blue Beard' tried to muster a force or fellowship of men about him. Kent here is the key.

The fact that the head of Suffolk had been found near Dover, and that the shipmen involved in the execution were men of Kent, inevitably placed that independent and sometimes recalcitrant shire under suspicion. The king's representative there threatened that the whole county would be laid to waste and turned into a deer park; but the men of Kent already had cause for complaint. The unsuccessful war against France had severely affected the maritime trade on which their prosperity relied. The coast was attacked with impunity by corsairs from France and Brittany. Agnes Paston wrote that a friend of the family 'had been taken with enemies, walking by the sea side'. She went on to pray that 'God give grace that the sea be better kept than it is now, or else it shall be perilous dwelling by the sea-coast'.

The beleaguered men of Kent rallied at Calehill Heath in the neighbourhood of Ashford at the end of May 1450; they gathered at a meeting place that had been employed for many hundreds of years. The old spirit of place asserted itself in times of uncertainty and danger. On this heath they elected as their leader and representative Jack Cade, and under his guidance they marched towards London; by 11 June they were encamped on Blackheath within sight of the capital. In their declaration they averred that 'they call us risers and traitors and the king's enemies, but we shall be found to be his true liege men'. Instead they attacked his advisers or, as they were commonly known, the 'evil counsellors'; as a result of their machinations, 'his lordship is lost, his merchandise is lost, his commons destroyed, the sea is lost, France is lost, himself so poor that he cannot afford his meat or drink'. They knew, by whispers or by rumours, the parlous state of his finances. The rebels also denounced the manifest perversions of local justice and the oppressions of local magnates, exposing indirectly the confused state of the entire realm.

Some among them, however, directed more personal criticism at Henry. William Merfield declared, at the market in the ancient hamlet of Brightling in East Sussex, that the king was 'a natural fool and would often hold a staff in his hands with a bird on the end, playing therewith as a fool'. This must refer to some children's toy; how Merfield came to know the fact is unclear. Harry Mase, a weaver from Ely, said that the king 'looked more like a child than a man' and that within a short time the ship imprinted on the coinage would be replaced by a sheep.

One of the words on the lips of Cade's men was 'common weal' or 'commonwealth', being the grand polity of king and kingdom, lords and commons; the subject owes obedience to the king, but the king must also strive for the welfare of the subject. All the estates of the realm were, or should be, united in an association of duty and responsibility. It was this association, by implication, that was being undermined by Henry and his advisers.

The forces of the king reacted quickly enough to the threat; while Cade's followers were encamped on Blackheath, emissaries from the king arrived on 13 June and ordered them to disperse. They also carried pardons with them. The king had wanted to go to them in person, emulating the bravery of the young Richard II seventy years before, but his advisers at first demurred. Several thousand men were gathered; 3,000 pardons, at least, were eventually issued. On the morning of 18 June Henry did advance upon Blackheath, with a large contingent of soldiers and guns, but the rebels had already dispersed under cover of the darkness of the previous night; they had been warned about the arrival of the royal army. It was a precautionary measure in another sense; to have fought against the king's banner was manifest treason. Some of the king's men, under the command of Sir Humphrey and Sir William Stafford, then pursued them; the rebels trapped them with an ambush, in which the Staffords were killed. The first blood had gone to the men of Kent.

The blood was soon avenged. Several lords rode into Kent where they exacted retribution, a measure of force that only provoked the rebels still further. A period of confusion followed in which the lords, faced with mounting reaction, quarrelled with one another and in which some soldiers deserted to the rebel cause. The king and his companions, together with the justices of the realm, then fled London and retreated as fast as they could to the safety of the midlands; the mayor of London had begged the king to remain in the capital, but he refused. It was another example of the king's lack of valour.

When they heard reports of the king's retreat, Cade and his followers reassembled on Blackheath at the end of June; on the following day they entered Southwark, and commandeered the inns and hostelries of that district. Cade himself – who had become known as 'the Captain' and as 'John Amend-All' – stayed at the White Hart Inn, along the high street, that became the headquarters for the rebellion. The white hart had of course been the emblem of Richard II.

On 3 July Cade and his men crossed London Bridge, cutting the ropes of the drawbridge so that it could not be later raised against them, and proceeded to occupy the guildhall. In that place of justice several royal servants were convicted of high crimes against the country, and summarily executed at the fountain opposite Honey Lane known as the Cheapside Standard. The sheriff of Kent, one of the most hated, was dragged to Mile End where he was beheaded. Cade retired to the White Hart, in order to formulate his plans.

The Londoners, alarmed at the scale of the riot and damage along the streets of their city, now determined to prevent Cade from entering London once more across the bridge. A force of citizens confronted the rebels and a pitched battle, or series of battles, ensued. Cade, thwarted, determined to burn down the drawbridge; the Londoners, joined also by the remainder of the king's servants who had escaped immediate justice, managed to close the entry-gate. Many perished in the flames of Cade's fire.

A truce among the parties, now on opposite sides of the Thames, was mediated by a group of churchmen led by the archbishops of York and Canterbury; they had remained in the Tower during the riots. It was also concluded that the rebels, having submitted their demands, would receive a royal pardon under the great seal on condition that they dispersed to their homes. The majority of them did so, gratefully enough, but Cade refused or repented his previous submission. He raised the standard of revolt once more, but he commanded too few followers to be a serious threat. He fled south, where he was pursued and cornered; he was arrested in a garden at Heathfield in Sussex and died of his wounds soon afterwards. The revolt had been put down, but not as a result of any of the king's actions.

At this juncture the duke of York returned from his unwelcome post in Ireland. It is of some interest that Jack Cade had called himself John Mortimer, thus aligning himself with the York family name; York had inherited the Mortimer lands and title twenty-five years before, when his mother, Anne Mortimer, had died while giving birth to him. Some of Cade's followers spread the report that he was the duke's cousin. This relationship is most unlikely, but it was suspected at the time that York had in some indirect way helped to foment the rebellion against the king's authority. He returned to England without the king's permission and was immediately seen as a potential threat to Henry's rule; it was at this time that the king appointed York's enemy, Somerset, as the Constable of England. In a series of formal public declarations, passing between the king and York, the duke averred that he had returned in order to clear his name of any unwarranted suspicions concerning the late rebellion; he announced that he had come in order to help to reform the king's household.

Henry duly invited him to join a 'sad [wise or serious] and sub-stantial council'.

This did not address the real problem concerning the enmity between York and Somerset after the debacle in Normandy. They blamed each other for the misconduct of the war, when in fact it was the king himself who should have incurred much of the responsibility for its failure. While Henry VI was still childless, York was the heir presumptive; but Somerset's supremacy in the council of the king provoked York into the fear that he was about to be disinherited.

In September 1450, York came to Westminster with 5,000 men; he called for the dismissal of Somerset as well as others whom he believed to threaten him. But he moved a step too close to anarchy and civil war; his supporters led a noisy demonstration in Westminster Hall, and an attempt was made to assassinate Somer-set. The Lords and Commons then intervened by promulgating a programme of reform in the king's household; a bill to recognize York as the heir apparent was defeated. York retired to his ancestral estates, discomfited, and Somerset was still pre-eminent.

There followed a sequence of skirmishes and confrontations in which neither side could claim victory for its cause; York exercised his power against other magnates without consulting the king, and at the beginning of 1452 denounced Somerset for the fall of Normandy and declared that his rival was about to surrender Calais to the French. York marched south with his supporters, but was forced to withdraw his challenge in the face of overwhelming numbers raised by the rest of the nobility. No large Yorkist 'party' was ready to fight for his cause, and the majority of the other magnates disapproved of what looked very much like armed rebel-lion. He was forced to submit and sue for pardon, protesting all the while that he had acted 'for the good of England'.

It seemed that Henry VI had prevailed but then, as has always happened in the history of England, an arbitrary and unforeseen circumstance turned the course of events. In the summer of 1453 the king fell into a stupor or, in the phrase of the period, his wit and reason were withdrawn. The origin of this malady is uncertain, and may lie in the series of humiliations and misfortunes that had beset the king since the beginning of his reign. But there was one precipitate and immediate cause. The last battle of the Hundred Years War had just been lost by the English. The citizens of Bordeaux had asked to be returned to English sovereignty, and an army was duly sent to assist them under the command of the earl of Shrewsbury; in the subsequent battle the English were routed and Shrewsbury, trapped beneath his fallen horse which had been killed by a cannon ball, was despatched with a hand-axe. This was also the battle in which the region of Gascony was finally surrendered to the French.

So Henry declined into a state of catatonic silence and despondency that was to endure for the next eighteen months. He could not walk or even rise from a chair without help; he had no awareness of time, and lost the power of speech. A child was born to him and Margaret of Anjou, in the autumn of this year, but even the arrival of a son and heir did not enliven him. The duke of Buckingham brought the infant to the king at Windsor Palace and, according to a contemporary,

> presented him to the king in goodly wise, beseeching the king to bless him; and the king gave no manner answer. Nevertheless the duke abode still with the prince by the king, and when he could no manner answer have, the queen came in and took the prince in her arms and presented him in like form as the duke had done, desiring that he should bless it; but all their labour was in vain, for they departed thence without any answer or countenance, saving only that once he looked on the prince and cast down his eyes again, without any more.

If he could have known or guessed the fate of the young prince of Wales, he would have had reason for his sorrow. Two months later the senior members of the council came to him, but 'they could get no answer nor sign'.

In the absence of effective leadership the king's council were obliged to turn to York; he was no longer heir apparent, according to the parliament house, but he was the senior nobleman in the kingdom. York had forgotten and forgiven nothing; he returned to London in the full heat of his anger. His great enemy, Somerset, was consigned to the Tower on the charge of betraying English possessions in France. York also declared that Somerset as well as the king and queen had effectively tried to isolate and to silence him. Margaret of Anjou had always opposed York, but her antipathy became all the more marked when it seemed possible that York might try to supplant her young son. Here were the seeds of the subsequent bloodshed. She turned York into an enemy by regarding him as one. She presented a Bill in which she was to be granted the power to govern the country and appoint the great officers of state but, in March 1454, York was declared to be Protector of the kingdom.

Five doctors had been appointed to watch over the ailing king. It was believed that the dung of doves, applied to the soles of the feet, induced healing sleep. Milk was very good for melancholy. But the eating of hazelnuts discomforted the brain. Green ginger, on the other hand, quickened the memory. Awareness returned to Henry slowly and by degrees. It was reported that 'the king is well amended, and has been so since Christmas day . . . On Monday afternoon the queen came to him and brought the lord prince with her; then he asked what the prince's name was, and the queen told him Edward; then he held up his hands and thanked God thereof. And he said he never knew him till that time, nor knew what was being said to him, nor knew where he had been whilst he was sick . . . He said that he was now in charity with all the world . . .'

It is not clear that he ever fully recovered from his affliction; the reports of his behaviour in succeeding years suggest that to some extent he had become feeble-minded. Yet the protectorate of York had now come to an end. He gave his resignation to the king at the palace in Greenwich; Somerset was duly released from the Tower and returned to the side of the monarch. Henry now also welcomed back to his councils the perceived enemies of York; he was behaving like the leader of a faction rather than as the ruler of the country. Naturally enough York deemed himself to be under threat. He felt obliged to make a preliminary strike but, in the process, he began the conflict that came to be known as the Wars of the Roses.

# 32

# Meet the family

In the absence of her husband Margaret Paston decided to attack those who had turned her out of the manor house at Gresham; the violent affair was mentioned in the previous chapter. She called on her husband to send handguns, crossbows, longbows and poll-axes; her servants wore body armour. In the same letter she asked for a pound (450 grammes) of almonds, a pound of sugar and some cloth to make gowns for the children. The ordinary life of the world continued even in the face of extreme violence. Or it could be claimed that violence was as ordinary, and as unremarkable, as almonds and sugar.

It is sometimes surmised that in the fifteenth century the expression of emotion is different from that of our own time. But where, if anywhere, does that difference lie? A delicacy of emphasis, not generally found in the register of contemporary speech, can perhaps be found in the Paston letters. Of the Paston servants we learn that 'they are sad [serious] and well advised men, saving one of them who is bald, called William Penny, who is as good a man as goes upon the earth, saving he will be a little, as I understand, a little cupshotten [drunk]; but he is no brawler, but full of courtesy . . .' Immense shrewdness is also evident. 'John Osborne flattered me,' John Paston wrote, 'because he would have borrowed money from me. In retailing of wood there it will be hard to trust him. He is needy.' Again, in another letter, we learn that one man 'had but few words but I felt by him he was right evil disposed to the parson and you; but covered language he had'.

In many respects it was a hard world, filled with threat. 'I pray you beware how you walk if he be there, for he is full cursed-hearted and lumish.' The meaning of 'lumish' is uncertain; it is a word that has gone forever. One husband believed that his wife's child was not his. 'I heard say that he said, if she comes in his presence to make her excuse, that he should cut off her nose to make her be known what she is, and if her child comes in his presence he said he would kill it.' That may of course have been an idle threat. A tendency to extravagance is found in the period. Of the earl of Arran, John Paston writes that 'he is the most courteous, gentlest, wisest, kindest, most companionable, freest, largest and most bounteous knight'.

Humour and irony are also to be found. When one son of Paston contracted a cold in damp Norwich he wrote that 'I was never so well armed for the war as I have now armed myself for the cold.' Resignation was a familiar theme. 'If it thus continue I am not all undone, nor none of us; and if otherwise then & . . .' Which is as much to say – well if we are undone, then so be it. There were striking phrases such as 'I know you have a great heart' and, sarcastically, 'this is a marvellous disposed country'. 'And so I am with the jailor, with a shackle on my heel.' 'This is a right queasy world.' Of an indiscreet man it was said that 'he is not secure in the bite'. Flattering an enemy was sometimes necessary because 'a man must some time set a candle before the Devil'. 'Towards me' is written as 'to me-wards'.

The syntax is often complicated with 'wherefore' and 'insomuch' and 'therein'; the sentences are often long and convoluted, but throughout there is an energy or earnestness of expression that drives the narrative forward. The intricate constructions, replete with double negatives at every turn, suggest a world of great formality; but one animated by the sheer struggle for survival. That is what lends the correspondence its pace and urgency.

The status of the Paston family itself indicates social movement and change. Clement Paston was married to a bondwoman (albeit she became, by a medieval paradox, heiress to her brother who was an attorney) and owned only a small farm in Norfolk; by dint of saving and borrowing he managed to send his son, William, to Eton College. In turn William Paston became a lawyer and was eventually appointed to be Justice of the Common Pleas; although his mother had been technically a villein he married into a gentry family. The next generation of the Paston family were themselves members of the gentry, and the male Pastons became knights of the shire. Within three generations the family had been transformed. This was a characteristic feature of English society.

Details in the Paston correspondence, assembled together, open up the world. 'I pray you that Pitt may truss up in a chest which I left in your chamber at London my tawny gown furred with black and the doublet of purple satin and the doublet of black satin, and my writing box of cypress, and my book of the meeting of the Duke and the Emperor . . .'

You can also hear the people speak. 'Forsooth when I came into the chamber there the first word I heard was this that you said to my Master, John Paston, "Who that ever says so, I say he lies falsely in his head."'

'Ya. You should have told what moved me to say so to him.'

'I could not tell that which I had not heard.'

'You should have examined the matter.'

'Sir it did not belong to me to examine the matter, since I knew full well that I should not be a judge of the matter for it belongs only to a judge to study *illam Sacre Scripture clausam* where Holy Job says "*Causam quam nesciebam diligentissime investigabam*".' So men were inclined, and able, to break into Latin when addressing one another.

Latin was also used for the ruder moments. Of two men in close alliance it was written that *singuli caccant uno ano* or 'they shit out of the same arse'. There is much talk of 'worship', meaning personal honour, and 'disworship'. Those in authority suggest that they will 'prove a good lord' or otherwise to their supplicants. It was a world of gossip, with many 'flyting words' passing around London. It was also a world of plots and machinations, of convenient alliances and accidental events, of endless litigation and pleas for patronage.

Domestic aspects of the Paston correspondence suggest that

the nature of human life is not greatly changed. Margaret Paston wrote to her husband while pregnant that 'I pray that you will send me dates and cinnamon as hastily as you may ... From your groaning wife.' In a previous letter she wrote, 'I pray you be not strange [slow] of writing letters to me between this time and when you come home; if I could, I would have one from you every day.' 'Forgive me,' one man writes, 'I write to make you laugh.'

Letters often begin with 'I greet you well'. They generally end with a religious salutation, 'the Blessed Trinity have you in his holy governance' or 'may God keep you and deliver you'.

One of the pleasures of the Paston correspondence, however, lies in the extent to which the life of the day is revealed. The actions of recorded history may be stirring or dispiriting, according to taste, but the busy concourse of human existence can be heard beneath the events recorded by the annalists and the chroniclers. The real life and spirit of the time are held in the innumerable remarks and encounters among the people going about their business in market and in town, in hamlet and in field. Those who pursue the process of living are those who create the history and traditions of the country in a million unacknowledged ways; they form the language of expression, and they preserve the stability of the land.

So in a period of war and domestic turmoil the general economy of the country was growing at a rapid pace. The diminution of population at the time of the Black Death in 1348 meant that there was more land, and more work, for fewer people; this in itself was the context for the relatively new experience of prosperity. It was a commonplace of observation that the English agricultural worker was better fed and housed than the French peasant. A Venetian diplomat remarked in 1497 that England was an under-populated country but that 'the riches of England are greater than those of any other country in Europe, as I have been told by the oldest and most experienced merchants, and also as I myself can vouch from what I have seen. This is owing in the first place to the great fertility of the soil which is such that, with the exception of wine, they import nothing from abroad for their subsistence ...

everyone who makes a tour in this island will soon become aware of this great wealth.'

The parish churches of the period are one of the most visible signs of affluence still to be observed in the English landscape, parish rivalling parish with the extent of its patronage; the screen-work and roof carvings are of the finest quality. It was the great age of the church tower, from Fulham in London to Mawgan-in-Pyder at St Mawgan in Cornwall. The majority of the stone bridges of the country were improved in the fifteenth century; London Bridge itself was rebuilt and widened. In the first half of that century a vogue for building libraries in the cathedrals, and in the colleges of the two universities, can be identified; fine examples can be found at Merton College and at New College in Oxford as well as in the cathedrals of York, Lincoln, Wells, Canterbury and All Saints, Bristol. The divinity school at Oxford began to rise in 1424 and was roofed in 1466.

Schools, almshouses and hospitals were constructed through-out the realm. It was the age of the large and unfortified country residences, where increasingly brick rather than stone was con-sidered the suitable medium. The wall around the town of Hull, constructed in the second half of the fourteenth century, was the first public edifice built entirely of brick. The public institutions of town and city were improved or built anew; between 1411 and 1440, for example, the present Guildhall of London was erected. The Guildhall at York was built in the 1450s. We have already mentioned Henry's meticulous concern for the building of Eton College and King's College, Cambridge; the foundation stone of the extraordinary King's College Chapel was laid by the king in the summer of 1446. Architecture was in the fullest possible sense the expression of the country, as it clothed itself in vestments of stone. It acts as a balance to the historical accounts which almost of necessity chronicle the violence and insecurity of the age. Most of what is now regarded as 'medieval' dates from the fifteenth century, and we can say with confidence that it remains physically close to us. The churches and libraries, the guildhalls and bridges, are still in use.

Periods of great economic activity succeeded periods of slump, so that the familiar cycle of overconfidence and anxiety was always in motion; yet what we now call the gross domestic product of the country materially increased. When a ship coming from Dieppe landed at Winchelsea harbour in 1490, it contained satin and pipes of wine, razors and damask, needles and mantles of leopards' skins, five gross of playing cards and eight gross of plaques stamped with the image of the Lamb of God. A trade in monkeys from Venice, described as 'apes and japes and marmosets tailed', flourished. An inventory of the household goods of Sir John Fastolf reveals that he purchased cloth from Zeeland (now part of the Netherlands), silver cups from Paris, coats of mail from Milan, treacle pots from Genoa, cloth from Arras and girdles from Germany. An old rhyme tells the story:

> Hops and turkies, carps and beer,
> Came into England all in a year.

In fact by the end of the fifteenth century, beer itself was coming out of England. It had once been imported from Prussia, but English merchants were soon carrying beer from London to Flanders.

Economic activity quickened in a variety of different spheres. A small native industry of glass-painting emerged, and carpet manufactories were established at Romsey in Hampshire. Great merchants now rivalled their competitors in Genoa or in Venice. William Cannynges of Bristol possessed, in 1461, ten ships and employed 800 sailors as well as 100 craftsmen. The ships of the merchants were in fact employed as a volunteer force working with the royal navy to patrol the seas and to defend the shores. The cities and towns that engaged in maritime trade, such as Bristol and Southampton, naturally flourished. John Cabot sailed out of Bristol for the New World in 1497, looking for new markets and new trade. The mercantile interest was successful in another sense; the more affluent merchants of the towns were now attending the parliament house, and pressing their demands for the exclusive management of what was not necessarily fair trade.

Iron from the Weald in Kent and the Forest of Dean in Gloucestershire was much in demand; other wooded areas, where timber was available to create the charcoal for smelting the ore, were fully exploited. In the Forest of Dean alone there were seventy-two forges. All Saints Church in the village of Newland, on the western edge of the forest, has a brass engraving of a miner. His leather breeches are tied below his knee, and he sports a wooden mine-hod over his shoulder in which to carry the iron ore; he holds a mattock or small pickaxe in his right hand, and between his teeth he carries a candle-holder or 'Nellie'. He would, of course, work and dress as a small farmer when he was not mining. The silver mines of Cornwall and Devon, Dorset and Somerset, were expanded. It was said at the time that 'the kingdom is of greater value under the land than it is above'. Productivity increased in the shipyards, the gunsmitheries and the bell foundries.

The reign of wool reached new heights during the rule of Henry VI and of his successor. The annual export of raw wool had declined a little from its peak in the fourteenth century but this was offset by a proportionate increase in the export of woollen cloth. Together they accounted for approximately 80 per cent of the country's exports. English cloths were taken to the shores of the Black Sea, and were traded at the fair of Novgorod as well as the Rialto in Venice; they went to Denmark and to Prussia. The merchant adventurers, in control of the cloth trade, were exporting approximately 60,000 rolls of cloth each year by the end of the century.

It was a business that engaged a significant part of the nation; the wool was given to village women to comb and to spin before being sent to the weaver; to this day, an unmarried woman is known as a spinster. Once the wool had been woven into cloth it was given to the fuller for dyeing and then passed on to the shearman for finishing. The dominance of wool is the reason why the Lord Chancellor of England, until 2005, always sat upon a woolsack in the House of Lords. The towns that were involved in the cloth trade – notably Colchester – became larger and stronger. The fulling mills of the West Riding and the west of England turned ever faster. Broadcloth came from the Cotswolds and the Stroud Valley. As York and Coventry decayed, so villages like Lavenham in Suffolk with its famous 'wool church' thrived.

Wool raw and finished was indeed the motor of the fifteenth-century English economy, and as a result more and more land was

preserved for the breeding of sheep. This in turn led to the
enclosing of land for that purpose. Villages were moved or even
destroyed to make way for the sheep-runs; the cultivation of grain
gave way to rearing. The shepherds lived in wheeled huts that
followed the flocks. In the late fifteenth century one Warwickshire
antiquary, John Rous, complained in his *Historia Regum Angliae* of
'the modern destruction of villages which brings dearth to the
commonwealth. The root of this evil is greed . . . As Christ wept
over Jerusalem so do we weep over the destruction of our own
times.' In his own county there are more than a hundred deserted
villages, the vast majority of them cleared in the fifteenth century.
The rights of freeholders and copyholders were in principle protected, but those who had dwelled on the land by custom could be
evicted with impunity. Much of the population moved a few miles,
perhaps, and continued working the land. A few were not so
fortunate. That rootless phenomenon known then as 'the sturdy
beggar' is first mentioned in the 1470s.

All things move in restless combination. There is a law of
contrast at work in human history, whereby one development
provokes a counter-development. Many people suffered from the
pace of economic change, but others benefited from it. The
successful small farmer was now paying rent for his land as a
tenant, rather than performing labour duties; the small freeholder,
known as the yeoman, is also more in evidence. The class of
villein or serf gave way to the labourer working for a wage. The
feudal economy had to a large extent been succeeded by a money
economy.

Yet the prosperity of England was by no means evenly shared,
and it is important to bear in mind the unimaginable extremes of
poverty beside the perceived affluence of certain county towns and
regions. The fact that the contrasts of life were more violent, and
the insecurity of existence more palpable, rendered the people more
passionate and more excitable. Theirs was a life more intense, more
sensitive, more arduous and more irritable than our own.

# 33

# The divided realm

Signs and portents of civil unrest, according to the native chroniclers, darkened the air of the mid-fifteenth century. A rain of
blood fell in different regions, and the holy waters of healing wells
overflowed. A huge cock was observed in the waters off Weymouth,
'coming out of the sea, having a great crest upon his head and a
great red beard and legs half a yard [45 centimetres] long'. Many
people heard a strange voice rising in the air, between Leicester
and Banbury, calling out 'Bows! Bows!' A woman in the county of
Huntingdon 'felt the embryo in her womb weeping as it were, and
uttering a kind of sobbing noise' as if it dreaded being born into a
time of calamity.

The houses of York and Lancaster were in fact two sides of the
same ruling family. The house of Lancaster was descended from
the fourth son of Edward III, John of Gaunt, duke of Lancaster;
the house of York was descended from the fifth son of the same
king, Edmund, duke of York, whose youngest son had married
the great-granddaughter of the third son. They are sometimes
described as the third and fourth sons respectively, but this omits
one male child who lived for six months. Their closeness, however,
bred only enmity and ferocity. Blue blood was often bad blood.
It was like a fight breaking out among a small assembly; slowly it
spreads, bringing in more and more people. But there is still a vast

crowd standing outside the arena of combat, watching silently and incuriously or going about their familiar business.

York and his followers retired to their estates after the recovery of the king from mental incapacity and the return of Somerset to power, but in the spring of 1455 they were summoned to attend a great council at Leicester. York feared that this would be the occasion for his arrest or arraignment, and so he forestalled events by gathering his supporters and marching down towards London. He was joined by the representatives of one of the great families of northern England; York's brother-in-law was Richard Neville, the earl of Salisbury, and the earl's son was another Richard Neville, the earl of Warwick. Their inveterate enemies in the north, the family of the Percys, had taken the side of Somerset. So local enmities exacerbated the general conflict. Salisbury and Warwick, who came to be known as 'Warwick the king-maker', proclaimed that they had taken up arms to remove 'our enemies of approved experience, such as abide and keep themselves under the wing of your Majesty Royal'.

They had at all costs to maintain the fiction that they were not marching against the king but against the king's councillors; otherwise they would have incurred the charge of high treason. Nevertheless York's army now faced the king's army in open battle at St Albans. There had been some attempt at preliminary negotiations, but York feared that Henry was wholly in Somerset's control and was therefore not to be trusted. So his forces entered the town at ten o'clock in the morning on 22 May 1455, and began a series of rapid raids in its main street and public spaces. They were looking for their enemies. Somerset and Henry Percy, the earl of Northumberland, had been marked for slaughter. They were tracked down and killed on the spot in a notable if not unique act of savagery. The king himself was wounded in the neck, as he sat beneath his banner in the market square, but he was not seriously injured. Sixty men were killed in the fighting, which lasted for only a couple of hours.

Once their victory was assured, York and the Nevilles submitted to the king. It was reported that they 'besought him of his Highness to take them as his true liegemen, saying that they never intended to hurt his person'. Henry then 'took them to grace, and so desired them to cease their people, and that there should no more harm be done'. York then escorted the king back to London, if escort is the appropriate word for an armed entourage, and four days later presented Henry with his crown in St Paul's Cathedral. It might legitimately have been asked who was in charge. A friend wrote to John Paston, on that day, 'as for what rule we shall have, yet I know never'. The king's forces had been defied, and the king himself wounded; the order of the world had been turned upside down, and the governance of the realm placed in utmost peril. Yet who could have known or guessed that the combat of St Albans was the prelude to an internecine war that would continue for thirty years, provoke seven or eight major battles on English soil, and lead to the killing of some eighty nobles of royal blood? It has all the ingredients of a revenge tragedy. 'By God's blood,' one Lancastrian noble screamed at the son of York on a later battlefield, 'your father killed mine, and so will I do to you and to all your kin!' We might be back in the days of the Anglo-Saxons, as if the years between had been a dream.

Within a short time after the battle the king had fallen prey to some malady, the nature of which remains unknown. It is easy to conjecture that he had relapsed into the same state of confusion as before, perhaps traumatized by his defeat, but he does not seem to have withdrawn completely from the world. He even managed to open the parliament in the summer of 1455. After a delay of some months York resumed the protectorate but the king, or his wife working in his name, let it be known to his councillors that he wished to be kept informed 'in all matters as touching his honour, worship and safety'. The royal family were now more wary and defensive; they feared that York aspired to being king in all but name.

York's most significant task was to defend the southern coast against French incursions and the northern frontier against the Scots; he was also obliged to protect the last remaining English settlement at Calais. So he named his ally, Warwick, as captain of that town. For all these preparations he needed money to be granted by the parliament house. That proved a complicated and arduous task, made infinitely more difficult when in February 1456 the king was brought by the lords to Westminster in order to abrogate the proceedings and effectively to overrule the protector. At that point York, resentful and weary, resigned or was made to resign from his post.

The king was now nominally in command, but the real power lay with his wife. Margaret of Anjou was according to a contemporary 'a great and strong laboured [strong-minded] woman' who arranged everything 'to an intent and conclusion to her power'. She was certainly more masterful than her husband. Her essential purpose was now to safeguard the interests of her infant son and to make sure that he succeeded his ailing father. In this respect, York was still the principal enemy made all the more dangerous by the death of Somerset.

She moved the king and court to the middle of her landed estates around Coventry, with the castle of Kenilworth as her stronghold, thereby setting up a base of power as an alternative to York who remained in London. The citizens had taken up his cause, and the queen did not feel safe among them. The councils of the realm were literally divided, and the course of affairs seemed likely to drift. One contemporary observed that 'the great princes of the land [pre-eminently York and Warwick] were not called to Council but set apart'.

For the next three or four years there is little mention of the king; he spent much of his time travelling through the midlands, staying at various favoured abbeys or priories. It is said that above all else he enjoyed sleeping. No speeches by the king are reported. He was 'simple'; he upheld no household, and he prosecuted no war. Little or no attempt was made at governance, apart from the routine business of finance and patronage. Even in these spheres, however, the queen's wishes and decisions were paramount. The Lancastrian court, and the Yorkist lords, watched each other eagerly and suspiciously; the air was filled with threat.

The court returned to Westminster, in the winter of 1457, accompanied by a force of 13,000 archers; it was widely believed that the king and queen had returned in order to overcome York and to overawe the city. Political life had always been a form of gang warfare, in a scramble for lands and riches. Now it showed its true face. The streets of the city were filled with supporters of the

Lancastrians and the Yorkists; the younger relatives of the Lancastrians who had been killed at St Albans had come for vengeance.

Another source of unrest arose in that winter. In the summer of the year a French fleet had landed at Sandwich and devastated the town, a signal example both of the failure of English policy and of English weakness. The merchants of London, in particular, were horrified and outraged at the threat to maritime trade. In such an environment no one could feel safe.

Confronted with the possibility of civil war breaking out in the capital between the supporters of both sides, the principal figures reached a form of compromise in which the relatives of the dead were offered financial compensation for their loss. Money, in England, is always the best policy. This agreement was followed by what was known as a 'love day', in which sworn enemies literally joined hands and proceeded to a solemn service in St Paul's Cathedral. But the love did not last. The royal court showed no favour to York or to the Nevilles, and in the spring of 1459 Henry ordered his loyal nobles to gather at Leicester with 'as many persons defensibly arrayed as they might according to their degree'. The king was, in other words, calling for the armed retainers of the lords to be put at his disposal. A great council was held in June at Coventry, to which York and his supporters were not invited. At this assembly the renegade lords were denounced for their disloyalty.

York and Warwick now gathered their forces, and marched towards Worcester where they held their own council. Richard Neville, earl of Salisbury, was intent upon joining them with 5,000 men. The queen's army intercepted him, however, on the road from Newcastle-under-Lyme; Salisbury beat off the attack, killing the queen's commander and scattering what must now be called the enemy. The battle, lasting for more than four hours, claimed the lives of 2,000 men; the battlefield itself became known as 'Deadmen's Den'. So it had come to this. The English were fighting and killing the English, the men of Yorkshire against the men of Shropshire, the men of Wiltshire against the men of Cheshire.

Despite Salisbury's victory, York and his allies were now

confronted by a large royal army bearing down upon them. They retreated from Worcester to Ludlow, where they established an armed camp. Yet it was clear enough that York was uneasy about confronting the king in open battle where he could be accused of high treason. A contingent of Warwick's forces from Calais then deserted and, knowing themselves to be vulnerable, York and the Nevilles fled under cover of darkness; York returned to his old fiefdom, Ireland, while Warwick and Salisbury sailed to Calais. Their lands were seized by the king and they were declared to be traitors. Their cause seemed to have ended ingloriously.

The coastal defences of the country were now strengthened, with the possibility of an attack both from Calais and from Dublin; meanwhile, in the spring of 1460, Warwick sailed to Ireland in order to consult York on the next move. It came in the form of invasion. In the early summer of 1460 Warwick and Salisbury landed at Kent and began a march to the friendly territory of London. The leaders of the capital welcomed them and even offered them money. The Nevilles said that they had come to 'rescue' the king from his evil councillors; they professed nothing but goodwill towards Henry himself; they were not rebels, but reformers of the body politic; they wished to lighten taxation and to reduce the king's debts; they pledged to reform the workings of the law and to lift the manifold oppressions of the king's courtiers. It was the standard rhetoric of the period, but it was received warmly by the citizens and by the people of south-eastern England. It seems likely, however, that York and Warwick had brooded on the possibility of killing the king together with his wife and son. It should be remembered that these were all vicious and ruthless men.

Warwick remained in the city for only three days before marching north in search of the king's army. He found it outside Northampton and, before sending his forces into battle, he ordered them to hunt down and kill the king's entourage; the senior nobility and the knights were not to be spared. The fighting lasted less than an hour, and the victory went to Warwick after the slaughter of the king's closest companions. Henry himself was taken into custody and once more escorted to London, where he was king only in name. 'I follow after the lords,' he is described as saying in a poem of the time. 'I never know why.' He was a puppet monarch.

Nevertheless the queen and her son, the young Prince Edward, were still at large.

York returned from Ireland ten weeks after the battle, and bore about him all the appurtenances of royalty. He no longer dated his letters according to the years of Henry's reign, as was the custom, and he bore the arms of England on his banners. He arrived as the parliament in Westminster, summoned by Warwick, was beginning its proceedings; his trumpets sounded as he made his entrance, and a drawn sword was carried before him. He then made his way towards the vacant throne and put his hand upon it as if to claim possession; this unexpected and unlawful act was greeted with surprise and dismay by the lords assembled. It looked as if York had miscalculated his popularity, and underestimated their residual loyalty to their rightful king.

He demanded to be installed as the monarch. When asked to make a courteous visit to Henry he replied that 'I know of no person in the realm whom it does not behove to come to me and see my person rather than that I should go and visit him.' The king himself was too frightened to encounter York. The lords demurred at York's demand, and passed the question to the judges; the judges in turn refused to meddle in such 'high matters' and passed the problem back to the lords. The question was 'above the law and past their learning'. In any case no man wished to perjure his oath of loyalty to the anointed sovereign. In his incapacity Henry had become the emblem of his age; the senior members of the realm were struck by indecision. Emptiness ruled at the heart of government.

Eventually the lords, in English fashion, proposed a compromise. Henry would retain the crown but, on his death or at the time of his willing abdication, York and his heirs should succeed him. Since York was ten years older than Henry, the lords were playing a game of wait and see. When the king accepted this proposal he was effectively disinheriting his son, and stripping him of his rightful inheritance. But he was in no position, and perhaps in no condition, to remonstrate on the matter. The feelings of Queen Margaret on the issue of succession are hardly in doubt; but for the moment she was on the run. She retreated with her son to Wales, but then fled to Scotland; she left her forces under the command of the earl of Pembroke, Jasper Tudor, half-brother to the king. So the Tudors properly enter English history. Jasper Tudor was the fruit of an unlikely marriage when Katherine of Valois, the widow of Henry V, became the wife of a junior courtier by the name of Owen Tudor. The older Tudor had joined his son on behalf of the queen. No one, however, could possibly have imagined the ultimate success of his family line.

By the end of 1460 the queen reappeared in the north of England, having persuaded the great lords of that region to support her against the Londoners and the south-easterners. She mustered some 10,000 armed retainers, as York and Salisbury marched north to meet them. Battle was joined outside Wakefield, in the course of which both York and Salisbury were despatched; it was for the Lancastrians some recompense for the slaughter at St Albans and Northampton. The head of York was wreathed in a paper crown, and placed on the southern gate of the city of York known as Micklegate Bar. It bore a sign saying 'Let York overlook the town of York.'

So it seemed that Margaret of Anjou had won, with the benefits flowing to her son as well as to a weak and feeble king; but Henry himself remained in London, in the control and at the mercy of Warwick. That magnate had not marched north with his allies, but had remained behind to protect what was now a Yorkist administration at Westminster. According to the agreement reached by the lords between the king and York, the heir to the throne had now become York's son, Edward of March. Two young Edwards, Prince Edward at the age of seven and Edward of March at the age of eighteen, were now pitted against one another.

Edward of March had in fact already taken to the field in defence of the Yorkist inheritance. He marched at the head of his army, with the aim of preventing the Welsh forces led by Jasper Tudor from aligning with the main body of Lancastrian troops in the north. At the beginning of February 1461 he encountered the Tudors in Herefordshire, at a place known as Mortimer's Cross. Before battle was joined the unusual appearance of a parhelion or sun dog became visible in the air, where by means of small ice crystals a second sun seems to appear beside the first. The soldiers on the earth knew nothing of ice crystals, of course, but the manifestation of two suns suggested some great change in the direction of the world. Two sons were, after all, in conflict. And there were about to be two kings of England.

The victory was won by Edward of March; Jasper Tudor fled, but his father was not so fortunate. Owen Tudor was taken to the block where he was heard to murmur that 'the head shall lie on the stock that was wont to lie on the lap of Queen Katherine', the widow of Henry V whom he had married. His head was carried from the scaffold and placed on the market cross of the local town. It was here that a madwoman combed his hair and washed the blood from his face.

Margaret was already marching towards London, emboldened by the death of York; the Tudors were unable to join her, of course, but still she moved steadily to the south. All the while she allowed her troops to pillage and plunder the lands of her Yorkist enemies through which they passed. Warwick mustered his army in London to prevent her from entering the capital, where most of his power and resources lay; he took the king with him, as a form of insurance. He must also have hoped that Margaret would not attack an army that effectively held her husband hostage.

His hopes were misjudged, however. On 17 February 1461, the Yorkists and Lancastrians met once more at St Albans, but on this occasion the Lancastrians were successful. The king was rescued; he had been placed for safekeeping a mile away, where it was said that he laughed and sang beneath a tree. Many of the leading Yorkist nobles were slaughtered. Warwick fled the scene with a handful of companions.

It is reported that Henry was overjoyed to see his immediate family once more and, in his excitement, he knighted his young son. The seven-year-old boy in turn knighted some thirty of his followers. Margaret, with the king in her possession, now stood close to the gates of London. It was reported in the chronicles that 'the shops keep closed, and nothing is done either by the tradesmen or by the merchants. Men do not stand in the streets or venture far from home'. They had heard the news of the devastation wreaked by Margaret's troops in the north of England. John Paston wrote to his father that they 'are appointed to pillage all this country, and give away men's goods and livelihoods in the south country, and that will ask a mischief'.

On hearing the news of Margaret's advance, Edward of March – who was now after his father's death the duke of York – left the site of his victory by the Welsh border and took his forces east to intercept her; he met Warwick in Oxfordshire, close to the Cotswolds, and together they moved towards London. Their purpose now was to occupy the city and to declare Edward to be the lawful king. The citizens were disposed to accept them, and the gates were shut against Margaret of Anjou.

When Edward arrived, he was greeted by the Londoners; the streets were crowded with his supporters and he took the crown almost by acclamation. His right to the title was proclaimed, at St Paul's Cross and elsewhere, while Henry VI was declared to have forfeited the throne by reneging on his agreement to make York his heir. On 4 March Edward entered St Paul's Cathedral, and then proceeded in state towards Westminster where he was crowned as Edward IV. All those present did homage to him, as he held the sceptre of Edward the Confessor. They chanted the refrain:

*Verus Vox, Rex Edwardus*
*Rectus Rex, Rex Edwardus.*

He was the true voice and the rightful king. He was nineteen years old and, at a height of 6 feet and 4 inches (1.9 metres), a commanding figure. He was every inch a proper king. The ambassador from Burgundy said that 'I cannot remember ever having seen a finer looking man'.

Yet Henry VI could still be construed to be the anointed sovereign; he was not dead, and he had not abdicated. So effectively two kings of England reigned. Two suns were visible in the sky. A seventeenth-century historian, Thomas Fuller, put it perhaps more vividly in *The Holy State and The Profane State* where he remarked that 'they lived in a troublesome world, wherein the cards were so shuffled that two kings were turned up trumps at once, which amazed men how to play their games'.

Edward took steps to resolve this unsatisfactory situation by going in pursuit of Margaret and of Henry. On 29 March the two armies met at Towton in Yorkshire, the royal family having taken the precaution of returning to York to await developments. They were right to do so. Edward won a signal victory on the battlefield; the conflict, held in a snowstorm, is thought to have involved some 50,000 soldiers of whom approximately a quarter perished. Much of the Lancastrian nobility were destroyed. Henry and Margaret, together with their son, escaped into Scotland. The old king, if we may call him that, was to remain at liberty for another four years as an emblem of the surviving Lancastrian claim to the throne. Only the first part of the Wars of the Roses was over.

# 34

# The world at play

Many miniature jugs have been found in the soil of medieval dwellings; they have been interpreted as toys for children. The son of Edward I was given a miniature cart as well as the little model of a plough. From an excavation in London was removed a toy bird, made out of lead and tin; in its original state it would have rocked on a horizontal rod, at the same time as its tongue would appear and reappear from an open beak. Miniature faces were made out of tin, with large ears and eyes and spiked hair. For the very young, rattles were made. Glove puppets were common. Dolls of wood or of cloth were known as 'poppets'. Tops were called 'scopperils' or things that jump about. Hobby-horses were small wooden horses. So the children played as they have always done. But the call of the world was not far distant. The boys were trained in wrestling and in shooting with bow and arrow. They were taught how to imitate the calls of birds, and how to tell the time from the shadows cast by the sun. The girls were trained in weaving, in sewing and in laundering.

Childhood did not last for very long. In the time of the Saxons the age of adult responsibility was twelve at which point the boy or girl could be set to proper full-time work, in the fields of the country or in the streets and markets of the town. In later centuries a boy was criminally liable from the age of seven and could make his will at the age of fourteen.

The more fortunate were granted an education. Some children were given to the monks at a very young age, and were never seen again in secular clothing. The child's hair was shaved from the round area of the scalp, so that he already resembled a monk. His cloak was taken from him at a special Mass as the abbot declared 'May the Lord strip you of the old man.' The boy was then given a monk's cowl with the words 'May the Lord clothe you with the new man.' One elderly monk recalled how in 1080, at the age of five, he began school in the town of Shrewsbury where 'Siward, an illustrious priest, taught me my letters for five years, and instructed me in psalms and hymns and other necessary knowledge'. A long tradition of clerkly learning already existed.

From the seventh to the eleventh centuries, in fact, the cloister schools of the monasteries provided the principal means of education; the lessons included those of grammar, rhetoric and natural science. The art of singing was also taught. They are not dead institutions. The school of St Albans, established in the tenth century, is still in existence at the beginning of the twenty-first century. The grammar school of Ely, now known as the King's School, also has an Anglo-Saxon origin; one of its boarding houses is reputed to be the oldest residential building in Europe. The present grammar school of Norwich was instituted in the eleventh century. Many other examples can be found.

It was widely believed that priests should also be schoolmasters, and a church decree of 1200 declared that 'priests shall keep schools in the towns and teach the little boys free of charge. Priests ought to hold schools in their houses . . . They ought not to expect anything from the relatives of the boys except what they are willing to give'. Such schools remained in use throughout the period of this book.

In the twelfth century a number of larger schools also emerged, as part of what has been called the 'renaissance' of that century in humane learning; they grew up beside the cathedrals, or beside the houses of canons, or in the towns reliant upon great monasteries. Their influence and reputation spread, and between 1363 and 1400 twenty-four new schools were founded. They became known as the grammar schools, despite the fact that grammar was not the only subject; the art of letter-writing was the subject of study, as well as the disciplines of record-keeping and commercial accounting. 'Business studies' began in the medieval period.

A fortunate male child received his education at the court of the king or the nobles. If a superior spoke to him, he was trained to take off his hat and to look steadfastly in that person's face without moving his hands or feet. He was taught to put his hand in front of his mouth before spitting. He was not to scratch his head and was to ensure that his hands and nails were always clean.

Other forms of education were also available. An apprentice was chosen between the ages of fourteen and seventeen, and entered a formal bond by which he agreed to spend between seven and ten years with his master while learning the 'secrets' of his chosen trade. It was by far the most common way of fully entering the adult world, although of course it had its risks. It was not unknown for masters to treat apprentices very roughly, or for apprentices to absent themselves without leave. Apprentices also had a reputation for being unruly and even violent; one of their favourite games, when they found themselves in a group, was known as 'breaking doors with our heads'.

By the middle of the twelfth century Oxford had become well known as a seat of learning and of scholarship. At the very beginning of that century Theobald of Etampes was calling himself *'magister Oxenefordiae'*. It was the one place in England 'where the clergy had flourished most', according to Gerald of Wales who in 1187 gave a public dissertation there on the topography of Ireland. By that date more than twenty teachers of arts, and ten teachers of canon law and theology, are listed; it was reported in 1192 that the town was so filled with clerks that the authorities of Oxford did not know how to support them. A deed for the transference of property in Cat Street, around 1200, attests the presence of a bookbinder, a scrivener, three illuminators and two parchment-makers; so the ancillary trades of learning were already in large supply.

Yet it was crime, rather than scholarship, that effectively formed the university. In 1209 a student killed a woman of the town and then fled. In retaliation the authorities of Oxford arrested the student's room companions and hanged them. All the teachers and students of Oxford left the schools, in disgust, and dispersed to other places of learning. A substantial number of them migrated to Cambridge, where the second English university was then established.

When the teachers of Oxford were persuaded to return in 1214 they insisted upon an official document to regulate the relationships between what at a later date would be called town and gown. That document, expressing the intention of electing a chancellor, became the source of the university's corporate authority. Cambridge followed the same principle as Oxford and its first chancellor is recorded in 1225. Scholastic communities also existed at Northampton and Salisbury, but eventually they withered on the vine; otherwise those two old towns might also have hosted great universities.

The universities had no public buildings, and the lectures were delivered in churches or in rooms hired for the purpose. The students lived in lodgings and inns. A Master of Arts could hire a large tenement, and advertise for scholars; he had created a 'hall' in which his pupils would live and learn. Tackley Inn, Ing Hall, Lyon Hall, White Hall and Cuthbert Hall were premises in which grammar was taught. Each of the halls specialized in a particular discipline or set of disciplines, but they were essentially unregulated. They could be riotous.

The colleges of Oxford were first erected for the poorer students. Balliol College, for example, was endowed as a home for poor scholars by 1266. The founders of the colleges were the most prominent ecclesiastics and nobles, particularly of royal blood; it was considered to be a religious duty, and the members of the college were pledged to sing innumerable Masses for the souls of their patrons. The fundamental intent of the college was to create learned clergy, and it was thus an adjunct of the Church in every sense. The fellows of Queen's College in Oxford wore purple robes as a memorial to the spilled blood of Christ. Teachers very gradually moved to the more regularized life of these institutions, which by the fifteenth century had become individual houses of learning.

The students themselves were classified as 'northern' or 'southern', with the river Nene (it rises in Northamptonshire, and runs for 3 miles (4.8 kilometres) between Cambridgeshire and Norfolk) being nominated as the boundary; the northern and southern contingents were often fiercely tribal, and the most trivial incident in a tavern or lodging house could provoke mass attacks one upon the other. Even the masters participated. A serious confrontation between southern and northern masters at Cambridge, in 1290, led to a general migration to the school of Northampton. The country was still in a sense divided into ancient kingdoms.

In 1389 some Oxford scholars from northern England fell upon their Welsh counterparts, shooting at them in the lanes and streets of the town; they called out 'War, war, slay, slay, slay the Welsh dogs and their whelps.' They killed some, and wounded others; then they dragged the rest to the gates. Before they ejected them they pissed on them and forced them 'to kiss the place on which they had pissed'. The chronicler adds that 'while the said Welshmen stooped to kiss it, they would knock their heads against the gates in an inhuman manner'.

Violent struggles also took place between the students and the townspeople. A skirmish at Swyndlestock Tavern, in the centre of Oxford, led to a bloody affray in 1354. The landlord's friends rang the bell of the church of St Martin, the signal to alert the people of the town. A crowd gathered and assaulted the scholars with various weapons, whereupon the chancellor of the university rang the rival bell of the university church of St Mary. The scholars, alerted, seized their bows and arrows; a pitched battle between the two factions lasted until night fell. On the following day the townspeople sent eighty armed men into the parish of St Giles, where many of the scholars lodged; they shot and killed some of them, when once again the university bell was rung and a large assembly of Oxford pupils set upon the townspeople with their bows and arrows. But they were outnumbered. 2,000 people of the town advanced behind a black flag, crying out 'Slay! Slay!' or 'Havoc! Havoc!' or 'Smite hard, give good knocks!' These were the war cries of the medieval period. A general carnage ensued, with many deaths. All the scholars of Oxford seem to have fled, leaving the university empty for a while.

34. The Battle of Crécy, which took place on 26 August 1346, was one of the most important engagements of the Hundred Years War, when the army of Edward III effectively crushed the French. This was the battle in which gunpowder cannon were first employed.

35. The tomb of the Black Prince behind the quire of Canterbury Cathedral. Its epitaph begins, 'Such as thou art, sometime was I. Such as I am, such shalt thou be.'

36. The image of Richard II from the 'Wilton Diptych'. Standing around him are King Edmund (saint and martyr), Edward the Confessor (saint), and John the Baptist (saint). He considered these to be his forebears and protectors.

37. A page from Wycliffe's Bible. This translation into Middle English is not the work of Wycliffe himself, but of several authors inspired by Wycliffe's example.

38. The cloisters of Gloucester Cathedral, with the earliest and perhaps the best fan-vaulted roof in England, were built in the latter half of the fourteenth century. The cathedral itself is of Norman origin based on an Anglo-Saxon original. In this, it does not differ from many other English cathedrals.

39. A scene from the Peasants' Revolt of 1381. It marked the greatest rebellion of the people against their masters in English history.

40. The coronation of Henry IV in Westminster Abbey, October 1399. Since he had gained the crown by conquest, it always lay uneasily upon his head.

41. The Battle of Agincourt, fought in the autumn of 1415, was an overwhelming victory for Henry V against the French. On his return from the field he was hailed by the English as 'lord of England, flower of the world, soldier of Christ'.

42. The wedding of Henry V and Katherine of Valois, daughter of the King of France, in the summer of 1420 at Troyes Cathedral. Henry died a little over two years later, but Katherine had given birth to a male heir.

43. An image of Joan of Arc, or 'the Maid of Orleans', whose victories in 1429 anticipated the English expulsion from the towns and cities of France two decades later.

44. Henry VI in full martial array. In truth he was not a very good soldier, and not a very able king.

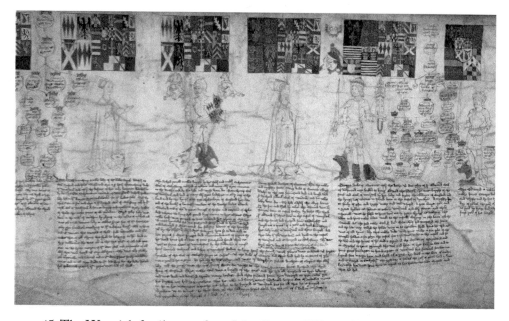

45. The Warwick family tree, from John Rous of Warwick's *De Regius Angliae*, showing Richard Neville, 16th Earl, his wife Anne Beauchamp, their daughter Isabel Spencer and her husband George, Duke of Clarence.

46. An image of Edward IV, whose greatest achievement was to consolidate royal authority after the weak and vacillating rule of Henry VI.

47. Elizabeth Woodville, wife of Edward IV. Unlike most royal brides she was English and, at the time of her marriage, already a widow with two children.

48 (*left*). Edward V, the unfortunate boy-king who reigned for just two months before being murdered in the Tower of London. He was never crowned.

49. Richard III standing on a white boar; the white boar was his personal badge or 'livery badge'. It may derive from the Latin name of York, *Eboracum*, since he was known as Richard of York.

50. Elizabeth of York and Henry VII, from a nineteenth-century illustration. From their union the rest of the Tudor dynasty sprang.

51. An allegory of the Tudor dynasty. The red dragon on the left represents the Welsh ancestry of Henry VII, for example, while the white greyhound on the right is taken from his father's coat of arms as first earl of Richmond. Surmounting all is the Rose of Tudor, incorporating the white rose of Yorkshire within the red rose of Lancashire.

Less violent diversions can also be cited. An inspection of the pupils of Magdalen College, Oxford, in the very early years of the sixteenth century, revealed that 'Stokes was unchaste with the wife of a tailor . . . Stokysley baptised a cat and practised witchcraft . . . Gregory climbed the great gate by the tower and brought a Stranger into College . . . Pots and cups are very seldom washed but are kept in such a dirty state that one shudders to drink out of them . . . Kyftyll played cards with the butler at Christmas time for money.' Other students were accused of keeping as pets a ferret, a sparrow-hawk and a weasel.

It is perhaps not surprising that, in a society of very young men, casual and sporadic violence was common. The students entered the university at an age between fourteen and seventeen, where they embarked upon a course of study that lasted for seven years. Grammar, rhetoric and dialectic were taught in the first three years; these disciplines were followed by arithmetic, astronomy, music and geometry. The students attended lectures and tutorials, but they also disputed among themselves in formal debates. Disputation was an important aspect of medieval life in every sphere. The examinations themselves were entirely oral and were prolonged for four days. The successful candidate would then be given the title of Master of Arts. The more learned moved on to the study of theology; that pursuit took another sixteen or seventeen years, more or less consigning its devotees to an academic life.

The learning promulgated in Oxford and Cambridge was not all of a scholastic kind. More informal schools, established in the two towns to take advantage of their general reputation, taught lessons in conveyancing, accountancy and commercial law; these were frequented by the sons of the greater farmers and landowners, and by the administrators of such estates, to keep abreast of the ever more complex world of property ownership and property speculation. A great enthusiasm for knowledge of a practical nature can be observed in this period.

The appetite for education was in any case instinctive, the natural child of emulation and ambition in an expanding world. By the beginning of the thirteenth century every town had its own school.

I would my master were an hare,
And all his books were hounds,
And I myself a jolly hunter:
To blow my horn I would not spare!
If he were dead, I would not care.

So wrote the author of a fifteenth-century poem, 'The Birched Schoolboy'. The schoolmaster sat on a large chair, often with a book in his lap, while the boys were grouped on simple benches around him. He would dictate the rules of Latin grammar, for example, while the boys would scribble them on wax tablets or chant them in unison. Schooling began at six in the morning and, with appropriate breaks, concluded at six in the evening. Another verse describes the life of the boy out of the schoolroom. When he was young, John Lydgate

Ran into gardens, apples there I stole,
To gather fruits I spared not hedge nor wall,
To pluck grapes from other men's vines
I was more ready than to say my matins,
My lust was to scorn folk and jape,
To scoff and mock like a wanton ape.

In a world of much casual and spontaneous violence the beating of children was customary and familiar. Agnes Paston beat her daughter, Elizabeth, 'once in a week or twice, and sometimes twice in one day, and her head broken in two or three places'. Elizabeth herself was twenty years old at the time. Agnes Paston also ordered her son's schoolmaster to 'truly belash him' if he was disobedient. The sentiment would be expected from a loving mother. It was advised that a child should be beaten until he or she admitted guilt and cried for mercy. But childhood was not simply a world of whips and blows. Many educational manuals espoused the cause of gentleness mixed with firmness; excessive punishment was generally denounced.

Thomas More, who was born in 1478, believed that three out of every five of the English people could read; that might be an overestimate, and he might only have been considering the men and women of London, but it is testimony to the growing literacy of the country. The development of the unfamiliar medium of printing, in the latter decades of the fifteenth century, created a new audience with new skills. This was the age in which the poster and the handbill came into use and in which some of the larger towns had libraries. The Guildhall Library, established in 1423, exists still. Four new grammar schools were established in London in the space of one year. In the last decades of the fifteenth century free schools were endowed at Hull, Rotherham, Stockport, Macclesfield and Manchester.

Schoolboys were not allowed to dice or to use bows and arrows on the premises; they were, however, given time and opportunity to engage in the more suitable sport of cock-fighting. 'Wehee!' was the cry of liberation from the schoolroom. It was an age of 'leaping about', of running and of wrestling. Birds were snared or brought down with sling and stone. Bede recalls that in his youth he had engaged in a primitive form of horse-racing.

The medieval schoolboy played croquet, football, skittles, marbles. Tennis was played against a wall rather than across a net, with the palm of the hand rather than a racket; rackets were not introduced until the end of the fifteenth century. 'Cambuc' was a form of golf, with a curved stick known as a 'bandy'. Skating, with skates made out of bone, was popular. A game known as 'tables' resembled backgammon. Chess was common and there were circular chessboards; stray chess pieces have been excavated from medieval dwellings. Card games were not introduced until the middle of the fifteenth century. Bowmanship was important; in 'penny-prick' an arrow was fired at a hanging penny coin. Dice were very frequent. 'You shall have a throw,' one schoolboy tells another in a schoolbook of the 1420s, 'for a button of your wristlet.' Play is as old, and as ever renewed, as the world.

# 35

# The lion and the lamb

The new king, Edward IV, was according to Thomas More 'a goodly personage, and very princely to behold . . . of visage lovely, of body mighty, strong and cleanly made'. A contemporary chronicler, Dominic Mancini, writing just after Edward's death, gave a more ambiguous account. 'Edward was of a gentle nature and cheerful aspect; nevertheless should he assume an angry countenance he could appear very terrible to beholders.' Of course it was one of the duties of a king to appear very terrible, especially one who had succeeded Henry VI; the previous king had been more lamb than lion. Mancini went on to report that 'he was easy of access to his friends and to others, even the least notable. Frequently he called to his side complete strangers, when he thought that they had come with the intent of addressing or beholding him more closely.' Come, he might have said. Look at me. Yes. I am your king. 'He was wont to show himself to those who wished to watch him, and he seized any opportunity . . . of revealing his fine stature more protractedly and more evidently to onlookers.' He had a voracious appetite and, like many gourmands, he often vomited in order that he might eat again. In time this affected his girth; More commented that in his later years he became 'somewhat corpulent and boorly, and nevertheless not uncomely'.

In his youth his pride was touched with vanity, and like many previous monarchs he indulged in the theatrical and spectacular aspects of kingship. In the first year of his reign the keeper of the great wardrobe spent a little over £4,784 on clothes and furs for the king's person, an extraordinary sum when the average annual wage of a labourer was approximately £6. He draped himself in cloth of gold and crimson velvet, in tawny silk and in green satin. He owned hundreds of pairs of shoes and slippers, hats and bonnets; he wore amethysts and sapphires and rubies in abundance. They were talismans as well as jewels. The amethyst gave hardiness and manhood; the sapphire kept the limbs of the body whole; if poison or venom were brought into the presence of the ruby it became moist and began to sweat. Edward possessed a toothpick made of gold, garnished with a diamond, a ruby and a pearl.

It was not just a matter of personal aggrandizement, although of course that played a large part in the acquisition of wealth. One of the purposes of becoming king was to become the richest person in the land. But it was also a way of asserting the wealth and status of the kingdom; it was a display of national power. So self-love, and self-aggrandizement, can be construed as devotion to duty.

Of course that kingdom was still divided or, at the least, unstable. The survival of Henry and his son was a serious embarrassment to the new monarchy, especially since the Lancastrian dynasty had many loyal followers in the west as well as the midlands of the country. Edward had no power at all in the far north, where the old king was just over the border in Scotland. The largest part of Wales supported Henry, who also commanded more supporters among the magnates of the country. Thirty-seven noble families had fought for him and with him; only three of those went over to Edward's side.

So the new king had to shore up his defences, as far as that was possible, partly in order to prevent the French from taking advantage of any internal confusion. He brought many previous Lancastrian supporters under the cover of his good lordship, principally by granting them territory; he was forced to trust, and to favour, those who had offended against him. Where the Lancastrians could not be reconciled, they were arrested or eliminated. The earl of Oxford and his son, for example, were beheaded at Tower Hill on charges of treason.

A commission of judges proceeded through twenty-five shires and eight cities in order to pursue political malcontents. No great set-piece battles were being fought but, in the first two years of his reign, there was probably more fighting than in any other period of the war; in 1461 he took under his control the estates of 113 enemies. This was the territory granted to his supporters. In that year he also created seven new barons.

The king then found it convenient to create a foreign crisis; it helped him to raise money for his own purposes and to unite his subjects in common enmity. In the spring of 1462 he claimed that the new king of France, Louis XI, was set to destroy 'the people, the name, the tongue and the blood English of this our said realm'. Edward can be considered the first English king who eschewed France altogether; he had no French possessions to defend, other than the garrison town of Calais, and was truly king of England only.

In the following year the exchequer was asked to provide the requisite funds to raise an army and a fleet against his manifold enemies at home and abroad. It was supposed that the king would march against the Lancastrian supporters in Northumberland and elsewhere, or that he would invade Scotland; in the event, none of this came to pass. He did not lead his troops into battle. 'What a wretched outcome,' one fifteenth-century chronicler reported, 'shame and confusion!' Yet it would be wrong to consider Edward as an inactive king. He arranged truces both with France and with Scotland. He took his court to York, and from there he supervised the slow domination of the northern shires.

From the beginning Edward proved himself to be a strong king; he was an expert administrator and had concluded that the survival of his throne depended upon financial and political stability. In an age of personal kingship this was necessarily a very heavy burden on the monarch, whose presence was required everywhere and whose authority had to be imposed directly. He kept a close scrutiny on commerce and on his customs revenues; he summoned members of the London guilds in order to guide or harangue them. Thousands of petitions were delivered to him every year. It was said that he knew 'the names and estates' of nearly all the people 'dispersed throughout the shires of this kingdom', even those of mere gentlemen. A king who had won his throne by force could not be aloof or detached; he had to remain at the centre of human affairs. He needed goodwill as well as obedience. That is why Dominic Mancini described him as being 'easy of access'. It has been said that Edward began the movement towards the 'centralized monarchy' that characterized the Tudor period; but in truth he had little choice in the matter. It was not a bureaucratic or administrative decision; it was personal instinct.

He had an interest in the administration of justice, too, and in the first fifteen years of his reign he travelled all over the kingdom for his judicial visitations. In the first five months of 1464, for example, he attended the courts at Coventry and Worcester, Gloucester and Cambridge and Maidstone. Several reasons can be adduced for this activity. Pre-eminent among them was his effort to check or punish violence between the noble families; he had a personal interest in preventing riot or disorder that might threaten the security of the various counties. He intervened in a struggle between the Greys and the Vernons of Derbyshire, for example, and closely interviewed the retainers of both sides. He made much use of the commission known as 'oyer et terminer', designed to hear and determine felonies or misdemeanours in an expeditious manner. It was composed of his own men, from the household or from the court, and of local magnates who could not be easily coerced.

The commissioners were not always successful, however, in summoning witnesses. The senior knights of Herefordshire con- fessed to them that 'they dare not present nor say the truth of the defaults before rehearsed, for dread of murdering, and to be mischieved in their own houses, considering the great number of the said misdoers . . .'. In the early years of Edward's reign, when the final outcome of the struggle between the Yorkists and Lancas- trians was still in doubt, private violence had by no means abated.

The king's own legal practice, however, was far from perfect. He regularly interfered with the process of the courts to ensure favourable judgments in the interests of his most powerful support- ers. He never prosecuted the retainers of those men upon whose loyalty he relied. This was of course not an unusual procedure for any king, whose rule relied more upon *realpolitik* than any judicial principle. Edward also had a vested interest in efficient or at least swift justice, since the revenues of the courts greatly augmented his income.

Another aspect of his character can be noted. One contemporary chronicler remarked that he had a liking for 'convivial company, vanity, debauchery, extravagance and sensual enjoyment'. These do not seem to be mortal offences in any king but, rather, the proper setting for the projection of authority and sovereignty. In the next sentence, after all, the chronicler goes on to praise the king's acute memory and attention to detail. Yet Edward made one decision in his private affairs that had more serious consequences. In the spring of 1464 he secretly united himself with a commoner in a marriage that emphasized his passion rather than his judgment. Elizabeth Woodville was a widow with two children; and, unlike most royal brides, she was English. She was not altogether common, however, since her father was a knight and her mother a widowed duchess. It was reported that, having decided that she would be a queen rather than a royal mistress, she had resisted the king's advances. Edward was known to be libidinous and to have had many sexual liaisons, but it seems that Elizabeth was the first to have refused him. A rumour spread through the courts of Europe that in desperation he had even put a knife against her throat. Yet she held out, to her ultimate satisfaction.

The king's choice was a cause of some dismay to those who believed that a king should only marry someone of royal blood. The fact that he married her in secret, slipping away from his courtiers on the first day of May 1464 with the pretence of going hunting, suggests that he himself knew that he had married beneath his rank. It was also believed preferable to marry a virgin. A newsletter from Bruges in the autumn of 1464 observed that 'the greater part of the lords and the people in general seem very much dissatisfied at this and, for the sake of finding means to annul it, all the nobles are holding great consultations in the town of Reading where the king is'. Richard Neville, earl of Warwick, had already begun negotiations with the French king on the matter of Edward's marriage to Louis XI's sister-in-law. Those plans were now in disarray. The 'consultations' of the lords, however, were meaningless. As a friend of Warwick remarked, 'we must be patient despite ourselves'. On 29 September 1464, Warwick and the duke of Clarence, the king's younger brother, escorted Elizabeth Woodville into the chapel of Reading Abbey where she was honoured by the assembled company as their lawful queen.

In the following summer Henry VI was captured; since the defeat at Towton he had retreated to Scotland and to the various loyalist castles of northern England. He was effectively a king in hiding, and such was his invisibility that Edward was not sure in which county he was being concealed. Margaret, in the meantime, had taken refuge on her father's lands in Anjou. The old king was seen at a dinner given by his supporters in Ribblesdale; he fled the area, but was betrayed by a monk. He was eventually caught in a wood known as Clitherwood, just on the border of Lancashire, and taken back to London on horseback with his legs tied to the stirrups; it is reported that he wore a straw hat, and was pelted with rubbish by some abusive citizens. He remained in the Tower for the next five years, with a small party of courtiers enlisted to serve the prisoner known only as Henry of Windsor.

The new queen's family, the Woodvilles, were in the ascendant at court and might be seen to threaten the position of Warwick and the other Nevilles. The king also arranged a series of marriages between Elizabeth's immediate relatives and various available aristocrats; since she had five brothers and seven sisters, this diminished the prospect of further patronage for many more distinguished families. Her younger brother, for example, was married off at the age of twenty to the sixty-five-year-old duchess of Norfolk; the duchess was a wealthy widow who had already buried three husbands, but she also happened to be the aunt of Warwick himself. Warwick's feelings at what was described at the time as a 'maritagium diabolicum' are not recorded. He would have been justified in thinking, in the language of the time, that the honour of his family had been disparaged and that his elderly relative had been made to look ridiculous. In fact the old lady outlived her young spouse, who ended on the scaffold. Louis XI disclosed the fact that he had received a letter expressing Warwick's dismay at Edward's behaviour; he hinted that Warwick might even try to supplant his sovereign, but all is lost in a mist of diplomatic surmise and posturing. The French king was not known for nothing as 'the spider king'.

A more tangible source of discord can be found in the foreign affairs of the nation. Warwick wished above all else for an alliance with France, while Edward favoured an accommodation with Burgundy and Brittany. Various strands of policy were involved. Warwick was receiving many favours from Louis XI, while the Woodvilles were related to the noble families of Burgundy. Burgundy was also the largest market for English cloth, and thus the principal trade partner of the English merchants. In any case the French were the ancient enemy who at this time were harbouring ambassadors from Margaret of Anjou.

In 1467 a commercial treaty was signed between England and Burgundy, swiftly followed by a peace accord and by the marriage of Edward's sister Margaret to the duke of Burgundy. In his defeat and disappointment Warwick retired to his estates in Yorkshire, where it was rumoured that he had begun conspiring against his sovereign; it was said that he had been able to suborn the duke of Clarence in a plot against the throne. A French chronicler, Jean de Waurin, reported that Warwick promised Clarence that he would give him his brother's crown. The old allies had fallen out.

Other rumours were circulating in the spring and autumn of 1467. The most astonishing of them was that the two inveterate enemies, Warwick and Margaret of Anjou, would enter an alliance and would invade England with the purpose of destroying Edward IV. It is not clear who proposed the bargain, but many observers suspected that the French king would do anything to stir up unrest and riot in the enemy country. Warwick and his kinsmen still attended the English court, however, and appeared to be on amicable terms with the king himself.

The break came in the summer of 1469. In June a rebellion in the northern shires was fomented by 'Robin of Redesdale' alias 'Robin Mend-All' alias Sir John Conyers who was a cousin of Warwick himself; it was in part a popular rebellion, inspired by those who were discontented with Edward's rule. The king was on pilgrimage to Walsingham, but on hearing news of the gathering insurrection he broke off his pious journey and marched with his retainers to Nottingham. He was hearing rumours from all sides of the treacherous designs both of Warwick and of his own younger brother; it was also reported that Warwick's brother, George Neville, the archbishop of York, was part of the insurrection. In a defiant spirit he wrote to the three of them, demanding their unconditional loyalty to confirm the fact they were not 'of any such disposition towards us, as the rumour here runneth'.

No such news reached the king. He was informed instead that the duke of Clarence was about to marry Warwick's daughter, despite the fact that he had already forbidden the union, and that the parties concerned were sailing to Calais for the ceremony. It was a clear act of defiance and disobedience.

From Calais, Warwick and his associates then issued a proclamation in which they took the part of the northern rebels against a king who was being governed by 'the deceivable covetous rule and guiding of certain seducious persons'; the last adjective suggests a modern mingling of seductive and seditious. These suspect persons were of course the Woodvilles, who had already been asked by the king to return to their home territories for safekeeping. Warwick invited his supporters to meet him at Canterbury on 16 July. It is possible that he intended to declare Edward illegitimate and to replace him with Clarence. This was not a struggle between Yorkists and Lancastrians, but between two factions of Yorkists.

Warwick and his newly aggrandized forces crossed the Channel and marched upon London, where Warwick himself was very popular; then they made their way towards Coventry, where they determined to join the men in league with Robin Mend-All. The king's army came up to challenge them, but a sudden attack by the rebels forced them to disperse. Some of the commanders of the king's army were taken on Warwick's orders, and in a gratuitous act of injustice he beheaded them on the following day.

Edward himself was by this time on the road to meet his army, and did not learn of its defeat until it was too late to turn back. His men promptly deserted him. This is the best to be made out of a confused narrative. He decided to turn back to London, accompanied by a small retinue, when he was surprised by the forces of the archbishop of York. The king was taken, with all due courtesies, and promptly confined to Warwick Castle. Two of the most prominent members of the Woodville family, the father and younger brother of the queen, were captured and beheaded on Warwick's order. He now controlled both the country and the king.

He could do nothing with either of them. The earl was in practice the ruler of the country, but he lacked legitimacy and moral authority. He could hardly rule on the king's behalf if he kept the king confined to a castle. Edward's council seems grudgingly to have accepted Warwick's direction, but the hiatus in national affairs provoked outbreaks of local violence and rebellion. Once more the great families of the realm could attack one another with impunity. Only one remedy offered itself. The king had to be released from custody and allowed to resume his sovereignty. So Edward IV returned to be met by a contrite earl, archbishop and younger brother who pleaded that they had acted only in the interests of the realm. Edward and his supporters then processed towards London, where they were met by the mayor and aldermen in their scarlet regalia. 'The king himself', John Paston wrote, 'has good language of the Lords of Clarence, of Warwick, and of my Lords of York and Oxford, saying they be his best friends.' But he added that 'his household men have other language'. His household, in other words, were inclined towards revenge.

Yet the king realized that the stability of the realm had to be regained at all costs. According to the chronicler Polydore Vergil 'he regarded nothing more than to win again the friendship of such noblemen as were now alienated from him . . .'. He invited Clarence and Warwick to join the sessions of a great council that was called to arrange 'peace and entire oblivion of all grievances upon both sides'. He also allowed his four-year-old daughter, Elizabeth, to be betrothed to Warwick's nephew. Warwick had of course only recently murdered the young girl's maternal grandfather and uncle. The politics of power are always realistic.

Nevertheless the earl had been dealt a grievous blow; it had been proved that he could not wield authority without the presence of the king. In the spring of 1470 he was once again implicated in armed rebellion. The revolt came from Lincolnshire where certain families, afraid of the king's justice or offended by the king's depredations, rose up with the intention of giving the crown to Clarence. When Edward took the field against them they cried out 'A Clarence! A Clarence!' and 'A Warwick! A Warwick!' It was all the evidence the king required. His army defeated the Lincoln-shire men with ease, and the site of the battle became known as 'Lose Coat Field' for the number of clothes bearing the livery of Warwick or of Clarence that the soldiers discarded in their flight. After his overwhelming victory, his two opponents fled to the safety of the court of Louis XI in France. Some of their collabor-ators were not so fortunate. One of Warwick's ships was seized at Southampton, where the gentlemen and yeomen on board were beheaded. A sharp stake was then driven through their posteriors, and their heads were impaled on top.

Warwick and Clarence were now joined by Margaret of Anjou. She, too, had left her familial lands and arrived at the court of the French king. Louis had three birds in his hand, but Margaret and Warwick had been fierce enemies for a long time. The king now entered into protracted negotiations in order to reconcile her to the man who had been 'the greatest causer of the fall of Henry, of her, and of her son'. He spent every day in long discussions with her until eventually she deferred to him. Margaret now agreed to conspire with her once inveterate enemies and to overthrow Edward IV. Her husband, still in the Tower, would regain the throne; her son Edward, prince of Wales, would marry another of Warwick's daughters and thus become brother-in-law to Clarence. The fam-ilies of York and Lancaster would therefore be finally united. The young couple were betrothed in Angers Cathedral.

Warwick and his new ally now began preparations for the great invasion of England. Edward kept his eyes upon the coasts but, in the summer of 1470, he was distracted by news of further rebellions in the north inspired by Warwick's cause; he was obliged to march to York and Ripon. He could not be sure where Warwick's fleet might land – anywhere from Wales to Northumberland – and he took a calculated risk in going northward. While he lingered in York, having successfully overcome the incipient rebellion, the news came in the middle of September that Warwick and Clarence had landed at Exmouth in Devon from where at once they began their march towards him. The king was in hostile country in any case, and it became increasingly clear that Warwick was acquiring supporters as he moved forward.

The public records of Coventry reveal that Clarence and Warwick 'drew to them much people' and that 'they were thirty thousand' by the time they reached the city. Edward had left York for Nottingham, but he was still in desperate circumstances. He had 'sent for lords and all other men', but to his dismay 'there came so little people to him that he was not able to make a field against them'. In the words of the public record Edward 'went to Lynn'. In fact he made a rapid retreat to what is now King's Lynn where he took ship and sailed towards the Low Countries. He had few men, and little money; such was his penury that he had to pay for his transport with the furred gown he was wearing.

Eventually he landed in Holland, where the governor of the province was known to him; he was in Burgundian territory, and the duke of Burgundy was an ally. The duke, having married Margaret of York two years before, was also the king's brother-in-law. So Edward was, for the time being, safe from his enemies. Elizabeth Woodville and her mother had already taken sanctuary in Westminster Abbey. The sanctuary stood at the bottom of the churchyard to the west of the abbey. It was described as 'a gloomy building, of sufficient strength to withstand a siege'. It was here that the queen was delivered of a son.

Warwick returned to London in order to confirm his supremacy. Margaret and her son remained in France, waiting for Henry VI to be given back his throne. So the once abandoned king was led from the Tower after an imprisonment of five years; he was wearing a long gown of blue velvet, but he was 'not so cleanly kept as should be such a prince'. In his captivity he sometimes quoted words from the seventh psalm to the effect that 'My help cometh of God, who preserveth them that are true of heart'. Now God had worked an unlooked-for wonder. Truly He moved in mysterious ways. At the opening of Henry's parliament the archbishop of York preached upon the text 'Turn, O backsliding children'.

But if Henry was once more king in name, Warwick was the puppet master. Henry was according to a contemporary chronicler no more than 'a crowned calf, a shadow on the wall'. Warwick now had to balance a variety of interests in order to preserve his rule; he had to satisfy his Lancastrian supporters as well as the Yorkists who had favoured Edward IV. He also had to manage the ambitions of Clarence, who might have wished the crown for himself. These various tensions and divisions did not augur for good rule. The noblemen of England had in any case become increasingly disenchanted with the protagonists on both sides, and were inclined merely to give their support to the strongest at any given moment. 'Trust not much upon promises of lords nowadays,' Margaret Paston told her son, 'that you should be the surer of the favour of such men. A man's death is little set by nowadays. Therefore beware of simulation, for they will speak right fair to you that would you fared right evil.'

Soon enough another reversal of fortune complicated a story already filled with strange turns and accidents. In the early spring of 1471 the duke of Burgundy agreed to finance an invasion of England by Edward, and on 14 March the exiled monarch landed at Ravenspur on the coast of Yorkshire; his reception was not at first encouraging. 'There came right few of the country [Yorkshire] to him,' according to a contemporary history, 'or almost none.' The men of Holderness turned him away, and he was only permitted to enter York on the declaration that he had come to claim his father's dukedom rather than the English crown.

Nevertheless he kept on moving towards London. He marched towards Doncaster and, learning that Warwick was gathering his forces in Coventry, turned towards that city. The duke of Clarence now deserted the earl in favour of his brother; with Henry VI back on the throne, and with Margaret of Anjou poised to return to England with her son, he may have realized that his chance of gaining the crown was now remote. He was also suspected by his erstwhile enemies; he was held, as a contemporary wrote, 'in great suspicion, despite, disdain and hatred with all the lords . . . that were adherents and full partakers with Henry'. But his actions may have had no logic to them at all; he was young, impressionable and impulsive with little control over his tongue or over his actions. He was a shuttlecock flying in all directions.

Edward, leaving Warwick embattled in Coventry, decided to move swiftly upon the capital and to announce himself once more to be king. The archbishop of York, brother of Warwick, tried to rally support by parading Henry VI through London; the king was still wearing the blue velvet gown in which he had been dressed when he left the Tower. Edward entered the city and urgently sought an interview with the old king. 'My cousin of York,' Henry told him, 'you are very welcome. I know that in your hands my life will not be in danger.' In this he proved to be mistaken. The unhappy monarch was once more consigned to the cold walls of the Tower, while Edward was united with his wife and his newborn son fresh out of sanctuary. Very little time could be spent in celebration, however, and on the following morning the king 'took advice of the great lords of his blood, and other of his council, for the adventures that were likely to come'. The adventures reached a climax on 14 April at Barnet, a small town north of London, where the Yorkists won the victory with a confused set of skirmishes in thick fog; in the subsequent rout Warwick himself was killed. The 'king-maker' was slain by the forces of the king.

The earl of Warwick is not a happy figure. Lands and wealth had been heaped upon him by an over-generous monarch, and as a result he became fractious and over-mighty; he proclaimed himself to be the representative of the rights of England, and yet he was merely the tool of faction and of family; he aspired to glory, but in victory he was cruel and vindictive; he was a politician without any grasp of political strategy, and a statesman who had a habit of opposing the national interest at every juncture. His vanity, and his ambition, destroyed him. In these respects, he was not so different from his eminent contemporaries.

Margaret of Anjou and her seventeen-year-old son, Prince Edward, had sailed from France without knowing of Edward's victory over Warwick. The news greeted her soon after her landing at Weymouth, in Dorset, with her followers. It was too late to flee; she could only fight. She made her way north towards Bristol, picking up supporting forces on the way, but Edward's army was approaching from the east. At this moment John Paston wrote to his mother, Margaret, that 'the world, I assure you, is right queasy'. On 4 May 1471, in a meadow just to the south of Tewkesbury in Gloucestershire, the Lancastrians were overtaken by the Yorkists;

in the subsequent mêlée Prince Edward was killed and Margaret was taken prisoner.

Edward IV returned in triumph to London less than three weeks later. On that same day, Henry VI was killed in the Tower of London. It was said that he had expired from melancholy, but the truth is no doubt more prosaic. He had been murdered on the orders of the victorious king, who wished to hold no hostages to fortune. It was claimed later that his assassin was Edward's youngest brother, the duke of Gloucester, but this inference may entirely be due to Gloucester's later fame as the inglorious Richard III. It seems appropriate, at any rate, that he should now enter this history of England as a man of shadows.

In any event the Lancastrian royal family, descended directly from Henry IV, was now extinguished. Henry's body was taken from the Tower to St Paul's Cathedral, where he was laid out 'open vysagid' so that all might recognize him. Margaret of Anjou was incarcerated in the Tower, where she remained for four years before being ransomed by Louis XI; she spent the rest of her days, impoverished, in France. Her life had been lived in a storm that had claimed her husband and her son.

A vignette of Henry VI may be included here. On one occasion, in the 1450s, he visited Westminster Abbey in order to mark out the site of his tomb. He ordered a stonemason to scratch with a crowbar the position and dimensions of the vault that he wished to be built in the floor of the abbey. He did not require a monumental tomb; he wanted to rest beneath the quiet stone. As he conferred with the abbot, he leaned on the shoulder of his chamberlain; the king was then only in his thirties, but he was already tired with the demands of the world. There has rarely been a wise king in England, let alone a good one. But it is still possible to concede a certain amount of sympathy to a man who seems to have been wholly unsuitable for the duties of kingship.

It is often said that the opposing sides in the Wars of the Roses were engaged in an act of mutual destruction, and that the noble families of England were noticeably thinned as a result of the fighting. In fact the pressure of time and circumstance always worked against the survival of any noble house, and it has been calculated that in any period of twenty-five years a quarter of the nobility left no sons to inherit their titles and so lapsed into inconsequence. There must always be a steady flow of 'new blood' to keep the governance of the land in good health. The Wars of the Roses did not interrupt what was essentially a continuing process.

In a larger sense, too, the world went on its own way despite the immediate disturbance of the wars. The fact of conflict of course weakened the body politic, and loosened the ties between the realm and the nobility, but there is no evidence of general desolation or dislocation. Few towns or cities were affected by the disturbances, and only those in the immediate vicinity of the battles would have suffered from the factional struggle. The vast resources of the Church were not touched, and in general the clergy remained as distant observers of the conflict. The law courts at Westminster were still in session and the judges rode on circuit throughout the country. The French chronicler and historian Philippe de Commynes remarked at the time that 'there are no buildings destroyed or demolished by war, but the calamities and misfortunes of the war fell only upon the soldiers, and especially on the nobility'.

There is also no sign of economic decline as a result of the wars. By the 1470s there was a resurgence of trade, a trend in which the king himself took an active interest. The author of the *Crowland Chronicle* states that Edward 'in person, having equipped ships of burden, laded them with the very finest wools, cloths, tin and other products of his realm, and like a man living by merchandise, exchanged goods for goods . . .'. The appearance of a merchant king helps to disperse any notion of economic degeneracy. 'There is no small inn-keeper, however poor and humble he may be,' an Italian observer wrote, 'who does not serve his table with silver dishes and drinking cups . . .'

In any case the life of a nation is perhaps better compared to a sea than to a pond. Exhaustion and renewal, decay and growth, occur simultaneously. So it was that in 1476 William Caxton established in the almonry of Westminster Abbey the first printing press in England. Ten years later the first water-powered pump was introduced to a coalmine at Finchale near Durham. In 1496 the first blast furnace in England was operating at Buxted in

Sussex. This industrial revolution was already provoking complaint. A parliamentary Bill of 1482 declared that hats, bonnets and caps made 'by men's strength, that is to say with hands and feet' were infinitely superior to those 'fulled and thicked in fulling mills'. At the same time very many humble people were still living on the land in the same conditions as their Saxon ancestors.

# 36

# The staple of life

Among the bare fields and deserted gardens of the derelict Roman villas grew wild garlic and onions. 'I grow very erect, tall in a bed,' runs one Anglo-Saxon riddle on the onion, 'and bring a tear to a maiden's eye. What am I?' The essential ingredient on the poorer tables, however, was that derisory 'mess of pottage' for which birthrights could be sold. The richer Anglo-Saxons ate wheaten bread, but bread of rye or barley was more common. They also consumed vast quantities of pork, the pigs grown fat on the inexhaustible supplies of acorns and beech-nuts to be found in the woods and forests of the country. The smallholder might also have a few razor-backed pigs on the common land. Venison and poultry were popular among the more wealthy Englishmen. Supplies of fish, among them salmon and herring, were plentiful. Horse-flesh was sometimes eaten. For many centuries large knives and coarse wooden spoons were the extent of the cutlery, the meals often eaten out of communal bowls. Then 'after the dinner they went to their cups,' according to one chronicler, 'to which the English were very much accustomed'. A weak ale, compounded with various spices, was the drink of choice. But the Anglo-Saxons also consumed a drink known as 'morat', essentially mulberry juice mingled with honey.

The diet of the Normans was not very different, since the

agriculture of the country was not materially changed by the invasion. The status of the lord, however, was such that he could eat only wheaten bread. When land was granted to him, it had to be capable of growing wheat; soil that could not bear that crop was of little value to him. That is why few Norman settlements were established in the higher and colder grounds of the Pennines, of Cumbria and other northern regions. The Normans were found among the wheat. They made their bread in the form of buns or cakes, often marked with a cross. They particularly enjoyed a form of gingerbread that was known as 'peppered bread'.

One difference was evident. They preferred wine to the native ale or mead, and much of it was transported from France. A twelfth-century philosopher, Alexander Neckam, stated that wine should be as clear as the tears of a penitent. He also declared that a good wine should be as sweet-tasting as an almond, as surreptitious as a squirrel, as high-spirited as a roebuck, as strong as a Cistercian monastery, as glittering as a spark of fire, as subtle as the logic of the schools of Paris, as delicate as fine silk, and as cold as crystal. The language of the wine connoisseur has not notably diminished in fancifulness over the centuries.

Through the medieval period little interest was evinced in what were once known as 'white meats', namely cheese and butter and milk. They were associated with the diets of common people, and were therefore to be avoided. Milk, however, was mixed in sweet confections. Olive oil, rather than butter, was used in cooking. Fresh fruit was considered to be unhealthy, and the most common vegetables were scorned except by the poor who considered them to be a kind of free food. The land was so fruitful that, in a good season, it may have been possible for a poor man or a wanderer to survive from the fields and hedges alone. Peas and beans, leeks and cabbages, could also be stolen from the small garden adjoining every cottage. 'I have no money,' Piers Plowman complains in the month before harvest. 'I have a couple of fresh cheeses, a little curds and cream, an oatcake and two loaves of beans and bran baked for the children. I have some parsley and shallots, and plenty of cabbages . . .' It is possible, therefore, that the diet of the poor was healthier than that of the rich.

By the thirteenth and fourteenth centuries, the meat had become highly flavoured with spices such as aniseed and liquorice. The richer families preferred strong and even coarse flavours. It is otherwise difficult to account for the attraction of the grampus and the porpoise even to royal appetites. The 'sea-calf', known in more recent times as the seal, was also a delicacy. The tongue of the whale, another royal dish, was either boiled with peas or roasted. Strongly flavoured birds, such as the peacock or the heron or the bittern, were also on the menu. 'Powdered salmon' was salmon sprinkled with salt. The smell of the conger eel was said by one enthusiast to be so wonderful that it would make a dead man sniff.

The first English cookery book, *The Forme of Cury*, was written in the late fourteenth century by Richard II's master cooks – 'cury' meaning the dressing of food. A dish of shelled oysters and hare's flesh must be flavoured with honey. Pork is to be fried and then mixed with saffron and raisins. Pheasant could be mingled with cinnamon and ginger. Spices were not used to disguise the taste of less than healthy meat; they were used for their own sake, and were part of the predilection for strong flavours. They were also used to colour the meats and other dishes; indigo turned the food blue, and saffron converted it to yellow; blood and burnt toast crusts provided the red and the black.

It is instructive that in *The Forme of Cury*, and in other compilations of recipes, there is seldom any mention of the quantities of the necessary ingredients. Medieval units of measurement are in fact always vague and imprecise. There was no need, or desire, for exactness. It was not a 'scientific' age. So gross underestimates and overestimates, at least by the standards of modern accuracy, were likely to be made. The monks of Ely believed that their isle measured 7 miles by 4 miles (11.2 by 6.4 kilometres), whereas in fact it had the dimensions of 12 miles by 10 miles (19.3 by 16 kilometres). It was declared, in the reign of Edward III, that there were 40,000 parishes in England; there were in fact fewer than 9,000, a huge error in one of the most basic measurements of the country. When we read in the sources that 'innumerable miracles' were attested at a site of pilgrimage, or that the king led an army of 'fifty thousand men', we may be given leave to doubt the claims.

Space and time were fluctuating and essentially indefinable. An acre of land (0.4 hectares) could be measured in three different ways. Various time systems, such as the regnal year or the papal year or the liturgical year, could be chosen. The charters and memoranda of the period were, before the thirteenth century, largely undated; a bond might give the year of transaction as 'after the espousal of the king of England's son and the king's daughter' or 'after Gilbert Foliot was received into the bishopric of London' which we know to have been 1163. Many people were unsure of their exact age; one old warrior, John de Sully, claimed to be 105 and to have fought at the battle of Najera in 1367. If that is correct, then he had carried arms at the age of eighty-seven. The father of another old soldier, John de Thirwell, was reported to have died at the age of 145. The hour of the day was measured by the shadows cast by the sun; clocks were not introduced until the fifteenth century, but they were heavy, cumbersome and not necessarily precise. The time measured by the church bell was that of the canonical day from prime to vespers. And everyone knew that a yard was the length of the king's arm. What else could it be?

# 37

# The king of spring

Edward IV was at last king without rival; the birth of a son to the queen in sanctuary at Westminster, followed soon after by that of another infant boy, suggested that the line of York might stretch onward indefinitely. But he had two brothers – George, duke of Clarence and Richard, duke of Gloucester – who at some later date might make their own claims for supremacy.

The younger brother, Gloucester, was rewarded for his loyalty during the commotions of the previous years. From the autumn of 1469 he was constable of England, and led his own supporters in the king's battles against the rebels; he had also sailed with Edward in flight from King's Lynn to Holland and, at the climactic battle of Tewkesbury, he had led the vanguard of Edward's army. For services rendered, therefore, in the spring of 1471 he was made Great Chamberlain of England; this was the position once held by Warwick. Gloucester was also granted much of Warwick's territory in the north of England and, from this time forward, he became the champion and warlord of the northern territories with his base in the great castle of Middleham in North Yorkshire. He was given the hand of Lady Anne Neville, Warwick's younger daughter, who had been married to the unhappy Prince Edward; the fifteen-year-old girl was now in alliance with the man who had helped to destroy her family, but it was of course more prudent to marry one of the victors. Romance was rarely to be found in the royal estate.

The older of the two brothers, Clarence, was the greater threat or perhaps just the greater nuisance. He had already proved himself to be disloyal to the king, in his temporary alliance with Warwick and Margaret, and now he turned furiously against his younger brother. He wanted to be Great Chamberlain; he wanted the Warwick lands of the north; he also wanted the lands owned by Lady Anne Neville herself. The brothers challenged one another in a set debate before the royal council, and both were applauded for their eloquence. Clarence, however, emerged as the temporary victor; he was given Warwick's estates in the midlands, as well as the title of Great Chamberlain. Yet Gloucester still retained his hold over the north.

In the period after his victory Edward prosecuted his erstwhile enemies with great dispatch. It was said that the rich were hanged by their purses and the poor were hanged by their necks, but in truth the king was interested in taking money rather than lives. The cities that had opposed him, such as Hull and Coventry, were deprived of their liberties and then fined for their restoration; individual magnates who had supported Margaret or Warwick were also penalized. The records of the parliament house are filled with reports of taxes, acts of settlement, attainders and forced contributions to the king's purse which were known without a trace of irony as 'benevolences'. Yet he could be generous as well as severe; many former foes were taken back 'into the king's pardon' and prominent Lancastrian clerics such as John Morton entered his service. Morton later became bishop of Ely and archbishop of Canterbury.

The great continental problem remained with Louis XI of France. The French king had aided Warwick and abetted Margaret of Anjou, in their claims to the control of the English throne, and he was still encouraging the rebel Lancastrians who sheltered in his dominion. He represented a threat that had to be rebuffed. But if Edward had the will, he did not necessarily have the means. He entered negotiations with the neighbours of France, the dukes of Brittany and Burgundy, on a proposal for a triple invasion. These two duchies were subjected by feudal ties to France, but were in practice independent. Edward succeeded, at least, with Charles the Bold of Burgundy.

On 4 July 1475 a large force of English troops sailed for Calais from Dover, prepared to meet up with the Burgundian forces. Edward was accompanied by the majority of the nobility, together with 15,000 men. He carried with him 779 stone cannon balls and more than 10,000 sheaves of arrows; he also transported cloth of gold, for sumptuous display, and ordered the building of a small house made of wood and covered with leather which he could use on the battlefield. It was a portable royal chamber.

Charles the Bold did not live up to his name, however, and arrived at the garrison town with only a few supporters. He had left most of his men engaged in the siege of a town in Flanders. Edward, apparently moved to great fury, almost immediately began talks with Louis XI in order to broker some kind of peace. The French king was eager to oblige, not wishing for the distraction of foreign soldiers on his soil, and a month later the two kings met on a bridge at Picquigny near Amiens.

A wooden barrier had been placed in the middle of the bridge, to ensure against any surprise attack, and the soldiers of both sovereigns were massed on either side. An impersonator, wearing the clothes of the French king, walked beside Louis. Three of Edward's retinue were dressed in the same cloth of gold as their sovereign. It was a precaution. Edward approached the barrier, raised his hat and bowed low to the ground; Louis reciprocated with an equally elaborate gesture. 'My lord, my cousin,' Louis said, 'you are very welcome. There is nobody in the world whom I would want to meet more than you'. Edward replied in very good French.

A solemn treaty was signed in which Louis agreed to pay the English king the large sum of 75,000 crowns as well as an annual pension of 50,000 gold coins on condition that English troops left the country. Satisfied by what amounted to a bribe, Edward returned to England. It was also agreed that his eldest daughter, Elizabeth of York, should marry the French king's eldest son. In the usual manner of these arranged royal marriages, the proposal came to nothing.

Edward returned richer if not exactly more glorious. He had

said in advance of the expedition that he wished to regain English possessions in France and even to advance himself upon the French throne. This was the rhetoric of the period, and was not necessarily believed. In any case the ambitions were misplaced. But if Edward had sailed with every intention of extorting a bribe from the French king, his mission had been admirably successful. Some evidence for this comes from a French historian who was with the court of Louis XI at the time. Philippe de Commynes states that Edward had begun to negotiate with Louis even before he left Dover. Commynes then goes on to speculate that Edward wanted to keep for himself all the money he had raised in England for the royal expedition.

In that event he had been engaged in an act of dissimulation on a very large scale; in the months before the planned invasion, the patent rolls reveal the combined efforts of 'carpenters, joiners, stonecutters, smiths, plumbers, shipwrights, coopers, sawyers, fletchers, chariot-men, horse-harness men and other workmen' in preparation for war. The truth may be that the English king was ready for a range of different results. He was simply waiting on events, to see what chance or fortune would throw in his way on the principle that when nothing is ventured nothing is gained. The historical record is made up of unintended consequences and unexpected turns of fate.

Edward did not publish all of the principles of the treaty made at Picquigny; but it soon became clear to the parliament house and the people of England that, as a result of the abortive French expedition, the king had been made richer and they had been rendered poorer. Yet Edward now was too strong to withstand.

He soon deployed that strength against his own brother. Clarence had effectively become ungovernable. According to the *Crowland Chronicle*, the most reliable source of information for the period, he 'now seemed more and more to be withdrawing from the king's presence, hardly uttering a word in council, not eating and drinking in the king's residence'. He had some cause for disaffection. On the death of his wife, after childbirth, it was suggested that he should marry the daughter of Charles of Burgundy; Edward refused to countenance such a union, because with the support of Burgundy, Clarence would become too powerful. For similar reasons Edward would not permit Clarence to marry the sister of the king of Scotland.

In April 1477 Clarence accused one of his wife's attendants, Ankarette Twynyho, of having murdered her mistress with 'a venomous drink of ale mixed with poison'; an armed gang of his men seized the unfortunate woman and took her to Clarence's town of Warwick where she was hanged. It was a form of judicial murder. Three months later one of the squires of his household was charged with necromancy in pursuit of the king's death and, on being pronounced guilty, was drawn to the gallows at Tyburn. On the following day Clarence came to the royal council and caused to be read a proclamation of the man's innocence; Clarence then withdrew. He had effectively challenged the king's honesty as well as his system of justice. Edward therefore summoned Clarence to appear before him and, in the presence of the mayor and aldermen of London, declared that he had acted 'as if he were in contempt of the law of the land and a great threat to the judges and jurors of the kingdom'.

At the beginning of 1478 a session of the parliament house was summoned where, in front of the lords, the king accused his brother of various crimes against the throne; some witnesses were called, but it was clear that they had been instructed in advance. The duke defended himself as best he could, even pledging to endure trial by combat, but the assembled lords declared him to be guilty of treason. The lords of the parliament were no doubt bound to support the king's wishes in the matter, and did not need to be duped into delivering their verdict. Yet the evidence was weak and perhaps concocted. Clarence was taken to the Tower where, a few days later, he was murdered by surreptitious means. It has often been stated that he was drowned in a butt of malmsey wine; this curious detail may, oddly enough, reflect its accuracy. It might indicate, however, that he was drowned in his bath; bathtubs were often made out of sawn-down wine barrels.

The king had killed the elder of his two brothers by dubious means. It was an act of ruthlessness that sealed the supremacy of the king. A soothsayer had prophesied that the reign of Edward would be followed by one whose name began with 'G'. So George, duke of Clarence, was despatched. The name of the younger brother, Gloucester, obviously did not occur to him. It was said at the time that the queen, and her Woodville relations, had also been eager to destroy Clarence; his eloquence and fair looks posed a challenge to her young sons in the event of Edward's death. Rumour was piled upon rumour; the murderous court was filled with shadows and suspicions. The path to glory for Edward IV had once been carved through the corpses of his enemies; now it mounted over the body of his brother. The king, according to the *Crowland Chronicle*, 'performed the duties of his office with such a high hand, that he appeared to be dreaded by all his subjects, while he himself stood in fear of no one'.

Apart from consolidating his rule, and maintaining his royal profits, Edward spent a great deal of time in arranging as many advantageous marriages as possible for his immediate kin. His investments in wool and cloth, as a working merchant, were small in comparison with the investment in his family. In all he had three sons and seven daughters; two of them died in infancy, leaving two sons and six daughters. The merry-go-round began, with daughters being betrothed to the heirs of Scotland, France and Burgundy. The prince of Wales, Edward, was played as a bargaining chip with Brittany. The king wanted hard money in exchange; he did not wish to pay the dowries for his daughters, in particular, and so engaged in prolonged negotiation to avoid that necessity. In fact none of his children were married by the time of his death, for the principal reason that they were still too young. All his plans, intentions and schemes came to nothing. The thousands of words spent in speeches and diplomacy vanished into the air.

His younger brother was more secure than ever. Richard of Gloucester remained the paramount lord of northern England. The Percy family were supreme in Northumberland, and the East Riding of Yorkshire, but the rest of the north came under the direct control of Gloucester. Edward had no reason to doubt his loyalty, however, and he seemed by far the best choice to be named 'Protector' of England and of the king's eldest son.

The moment came sooner than expected. In the spring of 1483 Edward IV became mysteriously and dangerously ill. It is reported that he caught cold on a fishing trip. Commynes says that he died of 'quaterre' or apoplexy. The *Crowland Chronicle* states that he lay down 'neither worn out with old age nor yet seized with any known kind of malady'. There is a suggestion of death by poison. In truth the only malady may have been that of self-indulgence; he ate and drank copious amounts; he had grown fat and debauched. Only a very pious king could avoid such a fate. Edward IV expired in his fortieth year.

Edward died without debts, the first king to remain solvent for 200 years. It was, perhaps, his greatest achievement. He had made no great legislative or judicial advantages, but he had at least consolidated the role and power of royal government. He had learned to make it work after the intermittently weak reign of Henry VI. That was the sum of it. The fact that England emerged from his reign more prosperous than before has everything to do with the underlying strength and purposefulness of a growing nation.

Edward was not strong enough, in any case, to ensure that his eldest son would be safely crowned as his successor. The warden of Tattershall College in Lincolnshire wrote to the bishop of Winchester that 'for now our sovereign lord the king is dead, whose soul Jesu take to his great mercy, we know not who shall be our lord nor shall have the rule about us'. Yet the transition appeared to have been immediate and graceful. Edward, prince of Wales, was acclaimed as Edward V.

The young heir apparent was at Ludlow, near the border of Wales, at the time of his father's death; he was in the company of his uncle, Anthony Woodville, Earl Rivers, when he was summoned back to London by his mother. A council had been called in the capital, of which the principal member was Lord Hastings. Hastings, like Gloucester, was loyal to the Yorkist monarchy rather than to the Woodville family; when he learned that the queen had asked her brother to guard her son's return to London with as large a force as he could assemble, he sensed the possibility of an unwelcome show of strength. He threatened to retire to Calais if the Woodvilles attempted to overawe the city, and at the same time he wrote to Gloucester with the troubling news.

Elizabeth Woodville then agreed to a compromise in which the young king would have an escort of no more than 2,000 men. Gloucester had been alerted to the possibility that the Woodvilles would control the king in more than name, however, and that they would supplant his role as the rightful Protector of the realm. He marched from his northern lands and joined his supporter, the duke of Buckingham, in Northampton at the end of April. This was just ten miles north of the place where the royal party had halted on their march to London; Stony Stratford was at the junction of Watling Street and the Northampton Road.

The two sides hailed each other with expressions of friendship. Rivers and his companions greeted the two dukes and entertained them at a house close to Northampton itself; they spent a convivial evening, but on the following morning Rivers was arrested and on charges of treason sent to a northern prison. Gloucester and Buckingham then rode out to Stony Stratford, and informed the young king that his uncle and others of his affinity had been engaged in a deep conspiracy against him. Edward objected, and protested that 'he had seen nothing evil in them and wished to keep them unless otherwise proved to be evil'. But the force of a fourteen-year-old will was no match for that of Gloucester. Gloucester also informed the king that Rivers had played some part in the dead king's debaucheries, thus fatally weakening him; this was in keeping with the strong moralism of his character. The young king remarked that he had full confidence in his mother, to which Buckingham replied that he should put no faith in women.

When the news of the arrest reached London the Woodville family and its supporters were in alarm. They tried to raise an army, but London was barren soil for them. So the queen took her other son and her daughters into the sanctuary of Westminster Abbey. This was the second occasion when she had sought the protection of the holy place, but the circumstances were now infinitely more dangerous. Two families were vying for control; no council was strong enough, and no group of nobles powerful enough, to come between them. The dead king should have foreseen the consequences of his actions, in building up two centres of over-mighty subjects, but he had made no effort to forestall them. So now the queen sat down among the rushes strewn on the floor of the sanctuary, surrounded by 'much heaviness, rumble, haste and business, carriage and conveyaunce of stuffe into Sanctuarie, chests, coffers, packs, fardels, trusses, all on men's backs, no man unoccupied, some lading, some going, some discharging, some coming for more, some breaking down the walls to bring in the nearest way . . .'.

Gloucester had taken immediate action to secure the person of the monarch in order to underline his authority in any struggle with the Woodvilles. He wrote to the council, and to the mayor of London, insisting that he had acted to preserve the life of the king and that he had no designs upon the crown. On 4 May he brought Edward V to London and, as a sign of his good faith, he insisted that all the lords and aldermen should swear an oath of fealty to their new monarch. Edward was taken first to Ely Place, but then was removed to the Tower of London as the appropriate place to prepare for his coronation.

Six days later Gloucester was appointed as Protector, although the length and extent of his protection was not made clear. The coronation itself was to be held on 22 June, and at that point the young king could declare himself ready to rule on his own account. That might be the wish of his mother. Henry VI had been fit to rule at the age of fifteen; Richard II assumed the duties of kingship at the age of seventeen. So in theory Gloucester had precious little time to enforce his authority. He may also have feared that the Woodvilles were set upon his destruction.

The fact that the queen herself remained in sanctuary demonstrated the uncertainty and danger of the situation. One of Gloucester's first actions as Protector was to remove the kin and allies of the Woodvilles from positions of influence. In that decision he seems to have had the support of the majority of the royal council, who did not see the dismissals as part of any plot to seize the crown. Gloucester also rewarded his allies. The duke of Buckingham, for example, was granted control of Wales and its border lands; it was a happy coincidence, perhaps, that he also usurped the power of the Woodvilles in that region.

The chroniclers of the period concur that by the end of May Gloucester had prepared himself to seize the crown; hindsight may be the real judge here. It is possible that Gloucester himself did not

know, or was not sure, what to do; he recognized as well as anyone, from the history of his own family, the power of chance and the unexpected.

The first real sign of his intentions came in a letter to his northern allies on 10 June, in which he asked them to come to his aid 'and assist us against the queen, her blood adherents and affinity, which have intended and daily doeth intend, to murder and utterly destroy us and our cousin, the duke of Buckingham, and the old royal blood of this realm . . .'. His words suggest fear and insecurity in equal measure. He did not mention Hastings as possible victim of these intrigues, because he now had cause to suspect him as well. It seems likely that Hastings had become aware of Gloucester's decision to supplant the young king, and had decided to resist the attempt; all of the chroniclers report his loyalty to Edward.

On 13 June, at nine in the morning, Gloucester joined the council at the White Tower of the Tower of London in a good humour. There is a lively account of the meeting by Thomas More, in his life of Richard III; the record has often been treated with scepticism, but More's principal source was undoubtedly John Morton who as bishop of Ely was present on the occasion. 'My lord,' the duke of Gloucester said to the bishop, 'you have very good strawberries in your garden in Holborn. I request you let us have a mess of them.'

'Gladly, my lord,' the bishop replied. 'Would to God I had some better things as ready to your pleasure as all that.' The bishop despatched his servant, and Gloucester retired to his chamber. He returned to the council, an hour later, in a much altered state. He was now in a sour and angry mood; he had a habit, when perplexed or enraged, of chewing his lower lip. 'What do those persons deserve,' he asked the councillors, 'who have compassed and imagined my destruction?'

Hastings was the first to answer. 'They deserve death, my lord, whoever they are.'

'I will tell you who they are. They are that sorceress, my brother's wife [Elizabeth Woodville] and others with her.' He then named Elizabeth 'Jane' Shore, who had been Edward IV's mistress, a most unlikely associate of the queen. At this point he pulled up

the sleeve of his doublet, and showed to the council his withered left arm. This deformity was not a new one – More says that the arm 'was never other' – but it served the purpose of proving witchcraft against his opponents. Then Gloucester turned on Hastings himself and furiously accused him of treason. Hastings was bundled away and summarily executed, beheaded on a log of wood that lay close to the door of the Tower chapel.

The *Great Chronicle of London*, compiled towards the end of the century, concluded that thus 'was this noble man murdered for the troth and fidelity which he bore unto his master', the 'master' being the young king held in the Tower. By swiftness and surprise Gloucester had managed to destroy the man whom he suspected of barring his path to the throne. It seems likely, too, that Gloucester had been given information that Hastings had decided to attempt a rescue of the young king from confinement; this may help to explain his impassioned letter to his northern allies on 10 June.

On 16 June Gloucester's personal troops surrounded the sanctuary at Westminster Abbey, where the king's younger brother was still being kept. The queen herself was persuaded to yield up her son by the persuasions of the archbishop of Canterbury, who argued that the heir apparent needed the company of his younger brother. The prelate declared that, on his 'wit and trouth', he would preserve the safety of the boy and that he would return him to her after the coronation. 'As far as you think I fear too much,' the queen replied, 'be you wel ware that you fear not too little.' She may have come to her decision in the knowledge that Gloucester's troops might force themselves into the sanctuary and remove her son by violent means.

She surrendered Duke Richard with the words 'Farewell my own sweet son, God send you safe keeping, let me kiss you once again before you go, for God knows when we shall kiss together again.' He was then escorted to the Tower to join his brother for the coming coronation. Nine days later the queen's brother, Earl Rivers, was beheaded in Pontefract Castle. 'I hold you are happy to be out of the press [of London]', an adviser wrote to the Lord Chancellor, 'for with us is much trouble and every man doubts other.'

The news of the death of Hastings had already provoked consternation in London, only quelled by the gentle ministrations of

the mayor who claimed that there had indeed been a plot against the Protector's life. Now the time had come for Gloucester to justify himself to the citizens and prepare them for his seizure of the crown. On 22 June a tame doctor of theology, Ralph Shaw, delivered a sermon at St Paul's Cross – the main centre for government proclamations in the period – in which he stated that Gloucester was the only legitimate son of Richard, duke of York, and thus the only true candidate for the throne. Another report, duly circulated at the time, declared that the two young princes in the Tower were also bastards. It is most unlikely that either claim had much substance, but it is possible that Gloucester believed one or both of them. Wherever a moral high ground was to be taken, he seized it with alacrity.

He could easily have convinced himself, for example, that Edward IV had what was called a 'pre-contract' with another woman and that his marriage to Elizabeth Woodville was thereby fraudulent. He had also seen at first hand the debauchery of Edward's court, and may have surmised that the occupant of the throne was in truth not king at all. Ambition might breed in him a false sense of duty. Fear also was an element in his calculation. Edward V, if he were crowned king, would have no compunction in destroying the man who had killed his uncle. Gloucester was obliged to move quickly.

Two days after Shaw's sermon the duke of Buckingham, Gloucester's paramount ally, made a speech to similar effect before the mayor and aldermen of London in the Guildhall. Once more the dubious claim to the throne was delivered with much earnestness and piety – and, as the *Great Chronicle of London* puts it, 'without the impediment of spitting'. The response of the Londoners was, by all accounts, lukewarm to the point of tepidity; the few calls of 'yeah, yeah' at the end were uttered 'more for fear than for love'. The servants of Buckingham roused one or two apprentices to cry out 'God save King Richard!' and as a result the event was deemed to have been a great success.

On the next day the parliament assembled at Westminster, and a roll of parchment announcing Richard's title to the throne was presented to the Lords and Commons. It was given unanimous consent by these various worthies from towns and shires, and on

26 June a large concourse proceeded with Buckingham to Gloucester's mansion in London, Baynard's Castle, where the roll was read out to him; he was then exhorted to take up the crown and, after a period of modest reflection, he decided so to do. He was therefore proclaimed as Richard III.

King Richard rode in state to Westminster Hall where he was seated in majesty upon the marble chair of King's Bench; this was the seat in which the monarch reposed when he was dispensing justice. Richard had immediately taken on the role of the wise and just king. He delivered a speech to the Lords and Commons, in which he pleaded for fairness and equity in the proceedings of justice. No man was outside the law. All parties should be treated equally. This may be considered a reproof to Edward IV, whose family interests often led him to break or bend the law for immediate profit.

Some in fact welcomed the advent of Richard's reign. He was known to be a good administrator, and a fine soldier. Surely his reign would prove superior to that of a fourteen-year-old boy under the thrall of his mother and his remaining Woodville relations? Edward V was king for eighty-eight days, a king for spring and early summer; he thus earns the unhappy distinction of enjoying the shortest reign of any English sovereign but in death his influence, as we shall see, was profound.

# 38

# Come to town

In the fifteenth century England was still predominantly a rural society, with only a fifth of the population living in approximately 800 towns. Only one city, London, could be compared with the cities of the European continent; the other urban centres were essentially large towns, with populations well under 10,000. York and Norwich were the exceptions, with populations of 30,000 and 25,000 respectively. The more important of them, such as York and Chester, were walled; so were the port towns such as Southampton. At the other end of this demographic range, the majority of towns contained populations of hundreds rather than thousands. Many of these smaller towns were simply ringed with a ditch.

A Venetian traveller, at the end of the fifteenth century, noted that the country was 'very thinly inhabited' with 'scarcely any towns of importance'. We may imagine a land with an uneven distribution of relatively small settlements, in utter contrast to the territories of the city-states in northern Italy. The small towns had not yet reached maturity; they were part of the great unconscious of England.

The most significant public buildings were constructed of stone; the churches were of stone, as were the bridges. But only the richest merchants built their houses of that material. The rest were constructed as before with timber or wattle-and-daub; the streets between them were narrow, dirty and malodorous, combining the less desirable aspects of the farm with the detritus of town life. Pigs and chickens roamed the streets and houses; there is a case from Girton in Cambridgeshire where, in 1353, a hen caused a fatal fire by scratching glowing ashes onto a child's bed of straw. Cattle were kept in the gardens of some town houses, and the back gardens resembled the 'strips' of the common farmland producing fruit and vegetables. Orchards and streams lent for a moment the illusion of open country. In many towns you would never be very far from the sound of running water.

The clamour was great, rising in a crescendo on market day, but a few minutes' walk would take the visitor into the relative silence of the fields or woods. The town gradually faded into the country, with dwellings and yards becoming fewer and fewer until pasture or field or wood became the landscape. The wind was fresher here, less contaminated by foul smells and the fear of infection, and the earth softer beneath the feet. Yet it would be ill-advised to create a picture of pastoral bliss; many trades were pursued in the cottages and hamlets of the countryside, among them cloth-making and leather-working. Fewer clothmakers resided in the town than in the country, where labour was cheaper and less regulated.

The towns were nevertheless the centre of commerce and of administration; they were the sites of assembly and of public entertainment. The market cross was the place where proclamations were made concerning the affairs of the town and the kingdom; this was the cross to which royal heralds would come with news of battle. Here, too, were the town stocks and the 'pound' or cage for offenders. Some towns were built in the shade of a castle or abbey, in which they found their most reliable and prosperous customers. Relations were not always harmonious, however, and the monks and citizenry of Bury St Edmunds were engaged in several violent confrontations; abbots did not make good landlords.

Other towns were built at the confluence of rivers, where trade was assured. A number of towns had a whole range of purposes. They grew organically without any plan or coordination; a new street would be laid out when traders multiplied; huts and houses were built outside the walls according to demand. They persisted and became hallowed by time. In towns as diverse as Winchester and Saffron Walden the building plots, the width of the streets, the topography of the market, still persist and are still visible.

The inhabitants of any town were deemed to be free after the residence of a year and a day, as we have observed, but the towns themselves were not centres of freedom. Many of them were subject to lords and bishops who took the proceeds of rents and taxes. Their internal administration was controlled by a hierarchy as rigid and as severe as any to be found in the nominally feudal areas of the countryside; the mayor and councillors were taken from the class of the richest merchants, and they effectively dominated all aspects of the town's life. They ran the guilds; they organized the courts; they regulated the markets. The merchants, owning property, were the 'freemen' or citizens. They lived in the same quarter of the town, often side by side, and their families intermarried as a matter of habit.

Specifically or predominantly urban crafts were in demand. The potter worked beside the mason and the tiler; the glover and the draper may have been found in the same small street; the skinner and the tanner were closely allied; the carpenter and the cooper frequented the same timber-yard. In the market at Salisbury were Oatmeal Row, Butchers' Row and Ox Row. In Newcastle there were Skinnergate, Spurriergate and Saddlergate. These men formed their own craft guilds, in part to defend themselves from the claims of the merchant guilds, but they were far inferior in status to the richer merchants who supervised and generally organized their working practices. Resentment, and even open confrontation, often arose between various members of the two groups; but the ties of commerce guaranteed that no general or permanent collapse of order could occur.

Beneath the craftsmen and the traders were the apprentices, the labourers and the household servants. There were always *potentes* and *inferiores*. Nothing in medieval England existed outside a formal social discipline of high and low. That was the nature of the world. At the lowest level of all were the poor or diseased people, attracted to the town by the possibility of begging or charitable relief. The late fourteenth and fifteenth centuries represented the great age of the almshouses and the hospitals. The larger towns had acquired schools by the fourteenth century, and in the following century one or two of them even possessed lending libraries. That is one pertinent difference between town and country; the level of literacy was higher in one than in the other. These public buildings in themselves expressed the civic pride of the town, exemplified also in the growing emphasis on civic ritual and procession. The mayor had become 'my lord mayor', preceded in ceremonial array by the sergeant carrying the sword and mace of the city. Spectacle and squalor resided, as always, on the same streets.

The Angelus or Gabriel bell rang at dawn to awaken the townspeople. Scores of bells pealed in each town, their particular sound alerting the people to begin or to end various tasks. After the Angelus had sounded, business began almost at once; the water-carriers congregated at the wells, and the butchers prepared the meat for their first purchasers. No traders were allowed to open their shops until six o'clock, however, and no goods could be sold before that time. In London no fish could be sold in the streets before Mass had been celebrated at certain stated churches. In the larger towns other bells rang out at nine or ten o'clock to signify that 'foreigners', or outsiders, could now begin to bargain in the markets. This was the hour when the first meal of the day was taken. The bells rang at midday for the consumption of the 'noonschenche' or noon-drink. This was also the time when builders and other labourers were allowed to sleep for an hour.

The afternoon was a less animated period than the morning; those who had travelled to the towns with their country produce now began to make their way back. Most shops closed at the dying of the light, but cooks and butchers could work until nine in the evening. That was the hour when the curfew bell was rung, ordering the men and women of the town to return to their dwellings. The workers in the fields now had to hasten home before the gate was closed against them. The bell tolled until the gate was shut. The town slept before beginning once more its customary round.

# 39

# The zealot king

Richard III was formally crowned on 6 July 1483, after a great procession that took him from Westminster Hall to the abbey. For a moment the uncertain events of the world changed into the order of ritual and spectacle. To the sound of trumpets heralds came out carrying the king's armorial insignia; they were followed by the bishops and abbots with their mitres and croziers, the bishop of Rochester bearing the cross before the archbishop of Canterbury. The earl of Northumberland followed the prelates, with the Curtana sword of mercy in his hands; Lord Stanley came after, bearing the mace, and then Lord Suffolk with the sceptre; the earl of Lincoln followed them with the cross and orb, while the earls of Kent and Surrey carried other swords of state. The Earl Marshal of England, the duke of Norfolk, now stepped forward carrying the crown. He was followed by the king himself, wearing a robe of purple velvet furred with ermine and clad in a surcoat of crimson satin. Four lords held a canopy above his head as he walked towards the great west door of the abbey. This was the prize he had wished for. Anne Neville, his wife and now queen of England, followed him with her own noble procession.

Soon after the coronation, Richard set out on a wide circuit of his kingdom both to parade his majesty and to reconcile himself with perhaps recalcitrant subjects. He travelled from Oxford on to

Gloucester and Worcester. In York he decided that he should be crowned for a second time, as if the ceremony in London had obtained the homage of only half his subjects. He was in many respects considered to be primarily a northern lord.

The image of Richard III has been outlined in letters of fire by William Shakespeare, who in turn derived much of his account from the history of Thomas More. More may have been a saint but he was also in part a fantasist, who had good partisan reasons for wishing to excoriate the memory of the last Yorkist king before the rise of the Tudor dynasty. Thus for More, and for Shakespeare, Richard was the smiling and scheming villain, the hunchback of dubious purpose, an abortive thing snatched violently from his mother's womb. There may be some truth in this caricature, but caricature it remains.

The king, for example, was not a hunchback. As a result of strenuous martial training one arm and shoulder were over-developed, thus leading to a slight imbalance, but nothing more. Shakespeare suggests that he was 'not made to court an amorous looking glass' but two early portraits reveal a face not devoid of handsomeness. He is relatively small and slight, at least in comparison with his elder brothers; he looks preoccupied, if not exactly anxious. A German observer noticed that he had delicate arms and legs, but possessed 'also a great heart' by which he meant magnanimity. The archbishop of St Andrews remarked that 'nature never enclosed within a smaller frame so great a mind or such remarkable powers'.

That 'great heart' was soon being called into question. Soon after the coronation had been celebrated, rumours and suspicions were whispered about the fate of the princes in the Tower. In the earlier months of the year the two boys had been seen shooting and playing in its garden. But then they disappeared from view. As the summer of 1483 turned to autumn the doubts grew louder and more persistent. Polydore Vergil, an historian as strongly biased against Richard as Thomas More himself, reports that the king decided upon the deaths while conducting his northern tour. In his account the king wrote to the constable of the Tower, Sir Robert Brackenbury, demanding that the boys be killed. When Brackenbury refused the king turned to a more compliant servant, Sir James

Tyrell, who arranged their deaths with the help of two accomplices. They 'suddenly lapped them up among their clothes, so bewrapped them and entangled them, keeping down by force the feather bed and pillows hard unto their mouths, that within a while smothered and stifled, their breath failing, they gave up to God their innocent souls . . .'. Other accounts of their fate included death by poison and death by drowning.

The most authentic commentary comes from another chronicler, Dominic Mancini, who reports that the two boys were drawn more and more into the inner chambers of the Tower and that their personal attendants were gradually dismissed. At the mention of the name of Edward V many men burst into tears but 'whether, however, he has been done away with, and by what manner of death, so far I have not at all discovered'. It was a mystery at the time, and has remained so ever since.

The fact is that the two boys themselves were never seen again beyond the walls of the Tower of London. There has been much speculation about their fate, but the only reliable conclusion must be that they were killed while they were in captivity. The occasion and nature of their death cannot now be known. Other candidates for the role of murderer in chief have also been suggested, including the duke of Buckingham and Henry Tudor who succeeded Richard to the throne. In the latter account Henry ordered their murder after his victory at the battle of Bosworth. But this is essentially a fancy. There can be little doubt that the two boys were murdered on the express or implicit order of Richard III. He may have persuaded himself that the two boys were indeed illegitimate, but that their baleful presence was a continuing threat to his regime.

The house of the Plantagenets, from Henry II to Richard III himself, was brimming with blood. In their lust for power the members of the family turned upon one another. King John murdered, or caused to be murdered, his nephew Arthur; Richard II despatched his uncle, Thomas of Gloucester; Richard II was in turn killed on the orders of his cousin, Henry Bolingbroke; Henry VI was killed in the Tower on the orders of his cousin, Edward IV; Edward IV murdered his brother, Clarence, just as his own two sons were murdered by their uncle. It is hard to imagine a family more steeped in slaughter and revenge, of which the Wars of the Roses were only one effusion. It might be thought that some curse had been laid upon the house of the Plantagenets, except of course that in the world of kings the palm of victory always goes to the most violent and the most ruthless. It could be said that the royal family was the begetter of organized crime.

There had been usurpers before, wading through gore, but Richard III was the first usurper who had not taken the precaution of winning a military victory; he claimed the crown through the clandestine killing of two boys rather than through might on the battlefield. This was noticed by his contemporaries. The god of battle was not on his side. The first example of his uncertain status came in an uprising of some southern nobles in the autumn of 1483. They were the prominent magnates of the shires south of the Thames and the Severn, many of them having served in the household of Edward IV. They were led by the duke of Buckingham, who had previously been one of Richard's most loyal and assiduous supporters. It has been presumed that Buckingham, believing Edward V to be still alive, had decided that the better course lay in supporting the young king's cause. He may, however, have wanted the crown for himself. Or it may be that horror at the news of the princes' deaths led him into precipitate action. Richard's reaction was one of fury towards 'the malice of him that had best cause to be true', as he wrote, 'the most untrue creature living'. In any event the rebellion was unsuccessful. Richard and his commanders rode down the rebels and Buckingham, captured at Salisbury, was summarily executed.

Another eminent figure was involved in this first rebellion. Henry Tudor, earl of Richmond, was a descendant of Edward III through the illegitimate (but later legitimated) issue of John of Gaunt. When Henry VI died in the Tower, Henry Tudor became de facto head of the Lancastrian household. As a result he found it necessary to flee to France, where he could escape the attentions of Edward IV and protect himself against the rise of the house of York.

At the time of the succession of Richard III Henry Tudor had become the most significant opponent of the new regime, therefore, made even more commanding by the troubled circumstances of Richard's accession. He was also aided by his mother. Lady Margaret Beaufort came into contact with Elizabeth Woodville, still claiming sanctuary in Westminster Abbey, through the agency of a Welsh doctor who ministered to both great ladies. It was agreed between them that Henry Tudor should marry Elizabeth Woodville's daughter Elizabeth of York, thus uniting the houses of York and Lancaster. This is also the best possible indication that Elizabeth the queen knew her two sons to be dead. Why else would she support another man's claim to the throne?

With this guarantee Henry sailed to England at the time of Buckingham's rebellion; all but two of his fifteen ships were scattered by a tempest and, when he hovered close by the coast of Dorset, he discovered that the revolt had ended ignominiously. So he returned to Brittany, followed by the rebels who had managed to evade the king's wrath. Henry Tudor set up what was in effect an alternative court.

Yet Richard was for the moment safe. He tried to make his position even more secure by promoting northerners into the positions previously held by the magnates of the south, although of course this proved less than popular with the southerners them-selves. They did not want 'strange men' in their shires, where rule was generally maintained by a closely knit group of relatives. Each shire was essentially a family business. The king was now stripping its assets.

The nature of his subsequent rule, however, has perhaps been judged unfairly because of its inauspicious beginnings. He had all the makings of a firm and even ruthless administrator. He set up a 'council of the north' to consolidate his power in that region, and it proved to be such a necessary tool of administration that it continued into the middle of the seventeenth century. Such was his zeal for public business that more than 2,000 official documents passed through his hands in the course of two years. Everything came to his attention, from the preparations for battle to the mowing of hay at Warwick. The high dignitaries of the Church, in convocation at the beginning of 1484, addressed his 'most noble and blessed disposition'. This may be the standard language of the supplicant, but differs so notably from the usual accounts of

Richard III that it deserves to be mentioned. The more benevolent view of the king is strengthened by the words of a popular ballad, 'Scottish Field', in which is described:

> Richard that rich lord: in his bright armour.
> He held himself no coward: for he was a noble king.

The king also gained the reputation of being a good law-maker. When at a later date an alderman of London disagreed with Cardinal Wolsey over a proposed exaction, he reminded the prelate that such forced taxation had been forbidden by a statute of Richard III. 'Sir,' Wolsey said in his usual high-handed manner, 'I marvel that you speak of Richard III which was a usurper and a murderer of his own nephews, then of so evil a man how can the acts be good?' The alderman replied that 'although he did evil yet in his time were many good acts made not by him only but by consent of the whole body of the realm which is in parliament'. So, contrary to the Tudor myth of the evil hunchback, memories of Richard III's good governance remained in London fifty years after his death. Francis Bacon, Lord Chancellor in a different reign, commented upon 'the politic and wholesome laws' passed in Richard's first and only parliament.

Piety, verging on moralism, seems to have been the most abiding aspect of his character. In the Act claiming his title to the throne the king denounced the rule of Edward IV as that of one who, determined by 'adulation and flattery and led by sensuality and excess, followed the counsel of persons insolent vicious and of inordinate avarice despising good virtuous and prudent persons . . .'. It seems likely that he did believe the Woodvilles to be of 'sensual' stock, and therefore justified to himself the murder of the two princes as a means of cleansing the body politic.

Two months after publishing this attack upon the Woodvilles he sent a circular letter to the bishops of England in which he declared that his fervent wish was 'to see virtue and cleanness of living to be advanced'. This might just be an act of public piety but, after the death of his wife and only son, he composed a prayer of more private intent in which he asked God 'to free me thy servant King Richard from all the tribulation, grief and anguish in which I am held'. His son, Edward, had died at the age of eleven in the spring of 1484; the insecurity of the York lineage was clear to all. His wife followed her child to the grave early in the following year. Richard was effectively alone in the world, prey to the 'grief and anguish' he lamented in his prayer.

Another intriguing aspect of his religious faith can be found. He owned a copy of the Wycliffite translation of the New Testament, as well as William Langland's *Piers Plowman*; both of these books had been condemned by a synod of the Church in 1408. They smacked of Lollardy and a more austere version of Catholicism. It can be safely concluded that Richard was interested in an unorthodox and more rigorous piety, wholly in keeping with what can be surmised of his stern character. He need have no scruples if he was doing the work of the Lord.

The death of his wife freed him for a further matrimonial alliance, and serious reports emerged at the time that he planned to marry Elizabeth of York, Elizabeth Woodville's eldest daughter, thus pre-empting her betrothal to Henry Tudor. It was even rumoured that he had poisoned his wife in order to hasten the new marriage. It never seemed likely, however, that he would be able to marry the girl whose brothers he had destroyed. Even by the standards of this harsh and cruel age, it would not be considered to be a blessed union. In any case his disdain for the Woodvilles was well known.

Yet the rumours persisted, to the point where Richard was obliged to summon a council in which he denied ever having wished to marry Elizabeth of York. Even his closest supporters had been horrified at the prospect and, according to one of the chronicles, declared to his face that the people 'would rise in rebellion against him, and impute to him the death of his queen'. There was widespread mistrust of him, especially of his harsh and unyielding temper. We have the paradox of a man of faith who was also a man of blood. But is it such a paradox, after all? Those of an austere faith may be the most ruthless and relentless, especially if they believe that they are acting in God's best interests. Richard III has often been accused of hypocrisy, but his real vice might have been that of zealotry burning all the brighter with his belief that he was surrounded by enemies.

Elizabeth of York was of course engaged elsewhere. In the

cathedral of Rouen, on Christmas Day 1483, Henry Tudor pledged that he would marry her on being crowned the king of England. His supporters, all the time swelling in numbers, then swore loyalty to him and to his claim. Polydore Vergil states that Richard III was now 'vexed, wrested and tormented in mind with fear almost perpetually'. He travelled around his kingdom, never staying in one castle or monastery for very long. He arranged for a force of soldiers to seize Henry Tudor from the duchy of Brittany but Henry, warned in advance, fled across the border into France.

It was from this country that he launched his invasion of England in the summer of 1485. An exile of twenty-two years was about to come to an end. Richard could not of course predict the point of invasion, despite the presence of his spies in Henry's entourage; so he settled on Nottingham as a convenient site for a court that was now essentially a war camp. Nottingham was in the middle of the kingdom and in any case close to his northern territories, from which most of his support would undoubtedly come. In that early summer, the king issued a general proclamation in which he denounced Henry Tudor as a bastard on both sides of the family and as a minion of the king of France; if he seized the throne he would 'do the most cruel murders, slaughters and robberies and disherisons that ever were seen in any Christian realm'.

On 7 August Henry landed at Milford Haven, in Pembroke-shire, with seven ships and 1,000 men. The French were happy to finance the venture as a way of distracting Richard from his designs to aid the old enemy of Brittany. Henry began moving northwards through Haverfordwest to Cardigan, where his forces were joined by some of his Welsh allies; Henry was the nephew of Jasper Tudor, earl of Pembroke, and was thus considered by Welshmen to be Welsh. A bardic song rang in the valleys:

> Jasper will breed for us a dragon –
> Of the fortunate blood of Brutus is he
> A Bull of Anglesey to achieve;
> He is the hope of our race.

Henry needed a myth to bolster his uncertain claim to the throne. In any case the Welsh affinity was of vital importance to

him. As he led his troops through Wales he flew the red dragon of
Cadwallader, from whom he claimed ancestry, on the white and
green colours of the Tudors. He advanced into England through
Shrewsbury and at Newport, in Staffordshire, he was greeted by his
first English adherents. His was still a vulnerable army, made up of
men from France and Brittany as well as Wales and England, and
might not have been considered powerful enough to confront the
king of England. Even by the time he reached Shrewsbury, however, it was clear to the king that a rebel army had come into
England without meeting any serious resistance.

Richard himself could not necessarily rely on the loyal support
of the magnates; he had alienated the great families of the south,
and of the midlands, by imposing upon their shires the members
of his northern affinity. He had a feudal, rather than a national,
sense of his kingdom, and his past actions made it impossible for
him to knit the nation into unity. From Nottingham Richard
marched to Leicester where he issued a call to arms, urging his
subjects on their utmost peril to join him. He had refused to
advance to Leicester until after the feast day of the Assumption,
another example of his overweening piety. He told his retainers to
'come with such number as you have promised, sufficiently horsed
and harnessed'.

The duke of Norfolk and the earl of Northumberland were
among those who obeyed his summons. The men of the north also
responded quickly, with the city of York sending eighty men 'in all
haste'. The duke of Suffolk made no move. Another great nobleman, Lord Stanley, held back on the excuse or pretext that he was
suffering from the sweating sickness; whereupon Richard seized his
son and told Stanley that, if he did not arrive with his forces, the
young man's head would be cut off. In the event Lord Stanley and
his brother arrived with sufficient men, but their loyalty was ever in
doubt. The king did not know whether they would enter battle as
his friends or as his foes.

When the armies met on Bosworth Field, on 22 August, the
advantage lay with the king. He had mustered 10,000 men, while
Henry commanded half that number. There are no authentic
descriptions of the battle itself, except that it began with the sound
of gunfire; both sides had artillery, including cannon and the

recently fashioned handguns. The bursts of fire solved nothing, and a bout of hand-to-hand fighting followed. At some point Richard decided to move up and attack Henry Tudor himself, in a deliberate decision to terminate the conflict as soon as practicable. It was a rule of war that an army would disperse or retreat as soon as its commander was killed. He may also have believed that some of his men were about to desert him.

Taking only his most loyal supporters with him he galloped hard into the mass of men around Henry Tudor, wounding and killing as many as he could reach with his sword. He is said to have cried out 'Treason! Treason! Treason!' He had made the mistake of separating himself from the main body of his army, but his sortie was effective for a while; then Sir William Stanley, who had stayed apart, now entered the battle on the side of Henry Tudor. In the ensuing chaos Henry's men surrounded the king and attacked him; he was engulfed, and his horse was killed beneath him. His blood ran into a small brook, and it was still being reported in the nineteenth century that no local person would drink from it. The dead king's prayer book was later found in his tent on the field of battle.

An hour's fighting had sufficed. After the battle was over, the crown that he had worn upon his helmet was found lying on the field. It was taken up and placed on the head of Henry Tudor. Richard's body was stripped of its armour and carried on a horse to the Franciscan house in Leicester where it was buried without ceremony in a stone coffin. The coffin was later used as a horse trough, and the bones of Richard III scattered. He is the only English king, after the time of the Normans, who has never been placed within a royal tomb. He had ruled for a little over two years, and was still a young man of thirty-two. The great dynastic war was over. The roses, white and red, were laid in the dust.

# 40

# The king of suspicions

The life of Henry Tudor, earl of Richmond, had been one of poverty and exile. On the triumph of Edward IV he had been hurried from Wales to Brittany by his uncle, Jasper Tudor. He would have remained an isolated and obscure scion of the Lancastrian affinity, an offspring of the bastard (but later legitimated) line of John of Gaunt, if the perverse actions of Richard III had not raised him up as a claimant to the English throne. The alienation of support suffered by the king, principally through the removal of the two princes, gave Henry the opportunity of stepping forward. It was his time.

After the victory at Bosworth Henry VII made a slow progress south. According to one who knew him, Polydore Vergil, he was 'slender but well built and strong' and his height was above the average; his appearance was 'remarkably attractive, and his face was cheerful especially when speaking'; his eyes were 'small and blue'. He had high cheekbones, hooded eyelids, a high-bridged pointed nose and thin lips. A picture of the king in majesty begins to develop. Vergil also notes, however, that in later years his hair grew white, his teeth were few and blackened with decay, and his complexion sallow.

The coronation was fixed for 30 October, and a parliament summoned for 7 November. It was proclaimed before the Lords and Commons that the reign of Henry had begun on 21 August, the day before the battle of Bosworth; by this sleight of hand Richard could be accused of high treason for opposing his sovereign lord even though he had at the time been the lawful king. The statute book has rarely contained any greater absurdity. Henry also desired to be crowned before the parliament convened because he did not wish it to be believed that his regal authority had been conferred by the assembly; what parliament could make, it might also unmake.

But by what right did Henry claim and hold the crown? It was not from the fact of birth. He derived all right of birth from his mother and, since she was still alive, the throne ought to have been hers. His promise to marry Elizabeth of York, thus finally uniting both principal families, was by no means sufficient or even appropriate; it might mean that he was crowned only because of his association with the house of York. If Elizabeth of York had died before him without issue, he might theoretically have to leave the throne and give place to the next in succession. It was not to be considered. That is the reason he postponed the wedding until after the coronation. He had to be king before he became husband.

The essential justification for his assumption of rule was simply that he had won on the field of Bosworth; the god of battles had blown Richard away. Victory was always seen to be a sign of divine favour, although the bewildering number of surprises and reversals in the feuds of the Wars of the Roses had led some to question that belief. The crown had changed by force five times in the preceding thirty years, and so its bestowal might be seen as a question of luck rather than of grace. The passing of the defeated king was not mourned; but the new king was a usurper whose rule might be endured rather than enjoyed. The power and significance of the crown itself might be considered to be a little tarnished. There was no sense of a glorious dawn. Eventually the king felt obliged to ask for a bull from the pope to guarantee his authority.

As king, therefore, Henry was not secure. Only in the last ten years of his reign did he achieve that happy state. He had spent his life in exile, and had little if any acquaintance with England and the English. He had never been involved in government, and had owned no great territories of English land. He was happier speaking French. The great families of the country could hardly have considered him to be one of their own, and had for the most part stayed out of his struggle with Richard. They were in effect neutral observers of his ultimate victory. Only two nobles fought with him at Bosworth and they, like him, were exiles. So at the age of twenty-eight he took up the burden of kingship without preparation or instruction.

He had to build up his support piece by piece. He was always cautious and circumspect, characterized equally by reserve and by suspicion. At the time of his coronation he established a royal bodyguard of 200 men, known as the yeomen of the guard; they wore jackets of white and green and carried weapons, part spear and part battle-axe, known as halberds. These men were the origin of the standing army of a later generation. Henry was emulating the French king, who had his own personal bodyguard; in this, as in other matters, he took the French court as his model. It was the one he knew best. He also extended his defences by other means, and sent garrisons to Plymouth and to Berwick in case of possible invasion.

He clothed himself in the mantle of pomp and power as a way of disarming any opposition to his rule. He claimed that he was descended from Brutus, the Trojan founder of London, and he identified himself with the supposedly saintly Henry VI. He spent much time and effort in an attempt to have the dead king canonized. He was the first king of England to put a stamp of his true image on the coinage of the country; the silver shilling showed him in profile, while the gold sovereign bore an image of him seated in majesty on a Gothic throne with the crown imperial upon his head. It was one of the many images of his 'majesty' popular during his reign. Despite his alleged parsimony he spent profusely on the magnificence of a court that became notable for its ceremonies and displays. He also refurbished the royal image by introducing the motif of the white and red roses intertwined as a symbol of regal unity. The red rose had never been a very important emblem for the Lancastrians, but it was of use to Henry as a device. So began the myth of Tudor renovation that was celebrated by Holinshed and Shakespeare.

He had every motive to justify and expand his royalty; a usurper is always in danger, and almost at once the Yorkist faction began to conspire against him. Some of the former king's supporters rose against Henry, at Worcester and in Wales, but they were easily dispelled. The throne was further strengthened by the birth of a son and heir at Winchester in 1486; this was the city in which the 'Round Table' was to be seen, and the infant was given the name of Arthur. Henry was eager to employ or to exploit any royal connection he could find.

Another attack upon his throne was launched at the end of this year by Yorkists who claimed that they had rescued the young earl of Warwick, son of the duke of Clarence and therefore a proper heir to the throne, from long imprisonment. This was enough to arouse all the hopes of the defeated. The fact that the real Warwick was even then immured in the Tower of London did not in any way diminish their enthusiasm. The boy had emerged in Dublin, and in that city on 24 May 1487 he was proclaimed as Edward VI. A crown had been taken from a statue of the Virgin Mary and placed in ceremony upon his head.

The real name of the supposed king was in fact Lambert Simnel. Of his earlier life, little enough is known. It seems that he was characterized by a pleasing appearance and an uncommon manner, leading some bold spirits to believe that he could indeed impersonate an earl. He also caught the attention of Edward IV's sister, Margaret of Burgundy, who would in future years do everything in her power to restore the Yorkist dynasty. Other Yorkist sympathizers, the earl of Lincoln and Lord Lovel among them, were eager to participate in the conspiracy. Its most surprising member, however, must be Henry's mother-in-law. Elizabeth Woodville, widow of Edward IV, might have been considered to be above suspicion. Her daughter, Elizabeth of York, was the reigning queen. What had she to gain in supplanting her son-in-law and effectively dispossessing her daughter?

It seems likely that she felt herself and her kin to have been humiliated by Henry's seizure of the crown. There were rumours that Henry was not treating his wife with due respect or kindness. He had delayed the wedding, and was still delaying the queen's coronation. He did not like the Yorkist connection; he had been fighting against it all of his adult life. He had married Elizabeth for reasons of state. So the mother turned against him, and supported the pretensions of Lambert Simnel.

Henry, alarmed at this threat to his rule, extracted the real earl of Warwick from the Tower and had him paraded through the streets of London. The young man also attended High Mass at St Paul's, where he was allowed to converse with those who were familiar to him. Simnel's supporters in Dublin of course denounced him as an imposter. From her palace in Flanders Margaret of Burgundy proceeded to hire 2,000 German mercenaries under the command of the earl of Lincoln. It was said by the Tudor chronicler, Edward Hall, that she was a 'diabolical duchess' and 'a dog reverting to her old vomit'; the vomit was directed against Henry Tudor.

The German mercenaries landed in Dublin as the army of the proclaimed Edward VI where they enlisted more soldiers and mercenaries. They sailed to England with the counterfeit king, and Henry rode out with his army against them. They met at East Stoke on 16 June, where the 12,000 men of Henry defeated the 8,000 men under the command of the earl of Lincoln. Lincoln himself was killed in the mêlée, and Simnel was captured. Lovel had fled the scene of battle. Francis Bacon, in his life of Henry VII, remarks that Lovel lived long afterwards 'in a cellar or vault'. It has been said that, during building work at Minster Lovell Hall in Oxfordshire at the beginning of the eighteenth century, an underground chamber was discovered; here was found the skeleton of a man, sitting in a chair with his head reclining on a table. Fortune had not favoured him.

Yet the battle of Stoke had been finely balanced. It is significant that some of the gentry had held back from supporting Henry with one excuse or another, and that many rumours or 'skryes' – commotions – were spread concerning the king's fate. The fortunes of battle are always uncertain, and the fragility of his rule was emphasized by the fact that he had been forced to fight for his crown only two years after Bosworth. The battle of Stoke may be considered to be the last battle of the Wars of the Roses. Yet the victor was relatively merciful. Lambert Simnel was employed by him as a turnspit in the royal kitchens, and later became the king's falconer. Elizabeth Woodville was removed to a nunnery in

Bermondsey, where she spent the rest of her life. At a later feast with the lords of Ireland Henry remarked that 'My masters of Ireland, you will crown apes at last'.

It was important for the king to stabilize and to strengthen his power. He preferred to govern through intimates rather than through the great men of the land; he did not exclude the aristocracy from his council, but he did not place his whole trust in them. Instead he surrounded himself with a retinue of self-made men who owed all their loyalty to the king. He preferred lawyers to magnates, and listened to the advice of great merchants rather than great lords. Of course he needed the nobility and the lords to control the counties in which they resided; in the absence of a police force and a standing army, he relied upon their support. But he was careful not to increase their number, and created only three earls and five peers in the whole course of his reign.

The king also worked through tribunals and courts which were under his control, principal among them the Star Chamber which was used to awe certain over-mighty subjects into submission. If they were guilty of perverting the course of justice, or of acquiring a small army of retainers, or of inciting disorder, they were quickly punished. Justice Shallow exclaims, in *The Merry Wives of Windsor*, that 'I shall make a Star Chamber matter of it . . . the Council shall hear it: it is a riot . . . Knight, you have beaten my men, killed my deer, and broke open my lodge.' The councillors were gathered in a chamber of which the roof was painted with stars. There was no jury, and no appeal. The *camera stellata* or *chambre de éstoiles* is first mentioned in the reign of Edward III, but Henry VII widened its powers for his own benefit.

Henry also involved himself in the close administration of royal finance, and the details of expenditure in the account books bear his initials; he went through them line by line. Throughout his reign he was determined to exact every possible claim and right he possessed; in that, however, he was not very different from his predecessors. He strengthened his personal hold over his cash when he diverted much of his earnings away from the exchequer, an official body, to his own private treasury. The revenue from the crown lands, the fees for the drawing-up of writs, the fines levied on prisoners, the old feudal payments, all flowed directly into his hands.

The foreign adventures of Henry were by no means over. He had consistently supported Brittany in its struggle against the power of France; it was to Brittany, after all, that he owed his earlier freedom. He had placed troops in the duchy armed and prepared for war against the French king, Charles VIII. Henry gathered a fleet and persuaded the parliament to raise a tax in order to subsidize the venture. He knew that the threat or promise of war could always fill his treasury. Charles VIII was of course eager to distract and destabilize the English king, and entered into negotiations both with Scotland and with Ireland to plan a campaign. The enemies of England only needed a cause.

So it was that in the late autumn of 1491 a young man of seventeen emerged in Cork claiming to be Richard, duke of York, the younger of the two princes murdered in the Tower of London. As Richard IV, he was the true Yorkist king of England. He was fluent and convincing about life at the court of his father; he recalled the details of his imprisonment in the Tower. He even remembered what he had said to the murderers of his brother. 'Why are you killing my brother? Kill me and let him live!' He was personable, and dressed in fine style.

He declared that he had been taken from the Tower and delivered to a certain lord for execution; but this lord, pitying his innocence and revering his royalty, sent him abroad after extracting an oath from him that he would not reveal his true identity until a number of years had passed. The time had now come for the rightful king to emerge into the light. Some were convinced of his identity on first observing him. He had the natural grace and dignity of the royal blood. His real name was Perkin Warbeck, and he was believed to be the son of a Flemish boatman.

The Irish deputy, the earl of Kildare, was not wholly enthusiastic about the young man's presence in the country; Kildare had supported the pretensions of Lambert Simnel four years before, and was understandably reluctant to commit himself again to a Yorkist revenant. But the great pretender had friends elsewhere. Warbeck readily accepted an invitation to travel to the court of

Charles VIII, where he was received with acclaim as the one and only king of England. He was known as 'Richard Plantagenet', and his retinue grew larger.

Henry was growing sick, perhaps with frustration and fear. The bills of his various apothecaries were seven times larger than before. He made a treaty with Charles VIII, who was himself eager to avoid war over the matter of Brittany; one of the clauses of the treaty stipulated that Charles would not harbour any of Henry's enemies. Warbeck then promptly crossed the border and made his way to the court of Margaret of Burgundy at Malines. 'I recognized him,' she wrote, 'as easily as if I had last seen him yesterday.' Others from the old court of Edward IV also claimed to know him, almost by instinct. He was now being called by Margaret of Burgundy the White Rose, the pure and fragrant emblem of the Yorkists.

The duchess also ensured that he acquired wealthy and influential allies. He was sent to the funeral of the Holy Roman Emperor, Frederick III, in Vienna where he met the great and the good; among them was Frederick's son, Maximilian, who now had command of the entire Habsburg Empire. Maximilian and the White Rose became fast friends. The pretender was soon coining silver groats in his own name; his armed guard was dressed in red and blue.

But Henry had not been idle. The danger was too acute for that. He applied trade sanctions against the Burgundian territories, where Warbeck was being sheltered. English goods, and in particular English cloth, were in turn barred from the Netherlands and elsewhere. The financial consequences were severe for merchants and workers on both sides, but the dynastic struggle took priority over economic affairs. Henry had also spent much money in trying to learn of Perkin Warbeck's real origins, and his envoys in Europe were now busily retailing the facts of his supposedly baseborn family.

The king feared that an invasion was imminent; he sent as many ships as he could find to patrol the seas along the Suffolk coast and ordered troops to guard the principal ports of the realm. He asked his supporters to supply men-at-arms who would be ready to fight at a day's notice.

He had spies in Warbeck's entourage also, listening to every conversation. It was said of the king that he handled every case 'circumspectly and with convenient diligence for inveigling, and yet not disclose it to the party . . . but keep it to himself and always grope further'. It was discovered that small clusters of Yorkist supporters, in Calais and Suffolk and elsewhere, were ready to rise on behalf of the claims of 'Richard Plantagenet'. Some of them were still working at Henry's court and in Henry's household. This was the moment to arrest and imprison them.

The most senior conspirator turned out to be in fact Henry's chamberlain, Sir William Stanley, the man who had engineered the king's victory at Bosworth. At his subsequent trial he was alleged to have said that 'if he knew for sure that the young man were King Edward's son, he would never bear arms against him'. Under other circumstances these would be unexceptionable sentiments but, in Henry's reign, the words meant a traitor's death.

On 3 July 1495, the White Rose and his mercenary army landed at Deal in Kent; but the invasion proved abortive. The forces of the pretender were overwhelmed, and Warbeck retreated to the relative safety of the seas. His captured soldiers were marched to Newgate or the Tower. Henry could draw even more comfort from the fact that the English had not rallied to Warbeck's banner; they had remained unexcited by his landing and unwilling to support him.

Warbeck had been rebuffed, but he sailed on to the old Yorkist haven of Ireland. He made the unlucky choice of Waterford as his point of entry, where the citizens actively resisted any attempt to enlist them into his war. For a few months he wandered through Ireland, a putative king without a kingdom, living in secrecy and fear. His fortune changed once again, however, when he was invited or invited himself to the court of James IV in Edinburgh. The young king of Scotland – approximately Warbeck's own age – was happy to take up any opportunity of embarrassing and weakening the old enemy of England. Warbeck provided the occasion. He arrived in the winter of 1495 and was greeted by the Scots as a conquering hero. He received more than promises, however; he obtained a bride. A close relative of the Scottish king, Katherine Gordon, was betrothed to him. She was not exactly a princess, but she was the next best thing.

So the White Rose and the Scottish king, now cousins by marriage, set about the invasion of England. James IV may have had in mind one of the border wars by which Anglo-Scottish hostilities were conducted, with the assumption that the English would then rise up in support of young Richard IV. Henry himself could not be sure of the outcome. He prepared to muster a force of 20,000 men, and launch a navy of seventy ships against the Scots; to widespread and furious resentment, he levied taxes and forced loans to pay for the proposed expedition. In the event the invasion proved to be a fiasco, and the White Rose professed himself to be horrified by the bloody depredations of the Scottish troops before they fled back over the border. Once again he was seen to be an unlucky prince.

He lingered in Scotland for a few more months, feeling increasingly unwelcome at the court of James IV, before venturing everything on another English assault. With his wife and a few supporters he sailed to Cornwall by way of Ireland. He had been informed that an army of Cornish rebels was waiting to greet him in the south-west of England, the men of Cornwall having marched a few months before towards London in protest against what they considered to be unjust taxation. They had been joined by men from the other western counties, all of them refusing to pay for the war against the Scots. Why should they finance a distant struggle in which they had no part? Like many such rebels, however, they marched as far as Blackheath before their leaders were cut down. Another opportunity now presented itself. They believed that they had found a leader of royal blood.

Once more Warbeck was singularly unsuccessful; some men from Devon and Somerset joined him, but the town of Exeter refused him entry. His followers, tired and hungry, began to desert his army; the king sent messengers among them, promising them pardons if they laid down their arms. Warbeck, sensing defeat, fled for sanctuary to the abbey at Beaulieu. Henry surrounded the church, and the pretender was persuaded to surrender. He came out of sanctuary dressed in cloth of gold, but his pride was soon extinguished. He was taken back to London, a trumpeter riding before him to blow mock flourishes into the air, where his confession was published. It is likely to have been written by the king's councillors, and to have borne as little relation to the truth as his original claim. Several versions of his life were soon circulating in England and in Europe. No one really knew the facts of his origin or his upbringing; it is possible that he was chosen for his role at an early age, and then brought up in the court of Margaret of Burgundy herself. It was said at the time that he was in fact an illegitimate son of Edward IV. Henry himself professed to believe that he was the illegitimate child of Margaret and a local bishop. Perkin is still wrapped in mist.

His end was in plain sight, however. He escaped from his guards at the palace of Westminster, where he seems to have been living as the king's confined guest, but was recaptured. He was then consigned to the Tower, the guest of the king in a more oppressive sense, where he lingered for more than a year. Yet the fears and the suspicions of the king still surrounded him. He was accused of plotting treason with another prisoner, none other than the young earl of Warwick who had been impersonated by Lambert Simnel. The king now took the convenient opportunity of killing the two young men who threatened his throne. Warbeck was hanged, and Warwick beheaded.

The earl of Warwick had been imprisoned, and killed, for the sole offence of being the Yorkist heir. He was an innocent and, in detention for fifteen years, it was said that he 'could not discern a goose from a capon'. He had to die all the same. A happier postscript may be found in the welcome provided to Perkin's young wife; Katherine Gordon settled down in the English court, and eventually remarried.

Henry was now believed to be securely placed upon the throne. 'This present state,' the Milanese ambassador reported, 'is most stable even for the king's descendants, since there is no one who aspires to the crown . . . His Majesty can stand like one at the top of a tower looking on what is passing in the plain.' The view from the tower is, of course, different from the view on the plain where there may be discordance and resentment. Two Spanish envoys suggested as much when they concluded that the king 'has established good order in England, and keeps the people in such subjection as has never been the case before'.

Yet Henry fell sick in the month after the executions; he

recovered, but his health was now gravely damaged. He was as devout as he was superstitious. He attended Mass each day but he also consulted astrologers and soothsayers. He listened eagerly to prophecies concerning the crown and the kingdom, at a time when he was pursued by private misfortunes. In the spring of 1502 his eldest son and heir, Arthur, died from disease or illness. On his death his strong and intelligent younger brother, Henry, became the heir. Six months before Arthur had married Catherine of Aragon, thus binding together the English and Spanish thrones, but Henry was now in turn betrothed to her. The king continually postponed any marriage, however, in the hope that a better prospect for his son might emerge. The young Spanish lady was caught in the middle of international events, starved of money and of affection.

In the year after the death of her eldest son, Elizabeth of York, the queen of England, suffered a miscarriage and succumbed to a post-partum infection. Henry was severely affected by this fresh sorrow, and it was said that he 'privily departed to a solitary place and would no man should resort unto him'. Elizabeth lay in state in the Tower, and was then given a ceremonial funeral in Westminster Abbey. Two years later the king sought another bride. He pursued the queen of Naples for her dowry as well as for her presumed attractions. He despatched envoys to Italy with the following questions. 'Whether she be painted, and whether her visage be fat or lean; whether there appeared to be any hair about her lips; whether she wore high slippers to increase her stature; whether her breath was sweet; whether she be a great feeder or drinker?' He then pursued Joanna of Castile, in the hope of governing that country as regent, even though the lady herself was known to be insane. The courtships came to nothing, and Henry never married again.

He did enjoy some success, the most prominent being the marriage of his eldest daughter to the king of Scotland. The wedding of James IV and Margaret Tudor in 1502 was the balm upon the wound inflicted by the advocacy of Warbeck. By his engineering of dynastic marriages, in fact, Henry did manage to consolidate the position of England among the ruling families of Europe. In so doing he abandoned the aggressive and expansionist policies of the Plantagenet kings. We may interpret that as a victory of his 'foreign policy'. In any case war was expensive; it also required taxation that stirred up the people.

Despite the brief interruption in the commerce between England and the Low Countries, as a result of Margaret's welcome for Warbeck, Henry did his best to foster the market in unfinished wool and finished cloth; they were now the principal exports, and the king wished to expedite the trade. He promoted English commerce in other areas, also, and there was scarcely a country in Europe with which he did not enter trade relations; Iceland, and Portugal, and the Baltic states, all came within his purview.

He was by no means a statesman striving for the common good; he was eager only to enjoy the fruits of the increase in customs revenue that went straight into his coffers. He traded on his own account, too, and in one year earned £15,000 from the import of alum used in the manufacture of soap. This was in theory a papal monopoly, but he considered the risk of excommunication less important than the making of profit. The figure of the king in 'Sing a Song of Sixpence' – in the counting house counting out his money – is likely to have been based on Henry VII.

The possibility of profit also promoted him to support the expedition of Bristol merchants over the seas to the 'isle of Brazil', better known as Newfoundland, where they found immense fishing grounds. He also gave John Cabot and his three sons a licence for a voyage of discovery in the western oceans, thus beginning the story of English exploration. Cabot touched down on the coast of North America, while all the time believing that he had reached Asia, and the colonial flag was raised. Hakluyt relates that the Bristol merchants brought back three native Americans from Newfoundland to Henry's court; they were 'clothed in beasts' skins and ate raw flesh, and were in their demeanour like to brute beasts'. Henry made sure that they were furnished with suitable lodgings in Westminster and, within two years, they were 'clothed like Englishmen and could not be discerned from Englishmen'. Hakluyt adds that 'as for speech, I heard none of them utter one word'. By the time that Sebastian Cabot reached Hudson Bay, on a subsequent voyage, the king was dead.

In his last years his suspiciousness intensified, to the extent that at the time of his death he was considered by many to be the tyrant of England. He had withdrawn further into the private world of majesty. Disturbed by the knowledge that senior members of his household had colluded with Perkin Warbeck, in an attempt to restore the Yorkist dynasty, the king decided to set himself apart from those who had customarily surrounded him. He created a Privy Chamber to which only his intimates had access. He lived and worked in a private set of chambers, secluded from the more open reception rooms of the Great Chamber and the Presence Chamber; now he could truly maintain his distance and, of course, keep his secrets. The royal household of the medieval period, established largely upon the retinue of men-at-arms surrounding the king and sharing his activities, was finally supplanted by the idea of a private court administered by servants and royal officials. In the last thirteen years of his reign he summoned only one parliament, in 1504.

Yet he maintained the magnificence of his court; as befitted a great king, jousts and processions and tournaments were organized on a grand scale. Tumblers and dancers were brought before him; he purchased or was given animals for the royal menagerie, and he liked to parade 'freaks' for the benefit of the courtiers. The king enjoyed gambling, too, and played card games such as Torment, Condemnation and Who Wins Loses. He liked to hawk and to hunt every day, and five falconers were enrolled in his entourage. He seems particularly to have enjoyed the company of 'fools' or jesters; at least five of them could be found in court at any one time, including Scot and Dick 'the master fools' and Ringeley 'the abbot of misrule'.

Medieval humour is now perhaps an arcane subject. One phrase became a catchword in the fourteenth century. 'As Hendyng says' or 'quoth Hendyng' was a way of encapsulating a piece of wit or wisdom. 'Friendless are the dead, quoth Hendyng' or 'never tell your foe that your foot aches, quod Hendyng' or 'Hendyng says, better to give an apple than to eat an apple' were repeated in street and field.

Many jokes or puzzles were posed, and a game of question-and-answer was called 'Puzzled Balthasar'. What is the broadest water and the least danger to walk over? The dew. What is the cleanest leaf among all other leaves? The holly leaf, for nobody will wipe his arse with it. How many calves' tails can reach from the earth to the sky? No more than one, if it is long enough. What is the best thing and the worst thing among men? Word is both best and worst. What thing is it that some love and some hate? It is judgment.

A thousand proverbs and sayings rose into the air:

Who can give more heat to the fire, or joy to heaven, or pain to hell?

A ring upon a nun is like a ring in a sow's nose.

Your best friend is still alive. Who is that? You.

The sun is none the worse for shining on a dunghill.

He must needs swim that is borne up to the chin.

An hour's cold will suck out seven years of heat.

The last sentence is redolent of the entire medieval period.

In the quieter times the king worked with his advisers undisturbed. Two of the most prominent of them, Richard Empson and Edmund Dudley, were set to harry and to prosecute the great ones of the realm. They dominated a small committee, called the Council Learned in the Law, specifically established to enforce the king's rights and to collect the king's debts. But they also had more informal ways of proceeding. If the eminent families spent little, and made no outward show, then they could spare a present of money to the king; if they spent lavishly, and lived in style, then they could afford to share their magnificence with the king. This was the 'fork' upon which the king impaled his victims.

Empson and Dudley also imposed fines or bonds upon the members of the nobility who had in any way breached the law. The earl of Northumberland was fined £5,000 for unlawful retaining. Lord Abergavenny was fined £70,000 for the same offence; Henry collected only £5,000 of that enormous sum, with the threat of seizing the rest if the lord did not behave satisfactorily. Anyone could be accused before a judge and, if he did not answer the summons, his goods could be confiscated and the presumed guilty party imprisoned at the king's pleasure. Thus did the king buy the obedience of those mightier subjects whom he did not trust. But he could not purchase their loyalty. He was feared by all, but he was not loved or admired by many. 'All things', wrote Thomas More of the king's reign, 'were so covertly demeaned, one thing pretended and another meant.'

As Dudley said at a later date, from the hindsight provided by a prison cell, 'the pleasure and mind of the king's grace was much set to have many persons in his danger at his pleasure, wherefore diverse and many persons were bound to his grace in great sums of money'. Dudley also confessed that he had illegally extorted money on the king's behalf from eighty victims. The king had in effect established a financial autocracy, an absolutism all the more feared because of exorbitant fines and the threat of endless imprisonment. This was the legacy that he left to his son and heir, who became Henry VIII. He kept notebooks in which he jotted down his caustic or suspicious thoughts and observations about those around him; when a pet monkey tore up one of these books, the courtiers were according to Francis Bacon 'almost tickled with sport'.

It could be said that, like Scrooge, Henry VII feared the world too much. Certainly, like Scrooge, he tried to protect himself with a wall of money. Yet he was avaricious with a purpose; he told one of his councillors that 'the kings my predecessors, weakening their treasure, have made themselves servants to their subjects'. He did not intend to beg or borrow, only to extort with menaces. In the process the annual royal income increased by approximately 45 per cent, and he was one of the few monarchs in English history to clear his debts and to die solvent. He was also the first king since Henry V to pass on his throne without dispute.

Money was power. It enabled the king to protect his throne and his dynasty; Henry told the Spanish ambassador that it was his intention to keep his subjects poor because riches would only make them haughty. He may have become more harsh, and more rapacious, in his last years; but it is equally likely that his natural tendencies were reinforced by age. He was in declining health, and in the final three years of his reign he was more or less an invalid. In his will he declared that 2,000 Masses should be said for the sake of his soul, within the space of one month, at sixpence a Mass. He died at his palace of Richmond on 21 April 1509, to general relief if not open rejoicing. 'Avarice', one noble wrote, 'has fled the country.' Yet the days of royal avarice were just beginning.

# A conclusion

When we look over the course of human affairs we are more likely than not to find only error and confusion. I have already explained, in the course of this narrative, that the writing of history is often another way of defining chaos. There is in fact a case for saying that human history, as it is generally described and understood, is the sum total of accident and unintended consequence.

So the great movements of the period, as described in the present narrative, may seem to be without direction and without explanation except in terms of day-to-day expediency; in that sense they are without historical meaning. What seem to be, in retrospect, the greatest and most important changes tend to go unnoticed at the time. We may take the slow progress of the English parliament as an example. The government of king with parliament was not framed after a model; the various parts and powers of the national assembly emerged from occasional acts, the significance of which was not understood, or from decisions reached by practical considerations and private interests. The entry of knights and townsmen, later to become known as 'the Commons', provoked no interest or surprise. It was a matter of indifference.

Everything grows out of the soil of contingent circumstance. Convenience, rather than the shibboleth of progress or evolution, is the agent of change. Error and misjudgment therefore play a large part in what we are pleased to call the 'development' of institutions. A body of uses and misuses then takes on the carapace of custom and becomes part of a tradition. It should be noticed, in a similar spirit, that most of the battles fought in medieval England were governed by chance – a surprise charge, or a sudden storm, might decisively change the outcome. This should come as no surprise. Turmoil and accident and coincidence are the stuff of all human lives. They are also the abiding themes of fiction, of poetry and of drama.

One result of historical enquiry is the recognition of transience; the most fervent beliefs will one day be discredited, and the most certain certainties will be abandoned. Opinions are as unstable and as evanescent as the wind. We may invoke, with George Meredith, 'Change, the strongest son of Life'.

The history of England is therefore one of continual movement and of constant variation; the historian, propelled onward by these forces, has scarcely time or inclination to glimpse the patterns of this ceaseless activity. Thomas Babington Macaulay once wrote, when surveying the passage of English history, that in the course of seven centuries a 'wretched and degraded race have become the greatest and most civilized people that ever the world saw'; at the beginning of the twenty-first century it would perhaps be difficult to pay the same compliment. We cannot find what he called 'progress' in the morals or in the culture of the English nation.

Yet we find something else of much greater interest and importance. From the beginning we find evidence of a deep continuity that is the legacy of an unimaginably distant past; there seems always to have been an hierarchical society with a division of labour and of responsibility. Yet there is a different kind of continuity, largely unseen and impalpable. The nation itself represents the nexus of custom with custom, the shifting patterns of habitual activity. This may not be a particularly exciting philosophy of history but it is important to avoid the myth of some fated or providential movement forward. Below the surface of events lies a deep, and almost geological, calm.

Many examples are to be found in this volume. The polity of England, for example, seems always to have been highly centralized; the political system was integrated; the legal and administrative systems were uniform. We have seen that, from at least the time of the building of Stonehenge, England has been a heavily organized and administered country. Unlike the provinces and sub-kingdoms of France or of Spain, or the fissiparous states and duchies of northern Europe, or the city-states of Italy, England was all of a piece.

Other forms of continuity are also evident. Modern roads follow the line of old paths and trackways. The boundaries of many contemporary parishes follow previous patterns of settlement, along which ancient burials are still to be found. Our distant ancestors are still around us. There is a history of sacred space almost as old as the history of the country itself. Churches and monastic communities were placed close beside the sites of megalithic monuments, as well as sacred springs and early Bronze Age ritual spaces. I have already noticed that the churchyard of the parish church of Rudston, in East Yorkshire, harbours the tallest Neolithic standing stone in England. The pilgrim routes of medieval Kent trace the same pattern as the prehistoric tracks to holy wells and shrines. We still live deep in the past.

Continuity, rather than change, is the measure of the country. It has been suggested that the cities and towns of England decayed at the end of the Roman occupation. But this is pure speculation. They may simply have changed their function while preserving their role as the centres of administration. The urban population remained, thus continuing a tradition of town living that can be glimpsed within a Neolithic settlement in Cornwall; in 3000 BC the enclosure, surrounded by a strong stone wall, accommodated 200 people. Can this be understood as an early English town? A village or small town at Thatcham, in Berkshire, has been in place for 10,000 years.

In the countryside, there is even greater evidence for continuity. The Anglo-Saxon 'invasion', for example, was once deemed to mark a decisive break with the past. Yet in fact there is no discernible change in agricultural practice. In historical terms there are no 'breaks'. We have seen that the same field systems were laid out by the Germanic settlers; the new arrivals preserved the old boundaries and in Durham, for example, Germanic structures were set within a pattern of small fields and drystone walls created in the prehistoric past. More surprisingly, perhaps, the Germanic settlers formed groups which honoured the boundaries of the old tribal kingdoms. They respected the lie of the land. The Jutes of Hampshire and the Isle of Wight took over the prehistoric lands of the Belgae; the East Saxons held the ancient territory of the Trinovantes, and the South Saxons established themselves within the prehistoric borders of the Regnenses. They even retained the same capitals. The sacred sites of the Saxons, at a slightly later date, follow the alignment of Neolithic monuments. All fell into the embrace of the past. The evidence suggests, therefore, that the roots of the country go very deep. Even now they have not been severed.

In this volume there have been endless variations upon the same principal theme or themes – the uneasy balance between the sovereign and the more powerful nobles, the desire for war pitted against the overwhelming costs of conflict, the battle for mastery between Church and sovereign, the precarious unity of monarch and parliament, are all part of this narrative. There are also enduring fault lines that create discord and crisis. We may mention here the barren attempts to regulate social life, the slow decay of the feudal order, the antipathy to central government in the shires, the rivalry of noble families in local affairs, the blundering efforts to regulate foreign and domestic trade. Identical political and constitutional problems recur again and again; it could even be said that change occurs only when the same factors combine in different ways.

Another salient fact arises from the history of England. All the monarchs from the time of the Norman invasion were, on the male side, of foreign origin. Only the last of them in this volume, Henry VII, was of island ancestry with progenitors from an ancient Welsh noble family. This does not consort well with the notion of English independence, but it fits more closely with the facts of the matter. The Normans were succeeded by the Angevins, who were in turn supplanted by the Welsh; the Welsh were followed by the Scots, who were removed by the Hanoverians. The English were a colonized people. I have written elsewhere about the heterogeneity of English culture, in *Albion: The Origins of the English Imagination*, but it is perhaps worth recalling that the great literary enterprises of the country derive largely from European originals.

A further point may be made. I had thought of including the histories of Wales, Scotland and Ireland within this volume but there was too great a risk of their seeming to become merely extensions of England in the process. Wales joined in a political and legal union with England in 1536, and Scotland entered a political union in 1707; but their cultures and their identities, like those of Ireland, are too dissimilar to warrant inclusion in this study. This may in turn lead to what has been called an 'anglo-centric' version of the past but, in a history of England, such a bias is hard to avoid. Only a history of the world could cope with the difficulty.

No philosopher, ancient or modern, has yet been able to divine the springs of human conduct or human character; so, on a more general scale, we can have little trust in historians who confidently describe the causes or consequences of such events as the Hundred Years War or the sealing of Magna Carta. In their vain attempt to follow the *ignis fatuus* or will-o'-the-wisp of certainty, their efforts will be at best uncertain and at worst contradictory. The wisest historians admit that their speculations may be misplaced and their interpretations incorrect.

History is about longing and belonging. It is about the need for permanence and the perception of continuity. It concerns the atavistic desire to find deep sources of identity. We live again in the twelfth or in the fifteenth century, finding echoes and reson-ances of our own time; we may recognize that some things, such as piety and passion, are never lost; we may also conclude that the great general drama of the human spirit is ever fresh and ever renewed. That is why some of the greatest writers have preferred to see English history as dramatic or epic poetry, which is just as capable of expressing the power and movement of history as any prose narrative; it is a form of singing around a fire. A drama, or a poem, is of course subject to manifold interpretations according to the judgment and imagination of the reader. Yet in that sense it resembles the events related within this volume. We might quote the words of Milton in *Paradise Lost*:

So shall the world go on
To good malignant, to bad men benign,
Under her own weight groaning . . .

Now we look ahead to the reigns of Henry VIII, Edward VI, Mary I and Elizabeth I, encompassing the great reformation of religion in the sixteenth century. We may in the process be able to glimpse, and perhaps restore, the poetry of history.

## THE END OF THE FIRST VOLUME

# Further reading

This is by no means an exhaustive list, but it represents a selection of those books I found most useful in the composition of this volume.

## 1: HYMNS OF STONE

Bradley, Richard: *The Passage of Arms* (Cambridge, 1990).
—— *An Archaeology of Natural Places* (London, 2000).
Collis, John: *The Celts* (Stroud, 2003).
Cunliffe, Barry: *Iron Age Communities in Britain* (London, 1991).
—— *Facing the Ocean* (Oxford, 2001).
Darvill, Timothy: *Prehistoric Britain* (London, 1987).
Harper, M. J.: *The History of Britain Revealed* (London, 2002).
Hawkes, Christopher and Jacquetta: *Prehistoric Britain* (London, 1943).
Hills, Catherine: *Origins of the English* (London, 2003).
James, Simon: *The Atlantic Celts* (London, 1999).
Mercer, Roger: *Farming Practice in British Prehistory* (Edinburgh, 1981).
Oppenheimer, Steven: *The Origins of the British* (London, 2006).
Pryor, Francis: *Britain BC* (London, 2003).
Slack, Paul and Ward, Ryk (eds): *The Peopling of Britain* (Oxford, 2002).
Stringer, Chris: *Homo Britannicus* (London, 2006).

## 2: THE ROMAN WAY

Arnold, C. J.: *Roman Britain to Saxon England* (London, 1984).
Burnham, B. C., and Johnson, H. B., (eds): *Invasion and Response* (Oxford, 1979).

Dark, Ken: *Britain and the End of the Roman Empire* (Stroud, 2002).

Faulkner, Neil: *The Decline and Fall of Roman Britain* (Stroud, 2004).

Frere, Sheppard: *Britannia: A History of Roman Britain* (London, 1967).

Millett, Martin: *The Romanization of Britain* (Cambridge, 1990).

Reece, Richard: *My Roman Britain* (Cirencester, 1988).

Salway, Peter: *Roman Britain* (Oxford, 1981).

—— *The Roman Era* (Oxford, 2002).

Todd, Malcolm (ed.): *A Companion to Roman Britain* (Oxford, 2004).

Webster, G.: *The Roman Invasion of Britain* (London, 1980).

## 3: CLIMATE CHANGE

Fox, Cyril: *The Personality of Britain* (Cardiff, 1938).

Jones, Martin and Dimbleby, Geoffrey (eds): *The Environment of Man* (Oxford, 1981).

Mackinder, H. J.: *Britain and the British Seas* (London, 1902).

Parry, M. L.: *Climactic Change, Agriculture and Settlement* (Folkestone, 1978).

Rackham, Oliver: *The History of the Countryside* (London, 1986).

## 4: SPEAR POINTS

Abels, R. P.: *Lordship and Military Obligation in Anglo-Saxon England* (London, 1988).

Arnold, C. J.: *An Archaeology of the Early Anglo-Saxon Kingdom* (London, 1988).

Blair, John: *The Anglo-Saxon Age* (Oxford, 1984).

—— *The Church in Anglo-Saxon Society* (Oxford, 2005).

Campbell, James (ed.): *The Anglo-Saxons* (London, 1982).

Chadwick, H. M.: *The Origin of the English Nation* (Cambridge, 1924).

Charles-Edwards, Thomas (ed.): *After Rome* (Oxford, 2003).

Higham, N. J.: *Rome, Britain and the Anglo-Saxons* (London, 1992).

—— *An English Empire* (Manchester, 1995).

Hill, Paul: *The Age of Athelstan* (Stroud, 2004).

Hodges, Richard: *The Anglo-Saxon Achievement* (London, 1989).

Jackson, Kenneth: *Language and History in Early Britain* (Edinburgh, 1953).

Jolliffe, J. E. A.: *Pre-Feudal England* (Oxford, 1933).

Kirby, D. P.: *The Making of Early England* (London, 1967).

Loyn, H. R.: *The Governance of Anglo-Saxon England* (London, 1984).

Morris, John: *The Age of Arthur* (London, 1973).

Myres, J. N. L.: *The English Settlements* (Oxford, 1986).

Pryor, Francis: *Britain AD* (London, 2005).

Randers-Pehrson, Justine Davis: *Barbarians and Romans* (London, 1983).

Reynolds, Andrew: *Later Anglo-Saxon England* (Stroud, 1999).

Stenton, F. M.: *Anglo-Saxon England* (Oxford, 1971).

Tatlock, J. S. P.: *The Legendary History of Britain* (New York, 1974).

Thomas, Charles: *Celtic Britain* (London, 1986).

Wood, Michael: *In Search of the Dark Ages* (London, 1994).

## 5: THE BLOOD EAGLE

Cavill, Paul: *Vikings* (London, 2001).

Dark, K. R.: *Civitas to Kingdom* (London, 1994).

Davies, Wendy: *From the Vikings to the Normans* (Oxford, 2003).

Faith, Rosamond: *The English Peasantry and the Growth of Lordship* (London, 1997).

Foot, P. G., and Wilson, D. M.: *The Viking Achievement* (London, 1970).

Hadley D. M. and Richards, J. D. (eds): *Cultures in Contact* (Turnhout, 2000).

Loyn, H. R.: *The Vikings in Britain* (London, 1977).

Sawyer, P. H.: *The Age of the Vikings* (London, 1971).

Smyth A. P.: *King Alfred the Great* (Oxford, 1995).

Stafford, Pauline: *Unification and Conquest* (London, 1989).

Whitelock, Dorothy: *The Beginnings of English Society* (London 1952).

## 6: The measure of the king

Poole, A. L.: *From Domesday Book to Magna Carta* (Oxford, 1955).
Harvey, Barbara: *The Twelfth and Thirteenth Centuries* (Oxford, 2001).
Wormald, Patrick: *The Making of English Law* (Oxford, 1999).


## 7: The coming of the conquerors

Barlow, Frank: *Edward the Confessor* (London, 1979).
—— *The English Church, 1000–1066* (London, 1979).
Brown, R. A.: *The Normans and the Norman Conquest* (London, 1969).
Clarke, P. A.: *The English Nobility under Edward the Confessor* (Oxford, 1994).
Fleming, Robin: *Kings and Lords in Conquest England* (Cambridge, 1991).
Garmonsway, G. M.: *Canute and his Empire* (London, 1964).
Lawson, M. K.: *Cnut* (Stroud, 2004).
—— *The Battle of Hastings* (Stroud, 2007).
Loyn, H. R.: *Anglo-Saxon England and the Norman Conquest* (London, 1962).
McLynn, Frank: *1066* (London, 1998).
Walker, I. W.: *Harold* (Stroud, 1997).
Williams, Ann: *Ethelred the Unready* (London, 2003).


## 9: Devils and wicked men

Barlow, Frank: *William Rufus* (London, 1983).
Douglas, D. C.: *The Norman Achievement* (London, 1969).
—— *William the Conqueror* (London, 1964).
Freeman, E. A.: *A History of the Norman Conquest of England* (Oxford, 1870–79).
—— *The Reign of William Rufus* (Oxford, 1882).
—— *William the Conqueror* (London, 1898).

Green, Judith: *The Government of England under Henry I* (Cambridge, 1986).

—— *The Aristocracy of Norman England* (Cambridge, 1997).

—— *Henry I* (Cambridge, 2006).

Hicks, Carola (ed.): *England in the Eleventh Century* (Stamford, 1992).

Hollister, C. W.: *Henry I* (London, 2001).

Maitland, F. W.: *Domesday Book and Beyond* (Cambridge, 1897).

Mason, Emma: *William II* (Stroud, 2005).

Rex, Peter: *Hereward* (Stroud, 2005).

—— *The English Resistance* (Stroud, 2006).

Rowley, Trevor: *The Norman Heritage* (London, 1983).

Strickland, Matthew (ed.): *Anglo-Norman Warfare* (Woodbridge, 1992).

## 10: THE ROAD

Cox, R. H.: *The Green Roads of England* (London, 1914).

Gelling, Margaret: *Signposts to the Past* (London, 1978).

Hoskins, W. G.: *The Making of the English Landscape* (London, 1955).

Jusserand, J. J.: *English Wayfaring Life in the Middle Ages* (London, 1889).

## 11: THE LAW IS LOST

Appleby, J. T.: *The Troubled Reign of King Stephen* (London, 1969).

Brooke, Z. N.: *The English Church and the Papacy* (Cambridge, 1931).

Chibnall, Marjorie: *The Empress Matilda* (Oxford, 1991).

Cronne, H. A.: *The Reign of Stephen* (London, 1970).

Crouch, David: *The Reign of King Stephen* (London, 2000).

Holt, J. C.: *Colonial England* (London, 1997).

Matthew, Donald: *King Stephen* (London, 2002).

## 13: THE TURBULENT PRIEST

Amt, Emilie: *The Accession of Henry II in England* (Woodbridge, 1993).

Barber, Richard: *Henry Plantagenet* (Ipswich, 1964).

Barlow, Frank: *Thomas Becket* (London, 1986).

Bloch, Marc: *Feudal Society* (London, 1961–62).

Dark, Sidney: *St Thomas of Canterbury* (London, 1927).

Grary, H. L.: *English Field Systems* (London, 1959).

Hall, Hubert: *Court Life under the Plantagenets* (London, 1899).

Norgate, Kate: *England under the Angevin Kings* (London, 1887).

Pain, Nesta: *The King and Becket* (New York, 1964).

Roberts, B. K.:*The Making of the English Village* (London, 1987).

Salzman, L. F.: *Henry II* (London, 1917).

Vinogradoff, Paul: *The Growth of the Manor* (London, 1904).

—— *Villainage in England* (Oxford, 1927).

Warren, W. L.: *Henry II* (London, 1973).

## 14: THE LOST VILLAGE

Beresford, Maurice: *The Lost Villages of England* (London, 1969).

Oswald, Alastair: *Wharram Percy* (York, 2004).

## 15: THE GREAT CHARTER

Appleby, J. T.: *England without Richard* (Ithaca, 1965).

Brundage, J. A.: *Richard Lionheart* (New York, 1974).

Church, S. D. (ed.): *King John* (Woodbridge, 1999).

Gillingham, John: *Richard the Lionheart* (London, 1978).

Holt, J. C.: *The Northerners* (Oxford, 1961).

—— *Magna Carta* (Cambridge, 1992).

Jolliffe, J. E. A.: *Angevin Kingship* (London, 1956).

Turner, R. V.: *King John* (Stroud, 2005).

Warren, W. L.: *The Governance of Norman and Angevin England* (London, 1987).

—— *King John* (Berkeley, 1961).
Wilkinson, Bertie: *The High Middle Ages in England* (Cambridge, 1978).

## 16: CRIME AND PUNISHMENT

Harding, Alan: *The Law Courts of Medieval England* (London, 1973).
Musson, Anthony: *Medieval Law in Context* (Manchester, 2001).
Musson, Anthony, and Ormrod, W. M.: *The Evolution of English Justice* (London, 1999).
Salzman, L. F.: *English Life in the Middle Ages* (London, 1926).

## 17: A SIMPLE KING

Burton, Janet: *Monastic and Religious Orders in Britain, 1000–1300* (Cambridge, 1994).
Carpenter, D. A.: *The Minority of Henry III* (London, 1990).
—— *The Reign of Henry III* (London, 1996).
—— *The Struggle for Mastery* (London, 2003).
Clanchy, M. T.: *From Memory to Written Record* (Oxford, 1993).
Harding, Alan: *England in the Thirteenth Century* (Cambridge, 1993).
Harvey, Barbara: *The Twelfth and Thirteenth Centuries* (Oxford, 2001).
Hennings, M. A.: *England under Henry III* (London, 1924).
Lloyd, Simon: *English Society and the Crusade* (Oxford, 1988).
Maddicott, J. R.: *Simon de Montfort* (Cambridge, 1994).
Powicke, F. M.: *King Henry and the Lord Edward* (Oxford, 1947).
—— *The Thirteenth Century* (Oxford, 1962).
Stacey, Robert: *Politics, Policy and Finance under Henry III* (Oxford, 1987).

## 18: The seasonal year

Hutton, Ronald: *The Rise and Fall of Merry England* (Oxford, 1994).
Postan, M. M.: *The Medieval Economy and Society* (London, 1972).
Powicke, J. M.: *Medieval England* (London, 1931).

## 19: The emperor of Britain

Jenks, Edward: *Edward Plantagenet* (London, 1902).
Knowles, David: *The Religious Orders in England, Volume One* (Cambridge, 1948).
Morris, J. E.: *The Welsh Wars of Edward I* (Oxford, 1901).
Morris, Marc: *A Great and Terrible King* (London, 2008).
Ormrod, W. M., (ed.): *England in the Fourteenth Century* (Woodbridge, 1986).
Pasquet, D.: *An Essay on the Origins of the House of Commons* (Cambridge, 1925).
Plucknett, T. F. T.: *Legislation of Edward I* (Oxford, 1949).
Prestwich, Michael: *Politics and Finance under Edward I* (London, 1972).
—— *The Three Edwards* (London, 1980).
Salzman, L. F.: *Edward I* (London, 1968).
Stones, E. L. G.: *Edward I* (Oxford, 1968).
Wilkinson, B.: *Studies in the Constitutional History of the Thirteenth and Fourteenth Centuries* (Manchester, 1937).

## 20: The hammer

Julius, Anthony: *Trials of the Diaspora: A History of Anti-Semitism in England* (Oxford, 2010).
Mundill, R. R.: *England's Jewish Solution* (Cambridge, 1998).

## 21: THE FAVOURITES OF A KING

Davies, J. C.: *The Baronial Opposition to Edward II* (Cambridge, 1918).

Fryde, Natalie: *The Tyranny and Fall of Edward II* (Cambridge, 1979).

Haines, R. M.: *King Edward II* (London, 2003).

Hamilton, J. S.: *Piers Gaveston, Earl of Cornwall* (London, 1988).

Howell, Margaret: *Eleanor of Provence* (Oxford, 1998).

Johnstone, H.: *Edward of Carnarvon* (Manchester, 1946).

Maddicott, J. R.: *Simon de Montfort* (Cambridge, 1994).

Raban, Sandra: *England under Edward I and Edward II* (Oxford, 2000).

Tout, T. F.: *The Place of the Reign of Edward II in English History* (Manchester, 1936).

## 22: BIRTH AND DEATH

Carey, H. M.: *Courting Disaster, Astrology at the English Court and University in the Later Middle Ages* (London, 1992).

Clay, R. M.: *The Medieval Hospitals of England* (London, 1909).

Finucane, R. C.: *Miracles and Pilgrims* (London, 1977).

Getz, Faye: *Medicine in the English Middle Ages* (Princeton, 1998).

Hunt, Tony: *Popular Medicine in Thirteenth Century England* (Woodbridge, 1990).

Rawcliffe, Carole: *Medicine and Society in Later Medieval England* (Stroud, 1995).

## 23: THE SENSE OF A NATION

Carpenter, D. A.: *The Reign of Edward III* (London, 1996).

Edwards, G.: *The Second Century of the English Parliament* (Oxford, 1979)

Given-Wilson, C. J.: *The English Nobility in the Late Middle Ages* (London, 1987).

Haines, R. M.: *The Church and Politics in Fourteenth Century England* (Cambridge, 1978).

Hewitt, H. J.: *The Organisation of War under Edward III* (Manchester, 1966).

Horrox, Rosemary (ed.): *The Black Death* (Manchester, 1994).

Keen, M. H.: *England in the Later Middle Ages* (London, 1973).

McFarlane, K. B.: *The Nobility of Later Medieval England* (Oxford, 1973).

McKisack, May: *The Fourteenth Century* (Oxford, 1959).

Mortimer, Ian: *The Perfect King* (London, 2006).

Ormrod, W. G.: *The Reign of Edward III* (Stroud, 2000).

Prestwich, Michael: *Plantagenet England* (Oxford, 2005).

Rubin, Miri: *The Hollow Crown* (London, 2005).

Stubbs, William: *The Constitutional History of England* (Oxford, 1874).

Waugh, S. L.: *England in the Reign of Edward III* (Cambridge, 1991).

## 24: THE NIGHT SCHOOLS

Aston, Margaret: *Lollards and Reformers* (London, 1984).

Dahmus, J. H.: *The Prosecution of John Wycliffe* (New Haven, 1970).

Lambert, M. D.: *Medieval Heresy* (London, 1977).

McFarlane, K. B.: *John Wycliffe and the Beginnings of English Nonconformity* (London, 1952).

—— *Lancastrian Kings and Lollard Knights* (Oxford, 1972).

Robson, J. A.: *Wycliffe and the Oxford Schools* (Cambridge, 1961).

Thomson, J. A. F.: *The Later Lollards* (Oxford, 1965).

Workman, H. B.: *John Wycliffe* (Oxford, 1926).

## 25: THE COMMOTION

Allmand, C. T. (ed.): *War, Literature and Politics in the Late Middle Ages* (Liverpool, 1976).

Bevan, Bryan: *King Richard II* (London 1990).

Bird, Ruth: *The Turbulent London of Richard II* (London, 1949).

Du Boulay, F. R. H. and Barron, C. M. (eds): *The Reign of Richard II* (London, 1971).

Fletcher, Christopher: *Richard II* (Oxford, 2008).

Fryde, E. B.: *The Great Revolt of 1381* (London, 1981).

Gillespie, J. L. (ed.): *The Age of Richard II* (Stroud, 1997).

Jones, R. H.: *The Royal Policy of Richard II* (Oxford, 1968).

Mathew, Gervase: *The Court of Richard II* (London, 1968).

Oman, Charles: *The Great Revolt of 1381* (Oxford, 1969).

Ormrod, W. G. (ed.): *England in the Fourteenth Century* (Woodbridge, 1986).

Saul, Nigel: *Richard II* (London, 1997).

Scattergood, V. J. and Sherborne J. W. (eds): *English Court Culture in the Later Middle Ages* (London, 1983).

Tuck, Anthony: *Richard II and the English Nobility* (London, 1973).

## 26: INTO THE WOODS

Keen, M. H.: *The Outlaws of Medieval Legend* (London, 1961).

Westwood, Jennifer and Simpson, Jaqueline: *The Lore of the Land* (London, 2005).

## 27: THE SUFFERING KING

Bennett, Michael: *Richard II and the Revolution of 1399* (Stroud, 1999).

Dodd, Gwilym and Biggs, Douglas: *Henry IV* (Woodbridge, 2003).

Kirby, J. L.: *Henry IV of England* (London, 1970).

McNiven, Peter: *Heresy and Politics in the Reign of Henry IV* (Woodbridge, 1987).

Mortimer, Ian: *The Fears of Henry IV: The Life of England's Self-made King* (London, 2007).

Williams, Daniel (ed.): *England in the Fifteenth Century* (Woodbridge, 1987).

Wylie, J. H.: *History of England under Henry IV* (London, 1884–98).

## 29: The warrior

Allmand, Christopher: *Henry V* (London, 1992).

Byrne, A. H.: *The Agincourt War* (London, 1956).

Earle, Peter: *The Life and Times of Henry V* (London, 1972).

Harriss, G. L. (ed.): *Henry V* (London, 1985).

Hutchinson, H. F.: *Henry V* (London, 1967).

Keen, M. H.: *England in the Later Middle Ages* (London, 1973).

Labarge, M. W.: *Henry V: The Cautious Conqueror* (London, 1975).

Lindsay, Philip: *King Henry V: A Chronicle* (London, 1934).

Myers, A. R.: *England in the Later Middle Ages* (London, 1952).

Perroy, Edouard: *The Hundred Years War* (New York, 1965).

Seward, Desmond: *Henry V* (New York, 1987).

Sumption, Jonathan: *The Hundred Years War* (London, 1990–2009).

Wylie, J. H. and Waugh, W. T.: *The Reign of Henry V* (Cambridge, 1914–29).

## 31: A simple man

Bagley, J. J.: *Margaret of Anjou* (London, 1948).

Gasquet, F. A.: *The Religious Life of Henry VI* (London, 1923).

Griffiths, R. A.: *The Reign of Henry VI* (London, 1981).

—— *The Fourteenth and Fifteenth Centuries* (Oxford, 2003).

Harriss, Gerald: *Shaping the Nation* (Oxford, 2005).

Jacob, E. F.: *The Fifteenth Century* (Oxford, 1961).

Macfarlane, K. B.: *The Nobility of Later Medieval England* (Oxford, 1963).

—— *England in the Fifteenth Century* (London, 1981).

Wolffe, Bertram: *Henry VI* (London, 1981).

## 32: Meet the family

Davis, Norman (ed.): *Paston Letters and Papers of the Fifteenth Century* (London, 1971–76).

Richmond, Colin: *The Paston Family* (Cambridge, 1990–6).

## 33 AND 35: THE DIVIDED REALM AND
## THE LION AND THE LAMB

Carpenter, M. C.: *The Wars of the Roses* (Cambridge, 1997).

Gillingham, John: *The Wars of the Roses* (London, 1981).

Goodman, Anthony: *The Wars of the Roses* (Stroud, 2005).

Hicks, Michael: *The Wars of the Roses* (New Haven, 2010).

Lander, J. R.: *Conflict and Stability in Fifteenth Century England* (London, 1969).

—— *The Wars of the Roses* (London, 1965).

Pollard, A. J. (ed.): *The Wars of the Roses* (London, 1995).

Seward, Desmond: *The Wars of the Roses* (London, 1995).

Storey, R. L.: *The End of the House of Lancaster* (London, 1966).

## 34: THE WORLD AT PLAY

Egan, Geoff (ed.): *The Medieval Household* (London, 1998).

Fleming, Peter: *Family and Household in Medieval England* (London, 2001).

Hanawalt, B. A.: *Growing Up in Medieval London* (Oxford, 1993).

Herlihy, David: *Medieval Households* (Cambridge, Mass., 1985).

Leach, A. F.: *The Schools of Medieval England* (London, 1915).

Orme, Nicholas: *Medieval Schools* (London, 2006).

Salusbury, G. T.: *Street Life in Medieval England* (Oxford, 1939).

Shahar, Shulamith: *Childhood in the Middle Ages* (London, 1990).

## 36: THE STAPLE OF LIFE

Abram, Annie: *English Life and Manners in the Later Middle Ages* (London, 1913).

Dyer, Christopher: *Standards of Living in the Later Middle Ages* (Cambridge, 1989).

Henisch, B. A.: *Fast and Feast* (Pittsburgh, 1976).

## 37: THE KING OF SPRING

Baldwin, David: *Elizabeth Woodville* (Stroud, 2002).

Brown, A. L.: *The Governance of Late Medieval England* (Stanford, 1989).

Chrimes, S. B., Ross, C. D. and Griffiths, R. A. (eds): *Fifteenth-century England* (London, 1972).

Dockray, Keith: *Edward IV* (Stroud, 1999).

Goodman, Anthony: *The New Monarchy* (Oxford, 1988).

Myers, A. R.: *The Household of Edward IV* (Manchester, 1959).

Ross, Charles: *Edward IV* (London, 1974).

Thomson, John: *The Transformation of Medieval England* (London, 1983).

Thornley, I. D. (ed.): *England under the Yorkists* (London, 1920).


## 38: COME TO TOWN

Beresford, Maurice: *New Towns of the Middle Ages* (London, 1967).

Britnell, R. H.: *The Commercialisation of English Society, 1000–1500* (Cambridge, 1993).

Dyer, Christopher: *Making a Living in the Middle Ages* (New Haven, 2002).

Green, Alice: *Town Life in the Fifteenth Century* (London, 1894).

Nicholas, David: *The Later Medieval City* (London, 1997).

Palliser, D. M. (ed.): *The Cambridge Urban History of Britain, 600–1540* (Cambridge, 2000).

Platt, Colin: *The English Medieval Town* (London, 1976).

Reynolds, Susan: *An Introduction to the History of English Medieval Towns* (Oxford, 1977).


## 39: THE ZEALOT KING

Dockray, Keith: *Richard III* (Stroud, 1997).

Hammond, P. W. (ed.): *Richard III* (London, 1986).

Hanham, Alison: *Richard III and his Early Historians* (Oxford, 1975).

Hicks, Michael: *Richard III* (London, 1991).

Hughes, Jonathan: *The Religious Life of Richard III* (Stroud, 1997).

Kendall, P. M.: *Richard III* (New York, 1956).

Pollard, A. J.: *Richard III and the Princes in the Tower* (Stroud, 1991).

Ross, Charles: *Richard III* (London, 1981).

## 40: THE KING OF SUSPICIONS

Bevan, Bryan: *Henry VII* (London, 2000).

Chrimes, S. B.: *Henry VII* (London, 1972).

Grant, Alexander: *Henry VII* (London, 1985).

Hunt, Jocelyn and Towle, Carolyn: *Henry VII* (London, 1998).

Loades, D. M.: *Politics and the Nation* (London, 1973).

Lockyer, Roger: *Henry VII* (London, 1968).

Rogers, Caroline: *Henry VII* (London, 1991).

Temperley, Gladys: *Henry VII* (Boston, 1914).

Wroe, Anne: *Perkin Warbeck* (London, 2003).

## A CONCLUSION

Andrews, J. P.: *The History of Great Britain* (London, 1794).

Buckle, H. T.: *History of Civilisation in England* (London, 1908).

Churchill, W. S.: *A History of the English-Speaking Peoples* (London, 1956).

Clark, Jonathan (ed.): *A World By Itself* (London 2010).

Davies, Norman: *The Isles* (London, 1999).

Fraser, Rebecca: *A People's History of Britain* (London 2003).

Green, J. R.: *History of the English People* (London, 1878–80).

Hibbert, Christopher: *The English* (London, 1987).

Keightley, Thomas: *The History of England* (London, 1837).

Lingard, John and Belloc, Hilaire: *The History of England* (New York, 1912).

Mackintosh, James, Scott, Walter and Moore, Thomas: *The Cabinet History of England, Scotland and Ireland* (London, 1831).

Smollett, Tobias and Hume, David: *The History of England* (London, 2008).

Trevelyan, G. M.: *History of England* (London, 1945).

Wood, Michael: *In Search of England* (London, 1999).

# Index

Aaron of Lincoln, 227
abbeys: built in Stephen's reign, 126
Abergavenny, George Neville, 3rd Baron, 439
Ackroyd, Peter: *Albion*, 446
Adam (bastard son of Edward II), 231, 240
Adam of Usk, 327
Aelric (of Marsh Gibbon), 99–100
Aethelbert, King of Kent, 56–8, 318
Aethelfrith, King of Northumberland, 52–3
Aethelric, Bishop of Chichester, 318
Agincourt, battle of (1415), 324–5
Agricola, Julius, 30
agriculture *see* farming
ale, 394–5
Alexander III, Pope, 135
Alfred the Great, King of West Saxons, 43, 64–8, 70, 74, 78, 101
almshouses, 413
Alnwick, Northumberland, 161
'Amesbury archer, the' ('king of Stonehenge'), 10–12
'Anarchy, the' (under Stephen), 126
Andrew of Winton, 306
Aneirin: *Gododdin* (poem), 52
Angevin Empire: and divine kingship, 79; beginnings, 130; fiefdom, 136; collapses, 162–3, 166, 175; John attempts to recover, 169; Henry III attempts to recover, 189; Henry II inherits territories, 339
Angles: colonize England, 47, 54–5
*Anglo-Saxon Chronicle*, 45, 62–3, 89, 100, 104

Anne of Bohemia, first Queen of Richard II, 286–7, 295
Anne (Neville), Queen of Richard III: marriage to Prince Edward, 387, 398; marriage to Richard, 398; Clarence covets lands, 399; at Richard's coronation, 415; death, 421
Anne, Queen: touches Samuel Johnson for scrofula, 80
Anselm, St, Archbishop of Canterbury, 108–10, 113
anti-Semitism, 227–8
Apollo (god), 19
apprenticeship, 372
Aquitaine (France), 154–5
archers *see* longbow
architecture: Perpendicular, 275; fifteenth-century, 355
aristocracy: prehistoric beginnings, 12, 15; early poetry, 52; *see also* hierarchies (social)
Arthur of Brittany, 159, 161–3, 167, 417
Arthur, King, 48, 213
Arthur, Prince (Henry VII's son): birth, 428; death, 436
Arundel, Richard FitzAlan, 11th Earl of, 289, 293–5, 301
Arundel, Thomas, Bishop of Ely, 290
Ashburnham, John, 238
Ashley, near Cirencester, 177
Athelney, Somerset, 64
Athelstan, King of West Saxons and Mercians, 69–72
Atrebates (tribe), 27

Augustine, St, Archbishop of Canterbury: mission to England, 57–8, 269

Augustine, St (of Hippo): *Soliloquies*, 78

Augustus, Roman Emperor, 26

Aurelianus, Ambrosius, 47

Avebury, Wiltshire, 7

Bacon, Francis: on Richard III's laws, 420; on Lovel, 429

Bacon, Roger, 226

Bagot, Sir William, 292

Baldock, 138

Ball, John, 144, 279, 283–4

Balliol, Edward de, King of Scotland, 252

Balliol, John de, King of Scotland, 218–19

Bannockburn, battle of (1314), 233–4

baptism, 247

Barnet, battle of (1471), 390

barrows *see* burial

bathing and bathhouses, 250

'Battle of Malden, The' (poem), 81

Beaufort, Cardinal Henry, Bishop of Winchester: as chancellor, 333–4, 336; advises Henry VI, 336, 338

Beaufort, Lady Margaret, 419

Becket, St Thomas, Archbishop of Canterbury: and church–state conflict, 110, 145; shrine and pilgrims, 121, 147; background and character, 132–3; relations and conflicts with Henry II, 132–5, 144–5; and crowning of Henry the Younger, 145; excommunicates Archbishop of York, 145; murdered in Canterbury Cathedral, 146–7; condemned by Lollards, 272

Bede, Venerable, 52–4, 57, 59, 377

Bedford, John of Lancaster, Duke of: in regency of Henry VI, 333, 335; and Joan of Arc, 335–6; death, 336

beer: trade, 356

Belers, Robert, 238

Belgae (tribe), 22, 56, 445

Belloc, Hilaire, 120

'benefit of clergy', 147

*Beowulf*, 54, 62, 86

Beresford (Esberfort), Lord Simon de, 244

Bernard of Clairvaux, St, 130

Berwick Field, battle of (1403), 311–12

Bible, Holy: English translations, 171

Bill of Rights (1689), 173

birth: conditions, 247

Black Death: outbreak in England (1348), 260; effects and mortality, 261–3, 283, 354

Blackheath: in Peasants' Revolt, 280, 284; Jack Cade's rebel camp at, 345–6

Blocking, John, 339

Blore Heath, battle of (1459), 363

Blount, Sir Thomas, 309–10

Bluestonehenge, 10

Bolingbroke *see* Henry IV, King

Bonefaunte, William, 182

Boniface of Savoy, Archbishop of Canterbury, 192

Bordeaux, 349

Borzeas (god), 19

Bosworth Field, battle of (1485), 423–6

Boudicca (or Boadicea), Queen of Iceni, 28–9, 54

Bouvines, battle of (1214), 169–70

Brackenbury, Sir Robert, 416

Bramwyk, Robert de, 182

Braose, Matilda de, 167

Braose, William de, 166

brigands and highwaymen, 216

Brigantes (tribe), 22, 28, 51

Bristol: merchants travel overseas, 437

Britain: origin of name, 19

Britons: defined, 41

Brittany and Bretons (France), 49, 384, 430, 432

bronze: manufacture, 16

Bronze Age, 12–15; customs, 24

Browne, Sir Thomas: *Hydriotaphia, Urn Burial*, 13–14

Bruce, David II, King of Scotland, 259

Bruce, Robert VIII, King of Scotland, 221–2, 229, 232–4, 239–40, 245; death, 252

Brunanburgh, battle of (937), 70

Buckingham, Henry Stafford, 2nd Duke of, 405–7, 417–18

Buckingham, Humphrey Stafford, 1st Duke of, 349

bureaucracy: increase under Henry I, 117, 126; and Henry III, 201

Burgh, Hubert de, 184–5, 188

Burgundy: Charles the Bold, Duke of, Edward IV forms alliance with, 384, 399–400; marriage to Margaret of York, 384, 388

Burgundy, John II (the Fearless), Duke of, 327

Burgundy, Margaret of York, Duchess of, 384, 388, 428–9, 432, 435, 437

Burgundy, Philip the Good, Duke of, 335, 337

burial: prehistoric, 7–14, 17; East Angles, 54; procedure, 250

Bury St Edmunds: parliament in (1447), 340; conflict between monks and citizenry, 411

Buxton: holy well of St Anne, 121

Byrhtferth (Benedictine monk), 43

Cabot, John, 356, 437

Cabot, Sebastian, 437

Cadbury (hill fort), 48

Cade, Jack, 56, 345–7

Caernarfon Castle, Wales, 214, 229

Caesar, Julius: invades England, 12, 25–6; on Druids, 21; *Comentarii de Bello Gallico*, 23

Calais: English capture, 253; Edward III in, 259, 264, 267; Thomas of Woodstock murdered at, 294, 296; Henry V marches on, 324, 326; Duke of Burgundy threatens, 337; remains in English hands, 343, 380; Duke of York protects, 361; Warwick in, 361, 364, 385

Calehill Heath, Kent, 344

calendar: and festivals, 204–6; *see also* space and time

Calvinists, 275

Cambridge University: founding and early development, 373–5

Cannynges, William, 356

canon law: Lanfranc introduces, 103

Canterbury: name, 55; archbishopric, 59; house density, 74; pilgrims, 120–1; Cathedral, 276; *see also* Becket, St Thomas

Cantii (tribe), 22

Canute, King of the English, Danes and Norwegians, 83–4, 97, 102

Caratacus, 27

Cartimandua, Queen of Brigantes, 28

Cassivellaunus, 26

Castillon, battle of (1453), 349

castles: Norman, 97–8, 100; in Wales, 213–14

Castor, Cambridgeshire, 34

cathedrals: built, 100

Catherine of Aragon, Queen of Henry VIII, 436

Catterick, 24

cattle: domesticated, 7

Caxton, William, 337, 392; *The Game and the Playe of the Chesse*, 342

Ceawlin (Saxon leader), 49

Cecilia (William the Conqueror's daughter), 88

Celtic church, 58

Celtic languages, 6, 41, 50

Celts: origins, 5

cemeteries and churchyards, 250

Cernunnos (god), 20

chancery: developed under Henry I, 117; under Edward I, 217

Channel, English: formed, 5

Channel Islands: retained by King John, 163

Charlemagne, King of Frankish Empire, 62

Charles I, King: and Petition of Right, 173

Charles IV, King of France, 240

Charles V (the Wise), King of France, 266, 279

Charles VI, King of France, 327

Charles VII, King of France: crowned, 335; captures Paris, 337; reoccupies Normandy, 342–3

Charles VIII, King of France, 431–2

Chaucer, Geoffrey: writes in English, 268; *Canterbury Tales*, 144, 147, 188, 268, 275; 'The Miller's Tale', 44; 'Tale of Melibee', 255; *Troilus and Criseyde*, 268

Cheddar Gorge, 2

Chester: footways, 140

childhood, 370–2, 376; *see also* education; schools

chivalry, 155–6

Christianity: introduced in Roman England, 36–7; under Anglo-Saxons, 51, 57; rich statues, 53–4; conversions under Augustine and Paulinus, 57; Roman Church prevails, 58; Church organization, 59–60; as unifying force, 59; Viking assault on, 62; prevails over Danish invaders, 65; Church reforms under Normans, 103; Church material wealth and landowning, 269–71; secular clergy, 269; practices and beliefs challenged by Lollards, 271–5; heretics burned at stake, 274–5; English saints, 275; tensions with sovereign, 445

*Chronique de la Trahison et Mort de Richard II*, 302

Church of England: in Henry V's reign, 329

Church, the *see* Christianity

churches: design, 75; Perpendicular style, 275–6; *see also* cathedrals

churchyards *see* cemeteries

Cicero, 27

Cistercians, Order: settle in England, 118, 126; practise eviction, 152

Clarence, George, Duke of: and recognition of Elizabeth Woodville as queen, 383; Warwick promises crown to, 384–5, 389; proposed marriage to Warwick's daughter, 385; Edward IV seeks friendship, 386; in Warwick's rebellion, 387–8; deserts Warwick for Henry VI, 389; rivalry with Edward IV, 398–9, 401–2; murdered in Tower, 402–3, 417

Clarendon, Constitutions of (1164), 134

class (social): system develops, 144; *see also* hierarchies

Claudius, Roman Emperor, 22, 27

climate: variability, 42–4; human effect, 43

clocks, 268, 397

Clyn, John, 261

coal: Romans and, 34

Coelius (Coel Hen; 'Old King Cole'), 39

coins and coinage: under Normans, 102; debased under Henry I, 114

Coke, Sir Edward, 173

Colchester (Camulodunum), 27–8; cloth manufacture, 138

Coleswain of Lincoln, 99

commerce *see* trade

common people: lives and conditions, 56, 222–4, 354, 393; effect of Black Death on, 262; dress and behaviour regulated by law, 263–4

Commons, House of *see* parliament

*communitas* (local self-rule), 176, 198

Commynes, Philippe de, 393, 401

*Complaint of the Poor Commons of Kent*, 56

Constantine the Great, Roman Emperor, 36

Conway Castle, Wales, 214, 299–301

Conyers, Sir John ('Robin of Redesdale'; 'Robin Mend-All'), 384–5

cooking *see* food and drink

Cornwall: Pytheas visits, 19; Celtic language, 50

coronations (royal), 78; *see also* individual monarchs

Cotton, Sir Robert, 172

Council Learned in the Law, 439

courtly love, 155–6

courts of law, 143

Coventry, 138

Crane, Matilda, 137

cranes (lifting), 268

Crécy, battle of (1346), 258–9, 267

crime: rises at times of harvest failure, 44; violent, 177–9, 181; and punishment, 179–80; prevalence under Henry VI, 341–2

*Crowland Chronicle*, 392, 401, 403–4

Crusade, Third, 156–7

Cunobelinus, 22

cursus monuments, 9

customs: prehistoric origins, 24; and continuity, 317–19, 443

customs duties: under Edward I, 215, 220

Cuthbert, St, 70

Danegeld (tax), 81

Danelaw, the, 65–6, 68, 83

Danes *see* Denmark

David I, King of Scotland, 123

'Deadmen's Den' (Blore Heath battlefield), 363

death *see* burial; mortality

*Deeds of Henry V, The*, 324, 329

Deira, kingdom of, 51–2

Denmark: Viking raiders from, 62–3, 81–2; invasions and settlement in England, 63–9; subjects fight on English side at Hastings, 85

Despenser, Henry, Bishop of Norwich, 287

Despenser, Hugh le (father and son), 236–7, 240–2, 245

diet *see* food and drink

doctors, 248–50

*Domesday Book* ('The King's Book'), 91, 98, 104–6

domestic life: in Paston letters, 351–4

Dominican Order, 187–8

Dover: name, 55

dress: in Bronze Age, 13; under Romans, 34; Anglo-Saxon, 53, 76; legislation on, 263

drink *see* food and drink

Druids, 20–2, 29–30, 264

drunkenness, 181–2

Dublin: as Norse trading centre, 69

Dudley, Edmund, 439–40

Dumnonii (tribe), 22

Dunstan, St, Archbishop of Canterbury, 78

Durham: Cathedral, 100; pilgrimages to, 120; Germanic structures, 444–5

Durotriges (tribe), 22, 49

East Anglia: settled, 54; Danes in, 63–4

East Saxons, 55–6, 445

East Stoke, battle of (1487), 429

economic activity: fifteenth century improvement, 355–6; *see also* trade; wool

Edgar Atheling, 86

Edgar, King of the English, 78

Edinburgh, 53

Edington, battle of (878), 65

Edith, Queen of Henry I, 113, 128

Edmund Ironside, King of the English, 83

education: children's, 371–2; university, 372–3; *see also* schools

Edward I, King: captures Gwynedd, 50; wars against Scotland and Wales, 189, 213–14, 218–22, 225; and de Montfort's war with Henry III, 196–7; imprisoned as hostage, 197; escapes and defeats de Montfort at Evesham, 201–2; on crusade, 202; accession and coronation, 210–11; attempted assassination, 210; interest in Gascony, 210, 215, 217, 219; soldierly qualities, 210–11; appearance and personality, 211; reclaims father's lost lands, 211–12; taxes and customs, 211–12, 214–15, 220–1; authority, 212, 217; and international finance, 213, 215; represses and expels Jews, 213, 225, 228; law and administration reforms, 215–17; raises paid troops, 216; and death of first wife (Eleanor), 217–18; remarries (Margaret), 219; death, 222

Edward II, King: acclaimed Prince of Wales, 229; birth and upbringing, 229; character and tastes, 230; coronation, 230; marriage and children, 230–1; relations with Piers Gaveston, 230–2; baronial opposition to, 232–3; conflict with Scots, 232–4, 239–40; and execution of Gaveston, 233; disgraced by Bannockburn defeat, 234; appoints Despenser chamberlain, 236; provokes civil war and violence, 236–9; authority and

Edward II, King (*cont.*)
tyrannical rule, 239–40, 289; calls parliament at York (1322), 239; dispute over Gascony, 240; Isabella rebels against, 241–2; deposed and killed, 243–4; supposed survival and peregrinations, 244–5; military ineptness, 252; Richard II and, 289

Edward III, King: father sends to France to do fealty for Gascony, 240; and rebellion against father, 242; character, 245, 251; crowned, 245; has Mortimer killed, 246; reign and administration, 251–2; wars with Scotland, 252, 259–60; claims throne of France, 253–4, 266; restores knightly virtues, 253–4; and conduct of Hundred Years War, 254–5, 258–60, 264, 266; as warrior, 254; taxation, 255–6; relations with parliament, 256; asserts authority, 257; invades Normandy, 258; and Black Death, 264; and capture of King John II of France, 265; accepts treaties and truces in France, 266; achievements, 267; death, 267

Edward IV, King (*earlier* Earl of March and Duke of York): Black Book, 319; in Wars of the Roses, 366–7; appearance and character, 368, 378–9; crowned, 368; extravagance and display, 379, 382; treatment of Lancastrians, 379–80; foreign policy, 380, 384, 399; strong rule, 380–1; view of French, 380; marriage to commoner (Elizabeth Woodville), 382–3, 409; sociability, 382; and Robin of Redesdale rebellion, 384–5; captured, confined in Warwick Castle and released, 385–6; defeats Lincolnshire rebels (1470), 387; and Warwick's 1470 invasion, 387–8; flees to Holland, 388; returns to England to counter Warwick, 389–90; defeats Warwick at Barnet, 390–1; participates in trade, 392; and succession, 398, 404; purges enemies,

399; treaty with Louis XI (1475), 400–1; has Clarence killed, 402–3, 417; arranges family marriages, 403; illness and death, 403–4; solvency, 404

Edward V, King (*earlier* Prince of Wales): marriage prospects, 403; accession and reign, 404, 410; confined in Tower and killed, 406–8, 416–17; and Richard III's seizure of crown, 409

Edward the Confessor, King of the English, 78, 80, 84–6, 102, 120, 186, 293

Edward the Elder, King of the Angles and Saxons, 68–9

Edward, Prince (Richard III's son): death, 420–1

Edward, Prince of Wales (Henry VI's son): birth, 349–50; mother protects, 362; as claimant to throne, 365, 387; and Wars of the Roses, 365–6; betrothal and marriage to Warwick's daughter, 387, 398; killed at Tewkesbury, 391

Edward of Woodstock, Prince of Wales ('the Black Prince'): military activities, 264–5; health decline and death, 266–7; sets up court at Bordeaux, 266

Edwin, King of Northumberland, 53, 58

Eleanor of Aquitaine, Queen of Henry II, 130, 148, 162

Eleanor of Castile, Queen of Edward I: death, 217–18; Crosses, 218; and birth of Edward II, 229

Eleanor of Provence, Queen of Henry III, 188, 192

Elizabeth I, Queen: authority, 78

Elizabeth II, Queen: coronation, 78

Elizabeth (Woodville), Queen of Edward IV: marriage, 382–3; twice takes sanctuary in Westminster Abbey, 388, 405–6, 419; children, 398; hostility to Clarence, 403; and son's succession to throne, 405; surrenders son Richard to Richard III, 408; and

Lady Margaret Beaufort, 419; supports Lambert Simnel, 428–9; sent to nunnery, 429–30

Elizabeth of York, Queen of Henry VII: marriage to Henry, 419, 422, 426, 428; Richard III's supposed plan to marry, 421; death, 436

Elmet (kingdom), 50

Eltham palace, 289

Ely: as centre of Hereward's resistance, 99; school, 371

Emma, Queen of Ethelred and of Canute, 83

Empson, Richard, 439

enclosures: in Bronze Age, 12–13; eighteenth-century Enclosure Acts, 74; and sheep breeding, 358

Engels, Friedrich, 17

England: early settlement, 1–5, 24; formed, 4–5; regional divisions, 6, 15; Romans invade and colonize, 12, 22–3, 25–31, 35; tribes, 22–3; government and social development under Romans, 32–6; early Christianity in, 36–7; incursion by northern tribes, 37–8; Roman rule ends, 38–9; post-Roman division and administration, 39–40; name, 41; under Anglo-Saxons, 50–1; converted to Christianity, 57–9; urbanization under Alfred the Great, 66–7; as Anglo-Saxon realm, 70; administrative units, 71–2; land ownership, 71–2; national identity formed, 86; involvement with France, 91; resistance to William the Conqueror, 97–9; under Norman rule, 102; frontier with Scotland defined, 108; development of bureaucracy, 117; Normans assimilated, 118; increased prosperity under Henry II, 136; archives and records develop, 164, 201; civil disorder under Edward II, 236–9; rivalry with France, 252–3; in Hundred Years War against France, 253, 258, 322, 335, 337, 339; popular discontent (1377), 278; established as nation under Henry V, 329; foreigners' views of, 331–2; loses possessions in France, 337, 339; economic fortunes in fifteenth century, 354–8, 392; prosperity under Edward IV, 404; historical change, 443; political and legal systems, 443–4; foreign-born monarchs, 445

English language: under Normans, 101; literary and official development, 268; prevalence under Henry V, 329

Epona (horse goddess), 20

Ermine Street, 28

esquires, 200

Essex: rebels in Peasants' Revolt, 282–3, 286

estates (landed), 72–3

Ethelred II ('the unready'), King of the English, 81–3, 184

Eton College, 337

Evesham, battle of (1265), 201–2

Evesham, monk of (chronicler), 286

Evreux, Louis, Count of, 229

exchequer: developed under Henry I, 117

fairs and markets, 136, 138

Falkirk, battle of (1298), 221

famines: (1086), 106; (1257–8), 193; (1314–17), 234

farming: beginnings, 7–8; Bronze Age, 12–13, 33; Iron Age, 19, 33; under Romans, 33–4; and climate change, 42–3; under Anglo-Saxons, 73–4; under Henry III, 190; and seasons, 204–7; regional diversity, 207–8; routines, 208–9; and a money economy, 358; *see also* harvest failures

Fastolf, Sir John, 342, 356

Faversham monastery, 162

fens: drained under Romans, 34

festivals and pastimes: seasonal, 204–7

feudalism, 102, 167

fields: formed, 12, 23, 444–5; regional diversity and patterns, 207–8

Fieschi, Manuel di, 244

Fishbourne, Sussex, 33

Fitz-Osbert, William (or William the Beard), 160

Fitzstephen, William, 146, 181

fitz Walter, Robert, 169–70, 174

Flanders: rebellion (fourteenth century), 282; English campaign in (1383), 287; French hold, 287–8

Flemings: settle in Pembrokeshire, 114

flint: artefacts, 1; tools, 5, 7; mining, 9

Flint Castle, Wales, 300

Florence: revolt (fourteenth century), 282

Foliot, Gilbert, 397

Folville, Eustace de, 238

Folville, John de, 238

Folville, Richard de, 238

food and drink: Bronze Age, 14; medieval, 394–6

Forest of Dean, 356–7

forest law, 100–1

forests *see* woods and forests

Formby Point, 3

*Forme of Cury, The* (cookery book), 396

Fortescue, Sir John: *De Laudibus Legum Angliae*, 342

Foxe, John, 223

France: English involvement with, 91; King John loses empire in, 163–4; Henry III in, 189; in Hundred Years War against England, 189, 253, 258, 265, 322, 335, 337, 339; power struggle with England, 252–3; Edward III claims throne, 253–4, 266; English depredations in, 264–5; Charles V's forces raid south coast, 279; Jacquerie riots, 282; alliance with Scotland against England, 287; threatens England from Flanders, 287–8; Henry V's campaigns in, 323–4, 328; Henry VI crowned king, 334–5; fleet sacks Sandwich (1457), 363; Edward IV's view of, 380; treaty with Edward IV (1475), 400; finances Henry Tudor's invasion against Richard III, 422

Franciscan Order, 187–8

Frederick II, Holy Roman Emperor, 188

Frederick III, Holy Roman Emperor, 432

free men: in towns, 75, 140, 413; legal rights, 143–4

French language: introduced by Normans, 101

Frisians: settle in England, 47

Froissart, Jean, 254, 286, 331

Fuller, Agnes, 182

Fuller, Thomas: *The Holy State and the Profane State*, 368

Galen, 249

games and sports, 377

Garter, Order of the: instituted (1348), 253–4

Gascony: Henry III in, 189; Edward I values and controls, 210, 217, 219; status of merchants, 215; Edward III does fealty to French king for, 240, 252; in Hundred Years War, 258, 266, 337–8; remains in English hands, 343; surrendered to French, 349

Gaul, Gauls, 23, 25–6

Gaveston, Piers, Earl of Cornwall, 230–3

gentlemen, 200

gentry, formed, 144, 200

Geoffrey of Anjou, 124, 130

Geoffrey, Prince (Henry II's son), 148–9

George, St, 156, 191

Germanic languages, 6

Germanic settlers: in England, 47–52, 56, 444–5

Germanus, Bishop of Auxerre, 40

Geyser, William, 178

Gildas, 20, 48

Girton, Cambridgeshire, 412

Glanville, Ranulph de: tutors King John, 165; *On the Laws and Customs of England*, 141

Glastonbury, 120–1, 213

Glendower, Owen, 310–11

Gloucester Cathedral: Perpendicular style, 276

Gloucester, Gilbert de Clare, 10th Earl of, 234

Gloucester, Humphrey, Duke of: as

protector in Henry VI's minority, 333–6; advises Henry VI on war with France, 338–9; arrest and death, 340–1

Gloucester, Richard, Duke of *see* Richard III, King

Gloucester, Thomas, Duke of (Thomas of Woodstock), 287, 289, 293–4, 296–7, 301, 417

Godiva (or Godgifu) Lady, 85

Gododdin (kingdom), 24, 52

Godwin, Earl of Wessex, 84–5

Gordon, Katherine, 433, 435

Gornay, Lord Thomas de, 244

Gothic art, 187

'Gough' map, 119

Gower, John, 264, 286

Gower Peninsula, 1

*Great Chronicle of London,* 408–9

Gregory the Great, Pope, 59

Guildhall Library, London, 377

guilds, 139, 413

Guinevere, Queen, 213

Guthrum (Danish leader), 65–6

Gwynedd, 50

Gytha (Harold's mother), 98


Hadrian, Roman Emperor, 31

Hadrian's Wall, 31, 36

Hailes Abbey, Gloucestershire, 121

Hakluyt, Richard, 437

Halidon Hill, battle of (1333), 252

Hall, Edward, 429

hamlets, 207–8

handwriting: development of cursive script, 164

Happisburgh, Norfolk, 1

Harald Hardrada, King of Norway, 89–90

Hardy, Thomas, 93; *Tess of the d'Urbervilles,* 22

Harfleur: Henry V besieges and captures, 323–4, 326

Harold Godwinson, King of the English, 86–91

Harold Harefoot, King of the English, 84

'harrowing of the north, the', 98

Harthacanute, King of Denmark, 84

harvest failures: early fourteenth century, 224, 234; *see also* famines

Hastings: burnt by French, 279

Hastings, battle of (1066), 89–90

Hastings, William, Baron, 404, 407–8

Hazlitt, William, 333

Heahmund, Bishop of Sherborne, 59

Helmsley, Yorkshire, 174

henge monuments, 14

Hengist and Horsa, 45

Henry I, King: and yard (measurement), 77; inheritance, 106; reign, 113–17, 126; and succession, 115–16, 122; death, 116; marriage, 128

Henry II, King: and king's touch, 80; administrative and judicial changes, 126–7, 136, 140–2, 150; succeeds Stephen, 127, 130–1; background and character, 130–2, 135; territorial victories, 131; expedition to Normandy, 132; relations and conflicts with Becket, 132–5, 144–5; assertion of authority, 134; temper, 134; speaks no English, 135; increases national prosperity, 136; and murder of Becket, 146; does penance for Becket's death, 147; disputes with sons, 148–9; succession question, 149–50; death and burial, 150; forbids tournaments in England, 155

Henry III, King: crowned, 183; regency council as minor, 184–5; reign, 184, 189–90, 193, 201; character and appearance, 185–7; piety, 185–7; and European affairs, 188–9; marriage, 188, 192; and increase in national prosperity, 190; court and advisers, 191, 194–5; opposed by native barons, 191–5; financial difficulties, 193–4; resumes sovereignty, 195; Simon de Montfort confronts, 195–6; defeat at battle of Lewes, 197–8; summons parliament (1236), 199; administrative complexity, 201; as hostage at battle of Evesham, 201; death and burial, 203, 210; and continuity in law, 319

Henry IV (Bolingbroke), King (*earlier* 1st Duke of Hereford): conflicts with Richard II, 295–7; exiled, 297–8; returns to England to oppose Richard II, 299–300; claims throne, 301–2; negotiates with Richard, 301; accession, 302–3, 308; and rumoured survival of Richard II, 308–9; seen as usurper, 308–9; assassination attempts on, 310; Percy family rebels against, 310–11; revenue raising, 310; defeats Hotspur at Berwick Field, 312; illness, 312–14; Scrope rebels against, 312; rule and administration, 313; and son Henry's ambitions for throne, 314–15; death and burial, 315–16; has Richard II killed, 417

Henry V (of Monmouth), King (*earlier* Prince of Wales): reburies Richard II at Westminster Abbey, 304; wounded at Berwick Field, 312–13; martial prowess, 313, 322, 329; as successor to father, 313–15; appearance and character, 320–1, 329; coronation, 320; piety, 320; campaigns in France, 323–4, 328; Agincourt victory, 324–6; acclaimed in England, 326, 329; builds up navy, 326; marriage, 327–8; death, 328–9; treaty with Charles VI of France (1420), 337

Henry VI, King: peaceful nature, 155, 336–7; ratifies Magna Carta, 173; infancy at father's death, 328, 333; minority, 333–4, 336; crowned as king of England and of France while boy, 334–5; character and appearance, 336, 378; piety, 337; seeks peace in war with France, 337–8; French demand renunciation of claim to crown, 338; marriage, 339, 344; bestows honours, 340; weak rule, 340–1, 362; loses Normandy to Charles VII, 343–4; debts, 344; and Jack Cade rebellion, 345–6; suffers stroke, 348–9; and York–Somerset enmity, 348; treatment and partial recovery, 350; wounded at St Albans, 360; suffers further malady, 361; in Wars of the Roses, 361, 366; captured at Northampton, 364; position challenged by York, 365; rescued at second battle of St Albans, 367; and crowning of Edward IV, 368; flees to Scotland, 369, 379; imprisoned in Tower, 383; released and reinstated, 388–9; Edward IV reconfines to Tower, 390; killed in Tower, 391, 417; marks out site of tomb, 391; Henry VII idealizes, 427

Henry VI, King of Germany, 158

Henry VII (Tudor), King (*earlier* Earl of Richmond): and murder of Princes in the Tower, 417; background, 418–19, 425–7, 445; rebels against Richard III, 418–19, 422; in Brittany, 419; marriage to Elizabeth, 419, 422, 426, 428; claim to throne, 422, 425–6; invades (1485), 422; defeats Richard at Bosworth Field, 423–6; appearance and character, 425, 427; coronation, 425–6; royal bodyguard (yeomen), 427; rule, 427, 438–40; Yorkist opposition to, 427–8; and Lambert Simnel conspiracy, 428–9; son Arthur born, 428; victory at East Stoke (1487), 429; financial stringency, 430, 440; supports Brittany against France, 430; and Perkin Warbeck conspiracy, 431–4, 438; health decline, 435–6, 440; piety and superstiousness, 436; remains unmarried after death of Elizabeth, 436; death, 437–8, 441; encourages overseas trade, 437; court, 438; isolation, 438, 440; reputation, 438, 440

Henry VIII, King: authority, 78; marriage to Catherine of Aragon, 436; legacy from father, 440

Henry, Bishop of Winchester, 122

Henry of Huntingdon, 116

Henry the Younger (Henry II's son): crowned as 'joint king', 144–5, 148; death, 148

heraldry, 200

herbs: medicinal, 249

Hereford, Henry Bolingbroke, 1st Duke of *see* Henry IV, King

heresy, 271–2, 321–2

Hereward the Wake, 99

hierarchies (social): prehistoric, 11–12, 15, 17–18; under Romans, 32; Anglo-Saxon, 50; medieval, 144; development, 200–1; survival, 200; in towns, 413; *see also* class (social)

Higden, Ranulf, 230, 332; *Polychronicon*, 243, 306

highway robbery, 120

hill forts, 18–19, 67

history: nature of, 446–7

Hoccleve, Thomas, 321

Holinshed, Raphael, 427

Homer: *Iliad*, 18

Honorius, Roman Emperor, 38

horse: as means of travel, 120

Hospitallers, Order of, 156

hospitals, 249, 413

houses: medieval design and construction, 92–6

Hugh, Bishop of Lincoln, 132, 159

Hugh de Neville, 162

Hull: brick wall, 138; wool exporters, 268

human sacrifice: in Iron Age, 21

humour: medieval, 438–9

humours, four, 249

Hundred Years War (1337–1453): conduct and campaigns, 154–5, 258–9, 265–6; origins, 189; and English claim to French sovereignty, 253; resumes under Henry V, 322, 329; continues, 335, 337; ends, 349

hundreds (administrative units), 71–2, 86, 102

hunting: by kings, 101

Iceni (tribe), 22, 28, 54

Icknield Way (track), 8, 46

illness and ailments, 248–9

imports: luxury goods in fifteenth century, 356

industry: in fifteenth century, 392–3

Inglewood, Cumbria, 307

Innocent III, Pope, 163, 167, 169–70, 174

inns: roadside, 119–20

inns of court, 142

Ireland: raiders against Vortigern, 45–6; Richard II in, 298; Warbeck in, 433

iron: as new technology, 16–17; under Romans, 34; demand in fifteenth century, 356–7

Iron Age: development, 5, 16–18, 22, 24; religion, 19–21, 24; art, 20

Isabella of Angoulême, Queen of King John, 163, 192

Isabella of France, Queen of Edward II, 230–1, 240–2, 245–6, 251

Isabella of France, second Queen of Richard II, 297

Isabella, wife of Emperor Frederick II, 188

Jack Straw's Castle, Hampstead Heath, 24

Jacquerie (France), 282

James IV, King of Scotland: shelters Perkin Warbeck, 433–4; marries Margaret Tudor, 436

James of St George, Master, 214

Jarrow, 62

jewellery: Bronze Age, 13–14

Jews: Edward I represses and expels, 213, 225, 228; early settlement and legal status in England, 225–8; as moneylenders and moneychangers, 225–6; popular hostility to, 226–7; accused of ritual murder of Christian children, 227–8; census (1239), 227

Joan of Arc, 334–6

Joanna of Castile: Henry VII courts, 436

John II, King of France, 265–6

John of Arderne, 248

John, King: kingship, 79; as 'Lackland', 148; nominated as king of Ireland, 149, 161; and succession to Henry II, 150; barons' rebellion against, 156, 170–1, 174–5; Richard pardons on return, 158–9; swears fealty to Philip II of France and usurps Richard's throne, 158; reputation and character,

John, King (*cont.*)
   160–2, 175–6; succeeds Richard,
   160–1; and death of Arthur of
   Brittany, 162–3; loses empire in
   France, 163–4, 169; raises revenues,
   164–7; travels throughout England,
   164–5; and administration of justice,
   165; campaigning in Britain, 166,
   168–9; dispute with pope over
   appointment of archbishops and
   bishops, 167–8; womanizing, 167;
   excommunicated, 168; accepts pope's
   demands, 169; assumes cross of
   crusader, 170; seals Magna Carta,
   171–4; defies Magna Carta, 173–4;
   death and burial, 175, 183; loses
   treasure in Wash, 175; calls
   parliament (1212), 199; protects
   Jews, 227; killings, 417
John, King of Bohemia, 259
John of Luxemburg, 336
John of Worcester, 123
Johnson, Samuel, 80
Joseph of Arimathea, 121
judges, 141–3
Julian, Roman Emperor, 35
Jurassic Way, 8
juries: origins, 142
Jutes: settle in England, 47, 55–6, 445

Katherine of Valois, Queen of Henry V:
   marriage to Henry, 327–8; remarries
   (Owen Tudor), 366–7
Kenilworth Castle: Edward II at, 242–3;
   John of Gaunt at, 278; Margaret of
   Anjou at, 362
Kent: settlers and administration, 55–6;
   popular revolts, 56; Danish invasion
   (1896), 67; condemns law under
   Henry VI, 341; coast attacked from
   France and Brittany, 344; and
   rebellion under Jack Cade, 344–6
Keston, Kent, 33
keyhold tenure, 93
King's College, Cambridge, 337
king's touch: as cure for scrofula, 80
kingship: origins and authority, 77–80;

and divine right, 80; and hunting,
   101; and lawlessness following death
   of, 122; Richard II and, 288–9, 292–3;
   tensions with nobility and Church,
   445
Knighton, Henry, 261
knights: under Normans, 102; status, 144,
   200; and chivalry, 155–6; and
   summoning of parliament, 199–200;
   'distraint of' (order), 215

labour: value following Black Death,
   262–3, 283
Lambarde, William: *The Perambulation
   of Kent*, 56
Lancaster family: in Wars of Roses, 359,
   361–3; extinguished, 391
Lancaster, John of Gaunt, Duke of:
   house burned by Tyler's rebels, 80;
   governs during Edward III's illness,
   267; unpopularity, 267, 281; and John
   Wycliffe, 270; as Chaucer's patron,
   275; Richard II fears as rival, 287;
   presides at Arundel's trial, 294; and
   son Bolingbroke's conflict with
   Richard II, 296; death, 298; marriage
   to Katherine Swynford, 334; and
   house of Lancaster, 359
Lancaster, Thomas of *see* Thomas, Earl
   of Lancaster
land ownership: and lordship, 71–4; as
   cause of disputes, 208; and social
   standing, 208; and land shortage, 224;
   in Black Death, 262–3
landscape: formed by farming and field
   system, 12, 23
Lanfranc, Archbishop of Canterbury,
   103, 107–9
Langland, William: *Piers Plowman*, 176,
   262, 268, 292, 306, 395, 421
Langton, Stephen, Archbishop of
   Canterbury, 167–71
languages: prehistoric, 6; *see also* English
   language
Laurence of St Martin, Sir, 273
law: under Normans, 101–2; reforms
   under Henry II, 140–3; under

Edward I, 215–16; custom and precedent in, 318–19; ineffectiveness under Henry VI, 341–2; Edward IV intervenes in, 381–2

lawyers: origins, 142

lead mines, 34

Leeds: founded, 137–8

Leeds Castle, Kent, 237

legal rights of free men, 143–4

*Leges Henrici Primi*, 170

Leofric, Earl of Mercia, 84–5

Leopold, Duke of Austria, 157

le Toruk, Jacob, 226

Lewes, battle of (1264), 197–8

Leyburn, Roger, 201

life expectancy, 250, 285

Lincoln: population, 74

Lincoln, John de la, Earl of, 428–9

Lincolnshire: revolt (1470), 386–7

Lindisfarne, 61–2

Lindisfarne Gospels, 86

Lindley Hall Farm, Leicestershire, 5

literacy, 376–7, 414

Lithere, Benedict, 182

livestock: in medieval period, 209

living standards: improve in fifteenth century, 355

Lollards, 272–5, 284, 321–2, 421

London: Boudicca attacks, 28–9; as Roman capital of Britannia Superior, 35; population, 74, 138; burned by Danish raiders, 81; medieval house design, 94–5; road links, 119; mayor and aldermen established, 138; plan, 139; communal government, 140, 176; citizens rebel against Richard I's taxes, 160; rebel barons occupy (1215–16), 170–1, 174; Prince Louis of France in, 183; supports de Montfort against Henry III, 196; Edward I imposes taxes on, 220; and rebellion against Edward II, 242; in Peasants' Revolt (1381), 280; Jack Cade rebels in, 346–7; improvements and rebuilding, 355

longbow: English mastery of, 259, 265, 268, 324

Lords, House of *see* parliament

lordship: and land ownership, 71–4; and feudalism, 102–3; *see also* aristocracy

Loudun Hill, battle of (1306), 222, 229

Louis VII, King of France, 146

Louis VIII (the Lion), King of France (*earlier* Prince), 174, 183, 186

Louis IX, King of France, 188–9

Louis XI, King of France, 380, 383–4, 387, 391, 399–401

Lovel, Francis, 1st Viscount, 428–9

Loveraz, Richard de, 179

Lud (or Nud; god), 20

Ludlow, Shropshire: in Wars of Roses, 364

Lutherans, 275

luxury goods: imported, 356

Lydgate, John, 376

Lynn (King's Lynn), Norfolk, 238–9, 388

Macaulay, Thomas Babington, Baron, 443

Maelbeath (or Macbeth), 84

Magna Carta (1215), 156, 166, 171–5, 184, 193, 199, 220–1, 255, 257

Maiden Castle, Dorset, 27

Maidstone Prison: prisoners freed, 279

Maine, France, 339

Malcolm III (Canmore), King of Scotland, 107–8

Malcolm IV, King of Scotland, 131

Maldon, battle of (991), 81

Malory, Thomas: *Le Morte Darthur*, 156, 254

Manchester: name, 30

Mancini, Dominic, 378, 417

manor: as centre of agrarian life, 105–6; court records, 136–7; at Wharram Percy, 151–2; accounts, 222, 263

Map, Walter, 141

March, Edmund Mortimer, 3rd Earl of, 302

March, Roger Mortimer, 1st Earl of *see* Mortimer, Roger

Margaret of Anjou, Queen of Henry VI: marriage to Henry, 339, 344; birth of son, 349; opposes Richard of York, 350; and threat to son's succession,

Margaret of Anjou (*cont.*)
350, 365; in Wars of the Roses, 362, 365–8; shut out of London, 368; flees to Scotland, 369; takes refuge in Anjou, 383; forms alliance with Warwick against Edward IV, 384, 387–9; taken prisoner at Tewkesbury, 390–1; incarcerated in Tower and ransomed by Louis XI, 391; Louis XI supports, 399

Margaret, Queen of Edward I, 219

Margaret Tudor, Queen of James IV of Scotland, 436

Margaret of York *see* Burgundy, Margaret of York, Duchess of

Markeby, John de, 182

Martin, St, 156

Mase, Harry, 345

Mass, the, 277

Matilda (*earlier* Edith), Queen of Henry I, 113

Matilda (Maud), Empress (Henry I's daughter): and succession to Henry, 115–16; conflict with Stephen over crown, 122–6; hailed as 'lady of England', 125; unpopularity, 125; retires to Rouen, 127

Maximilian I, Holy Roman Emperor, 432

measurement: inexactness, 396; *see also* yard

Meaux, siege of (1421), 328

medicine: practice of, 248–50

megaliths, 9, 23, 444; *see also* Stonehenge

melancholy (humour), 248–9

merchant adventurers, 356

Mercia, kingdom of, 55, 61

Meredith, George, 443

Merfield, William, 345

Meriden, Warwickshire, 5

Mesolithic people, 3–4, 7

Middle Saxons, 55

Middleham, north Yorkshire, 398

Milton, John: *Paradise Lost*, 446–7

minsters (communities of priests and monks), 59–60

miracle and mystery plays, 139

monasteries: established by Normans, 100; children recruited to, 371

Mons Badonicus, battle of (490), 47

Montfort, Eleanor de, Countess of Leicester, 195

Montfort, Simon de, Earl of Leicester: opposes Henry III, 195–8; and summoning of parliament, 199–200; defeated at Evesham (1265), 201; death and burial, 201–2

Morast (fruit drink), 394

More, Sir Thomas: personal display, 133; on literacy in England, 376; on Edward IV, 378; on Richard III, 407–8, 416; on Henry VII, 440

*mort d'ancestor* (legal procedure), 143

mortality: age of, 76; infant, 247

Mortimer, Anne, 347

Mortimer, Roger, 1st Earl of March, 240, 243, 245–6, 251

Mortimer's Cross, battle of (1461), 366–7

Morton, John, Archbishop of Canterbury (*earlier* Bishop of Ely), 399, 407

Motte, Agnes, 238

Mowbray, Thomas *see* Norfolk, 1st Duke of

murrain (disease), 207, 235

names: changes under Normans, 128–9

navy: King John constructs, 164; Henry V builds up, 326

Neckam, Alexander, 395

Nefyn, Wales, 214

Neolithic: as term, 3, 7

Neolithic period, 7–12, 444–5

Neville family: support Yorkists in Wars of Roses, 360, 363–4

Neville, George, Archbishop of York, 385, 390

Neville's Cross, battle of (1346), 259

Newfoundland, 437

Norfolk, John Howard, 1st Duke of, 415, 423

Norfolk, Roger Bigod, 4th Earl of, 194, 219–20

Norfolk, Thomas Mowbray, 1st Duke of, 295-8

Normandy: Henry I invades and conquers, 113; Henry II's expedition to, 132; King John loses to Philip Augustus, 163-4; Edward III invades, 258; Henry V in, 323, 326-8; France reclaims, 337, 342-3

Normans: and separation of Church and state, 59; Ethelred marries into, 82; Edward the Comfessor's loyalty to, 84; under William, 87-8; invade and conquer England, 88-90; oppressive rule and occupation of England, 98-100; buildings, 100; introduce French language, 101; assimilated, 118, 164; names, 128-9; council, 199; wheat-growing and eating, 394-5; dynasty, 445

Norsemen *see* Vikings

North America: English exploration and settlement, 437

North Sea: formed, 4

Northampton: parliament (1380), 279; scholastic community, 373-4

Northampton, battle of (1460), 364

Northumberland, Henry Percy, 1st Earl of, 290, 299-300, 310, 312

Northumberland, Henry Percy, 2nd Earl of (Hotspur), 299, 310-12, 360

Northumberland, Henry Percy, 4th Earl of, 423

Northumberland, Henry Percy, 5th Earl of, 439

Northumberland, kingdom of: power, 61; Vikings conquer, 64; Malcolm IV surrenders to Henry II, 131

Norway: Viking raiders from, 61-2

Norwich: population, 74, 138, 411; social divisions, 139; grammar school, 371

Noseles, Philip, 136

Noteman, Andrew, 137

Offa's Dyke, 61

Oldcastle, Sir John, 321-2

Orderic Vitalis, 99, 116-17

Ordinance of Labourers (1349), 262

Orkney: surrendered to Scotland, 69

Orleans: Joan of Arc lifts siege, 334-5

Orleton, Adam, Bishop of Hereford, 243

Osborne, John, 351

Otto IV, Holy Roman Emperor, 169

Oxford, John de Vere, 12th Earl of, 379

Oxford, Provisions of (1258), 194

Oxford University: teaching of law, 142; origins, 372-3; student violence and misbehaviour, 374-5; learning, 375

'oyer et terminer' commission, 381

Page, John and Agnes, 223

Palaeolithic: as term, 3

Palfrey, William, 178

Pandulf (papal legate), 184

papacy: and appointment of archbishop of Canterbury, 167-8; *see also* Christianity

Paris: Treaty of (1259), 252; in Hundred Years War, 258; falls to Charles VII, 337

Paris, Matthew, 160, 168, 192-3

parish: development, 75; numbers, 396

parish churches: as communal centres, 276-7; show evidence of affluence, 355

parish priests, 75, 269-70

Parisii (tribe), 22, 51

parliament: origins and development, 198-200, 442; Edward I summons, 212, 214; first records (1316), 217; Edward II summons, 239; and consent to taxation, 255-6; growing power during Hundred Years War, 256; relations with Edward III, 256-7, 267; 'Good' (1376), 267; in Westminster Hall, 288; conflict with Richard II, 289-91, 293-4; 'Wonderful' (1386-7), 290; 'Merciless' (1389), 291; relations with Henry IV, 310; meets in Bury St Edmunds (1447), 340; Henry VII ignores, 438

pastimes *see* festivals and pastimes

Paston family: life and letters, 341, 351-4

Paston, Agnes, 344, 376

Paston, Clement, 352

Paston, Elizabeth, 376

Paston, John, 341–2, 351–3, 361, 367–8, 386, 390
Paston, Margaret, 351, 354, 389
Paston, William, 353
Patrick, St: *Confessions*, 40
Paulinus (missionary), 57
peasantry: and village life, 73; houses, 93; condition improves in Black Death, 262–3, 268, 354; *see also* serfs
Peasants' Revolt (1381), 56, 279–85
Pembroke, Jasper Tudor, Earl of: commands Queen Margaret's forces, 366–7; and Henry Tudor's invasion, 422; sends Henry to Brittany, 425
Pembroke, William Marshal, 1st Earl of, 184
Pembrokeshire: Flemings in, 114
Penny, William, 351
Pepys, Samuel, 69
Percy family: rebels against Henry IV, 310–11; power in north, 403
Percy, Henry (Hotspur) *see* Northumberland, 2nd Earl of
Perpendicular style (architecture), 275–6
Perrers, Alice, 266–7
Peter de Blois, 132
Peter des Rivaux, 188, 191
Peter des Roches, Bishop of Winchester, 184–5, 188, 191
Peter of Savoy, Earl of Richmond, 192
Peter, St, 271
Peterborough: Bronze Age remains, 15
Peterborough Abbey: suffers under Henry I, 114; and warfare between Stephen and Matilda, 126
Petition of Right (seventeenth century), 173
Philip II (Philip Augustus), King of France, 158, 163, 169, 174
Philip VI of Valois, King of France, 253, 258–9
Philippa of Hainault, Queen of Edward III, 241
Pickering, Vale of, Yorkshire, 3
Picquigny, treaty of (1475), 400–1
Picts: land of (Prydyn), 19; harass Romans and English, 35–6, 40, 45–6

pilgrims, 120–1
Pilgrims Way, The, 8, 120
Pistor, John, 223–4
Pius II, Pope, 336
plague: in 540s, 49; *see also* Black Death
Plantagenet dynasty: succession, 130; killings, 417–18
Plautius, Aulus, 27
Pliny the Elder, 21
poems, songs and tales: heroic, 18, 52–3
Poitiers, battle of (1356), 265
Poitou, 189
poll tax: introduced (1377), 267; (1380), 279
Poppelau, Nicholas von, 331
population: in Neolithic period, 7–8; increase in Bronze Age, 12; in Iron Age, 19, 22; reduced by plague (1540s), 49; towns, 74, 138, 411; increase in Henry III's reign, 190; falls in fourteenth and fifteenth centuries, 234; reduced by Black Death, 261, 354
portents: and civil unrest, 359; of two kings, 366, 368
Pounchon, William, 223
Poundbury, Dorset, 36
Prasutagus, King of Iceni, 28
Preseli Hills, south-west Wales, 11
prices: rise under King John, 165–6; increase under Henry III, 190; rise during harvest failures, 224, 235
priests *see* parish priests
Princes in the Tower *see* Tower of London
printing, 377, 392
Procopius of Caesarea, 38
property: inheritance under Normans, 103; legal disputes over, 142
*Prophecies of Merlin*, 214
proverbs, 439
public houses, 120
punishment: for crimes, 179–81
Puttock, Stephen, 222–3
Pytheas, 19

Quernbetere, Alice, 182

rabbit: introduced to England, 114
Radcot, battle of (1388), 291
Ralph de Crockerlane, 94
Ravenspur, Yorkshire, 389
Redwald, King of the East Angles, 54
Reformation, the, 275
Regenbald, chancellor, 97
Regnenses (tribe), 56
religion: Iron Age, 19–21; *see also*
    Christianity; Druids
Restitutus, Bishop of London, 37
Rheged (kingdom), 52
Riccardi bankers (of Lucca), 213, 215
Richard I (Lionheart), King: kingship,
    79; and 'legal memory', 141; disputes
    with father and brothers, 148–50;
    background and character, 154–7;
    coronation, 154; on Third Crusade to
    Holy Land, 156–7; captured and
    ransomed, 157–8; returns to England
    and pardons John, 158–9; and
    succession, 159–61; troubled reign,
    159–60; and Jews, 227
Richard II, King: authority, 79–80,
    288–95; peaceful nature, 155, 288;
    crowned aged ten, 278; confronts
    Peasants' Revolt, 280–3, 285;
    appearance and manner, 285–6, 293;
    first marriage (to Anne of Bohemia),
    286–7; campaign against Scots, 287;
    court and favourites, 287; conflict
    with parliament, 289–91, 294;
    deposed and reinstated, 291; mediates
    between Lords and Commons, 292;
    piety, 293; purges lords, 294–5; exiles
    Bolingbroke, 297–8; halts
    Bolingbroke–Mowbray duel, 297;
    second marriage (to Isabella), 297;
    sails to Ireland, 298; returns to
    England to oppose Bolingbroke,
    299–300; Bolingbroke negotiates
    with, 301; renounces throne in favour
    of Bolingbroke, 301–3; death and
    burial, 303–4, 417; rumoured survival,
    308–9, 311; posthumous support for,
    309–10; kills Thomas of Gloucester,
    417

Richard III, King (*earlier* Duke of
    Gloucester): reputation, 160; and
    Princes in the Tower, 163, 416–19; as
    rumoured murderer of Henry VI, 391;
    background and service to Edward
    IV, 398; and succession to throne,
    398, 403, 406–7; power in north, 403;
    and Edward V's accession, 405; seizes
    and confines Edward V, 405–6;
    appointed Protector, 406; deformed
    arm, 408; has Hastings executed, 408;
    claims crown, 409–10, 418; crowned,
    415–16; makes circuit of kingdom,
    415–16; appearance and character, 416;
    rebellions against, 418–19; rule,
    419–20; piety, 420–1, 423; and threat
    of Henry Tudor, 422; and Henry
    Tudor's invasion and campaign, 423;
    killed at Bosworth Field and bones
    scattered, 423–4
Richard of Crudwell, 177
Richard, Duke of York: confined in
    Tower and murdered, 408, 416;
    Perkin Warbeck impersonates, 431
Richard, Earl of Cornwall and King of
    the Romans (Henry III's brother),
    185, 189
Richard le Brewer, 182
Riche, Geoffrey, 182
Rivers, Anthony Woodville, 2nd Earl,
    404–5, 408
roads and trackways: prehistoric, 8;
    pilgrim routes, 23–4, 120;
    development and maintenance,
    119–20; continuity, 444
Robert, Duke of Normandy, 106–8,
    113–14
Robert, Earl of Gloucester, 123–5
Robert of Reading, 236
Robert of Wetherby, 305
Robin Hood, 202, 305–7
Robin of Redesdale *see* Conyers, Sir
    John, 384
Rochester castle, 174
Roger of Hoveden, 181
Roger of Portland, 238
Roger of Wendover, 160

Roland the Farter (jester), 131–2

Roman Catholicism: Church prevails in England, 58

Rome (ancient): invades and occupies England, 12, 22–3, 25–31; imperial frontiers, 31, 36; social and cultural influence in England, 31–6, 444; taxation, 34; Christianity in, 36–7; disputes over imperial power, 38; rule in England ends, 38–9

Rouen: Henry V besieges, 327

Rous, John: *Historia Regum Angliae*, 358

Rudton, East Yorkshire, 23, 444

Runnymede, Surrey: Magna Carta signed at, 171

Rye: plundered by French, 279

Saffron Walden, 413

St Albans: first battle of (1455), 360–1; second battle of (1461), 367; cloister school, 371

saints: and medical cures, 249–50; English, 275

Saladin, Sultan, 157

Salisbury: scholastic community, 373

Salisbury, John Montague, 3rd Earl of, 299–300

Salisbury Plain: prehistoric, 9–10, 17; under Romans, 34

Salisbury, Richard Neville, 1st Earl of: killed at Wakefield, 36; supports Richard of York in Wars of the Roses, 360, 363–4, 366; invades England with Warwick, 364

Salisbury, Thomas Montague, 4th Earl of, 328

salt: trade in, 19

Samain (festival), 24

sanctuary, 181

Sandwich, Kent: raided by French (1457), 363

Savoy Palace, London: burned in Peasants' Revolt, 280

Savoyards: at Henry III's court, 192, 195

Sawtré, William, 274–5

Saxon Shore, 35, 37

Saxons: early settlers, 40–1; recruited as mercenaries, 45–6; spread and colonization, 46–50

Scarborough, 138

schools, 371–2, 375–7, 414

Scone Palace, Scotland, 218

Scot, John, 177

Scotland: Romans reach, 30; Athelstan subdues, 69; border with England, 108, 114; Stephen defeats (1138), 123; war with Henry II, 147; Edward I's wars with, 189, 218–22, 225; conflict with Edward II, 232–4, 239–40; Edward III's wars with, 252, 259; alliance with France against England, 287; Edward IV negotiates peace with, 380; Perkin Warbeck in, 433–4; union with England (1707), 446

Scots: harass Romans, 35–6

Scrope, Richard, Archbishop of York, 312

seasons, 204–7

serfs, 32, 143–4, 268; *see also* peasantry

Shakespeare, William: depicts King John, 160; on Tudors, 427; *Henry IV, Pt.2*, 314; *Henry V*, 314, 321, 329; *The Merry Wives of Windsor*, 430; *Richard II*, 302; *Richard III*, 416; *The Tempest*, 209

Shaw, Ralph, 409

sheep: domesticated, 7, 73; introduced, 7; numbers in Bronze Age, 13; numbers in Henry III's reign, 190; and enclosures, 358; *see also* wool

Sheppey, isle of, 63

sheriffs, 72, 102, 199

Sherwood forest, 307

Shetland: surrendered to Scotland, 69

shires, 71–2, 86, 102

Shore, Elizabeth ('Jane'), 407

Shrewsbury, John Talbot, 1st Earl of, 349

Sigeberht, King of Kent, 58

Silbury Hill, 11

Silchester, 37, 39

Silures (tribe), 5

silver: imported, 165, 190; mines in west country, 357

Simeon of Durham, 100

Simnel, Lambert ('Edward VI'), 428–9

slaves: in Iron Age, 17; under Anglo-Saxons, 50, 71; in *Domesday Book*, 105

Sluys: English naval victory over French (1340), 258, 267

Smith, William (of Leicester), 273

Somerset, Edmund Beaufort, 2nd Duke of, 341–2, 347–50, 360

Somerset, John Beaufort, 1st Duke of, 338

*Song of the Husbandman*, 220

*Song of Lewes, The* (poem), 197, 217

South Saxons, 55–6, 445

space and time: loosely defined, 396–7

sports *see* games and sports

Stafford, Edmund, 3rd Earl of, 312

Stafford, Sir Humphrey, 346

Stafford, John, Archbishop of Canterbury, 343

Stafford, Sir William, 346

Stamford Bridge, battle of (1066), 89

Standard, battle of the (1138), 123

standing stones *see* megaliths

Stanley, Thomas, Baron (*later* 1st Earl of Derby, 423

Stanley, Sir William, 424, 431

Stapledon, Walter le, Bishop of Exeter, 242

Stapleford Park, Leicestershire, 151

Star Carr, Yorkshire, 3

Star Chamber, 430

Statute of Jewry (1253), 228

'Statute of Westminster the First' (1275), 213, 215

Statute of Winchester, 215

Stephen, King: succeeds to throne, 115, 122–3; conflict with Matilda, 123–6; financial problems, 123; captured and imprisoned, 125; mistrusts centralized bureaucracy and devolves power, 126; succeeded by Henry II, 127

Stirling Bridge, battle of (1297), 219–20

stone of destiny (Lia Fáil; stone of Scone), 218–19

Stonehenge, 1, 9–11

Stony Stratford, 405

Stowe, John, 320

Strabo, 26

Stratford, John, Archbishop of Canterbury, 256–7

Stratford-upon-Avon: plan, 138

Strathclyde (kingdom), 52

Stratton, Adam de, 217

Suetonius, 22, 29

Suffolk, John de la Pole, 2nd Duke of, 423

Suffolk, Michael de la Pole, 1st Earl of, 289–90

Suffolk, William de la Pole, 1st Duke of, 339, 343

Sully, John de, 397

surnames: introduced by Normans, 128–9

Sutton Hoo, 54

Sutton, Robert, 238

Swein Forkbeard, King of Denmark, 82–3

Swynford, Katherine, 334

Tacitus, 5–6, 29–31, 56

Tailboys, William, 341, 343

taxation: Roman, 34; and kingship, 79; under William the Conqueror, 97, 102; under Henry I, 117; under King John, 165–6; in Magna Carta, 172; under Edward I, 212–15, 220–1; raised during Great Famine (1313–17), 235; Edward III's, 255–6; and Peasants' Revolt (1381), 278, 281

Templars, Order of, 156

Tewkesbury Abbey, 126

Tewkesbury, battle of (1471), 390–1

Thame, Oxfordshire, 137

Thames, river: Bronze Age weapons and artefacts in, 14; prehistoric skulls in, 21; freezes (1309–10), 44

Thanet, Kent, 46–7

Thatcham, Berkshire, 4, 444

thegns, 72–3, 102

Theobald, Archbishop of Canterbury, 133

Theobald of Etampes, 372

Thirwell, John de, 397

Thomas, Earl of Lancaster: as rival to
    Edward II, 231–4, 236; executed, 237,
    240; posthumous miracles, 237; on
    Richard II, 286
Thomas of Eldersfield, 179–80
Thomas of Woodstock *see* Gloucester,
    Thomas, Duke of
Thorpe, Norfolk, 151
Thurkill of Arden, 99
time *see* space and time
tin, 16
Tinchebray, battle of (1106), 114
Tiptoft, Sir John, 321
Tirel, Walter, 111
tithings, 86, 102
tombs: prehistoric, 9; *see also* burial
Tostig, Earl of the Northumbrians, 87
tournaments, 155
Tower of London: in Peasants' Revolt,
    280–1; Edward V and Richard of
    York confined and murdered in
    ('Princes in the Tower'), 406–7,
    416–18
towns: Anglo-Saxon development, 74–5;
    populations, 74, 138, 411; free men in,
    75, 140, 413; fortified, 126, 411; grow
    under Plantagenets, 137–40; trade and
    manufacture, 138–9; communal
    government, 176, 413; character and
    conditions, 411–12; crafts and
    businesses, 413; civic rituals and
    routines, 414; literacy levels, 414;
    origins, 444; post-Roman, 444; *see
    also* villages
Towton, battle of (1461), 369
toys (children's), 370
trade: Bronze Age, 15–16; in iron, 17, 19;
    with Vikings, 62, 66; wool, 262, 268,
    357; fifteenth century, 356–7, 392
trailbaston (courts), 216
travel: in medieval period, 120
Tresilian, Robert, 291
Trevelyan, George Macaulay, 12
Trevet, Nicholas, 211
trial by ordeal, 180–1
Trinovantes (tribe), 56, 445
troubadours, 155

Tudor family, 366
Tudor, Jasper *see* Pembroke, Earl of
Tudor, Owen, 366–7
Tusser, Thomas, 206
Twynyho, Ankarette, 402
Tyler, Wat, 56, 280, 282–3

umbrella: introduced, 126
universities, 372–5
urn fields, 13
Usamah ibn Munqidh, 157

Varausius, 35
Vergil, Polydore, 386, 416, 422, 425
Verulamium, 39–40
Vespasian, Roman Emperor, 27
Vikings (Norsemen): raids, 61–3, 81–2
villages: beginnings, 8, 24, 137, 152–3;
    Iron Age, 17; regional variations, 43;
    Anglo-Saxon, 72–4; thrive under
    Henry II, 136–7; customs and
    traditions, 137; deserted, 151–3, 358; *see
    also* towns
villeins, 140, 144
violence: prevalence in medieval times,
    177–8
Visigoths, 37
*Vita Edwardi Secundi*, 332
Vortigern (or Wyrtgeorn), 45–7
Voxe, John, 223

Wakefield, battle of (1460), 366
Wales: Agricola conquers, 30; name, 51;
    subdued by Harold and Tostig, 87;
    William Rufus moves against, 108;
    Henry I's settlements in, 114; King
    John subdues, 166; Edward I
    campaigns against, 189, 213–14;
    castles, 213–14; Edward II born in,
    229; supports Henry VI, 379; and
    Henry Tudor's bid for throne, 422–3;
    and English monarchy, 445; union
    with England (1536), 446
Wallace, William, 219, 221
Walsingham, 121
Walsingham, Thomas, 294
Walter of Maidstone, 223

Walworth, William, 281–2

Wansdyke, 48

Warbeck, Perkin ('Richard IV'), 431–5, 437–8

warrior aristocracy: in Bronze Age, 15

Wars of the Roses: origins, 333, 340, 343; outbreak, 350, 361; conduct of, 363–4, 369; effect on English noble families, 391–2; end, 424; and claims to throne, 426

Warwick, Edward, Earl of (Clarence's son), 428–9, 435

Warwick, Richard Neville, Earl of ('the kingmaker'): supports Richard of York in Wars of the Roses, 360–1, 363–4, 367–8; commands forces in Calais, 361, 364; invades England with Salisbury, 364; and Edward IV's marriage, 382–3; alliance with Margaret of Anjou, 384; seeks alliance with France, 384; instigates rebellion of Robin of Redesdale, 385; as effective ruler after capture of Edward IV, 386; and Lincolnshire rebellion (1470), 386–7; lands at Exmouth with Clarence (1470), 387; rules after release of Henry VI, 388–9; and Edward IV's return from continent, 389–90; killed at Barnet (1471), 390; character and achievements, 390; Louis XI supports, 399

Warwick, Thomas de Beauchamp, Earl of, 293, 295

water: significance in Bronze Age, 14

Watling Street, 8

Watton, Yorkshire, 177

Waurin, Jean de, 384

Wessex (and West Saxons): settled, 55; power, 61; threatened by Vikings, 64

Westminster Abbey: Henry III rebuilds, 186–7, 202; Richard II reburied in, 304; Elizabeth Woodville takes sanctuary in, 388, 405–6

Westminster Hall: parliament in, 288

Wharram Percy, Yorkshire, 151–3

wheat: cultivation, 395

*White Ship*: sunk (1120), 115

Whittlesford, Cambridgeshire, 178

William I (the Conqueror), King: relations with pope, 10–14; employs Breton forces, 49; oath of loyalty to, 71; kingship, 79; claims English crown, 86–7; background and character, 87–8, 123; invades and conquers England, 88–91; rule in England, 97, 100–2; and English rebellions, 98; hunting, 101; commissions *Domesday Book*, 104–5; death, 106; brings Jews to England, 225

William I (the Lion), King of Scotland (1209), 168

William II (Rufus), King of England: reign, 106–10; death, 111–12; achievements, 112–13; calls assembly, 199; policy on Jews, 226

William Adeline, Prince (son of Henry I), 115, 117

William of Norwich, 227

William of Savoy, 192

William of Wakeham, 273

Wilton Diptych, 293

Winchester: Roman name (Venta Belgarum), 22; as Camelot, 48; pilgrimages to, 121; street plan, 413

windmills: first constructed, 136

Windsor Castle: Edward III rebuilds, 254

wine: imported by Normans, 395

witenagemot, 102, 198

Wolsey, Cardinal Thomas: relations with monarch, 133; on Richard III as usurper, 420

wolves: in England, 179

women: dress legislation, 263–4

woods and forests, 307

Woodville family, 383–6, 404–5, 420–1

wool: products under Romans, 34; exports under Henry III, 190; taxed, 212–14, 220, 255; exports maintained during Black Death, 262; English exporters exceed foreign, 268; cloth exports increase in fifteenth century, 357; economic importance, 357

Wroxeter, 39
Wulfstan, Bishop of Worcester (and
    Archbishop of York), 82, 175
Wycliffe, John, 270–2, 274–5, 284

yard: as unit of measurement, 77
Yeavering, Northumberland, 53
yeomen of the guard, 427
Yevele, Henry, 275
York (city): as Roman capital of
    Britannia Inferior, 35; Constantine
    appointed emperor at (306), 36;
    archbishopric, 59; Athelstan conquers,
    59; Danish Vikings capture, 64;
    wealth and power under Danes, 66,
    69; population, 74, 411; William the
    Conqueror attacks, 98; self-
immolation of Jews, 226–7; guildhall
    rebuilt, 355
York family: in Wars of Roses, 359,
    361–3
York, Edmund of Langley, 1st Duke of,
    303, 359
York, Richard, Duke of: commands
    English forces, 338, 361; as heir to
    throne, 341; protects John Paston,
    342; return from Ireland and conflict
    with Somerset, 347–8; claim on
    throne, 349–50, 365; in Wars of
    Roses, 360, 363–4, 366; and
    protection of Calais, 361; reigns, 362;
    killed at Wakefield, 366

Zosimus, 38

Plague—"Black Death"

Summer 1338
       1361
       1369
       1374